KASHMIR CRISIS

KASHMIR CRISIS
Unholy Anglo-Pak Nexus

SAROJA SUNDARARAJAN

KALPAZ

Kashmir Crisis . Unholy Anglo-Pak Nexus

Rs. 850

ISBN: 978-81-7835-808-6

Published in 2010 in India by
Kalpaz Publications
C-30, Satyawati Nagar,
Delhi-110052
E-mail: kalpaz@hotmail.com
Phone : 9212729499

Laser Type Setting by: Rudra Computer Graphics, Delhi
Printed at : Gian Ridhi Offset Printers, Delhi

Contents

Preface

There are many classic works on Kashmir by renowned authors covering all epochs in her history from the ancient times up to the present. Books on the Kashmir problem viewed from different angles are legion. However, I felt it was very essential to present to readers of history, a cogent account of the Kashmir crisis from the perspective of the British policy on Indo-Pakistan relations and its impact on India. I was contemplating a book on this aspect of the Kashmir imbroglio when my attention was drawn to the release by the National Archives, London, of some very crucial files containing material germane to this subject. This spurred me on to go ahead with the intended work. My stay in London for about six months in 2005 enabled me to acquire immeasurable wealth of source material from the archives and libraries in the United Kingdom.

The core of the book being Britain's partisan attitude towards the two Commonwealth countries in the sub-continent, it seeks to review critically the post-partition era which witnessed a new dimension of British diplomacy *vis-à-vis* the history of the sub-continent, the consistency in the partiality of the British mindset towards the two populations of the sub-continent it divided and the great historical betrayal of India's trust by the British Government and its faithful supporters including Mountbatten.

Apart from a brief introduction, the book comprises 19 Chapters. It commences with the past glory of the Hindu State of Kashmir (Chapter 1) and concludes with the Third Indo-Pakistan War on Kashmir in 1971 (Chapter 18). The Epilogue (Chapter (19) discusses succinctly the aftermath of the 1971 War by which time there were signs of Britain giving up her policy of involvement in the Indo-Pakistan disputes.

The full text of Jawaharlal Nehru's letter of 19 November 1962 to President Kennedy, about which there is still a controversy, is reproduced verbatin in Chapter 13.

The book is based mainly on information culled out from original sources. If there are any dark spots, they should be attributed to inaccessibility to certain crucial records and private collections/papers relevant to the title housed in the archives and libraries of India and Britain.

Coimbatore
15 May 2009.

Saroja Sundararajan

Acknowledgements

I owe a deep debt of gratitude to the following institutions and persons for their help in the preparation of this book:

United Kingdom

National Archives, London.

Oriental and India office collections (OIOC), British Library, London.

National Army Museum, London.

Churchill Library, Cambridge.

India

New Delhi

Parliament Library.

Nehru Memorial Museum and Library.

Chennai

Adyar Library and Research Centre.

Madras Institute of Development Studies.

My greatest debt is due to Prof. (Dr). J.L. Azad, Ex-Chief (Education Division), Planning Commission, who was kind enough to peruse the chapters and offer valuable suggestions.

I am much obliged to my erstwhile colleague and Member of Parliament, Dr. K. Dhanaraj, who was responsible for getting me access to the Parliament Library.

I am in a very special sense beholden to Shri P.D.T. Acharya, Secretary General, Lok Sabha and Dr. Ravinder Kumar Chadha, Joint Secretary, Lok Sabha Secretariat, for having kindly accorded me permission to use the Parliament Library. I am equally grateful to the Joint Directors and their staff in the Library for their uniform courtesy in supplying books and back issues of newspapers to me.

My sincere thanks are also due to Prof. A.R. Venkatachalapathy, Librarian Ms. R. Seetha and the staff of the Madras Institute of Development Studies as well as the staff of the Adyar Library and Research Centre for permitting me to consult the books in their Libraries.

My grateful acknowledgements are due in a large measure to Shri Amit Garg, Director, Gyan Books Pvt Ltd., Delhi, for having kindly accepted to publish the book.

Acronyms

CFL (Cease Fire Line)
CRO (Commonwealth Relations Office)
FRUS (Foreign Relations of the United States)
EPAL (East Pakistan Awami League)
HMG (Her/His Majesty's Government)
LOC (Line Of Control)
NEFA (North East Frontier Agency)
NWFP (North West Frontier Province)
POK (Pakistan Occupied Kashmir)
SWJN(Selected Works of Jawaharlal Nehru)
UK HC(I) (United Kingdom High Commissioner in India)
UK HC(P) (United Kingdom High commissioner in Pakistan)
UNCIP (United Nations Commission for India and Pakistan)
UKD to UN (United Kingdom Delegation to United Nations)
UNMOGIP (United Nations Military Observers Group for India and Pakistan)

Introduction

The British Empire was built in the eighteenth century with "money, courage, cruelty and brains in full accord with the international morals" of that age. It reached its colossal dimensions and became the foremost political power in the world with its two proudest bastions – India in the east and Canada in the west. Hence Britain's boast "The Sun never sets on the British Empire."

In India, the British rulers' attitude was racist. Barring a handful of rare and exalted souls, who had real concern for the material well-being of the governed, the generality of the Englishmen who came to India, totally lacked the spirit of *bon camaraderie.* To such Englishmen contact with the colonial population was *infra dig*. The Englishmen sent to India were young, almost boys. But as Edmund Burke put it: "As English youth in India, they drank the intoxicating draught of authority." They came to India, their biggest possession, to amass fortune as quickly as possible and return home to live in ostentatious luxury. Every rupee of profit made by an English man was lost for ever to India. Motivated by racial arrogance, the ruling race consciously insulated itself from the colonial people who were derogatively called "natives." And these "natives," millions of whom were dumb agriculturists, sincerely believed that the white-skinned rulers were Almighty's alter ego!

Steeped in the notion that civilisation was a purely European phenomenon, the occidental mind could not understand the greatness of the orient. The British, who came as traders but stumbled on an empire, could not bring themselves to think that the territory under their control was an intellectual, populous and polyglot sub-continent. This explained their long failure to work towards a productive relationship with the Indian society.

Gradually, wisdom dawned on the rulers and they realised that they could not administer the vast sub-continent of India without the assistance of the Indians. This prompted them to create facilities for the Indians to learn English. Though this provision was extended to all the Indians, initially only the Hindu community, particularly the Brahmans, availed themselves of the opportunity offered for their material advancement by the British. This brought a change for the better in the attitude of the rulers towards the English educated Hindus who served them as clerks. Thus English became the major binding factor where the Hindus were concerned. But the British relations with the Muslims remained far from friendly. In fact, during the Governor Generalship of Ellenborough (1842-44), the British made no secret of their dislike for Muslims when they openly stated that the Government's "true policy is to conciliate the Hindus." After the Great Indian Revolt of 1857, the hatred towards the Muslims became more pronounced. Although both the Hindus and the Muslims united against the British during this Revolt, the Muslims were looked upon as the spearhead of the anti-British resistance. Believing that they were contemplating a *jihad* ("holy war") against the white rulers, the Muslims were "singled out for official disfavour." This did not however mean that the Government's rapport with the Hindus remained unimpaired. Its animosity towards the Muslims and amity towards the Hindus were reversed by the last quarter of the nineteenth century.

The past tendency of Britain to cultivate the goodwill of the Hindus suffered a great setback with the founding of the Indian National Congress in 1885. The fact that the British Administrator A.O. Hume had a decisive role in this was ignored because he was a great friend of India. The avowed objective of the Congress at that point of time was to demand a greater share for the Indians in the governance of their country. But the alien Government panicked over the growing popularity of what it called the "Hindu" Congress. The organisation had, of course, become a formidable force within a short period of its birth.

A Retrograde Move

Thanks to the British, the advent of the Congress heralded a new era of enmity between the Hindus and the Muslims. The British Indian Government spared no effort to create bad blood between the two communities which had hitherto lived in harmony. With the view of throttling the nascent Congress, many measures were introduced to pit the one community against the other and thereby wean away the Muslims from that organisation.

Towards the end of the nineteenth century, Theodore Beck, the English Principal of the Aligarh College, who was hell-bent on segregating the Muslims from the Hindus, ignited communal passions. He was a confidant and adviser of Sayyid Ahmad, a judicial officer, British loyalist and founder of the Aligarh Movement. Beck was responsible for converting this Movement which was launched for the educational advancement of the Muslim community into a separatist movement fomenting anti-Congress feelings. He thoroughly exploited Sayyid Ahmad's antipathy towards the Congress to the advantage of the Muslims. Very soon, with this Englishman's help, Ahmad succeeded in making a large number of Muslims look upon the Congress with disfavour. He injected into the impressionable minds of the Indian Muslim youth the idea that communalism in political agitation was an indispensable factor. He wanted to carve out a distinct Mohammadan nationality and many Muslims blindly followed his leadership.

On 1 September 1905, took place the partition of Bengal, the crowning folly of Viceroy Curzon (1898-1905). It was done ostensibly to bifurcate the area which was too large to be administered by a single Lieutenant Governor but really to benefit the East Bengali Muslims by dealing out a political blow to the "Hindu" Congress. This vile act of cutting Bengal to pieces gave a tremendous impetus to the process of separating the two Indian communities. About 62 million Muslims were pulled back from joining the "seditious opposition" of the Congress. The best part of the whole drama was the public declaration of the Lieutenant Governor Fuller Bampfylde of the new province of East Bengal that "he had two wives, one Hindu and one Moslem but that the Moslem wife was his favourite." Though the partition was revoked on 12 December 1911, the seeds of hatred between the two communities sown by the British Indian administration had taken deep roots. In 1906, the Government encouraged the launching of the Muslim League as a counterblast to the Indian National Congress. The British stood as a wedge between the two communities and there was evidence of this fact in the communal electorate created. In 1909, by the Indian Council's Act, the Muslims were constituted into separate Muslim electorates.

For a short time, much to the discomfiture of the Government, both the communities united first under the Congress-League Pact at the Lucknow session of the Indian National Congress in 1916 and then during the *Khilafat* agitation against the shabby treatment meted out to the Caliph of Islam by the British Government during the First World War. At the Lucknow session, by the acceptance of separate electorates for the Muslims and by the agreement on the number of the Muslim seats in the Provincial and Imperial Legislative Councils, the Congress actually sacrificed a principle on which it had until then taken a definite stand. As a reputed historian wrote: "In its endeavour to forge unity for achieving a temporary gain, the Congress surrendered to Muslim communalism and thereby made its own contribution to the forces of separatism which led to the creation of Pakistan."

To Britain's great relief, the unity forged between the two communities was short-lived. It enabled the British Government to continue the game of *divide et impera* to such an extent as to make the fusion of the two communities impossible. Englishmen of stature like Sydney Olivier, Secretary of State for India, had admitted on the authority of their own "close acquaintance with Indian affairs," that there was a predominant bias in the British officialdom in India in favour of the Muslim community, partly on the ground of closer sympathy, but more largely "as a makeshift against Hindu nationalism." Responsible Indians had attested to the charge that the Government's behaviour was dictated by "a deliberate desire to maintain communal trouble as testimony against the possibility of constitutional progress."

The policy of perpetrating the Hindu-Muslim disunity was brought to a finale with the partition of the sub-continent of India which was also the handiwork of the British to keep the Muslims in good humour. The new nation of Pakistan became congenitally hostile to India.

White Hall-Karachi Axis

The post-partition era witnessed the new dimension of British diplomacy *vis-à-vis* the history of the sub-continent. There was a consistency in the partiality of the British mindset towards the two populations of the sub-continent it divided. There was an undercurrent of affability towards the militant Islamic Pakistan and hostility towards the democratic secular India exposing the truth that Britain had not reconciled itself to the loss of India. Britain's contradictory attitudes helped communalism to penetrate deep into the fabric of Pakistan's public life. And India became her hereditary enemy.

For a variety of reasons, Britain's desire that Kashmir should go to Pakistan had been constant. She was almost sanguine about it simply because it had a large Muslim population. One of the tasks entrusted to Mountbatten, the last British Viceroy of India (1947-48), was to achieve this. It was with this view that the propaganda against the "misrule and autocracy" of Maharaja Hari Singh of Kashmir was intensified by the British-Indian Government in the last days of its hegemony over India. After August 1947, blatantly propagandistic vehicles were used in Pakistan to project a distorted picture of the Maharaja and his cruelty to his Muslim subjects in order to induce the Muslims throughout the world to believe the deliberate falsehoods.

When Britain's fond hope of having Kashmir acceded to Pakistan did not materialise, she was really terrified out of her wits. Though the British Government knew that Kashmir's accession to India was legal, its utter disillusionment with the Maharaja's action forbade it from welcoming the event. Britain's attitude towards India thereafter was one of "unmixed malice." Instead of being on the side of a large, progressive, non-sectarian democracy, Britain favoured a military dictatorship in a religious state which was harping day in and day out on *jihad* against India. To put it more precisely, religion was allowed to penetrate deeply into the political sphere.

When Kashmir joined India, Britain exercised all powers at her command to ensure that Pakistan stood firm on her refusal to recognise the State's accession to India which, in her view, was achieved "fraudulently." The members of the British Delegation to the UN and the British army officers of the sub-continent, many of whom opted to serve in Pakistan after August 1947, had a substantial share in the strategies adopted to nullify all the painstaking efforts of India to have the matter settled amicably. They freely indulged in highly disturbing activities, certainly not without the connivance of the higher echelons in the Home Government, to spite India. There were cases where such officers who were staunchly pro-Pakistan and rabidly anti-India, were richly rewarded by the British Government.

Astonishingly, even high-ranking British political personages like the Secretaries of State chose to play an unworthy role in this matter. Philip Noel-Baker's handling of the Kashmir case brushing off all code of conduct was a case in point. He joined the British Cabinet as the Commonwealth Secretary in 1947. If, by virtue of the position he held, Noel-Baker had viewed the Kashmir issue in the right perspective, the matter would have been settled in 1948 itself. But he chose to treat the issue with extraordinary contempt and stoutly opposed India's claim that Kashmir was part of her by the Maharaja's act of accession. He minced no words in stating that Mountbatten's approval of Kashmir's accession to India had absolutely no validity in either the British or the International Law. He did not even hesitate to send an elaboration of his theory of the invalidity of the accession to the *Manchester Guardian.* He wrote to the Editor of the newspaper on 20 February 1957 that if a competent authority highlighted the unsoundness of the Indian case in the columns of his paper, it would weaken India's case substantially. In requesting the Editor to keep his identity highly confidential, Noel-Baker wrote, "because having handled the matter officially, it will do no good if I come into conflict with Nehru." Noel-Baker cannot certainly be absolved of the responsibility for the unsettlement of the Kashmir dispute and the consequent miseries inflicted upon the people of the entire Indian sub-continent for more than six decades.

Philip Noel-Baker, who adorned the lofty Chair of the Commonwealth Secretary, had no scruples about taking cognizance of a letter from Mountbatten to Nehru which was a top secret document, sharing its contents with Archibald Nye, British High Commissioner in India and warning him against ever showing a soft corner to Nehru in any discussion on Kashmir.

Philip Noel-Baker, it must be remembered, was the recipient of the Nobel Peace Prize 1959 for his contribution to International peace and cooperation!

All these highlighted the way the wind was blowing where the White Hall-Karachi Axis was concerned. The special correspondent of the *Indian News Chronicle* learnt from the diplomatic quarters in New Delhi that the Pakistani Prime Minster's replies to Nehru's telegrams were either drafted or vetted in the White Hall or in the UK High Commissioner's Office in Karachi.

The hostile posture Britain adopted towards India on Kashmir encouraged Pakistan to freely revile India. She delivered immoderate speeches replete with warlike expressions and virulent criticisms of Indian leaders and their handling of the Kashmir question. Such vituperative attacks were made not only by firebrands but also by responsible politicians of Pakistan. Zafrullah Khan, Zulfilkar Ali Bhutto and leaders of their ilk always breathed fire and spewed venom on India during discussions on Kashmir at the Security Council. Whenever Pakistan had internal problems, which she always had in a large measure, to divert the attention of the public, she would start a hate-campaign against India. Even when the State of Jammu and Kashmir was enjoying absolute peace, her spokesman would cry that the people there who were unreconciled to their Indian "occupation" had risen in open rebellion and that there was a dire need for the Security Council to hear their voice. Even if the British Government knew for certain that these were all Pakistan's own concoctions, it would, just to placate Pakistan, go out of the way to arrange a meeting of the Security Council in order to get a resolution tabled there.

The instances cited will bear out the belligerent and aggressive nature of the British officers in their dealings with India on Kashmir. As a renowned Indian journalist put it, there was "as much national unity" on the Kashmir issue "as there was against Hitler." The most perplexing feature of the whole game was Britain's readiness to condone Pakistan every time she threw Kashmir into turmoil. Britain, renowned for her sense of justice and contempt for aggression as "the most heinous of all crimes in the international calendar," felt no compunction about allowing and encouraging Pakistani aggression against India who was also her friend as well as a Member of the Commonwealth.

A columnist of a reputed Indian Newspaper observed :

> "Among the thousands of sentences published by the British newspapers on the Kashmir crisis, I cannot recall a single one where the words 'Pakistan' and 'aggression' were linked together...There has at the most been a perfunctory and parenthetic allusion to Pakistan's 'wrong doing' and the editorials notably those in the *Guardian* have been passed on hastily to excoriate India in stern language for its folly and blindness. One can only conclude that the concept of aggression has no longer much meaning or validity to British policy makers and opinion framers."

Nehru's deep distrust over the raid on Kashmir, his assertion of Pakistan's aggression against India and his annoyance at her refusal to vacate the aggression exasperated the British officialdom beyond measure. It accused India of "beating the drum of Pakistani aggression as loudly as ever" and pronounced that "Nehru falls short of being a great statesman over Kashmir."

In treating India on par with Pakistan who was the aggressor and incessantly blaming India of sabotaging the efforts to conduct a plebiscite, Britain deliberately ignored the crucial fact that Pakistan observed the ceasefire agreement of January 1949 only in the breach and refused to create conditions necessary for a plebiscite.

Britain was far from being judicious in assessing the Indian leaders or their policies. Her fulminations against India on the Kashmir crisis were as acrid as those of Pakistan. In fact the activities of some of her officers who involved themselves in the dispute greatly lowered her credibility apart from exposing her total lack of transparent honesty in her dealings with India.

In all its correspondence/notes/summaries on the Kashmir dispute, the British Government would amply emphasise the failure of the UN to reach a settlement but would never say a word that its failure was entirely owing to Pakistan's persistent intransigence and continued aggression against India. It would describe Azad Kashmir at the best as a region "established on the Pakistani side of the Cease-Fire-Line," that "its constitutional links with Pakistan are not clearly defined" and that the Pakistan Government "exercises an effective control over it" but never as an Indian territory under the forcible and illegal occupation of Pakistan since October 1947. This grave international crime has never been questioned by Britain.

1

The Hindu Kingdom of Kashmir Its Glorious Past

Kashmir, "the jewel of Asia," covers an area of 2,22,236 square kilometres extending from 32° 15′ and 37° 05′ North latitude and 72° 35′ and 83° 20′ East longitude.[1] This scenic "intermontane valley" is between the main Himalayan ranges in the northeast and the Pir Panjal range in the southwest in the northwestern India. The State has within her the lofty peaks of Mount Godwin Austen and the Nanga Parbat with their tremendous summits. The river Indus and her major tributary Chenab flow through Kashmir. Since Jhelum, another principal tributary rises within Kashmir, the Vale is said to be the "Gift of Jhelum." Ravi, yet another principal waterway of the Indus, enters the territory for some miles.

Kashmir's boundaries abut on five countries – Russia, China, Afghanistan, Pakistan and India. But many of the borders particularly the huge length of about 1450 Kilometres running along Sinkiang and Tibet have not been internationally defined. It is screened from Russia and China by the Himalayas and the Pamirs. It is bordered by Tibet on the east, the Sinkiang Province of China on the northeast and Afghanistan on the north. Since the partition of India in 1947, the full length of Kashmir's western frontier from which emerge its most important roads and trade routes, is bounded by Pakistan. Only the southeastern areas fringe India. The entire territory comprising Baltistan, Dartistan, Muzaffarabad, Mirpur, Poonch, Jammu, Ladakh, the Vale of Kashmir and other mountain tracts has always been a part of India.

Though the whole territory is called "Kashmir," in reality, it is the name of just one part of the State – the Vale. This much coveted beautiful strip of land which covers approximately a length of 140 kilometres, width of 40 kilometres and a mean height of 5600 feet above sea level, lies in the very heart of the Himalayas.

Kashmir is sparsely populated. Since a large portion of the State is mountainous and barren, its population is disproportionate to its size. According to the 2001 census, the State of Jammu and Kashmir has a population of 1,00,69,987[2] which includes Muslims, Hindus, Sikhs and Buddhists. While in the Kashmir Valley the Muslims are predominant, in Jammu, the Hindus constitute a substantial majority.

In the north of Kashmir is the vast Gilgit Agency with its wide range of local dialects and cultures; and in the northeast, between the Kashmir Valley and Tibet lie Baltistan and Ladakh occupied mainly by the Karakoram ranges. While in Baltistan, the Shia Muslims constitute the majority, in Ladakh, also called "Little Tibet," the Buddhists with close religious and linguistic affinity are the largest numerically, particularly in the southern part.

In the south, where the Jammu province lies amid the lowest foothills of the Himalayas, Dogri is widely spoken by the Muslims in the west and the Hindus in the east; in the centre where the Kashmir Valley proper lies with its capital at Srinagar, Kashmiri is the dominant language spoken by the Muslim majority and the Hindu minority. The strip of territory that lies along the Pakistan border in the western extremity of Jammu comprises Muzaffarabad, the Mirpur districts and the Poonch *jagir*. This is a predominantly Punjabi-speaking area with a Muslim majority. There are large number of Hindus and Sikhs also especially in Mirpur.

This chapter attempts to give glimpses of the history of the Hindu kingdom of Kashmir up to the onslaught of the Muslim forces on it.

Of the 562 Princely States in India covering a total area of 15,49,177 square kilometres which was two-fifths of the total area of India with a population of 68,652,974 (one-fifth of the country's population), Kashmir was territorially the largest State to be ruled by a Hindu monarch. Many outstanding voyagers from both the east and the west have bequeathed to posterity their accounts of the breath taking beauty of Kashmir. Thomas Moore says that in the "Happy Valley (of Kashmir) the world comes to an end and the paradise begins." The most appealing description of the special charm of Kashmir emanates from the pen of the seventeenth century French traveller, Francois Bernier, who was the first European to visit Kashmir. Writing in 1665, he says

"In truth the kingdom surpasses in beauty all that my warmest imagination had anticipated...It is not indeed without reason that the *Mogols* call *Kachemire* the territorial paradise of the Indies."

But a more fascinating depiction than the most moving pictures of the place emerges from Jawaharlal Nehru, who hailed from Kashmir. Speaking of his kinship with Kashmir, he wrote in 1940 when he visited the State after an interval of 23 years:

> "...Like some supremely beautiful woman, whose beauty is almost impersonal and above human desire, such was Kashmir in all its feminine beauty of river and valley and lake and graceful trees. And then another aspect of this magic beauty would come to view, a masculine one, of hard mountains and precipices, and snow-capped peaks and glaciers, and cruel and fierce torrents rushing down the valleys below. It had a hundred faces and innumerable aspects, ever-changing, sometimes smiling, sometimes sad and full of sorrow...I gazed at it, it seemed to me dreamlike and unreal, like the hopes and desires that fill us and so seldom find fulfilment. It was the face of the beloved that one sees in a dream and that fades away on awakening..."

This loveliest State of India could be characterised *sui generis* with no parallel at any time anywhere in Asia.

Taken as a common noun, Kashmir means "saffron" owing to its luxuriant growth there. Legend goes that the entire land was originally filled with the waters of an immense lake on which Goddess Parvati sailed in a pleasure boat from the Haramukh Mountain in the north to the Konsanag Lake in the south. In her honour, the lake was called *Satisaras* – the Lake of Sati (Durga). The countryside of the State was tormented by a ferocious demon called Jalodbhava. The terrified people fervently appealed to sage Kashyapa who saved them from the devastations caused by the demon. According to the *Mahabharata,* Kashyapa was the son of Marichi and grandson of Brahma, who was the source from which all beings sprang.[3] Since the demon was eluding the sage hiding under the water, Vishnu intervened, struck the mountains at Baramulla[4] and caused the waters of the lake to rush out while Goddess Parvati cast a mountain on the wicked demon and destroyed him. The land that emerged out of the water was named "Kashmir" after its mythical founder Kashyapa. The mountain became "Hari Parbat" – "the Olympus[5] of the Hindus." In fact, some authorities refer to Kashmir as "Kashyapi" or "Kashyapuri." According to *Srimad Bhagavatam*, acknowledged as the most complete and authoritative exposition of Vedic knowledge, the tract of land in

Bharata Varsha called "Kashmir" is accepted as *bhauma svarga* – one of the three divisions of heaven.[6]

According to the *Nilamata Purana,* named after Nila, the patron saint of Kashmir, the Kingdom was originally inhabited by the Nagas – worshippers of serpents – who were conquered by the Dard[7] branch of the Aryans. The latter's language was Paisachi[8] which was akin to Prakrit and which formed the basis of the modern Kashmiri language.

National Integration through Sanskrit

Kashmir has been acclaimed as the cradle of Sanskrit lore and learning. Despite its geographical isolation, the Valley's cultural contributions to and historical affiliations with the rest of India have been enormous. Notwithstanding the "Indianness" that one could perceive in the cultural life of entire India, each State has had its own culture and intellectual attainments. But the unique feature of Kashmir has been that though hemmed in between huge mountain-barriers, the territory could evolve a culture untainted by narrow parochial attitudes. What facilitated her to achieve this was that both by faith and by conviction, Kashmir could look not only beyond her mountains but also beyond her own self.[9] This liberal attitude has enabled Kashmir to bequeath to the posterity of the whole nation a peerless legacy of aesthetic and intellectual attainments.

Who can deny that the heritage of India has come down to us through the medium of Sanskrit and that the birthplace of this "language of gods" is Kashmir? In this ancient and rich language is enshrined all the essentials of Hindu culture. The renowned Sanskrit Professor V. Raghavan says, "If there is a prominent Indian Aesthetics which could be applied to all fine arts, it is to Kashmir we owe it." The Vedic art and culture grew in Kashmir. Some of the earliest Vedic hymns are said to have been composed in Kashmir. The eminence of the Kingdom in the realm of learning has earned Kashmir the reputation of being the "special abode" of Sarasvati, the Goddess of Learning. The Kashmiri minstrel Bilhana of the eleventh century called Kashmir "Sarada Desa." For millennia people throughout India have been celebrating Sarasvati *Puja* most piously to seek Her blessings to acquire knowledge. People living in the south of India observe it on the ninth day of *Navaratri* ("Festival of Nine Nights") and on the following day – *Vijaya Dasami* – initiate their wards into learning. From time immemorial, it has been the practice of the South Indians to look to the north soon after rising and folding their palms together in supplication chant *Namaste, Sarada Devi, Kashmira Mandala Vasini* ("I salute the Goddess of Learning who resides in Kashmir.") According to some authorities, the worship of *Srividya* and *Srichakra* originated in Kashmir whose capital was called "Srinagara" ("City of Wealth of Knowledge") in view of its spiritual and material wealth.

Centuries before the Christian era, Sanskrit played a seminal role in cementing the bond between Kashmir and the other parts of India. Had it not been for this cultural unity forged by Sanskrit, "India could never have retained its identity through the dark centuries of oppression and foreign rule."[10] The all pervasive nature of the Kashmiri Pandit cultural heritage stood as a monument to the State's recognition of Sanskrit as a national and not a local heritage. The Kashmiri Pandits were "a cultural hybrid" constituting a highly literate and sophisticated group. They wrote extensively in Sanskrit. Their origin is, however, veiled in obscurity. It is not known when or from where they migrated to Kashmir. The celebrated Kashmiri chronicler Kalhana of the twelfth century speaks of their earliest appearance as recipients of *agraharas* from the first beneficent monarchs of Kashmir. The *Nilamata Purana* which is the earliest standard text for the Pandits traces their descent from Kashyapa Muni, the creator of Kashmir.

Kashmir has given lavishly to fine arts also. The undated *Bharata Natya Sastra* – the most popular treatise on classical dance – authored by sage Bharata was written in Kashmir. It is the earliest authoritative work on dance, music and drama, the last one being the sage's primary theme. The celebrated grammarian Patanjali of the second century BC compiled his compendium on the *Yoga* in Kashmir. The *Panchatantra*, a collection of ancient tales and fables in prose and verse in Sanskrit, is also said to have been produced in Kashmir between the first century BC and early centuries of the Christian era. This work, generally attributed to a Brahman by name Vishnu Sarma, is popular throughout the world having been translated into several languages of the east and the west. The Kashmiri Kshemendra of the early eleventh century also wrote profusely. His celebrated *Brihatkathamanjari* written in 1037 is a book of stories condensing the Prakrit *Brihatkatha* in Sanskrit. He reckons Buddha as the ninth incarnation of Vishnu in his *Dasavataracharitra*. Somadeva Bhatta, also a Kashmiri of the same century, was a renowned poet and story-teller. He was patronised by the kings of Kashmir. His *Katha-Sarit-Sagara* ("The Ocean of the Streams of Story") written between 1063 and 1081 is a repository of the "River of Stories" which was really intended for the amusement of the Queen of King Ananta of Kashmir. This work comprises 22,000 verses and prose. Bilhana of the late eleventh century, to whom reference has already been made, is the author of the renowned work *Vikramankacharita*. He was patronised by the kings of the Kalachuri dynasty who honoured him with the title of *Vidyapati*.

The great Sankara, who expounded the fundamentals of his *Advaita* ("Monism") philosophy with unsurpassed wisdom and brilliance, visited Kashmir in the ninth century AD. Another saint from the south, Ramanuja, who belonged to the Vaishnava school of Hinduism and founded the epochal new philosophy, *Visishta-Advaita* ("Qualified Monism"), also visited Kashmir in the eleventh century AD. He wanted to fulfil his life's ambition of giving a final coat of brilliant polish to his monumental work *Sribhashya*. For this, he had to access the ancient document *Bodhaayana Vritti* which was housed only in the Royal Library of Kashmir. It was none too easy for him to consult it for any length of time. Fighting against heavy odds, with the assistance of his disciple Kooresa (also called Koorat Aazhvar), who had an extraordinary memory, Ramanuja succeeded in incorporating the relevant authentic passages of the *Vritti* into his *Sribhashya*.[11]

The influence of Sanskrit on Buddhist thought and literature, which flourished in Kashmir over two millennia ago, has been equally admirable. At a time when Pali was the language of the Buddhist literature in the rest of India, all the Buddhist literature produced in Kashmir was in Sanskrit. The Buddhist monks of Kashmir for their part carried Kashmir's civilization to Central Asia and China.

It is significant that the women of Kashmir had effortlessly mastered the Sanskrit language. Bilhana records that the women of Kashmir spoke both Sanskrit and Prakrit fluently. This is evidence of the high status the women of Kashmir enjoyed in those days.

That Kashmir was a great centre of learning from early times has been testified by the existence there of a university which was as famous as the universities of Takshasila (in north-west near Rawalpindi now in Pakistan), Nalanda (Bihar) and Ghatikasthana (Kanchipuram in Tamil Nadu). In fine, Kashmir was not only the *Saradapitha* but also the *Sarvajnapitha*.

The European scholar George Bashier who came to India in the middle ages in search of some Sanskrit manuscripts was much disillusioned when he could not find them in most of the States in India where the language had lost the high status it once enjoyed. In fact, it was relegated to the "Pantheon of dead languages." Finally Bashier went to Kashmir where he was much delighted to find the manuscripts he was searching for. This bore eloquent testimony to Sanskrit being still in its halcyon days in Kashmir when it was in eclipse in the other parts of India. Bashier could easily contact 22 Sanskrit speaking Pandits in Kashmir. He was also happy to find some traders and officials who had preserved a good collection of rare manuscripts in Sanskrit.

Kalhana: Dominating Figure of Kashmir

Many creative minds have lived and made substantial contributions in the realms of literature, art and culture through millennia on the soil of Kashmir. Their priceless creations verily constitute a golden chapter in the history of Kashmir. The period of 400 years from the ninth to the twelfth century marks the existence of the brightest luminaries in Sanskrit literature who have shone on the firmament of Kashmir. In fact, Kashmir of the mid-twelfth century in particular, was a brilliant epoch of Sanskrit culture having produced more innovative literature than perhaps any other country in South Asia.

It is sad, very sad indeed, that the land which was fertile in the production of geniuses in several fields did not, like the rest of India, give a historian-genius until the twelfth century. A.A. Macdonell, historian and Sanskrit scholar, was absolutely right when he said while dwelling on the lack of historical sense in India up to the twelfth century: "History is the one weak spot in Indian literature. It is in fact non-existent." The only trustworthy source preserving the early history of Kashmir is the *Rajatarangini* in Sanskrit authored by Kalhana, son of a judicial officer, who certainly brought fame and lustre to Kashmir by his marvellous work. He towered over a galaxy of men of erudition like Ruyyaka, Trailokya, Jinduka, Jalhana and Alankara, who were his contemporaries.[12] There were extensive works containing royal chronicles of very ancient times but they were all lost. Kalhana himself admits that he was not the first historian of Kashmir.

Scholars owe a deep debt of gratitude to the Hungarian-British archaeologist and geographer Aurel Stein but for whose painstaking dedication, Kalhana's real historical work would have gone unrecorded. Stein rescued this only known surviving ancient Indian historical work from oblivion. He first published his Sanskrit edition of this work and then his English translation of it in 1900 under the title *Kalhana's Rajatarangini: A Chronicle of the Kings of Kashmir*.

Kalhana disassociated himself from politics and dedicated his life to writing his monumental work with true historical instinct. Apart from his personal knowledge of life in contemporary Kashmir and critical analysis of whatever earlier chronicles – they were indeed very few – were available, Kalhana also made extensive use of official documents like land grant deeds and foundation charters of temples. About *Rajatarangini*, it is said: "Though dealing with only a small part of South Asia, it has a richness of detail unequalled in ancient southern Asia except in Ceylon."[13] He commenced his work in 1148 (*Saka* year 1070) and completed it in 1150 when Jayasimha of the Lohara dynasty, who succeeded King Harsha[14] on his death, was ruling Kashmir. Situation in contemporary Kashmir was then "stormy and bloody." Though Kalhana did his work under Jayasimha, he did not indulge in prodigious panegyric of his king which was invariably the practice with normal court poets. His forthright account speaks of certain avaricious Hindu kings who defiled idols to make money. He does not also shrink from condemning the sacrilegious acts of the Hindu ruler Harsha of Kashmir. However, not many are aware that the *Naishada* of king Harsha is regarded by Indian critics as a *Mahakavya.*

Though the title of Kalhana's work suggests that it is a story of the kings, the royal families and the nobility and not of the common people of Kashmir, it is actually much more than a record of the activities of the royalty. It contains information – political, social and also economic – of the Kingdom to some degree.

The narrative poem *Rajatarangini* or *River of Kings* comprises in all eight cantos each of which is called *Taranga* ("Wave"). Kalhane dispassionately assesses the merits and demerits of his own countrymen and his judgements of them have been "abundantly confirmed by history."[15]

Kalhana commences his work from about the third millennium BC. The opening scene of his long narrative is Gandhara (East Afghanistan). He mentions Gonanda, a relative of Jarasanda, who gave battle to Lord Krishna, as the first king of Kashmir. But the chronicles of these centuries contain no dates as the record of all these rulers had apparently disappeared by Kalhana's time. Being also a *Kavi* ("poet-seer") he gives his account of this period in the form of *Kavya* ("work of art").[16] After the early cantos which are pre-eminently a work of art, Kalhana's history is a faithful and authentic record of the kings of Kashmir. He is credited with painting the characters of the kings with a "rare acuteness."

The following is a brief account of a few kings – good and bad – whose activities were fundamental to the growth or decadence of the Kingdom.

In the *Rajatarangini*, the first historical figure of the chequered career of Kashmir is Asoka the Great of the Mauryan dynasty who founded the capital city of Srinagar about twenty-three centuries ago. During his reign, the valley and its neighbourhood were brought under the vast Mauryan Empire. He first founded the capital Srinagar which was later shifted by King

Pravarasena II about the end of the sixth century AD to the adjoining site of the modern Srinagar. The ancient site known as Puranadhisthana, is now called Pandrethan.[17]

Asoka's role in making Kashmir the fountain head of Buddhism is too well known to need elaboration here. Buddhism was introduced here by the Buddhist monk Majjhantika who was sent by Moggaliputta, Asoka's adviser. It was noteworthy that Asoka had a great respect and consideration for the Hindu religion which continued side by side with Buddhism. In fact, until the fourteenth century, there was a total absence of religious persecution in Kashmir.

After Asoka, the next important landmark in the history of Kashmir was its conquest by Kanishka, the greatest of the Kushan kings of Gandhara. Generally accepted to be the founder of the *Saka* era in 78 AD, this enlightened ruler, who was called the 'Second Asoka,' contributed immensely to popularise Buddhism in Kashmir. At the Fourth Buddhist Council held under his patronage in Kashmir, Kanishka directed the Buddhist theologians including Asvaghosha, philosopher and author of *Buddha Charita*, to codify the Buddhist doctrines in a summary called the *Mahavibhashya.*

In the four centuries following Kanishka, there was no famous historical figure connected with Kashmir. About the second quarter of the sixth century, the State had the misfortune to come under the control of the ruthless Hepthalites or white Huns. It was a time when entire north India relapsed into bondage and chaos. Though both the Hun invaders from Sialkot – Toramana and his son Mihirakula (also called Mihiragula) – indulged in most monstrous acts, the son excelled the father in barbarity. His acts were done not with insensibility only, but with levity – with laughter! Stories of his sadistic tyranny are still current in Kashmir. Kashmiris still point to the ridge in Hastinavat on the Pir Panjal range where Mihirakula would amuse himself by his blood-curdling deeds. Once while crossing the Pir Panjal Pass, one of the elephants in his train slipped and fell. The cries of the animal were so pleasing to Mihirakula's ears that he subsequently drove one hundred elephants over the precipice, caused their fall down the hill and enormously enjoyed hearing the terrified shrieks of the agony of the dying elephants. The dangerous precipice is named "Hastivanj" ("the destroyer of elephants") after him.[18] Mihirakula had "no pity for children, no compassion for women and no respect for the aged."[19] He was called the "Indian Nero." He had destroyed many monasteries and killed the monks residing there. The Gupta king Baladitya, who defeated and made Mihirakula a prisoner, mercifully spared him. Mihirakula reciprocated this kind gesture by treacherously murdering his benefactor while taking refuge in Kashmir. His son and successor Baka was a total contrast to him. Kalhana portrays him as "a most virtuous prince and a comforter of humanity." His reign was marked by his genuine efforts to right the wrongs done to the people especially the Brahmans by his predecessor and to advance their interests. Kalhana also refers to Baka's supernatural death at the hands of a sorceress.[20]

Since Kashmir remained a renowned centre of Buddhist learning even in the seventh century AD, the celebrated Chinese pilgrim Yuwan Chuwang visited it in 631 and stayed there for two years in pursuit of Buddhist scriptures. The reigning monarch was King Durlabhavardhana, son of a Naga Karkota, and the first king of the Karkota dynasty to rule Kashmir from 627 to 663. He provided the Chinese traveller with 20 clerks to copy out the sacred books and *Sastras* and five men to wait upon him. Kashmir had then a Buddhist monastery with 300 monks and a sacred *stupa* believed to have been built over a tooth relic of the Buddha.[21] Yuwan Chuwang also mentions his visit to the magnificent city of Pravarapura built by Pravarasena II on the site of the modern capital of Srinagar and calls it the "new city."

Durlabhavardhana's grandson Muktapida Lalitaditya (724-760) also played a praiseworthy role in the politics of the Gangetic plain. He was the most reputed Hindu ruler of the Karkota dynasty. He undertook extensive campaigns and lost his life in a military expedition against the Tibetans. During his reign, the imperial power of Kashmir was felt even beyond India's northern, north-western and western frontiers. During the reign of this king and his predecessors, Kashmir maintained good military relationship with China and Lalitaditya received an investiture from the Emperor of China. Kalhana credits him with the construction of the famous Vishnu temple of Martanda. He also built the imposing city of Paraspur (Parihasapura) but to give it pre-eminence, he burnt down the equally splendid city of Pravarapura. Though Hinduism was the State religion, Lalitaditya patronised Buddhism also. He erected a monastery and a *stupa* in Uskur – the town founded by Huvishka, successor of Kanishka. What had immortalised Lalitaditya's name has been the most sublime piece of advice he gave his subjects. He told them to abjure internal feuds; keep the forts in good repair and well provisioned so that they would not fear any foe; living as they did in a country shut in by mountains they must observe strict discipline; and agriculturists should have no more grain than what was needed for a year because their interests should be strictly subordinated to the comfort of the city.[22] These words uttered more than 1300 years ago are as good today as in the eighth century.

Avantivarman (855-883), who ruled a century after Lalitaditya, was a humble but able ruler. He was the grandson of Utpala, founder of the Utpala dynasty. Unlike Lalitaditya, he was a peace-loving monarch who concentrated on engineering works carried out through Suyya,[23] a renowned engineer in his service. It is said that Suyya "made the streams of Indus and Jhelum flow according to his will, like a snake-charmer his snakes."[24] He lowered the water level of the Jhelum by removing obstructions in the river bed below Baramulla. His concern for his people made him reduce the price of rice from 36 to 20 *Dinnaras* per *khaewar*.[25] Avantivarman had his capital at Avantipur, which he founded in Anantnag district southeast of Srinagar. Though the kings who ruled Kashmir after Asoka had their own capitals in different parts of Kashmir, Srinagar never lost the status it enjoyed from the period of Asoka. The last of the strong Hindu rulers of Kashmir who belonged to the Utpala dynasty was Queen Didda (980–1003). King Kshemagupta of Kashmir married Didda, daughter of Simharaja, Chief of Lohara. This marriage brought Kashmir under the rule of the Lohara family. From her mother's side, Didda was a scion of the noble stock of the Shahis mentioned by Alberuni in his list of the "Hindu Shahiyas of Kabul." This romantic granddaughter of Bhima Shahi had inherited much of the administrative acumen and energy of the Shahis which contributed to her remarkable governance of Kashmir for close on a quarter of a century. Stories of her amours are said to be still current in Kashmir. She repented for the sins she committed by founding shrines and monasteries.[26] Her sin was her unfeeling and cruel treatment of the culprits who organised a dangerous rebellion against her. She wreaked her vengeance on the captured rebels by executing them and exterminating their families.[27] On her death in 1003, her nephew Sangramaraja of the Lohara dynasty became the ruler of Kashmir. There were signs of decay from then on and the weak kings of the Lohara dynasty could not save their kingdom falling a prey to civil war and violence. The last ruler of this dynasty was Jayasimha (also called Simhadeva) during whose reign a new storm was breaking over in Kashmir. In 1128, the Tartar, Khan Dalcha invaded Kashmir and caused great havoc throughout the kingdom.

Though monarchy was the form of Government throughout the Hindu period, the king was bound by the advice of his councillors. Kalhana's chronicle refers to two cases of the Privy Council deposing the king and vetoing the king's nomination of his successor.[28]

Co-existence of Faiths

For centuries, the various sects of Hinduism as well as the Buddhist creed existed peaceably side by side. Kalhana gives copious proofs of the co-existence of Buddhism and the orthodox creeds of Saivism, Vaishnavism and Saktism despite the temporary setback to that harmony by the advent of Nagarjuna, the great Buddhist monk-philosopher on the scene in the first century AD. During this era, the power of the Buddhists, who were protected by Nagarjuna, predominated Kashmir. These disputants, who were opponents of the Vedas, defeated the Vedic scholars in open debates thus cutting at the root of the religious rites prescribed in the *Nilamata Purana*.[29] Fortunately, this set-back was short lived.

It is noteworthy that Saivism received official patronage alongside Vaishnavism. Kashmir is well-known for the recondite system of Saiva philosophy called Kashmir Saivism. It is also called *Trika* or *Triad*. The originator of this profound philosophy was Vasu Gupta. The greatest exponent of this cult was Abhinava Gupta, who belonged to the *Dhvani* School. He was also a very prolific writer and was most popular for his contribution to Sanskrit literature. He was famous for his commentary on the *Natyasastra*. He was also a philosopher. His disciples, admirers and later Kashmiri authors extolled him as *Mahamaheswara*. Saivism, which is one of the oldest religious systems of India, exists in three recognised forms: the *Satstala Veera Saiva Siddhanta* in Karnataka, the *Saiva Siddhanta* in Tamil Nadu and the *Advaita Saiva* or *Trika* doctrine in Kashmir. The Kashmir Saivism aims at dispelling the innate ignorance that separates the universe from its creator and does not recognise any discrimination on the basis of caste, creed and colour. The verses comprising the lofty teachings of Kashmir Saivism were composed by Lalla, a lady philosopher of Kashmir. Kashmir Saivism as elaborated by Kshemendra, Kshema Raja and Yoga Raja spread far and wide. In the ninth and the succeeding centuries, Kashmir produced illustrious teachers who are reckoned among the greatest exponents of the Saiva doctrine.

Being monistic, the Kashmir Saivism shares Adi Sankara's doctrine of *Advaita*. It is generally accepted that Adi Sankara visited Kashmir in the second decade of the ninth century AD to preach the essentials of the *Advaita* doctrine. According to an anecdote, in a contest with the Sakta Pandits, Sankara emerged victorious but it was not easy to achieve it in the abode of Sri Sarada. It would appear that Sankara challenged the existence of *Sakti* and in consequence became extremely weak, having lost all human energy. He then realised his folly in attacking the doctrine of *Sakti*, the supreme energy and atoned for his transgression by composing and singing then and there 102 verses which were a paean of praise on *Sakti.* This prayer-poem in the *Sikharini* metre is the most popular *Soundaryalahari* which bears evidence not only to the discussions he had with the propounders of the Saiva faith but also to the influence which the Kashmir Saiva Acharyas had on him. Can there be a better proof than this of the national integration of India from Kashmir to Kanyakumari marked by a phenomenal unity amidst diversity?

It would be of interest to know that western intellects especially the Americans are avowedly studying the Kashmiri culture and spiritualism particularly its Saivism. Prof Paul Muller, who visited Kashmir, described Abhinava Gupta as the "greatest genius India has ever produced." It is said that in this era of information technology "Kashmir Saivism is bound to produce a new synthesis between science and spiritualism."[30]

Kalhana dwells at length also on the flourishing trade and commerce of Kashmir. He speaks of the shawls, which have been the most celebrated manufacture of Kashmir. It is universally acknowledged that weaving of finest shawls has nowhere been done to such perfection as in Kashmir. Most of the woollen fabrics of Kashmir were in olden days made in *pashmina*, the wool of a certain mountain goat. According to Bernier to whom a reference has already been made, shawls were manufactured in Kashmir on a "prodigious scale" and brought her extensive revenue.[31] Kalhana says that the Kashmiri merchants who were dealers in different wares were from all regions of the sub-continent. Elaborating on Kalhana's impression of the trading genius of the Kashmiris, the Scot traveller John Bogle observes that the natives of Kashmir "scatter themselves over the Eastern kingdoms of Asia...Their agents stationed on the coast of Coromandal, in Bengal, Benares, Nepal and Kashmir furnish them with the commodities of these countries..."[32] Kashmir is also noted for sandal and apples besides saffron. Kalidasa's poems describe the sandal of Kashmir.[33]

Aurel Stein makes this most authentic statement in his English translation of the *Rajatarangini*: "The favours with which nature has lavishly endowed 'the land in the womb of Himalayas' are not likely to fade or vanish. But those manifold remains of antiquity which the isolation of the country preserved and which help us to resuscitate the life and conditions of earlier times are bound to disappear more and more with the advance of western influence."[34]

References

1. *India 2009 A Reference Annual,* pp. 1064 & 65. This area includes 78,114 sq. km under the illegal occupation of Pakistan, 5180 sq. km illegally handed over by Pakistan to China and 37,555 sq. km under the illegal occupation of China.

2. *Ibid.* This figure excludes the population of areas under the illegal occupation of Pakistan and China where census could not be taken.
3. John Garrett, *A Classical Dictionary of India*, p. 281.
4. A corruption of the ancient Varaahamoola. The place enjoyed great sanctity in early times as the abode of Vishnu in his primeval boar incarnation. The famous Aadi Varaaha Temple here was destroyed by Sikandar, the notorious iconoclast.
5. Mythical abode of the greater Grecian gods in North East Greece on the boundary between Thessaly and Macedonia.
6. The three divisions of *svarga-loka* or heaven are: *divya-svarga, bhauma-svarga and bila- svarga.* (Swami Prabhupada, *Srimad Bhagavatam*, Fifth Canto, p. 596.)
7. People who speak the Dard group of languages spoken in Kashmir, northern Pakistan and eastern Afghanistan including Kashmiri.
8. So-called because the speakers were cannibals and thus styled *Pisachas*, eaters of raw flesh, by their neighbours.
9. K.N. Dhar, *Glimpses of Kashmiri Culture*, Series I.
10. Karan Singh's Foreword to K.S. Nagarajan's *Contribution of Kashmir to Sanskrit Literature*, p. 3.
11. Devarajan, *Vainavamum Aazhvarkalum* (Tamil), Part 2, pp. 1105-07; M.K. Sudarshan, "A Great Disciple of Ramanuja," *The Hindu*, 30 June 2000.
12. *Literary Cultures in History, Reconstructed from South Asia*, p. 44.
13. *Dictionary of World History*, p. 1254.
14. Different from the famous King Harsha Vardhana of the seventh century who was the ruler of Sthaneswar and Kanauj.
15. A.B. Keith, *A History of Sanskrit Literature*, p. 196.
16. Ranjit Sitaram Pandit, *Rajatarangini The Saga of the Kings of Kashmir*, pp. xxxviii &xxxix.
17. Debala Mitra, *Pandrethan, Avantipur and Martand*, p. 9.
18. M.J. Akbar, *Kashmir Behind the Vale*, p. 13.
19. Jawaharlal Nehru, *Glimpses of World History*, p. 107.
20. M.A. Stein, *Kalhana's Rajatarangini A Chronicle of Kings of Kashmir*, p. 78.
21. *Pandrethan, Avantipur and Martand, op. cit.*, p. 12.
22. *Imperial Gazetteer of India*, Vol. XV, p. 91.
23. Modern Sopore or Suyyapur has been named after him.
24. A.L. Basham, *The Wonder that was India*, p. 195.
25. *History of Kashmir*, Christian Literature Society for India, p. 6.
26. *Rajatarangini, op. cit*, pp. 244 & 259.

27. *Kalhana's Rajatarangini, op. cit*., P. 105.
28. *The wonder that was India, op. cit.*, p. 100.
29. *Rajatarangini, op. cit.*, verses 173, 177 &178, First Taranga, pp. 28 &29.
30. The *Variegated Plumage Encounters with Indian Philosophy, A Commemoration Volume in honour of Pandit Jankinath Kaul "Kamal,"* p. 64.
31. *The Gazetteer of India, History and Culture*, edited by P.N. Chopra, Vol. Two, p. 499.
32. Cited in John Mac Gregor, *Tibet: A Chronicle of Exploration*, p. 149 reproduced in *Kashmir: Garden of the Himalayas*, p. 15.
33. A. B. Keith, *A History of Sanskrit Literature, op. cit.*, p. 80.
34. Cited by K.S. Nagarajan, *Contribution of Kashmir to Sanskrit Literature*, p. iii.

2

Hindu Kashmir Becomes Muslim Kashmir

Kalhana's monumental work *Rajatarangini* was continued by the famous commentator Jonaraja until his death in 1459. He covered the troubled period from the last of the Hindu dynasties and of the first Muslim rulers up to the ascendancy of the popular ruler Zain-ul-Abidin, whose reign began in 1420. It is generally held that Jonaraja carried the work in the style of Kalhana. After him his pupil Srivara carried the narrative from where his *Guru* had left to the ascension of Fateh Shah in 1486 in his four works titled *Jaina Rajatarangini*. Following him, Pranjnya Bhatta and his pupil Suka Rajavalipataka brought the record down to 1586 when Akbar conquered Kashmir. A.B. Keith, the reputed Professor of Sanskrit and Comparative Philology, does not speak well of the later works. To him, they are of minimal value devoid of originality or merit. He says "they come nowhere near *Rajatarangini* and are far less accurate in matters of topography than Kalhana." Fortunately, other authentic sources of information for the period from twelfth century are by no means scarce.

After the reign of the celebrated Avantivarman of the Utpala dynasty, Kashmir suffered the misfortune of a long succession of weak rulers. But they were considerably helped by the Gurjara-Pratihara kings like Jayapala, Anandapala and Trilochanapala in defending the northwestern gates of India against the depredations of Mahmud of Ghazni first and Mohammad of Ghor later. Until the fourteenth century, Islam, which made spectacular progress almost throughout northern India forcing many kingdoms to succumb to the

Muslims, failed to establish itself in Kashmir. Despite a succession of wars and internal dissensions after Avantivarman, even Mahmud of Ghazni could not gain a foothold in Kashmir. The mountain territory triumphantly checked and repulsed his invasion. It was indeed Kashmir's good fortune that nature saved her from Mahmud of Ghazni when he swooped upon the territory with a huge army over the Pir Panjal Pass during one of his invasions in the eleventh century. In the twelfth century, a descendant of Chengiz (also called Genghis) Khan "the Mongol shaker of the earth," made an unsuccessful attempt to plunder Kashmir. Unable to brave its severe winter, he did not enter the Vale and left it through the Banihal pass and died in a blizzard in 1203. His grandson Kublai Khan ruled Kashmir for a short period.

It is significant that Marco Polo (1254-1324), the Venetian traveller, who visited Kashmir sometime in the last quarter of the thirteenth century, makes mention of two things in his travelogue *Il Milions* known in English as the *Travels of Marco Polo* which became famous as a "Geographical classic." One was the presence of Saracens[1] in Kashmir in his time. The other was the existence of evil practices like sorcery and "devilries of enchantment." This could be because some of the poor, credulous and simple minded Kashmiris being reduced to penury during the reigns of some irresponsible and cruel kings, who used "shameless methods" for extortion, gradually resorted to earning their livelihood as quacks, alchemists and through other dishonest practices.[2] This unfortunately added to the moral decadence and economic decay of the Hindu State which was on the brink of collapse when "adventurers were hovering round like vultures on a dying beast."[3] In the *Rajatarangini*, there are many references to witchcraft and sorcery. Even "kings desirous of sovereignty in this kingdom use witchcraft and other foul means against elders," says Kalhana.[4] It is said that Kalhana "quite cheerfully accepts witchcraft as a legitimate cause of deaths."[5] Marco Polo also says that "Kashmir is the very source from which idolatry spread abroad."[6]

Muslim Inroads into Kashmir

Of the numerous Muslim raids of Kashmir, the first and the most devastating was the one launched during the reign of Suha Deva in early fourteen century. It was launched by Dalcha believed to be a vassal of the Chagtay Mongol Khanate. The raid which lasted eight months witnessed the forcible conversion of the Hindus of Kashmir to Islam. While leaving the Valley, Dalcha took with him 50,000 Brahman Pandits as slaves. But he, his troops and the enslaved Brahman Pandits perished in the snowstorm they encountered while crossing the Devasar Pass. This Pass was consequently named "*Bata Gajan*" meaning the "Brahmans' Death Oven."[7] As a result of the frequent raids of Kashmir by the Muslims, its classical Sanskrit tradition suffered a great set-back yielding place to Persian. A more tragic result was the conversion of the Hindu Kingdom of Kashmir into a Muslim State. Since then the Muslim rulers have all been extremely cautious to preserve the newly acquired Muslim character of the Hindu State of Kashmir. Anything done for the good of the Hindu community, which was reduced to a minority, was considered a conspiracy to change the Muslim- majority character of Kashmir.

Islam was first popularised in Kashmir by the Tibetan Prince Rinchan Shah who usurped the throne of Kashmir in 1317 with the help of Shah Mir, a Muslim adventurer of Swat (now in Pakistan). Both Rinchan Shah and Shah Mir were friendly with Ram Chand, the intrepid and patriotic Commander-in-Chief of Kashmir assisting him to maintain some semblance of authority in Kashmir. Later, Rinchan Shah quarrelled with Ram Chand and killed him with the help of the Ladakhis. He married Kuta Rani, daughter of Ram Chand. When his avowed desire to convert to Hinduism was thwarted by the Kashmiri Pandits, Rinchan Shah turned to a Transonian Muslim mystic who converted him to Islam. He was the first Muslim ruler of Kashmir. Many of his subjects followed in his footsteps and embraced Islam. He died having reigned for just two years and a half. Following Rinchan Shah's death, Udayanadeva, the brother of Rajasimhadeva of Lohara dynasty married his widow Kuta Rani and ruled Kashmir. On his death, Kuta Rani ruled for a short while and committed suicide to escape marrying Shah Mir. The latter declared himself King of Kashmir and established the Sultan dynasty in Kashmir in the fourteenth century.

Towards the close of the fourteenth century began the tide of barbarism. The Hindu Kingdom of Kashmir came under the control of fanatical rulers beginning with Sultan Sikandar (1394-1416). Since then fomenting violence against the Hindus in their homeland became the order of the day. Desecration and destruction of the temples of the Hindus, many of which had been in existence for more than a millennium, was the pastime of a many a ruler. In many cases, mosques were raised on their foundations. Sikandar, the iconoclast, destroyed the ancient temple of Vishnu Adi Varaha. He delighted in pulling down the temples and throwing away the idols made of precious metals after mutilating them. For "achieving" such "noble" acts, the Sultan earned the epithet *Butshikan* ("idol breaker"). The demolition of the temples was carried out by piling in the temple heaps of timber which were set ablaze.[8]

Shockingly, the Sultan's chief agent, who planned the demolition, was his Minister Suhabhatta, a Brahman convert to Islam.[9] Muslim India's famous historian Firishta also refers to the Sultan's demolition of the temples and the inhuman treatment meted out to Kashmiri Pandits. Abul Fazl also speaks of Sikandar's iconoclastic zeal and persecution of non-Muslims. Jonaraja presents a detailed account of the persecution of the Pandits of Kashmir and the wholesale destruction of the temples down to 1459.[10]

There were of course benevolent monarchs among the Muslim rulers like Zain-ul-Abidin (1420-70) called "the Badshah." He was wise, virtuous and very tolerant to the Hindus. He remitted the poll-tax imposed on Hindus and reversed the bigoted policy of Sikandar. He was fondly described as "The Akbar of Kashmir." He patronised scholars of all faiths and was instrumental in bringing out a Persian translation of the *Mahabharata* by Mulla Ahmed Kashmiri. Towards the close of his good reign, the Chakks, a turbulent and brave clan rose to prominence. Though the Sultan drove them out, they returned during the period of his weak successors and eventually seized the Government of Kashmir. The Chakks were poor administrators and hence internecine quarrels among them robbed Kashmir of peace and tranquillity. This disquiet continued until 1586 when Kashmir was annexed to the Mogul Empire by Akbar. Actually in 1580 itself, Akbar had a chance to interfere in the internal affairs of Kashmir. Yusuf Shah, the last of the Chakks expelled by his cousin who usurped the throne of Kashmir, fled to Akbar's court to solicit his help to retrieve his throne. Akbar agreed to help him and was on the verge of invading Kashmir, when the Kashmiri nobles dreading the invasion of their kingdom by the imperial army, promised to reinstate Yusuf Shah on the throne if he returned to Kashmir alone. Yusuf Shah accepted the condition and regained his lost throne, without the assistance of Akbar.

Six years later, Akbar ordered two invasions into Kashmir. The first expedition in February 1586 led by Raja Bhagwan Das, heir of the Rajput chief Bihari Mal of Amber, resulted in the submission of Yusuf Shah. He surrendered on the understanding that Akbar required nothing more than his personal submission and a promise of tribute and that he could return to his kingdom as the Emperor's vassal. Akbar was disenchanted with these terms. He ratified the treaty but having done that, detained Yusuf Shah as a State prisoner and sent a second expedition to Kashmir under Mohammad Kasim Khan to complete the subjugation of the kingdom. On 15 October 1586, Kashmir was formally annexed to the Mughal Empire though Yusuf Shah's son Yakub Khan surrendered only in August 1589. Akbar ruled Kashmir for sixteen years. When he visited Kashmir in 1589 he called it "My Private Garden." He was a great admirer of Kashmir shawls ornamented with gold and silvery thread. In 1599, Akbar introduced a lighter assessment of revenue and opened public works measures which alleviated the distress of the people who were famine-stricken. He also dispensed with forced labour.[11] His son Jehangir (1605-27), a nature lover, was equally enamoured of the idyllic Valley of Kashmir. His fascination for the enchanting Kashmir is discernible in his ecstatic outburst on the occasion of his first visit to the Valley in these words in Persian:

Agar firdous bar rooye zamin ast:
Hamin ast, hamin ast, hamin ast.
("If there is a paradise on the surface of this earth;
It is here, it is here, it is here.")

Being skilled in the art and practice of laying out gardens, he was responsible for as many as 777 lovely pleasure gardens in Kashmir including the loveliest Shalimar Bagh, all yielding a revenue of one lakh of rupees from roses and bed musk. This is what Jehangir says about Kashmir in his *Tuzuk-I-Jehangir* ("*Memoirs of Jehangir*"): "Kashmir is a garden of eternal spring or an iron fort to a palace of kings – a delightful flower bed and a heart-expanding heritage for derwishes. Its pleasant meads and enchanting cascades are beyond all description. There are running streams and fountains beyond count..."[12] There is one rare information about a tree that Jehangir had planted in Kashmir. It was massive chinar whose trunk attained a girth of 56 feet. This celebrated tree, which was in the Moghal Garden at Bijbehara in the Srinagar-Jammu highway, was a great tourist attraction for more than three centuries. It fell down in 1970 under the weight of the unseasonal snow in Kashmir, at the age of 350. It was evidently planted by Jehangir in the early 1620s. His son Shah Jehan (1627-58) also had left his imprints on the valley. Apart from introducing fresh laws and abolishing unfair taxes, he was also immensely fascinated by the beauty of Kashmir. With his abiding interest in the designs and plans of buildings, he too adorned Kashmir by many exquisite gardens and stately buildings.[13] In short, the sixty years from 1589 constituted an era of amazing construction of buildings and gardens in Kashmir.

Resumption of Fanaticism and Oppression

For about six decades the people of Kashmir enjoyed a quiet life and prosperity owing to the benevolence of the three Moghal rulers. But in the third quarter of the seventeenth century, their even life was again disturbed more violently than before during the reign of Aurangzeb. His policy of religious persecution and demolition of temples including those of the Sikhs incensed the latter. Under Tegh Bahadur, son of Har Govind, the sixth Sikh spiritual Guru, they protested against the religious policy of Aurangzeb. Tegh Bahadur also encouraged the Pandits of Kashmir to oppose the Moghal ruler's religious intolerance. Aurangzeb known for his extreme fanaticism arrested him and gave him a choice between conversion to Islam and death. Tegh Bahadur who valued his faith more than his life submitted to his execution in 1675.

The next consequential incident in the history of Kashmir was the third invasion of Ahmad Shah Abdali, an Afghan of the Abdali clan, who later crowned himself *Durrani Padishah* ("Pearl among Kings") in 1751. He conquered Kashmir after defeating the weak Moghal Emperor Ahmad Shah but the disturbances at home compelled his immediate return to Afghanistan. But in 1756 he came to India for the fourth time and made the Moghal Emperor cede Kashmir to him. He came thrice more to India – in 1759, 1764 and 1767. The oppressive rule of these Afghans for about seven decades was a period of "brutal tyranny unrelieved by good works, chivalry or honour" in the history of Kashmir. There was active persecution of Hindus especially the Pandits throughout their rule. The assiduous efforts to banish them from Kashmir, their homeland, were in full swing paving the way for the Muslim converts to constitute a large majority in the State. Speaking of the precarious status of the Hindus in their own land, Francis Younghusband writes that the Afghans "thought no more of cutting off their heads than of plucking flowers." Their inhuman treatment of the Hindus smacked of the gladiatorial combats of ancient Rome where the slaves were tortured by wild animals to the delight of the public. The Afghans delighted in "tying up the Hindus, two and two, in grass sacks and sinking them in the Dal Lake."[14] As if the cruelties perpetrated by the rulers were not enough, famines also struck Kashmir, the worst one occurring in 1773.

One significant result of Durrani's invasions was the rise of the Sikhs whose martial prowess was matchless. They played a very crucial role in shaping the history of Kashmir. The people of Kashmir oppressed by the Afghan rulers invited the Sikh supremo Ranjit Singh, "the Lion of Punjab," to rescue them from the Afghan clutch. This presented the much awaited opportunity to the Punjab ruler who had covetous eyes on this enormously enchanting Kingdom. Well known for his iron will, avarice and perseverance, Ranjit Singh rushed to the succour of Kashmir, defeated the Afghan Governor of Kashmir and annexed the territory to his dominion.

A British historian of India rightly observes that Ranjit Singh "possessed just that combination of virtues and vices which is best adapted for building up an oriental empire." By 1820, he was the master of nearly the whole of the Punjab and Kashmir. A diplomat of the first order, he secured the friendship of the English. He promised and did help them to keep the Mahrattas out of the Punjab. Wisely recognising the mighty English, Ranjit Singh remained loyal to them until his death in 1839 at the age of 54.

The Kashmiris were not happy with their Sikh rulers either, as they taxed them exorbitantly. A great number of them facing starvation at home fled to the plains of Hindustan. To be brief, the Sikhs also were tough masters if not so "barbarically cruel as the Afghans." The accounts of foreign travellers of Kashmir during this period are not in the least complimentary about the Sikh governance. According to Moorcroft, who visited Kashmir in 1824, the people throughout the State were in the most abject condition being taxed excessively by the Sikh Government and "subjected to every kind of extortion and oppression by its officers...not one-sixteenth of the cultivable surface is in cultivation and the inhabitants starving at home, are driven in great numbers to the plains of Hindustan." The famous shawl industry of Kashmir was the worst affected during the Sikh regime. Moorcroft says that "every shawl was taxed 26 per cent upon the estimated value, besides which there was an import duty on the wool with which they were manufactured and a charge was made upon every shop of workman connected with the manufacture."[15]

Unfortunately, the Kashmiris sadly lacked valour. The gentle, graceful and friendly Kashmiris possessed very little physical stamina to face trouble. They had a loud bark but no bite at all. It was their "pathetic incompetence" writes Lord Birdwood that was "successfully exploited by the Scythian Hindu Princes, Mughal Emperors, Durranis of Kabul and Ranjit Singh, the Sikh." The British historian of India, Vincent Smith also attributes the ills of Kashmir "partly to the cowardly character of the population, which invited oppression."[16] Kalhana describes the Kashmiri as "fair and false and fickle" and condemns the soldiery for being "disorderly and cowardly." Mohammad Iqbal, himself a Kashmiri, very dejectedly writes that "the Kashmiri has come to hug slavery to his bosom...A stranger to the dignity of self, ashamed of his ego." The unkindest cut came from Zafrullah Khan who, as the Foreign Minister of Pakistan, said once while addressing the Security Council that "one soldier armed with no more than a bayonet could drive 4,000 Kashmiris in whatever direction he desired."[17]

Sale of Kashmir

After Ranjit Singh's death in 1839, the fate of north India was once again in the melting pot. His military kingdom was not destined to live long. It broke up paving the way for two Anglo-Sikh wars. In the first war of 1845-46 which related to Kashmir, the English vanquished the Khalsa army. By the Treaty of Amritsar that followed in March 1846, the Sikhs ceded to the British the hill districts between Beas and Indus including Kashmir and Hazara. In the case of Kashmir, as per the Treaty, the Sikhs had to pay the British an indemnity of a million pound sterling and a half or cede Kashmir with half a million sterling. By an extraordinary stroke of luck, Gulab Singh, the Dogra Hindu Rajput[18] ruler of Jammu stood to gain enormously from the transaction. The Sikh preferred the latter alternative offered by the English. The sequel was the sale of the rich and idyllic Vale of Kashmir for just one million sterling by the British to Gulab Singh who remained neutral in the war.

A brief mention of the background of Gulab Singh, the first Maharaja of Kashmir, is necessary in this context. Talented Gulab Singh who was "a running footman" to Ranjit Singh to start with, was a descendant of Raja Dhruv Dev, a Dogra Rajput, who came into prominence in the area surrounding Jammu after the invasion of Nadir Shah of Persia in 1739. These Hindu Chieftains often attacked other minor rulers, both Muslim and Rajput, for local ascendancy. Being far removed from the Punjab plains, their activities went unnoticed by the Mughals. In 1780, when the then Dogra Rajput ruler died, there was a succession dispute between his sons who invoked the intervention of the Sikhs. This resulted in Jammu becoming a tributary to the Sikh power. It was given to the three grandsons of the youngest brother of the deceased Dogra ruler to restore the fortunes of the dynasty. The three youths one of whom was Gulab Singh took service with the Sikhs who rewarded them in 1820 with the fiefs of Poonch, Ramnagar and Jammu for their military exploits. The brothers soon consolidated their rule over most of the hill territory between the Punjab and the watershed beyond which lay the Valley of Kashmir. Jammu fell to the lot of Gulab Singh. He conducted two campaigns to the northeast and added to his conquests Ladakh, the quasi-independent Buddhist feudatory of Tibet for centuries. He then turned to the north and annexed Baltistan. Still he continued to acknowledge the Sikh suzerainty. Though during the first Anglo-Sikh war he held himself aloof, after the battle of Sobraon, which marked the final defeat of the Sikhs, he played the mediator. Since the Sikhs were unable to pay the British the war indemnity as per the Treaty of Amritsar that ended the war, in 1846, they relinquished their hill feudatories beyond the Punjab. As a reward for Gulab Singh's benevolent neutrality and other services rendered, the British allowed him to pay the indemnity and take the territories which included his own fiefs and conquests, the fiefs of his two dead brothers and the Valley of Kashmir.[19]

It was thus to further weaken the Sikhs that the English Government separated Kashmir from the Sikh Kingdom and sold it to Gulab Singh. Viceroy Hardinge (1844-48) wrote to Ripon,[20] President, India Board: "A Rajpoot State independent of the Sikhs on the right flank of our Beas frontier would strengthen us and weaken the Sikhs – and this I consider most desirable."[21]

Thus, Kashmir once again came under the Hindu rulers after a long span of nearly five centuries. *But by mid-nineteenth century, nine-tenths of her Hindu population had been converted to Islam.*

On 16 March 1846, a separate treaty was signed with Gulab Singh by which Kashmir and the Hill States from the Indus to the Beas were detached from the Punjab and transferred to Gulab Singh as a separate sovereignty for a sum of one million sterling. By Article 1 of this Treaty, the territory of Jammu and Kashmir comprising an area of 2,22,236 square kilometres was "transferred and made over for ever in independent possession to Maharaj Gulab Singh." Since the British faced no problem from Russia at that time, Article V of the Treaty merely said that any disputes with neighbouring States must be referred to the arbitration of the British Government whose decision was final. No resident was appointed to Kashmir. It was an open secret that the Maharaja became a vassal of the East India Company. The Maharaja had no illusion about his position. In token of the British Government's supremacy, he agreed to present it annually "one horse, twelve perfect shawl goats of approved breed (six male and six female) and three pairs of Kashmiri shawls." Gulab Singh further promised "to join...the whole of his military force (with the) British troops when employed within the hills or in the territories adjoining his possessions." The British Government on their part promised to give its aid to Gulab Singh in protecting his territories from external enemies. The Governor of Kashmir, who was appointed by the Sikh Government, treated with great contempt the sale of Kashmir to Gulab Singh, a scion of the Sikh rivals.[22] When he attacked Gulab Singh with the aid of feudatories, the British came to the latter's aid and the British officer Sir Henry Lawrence accompanied him to Srinagar. Gulab Singh was able to establish his rule only by the end of 1846. The credit for the amalgamation of the modern State of Jammu and Kashmir goes to the Kashmiri Dogras. About a century later, referring to this, Pakistan accused Britain of having sold the Kashmiri Muslims into slavery to a Hindu dynasty.

It was reported that in 1850, Maharaja Gulab Singh, who was much upset about the extremely large scale conversion of the Kashmiri Hindus to Islam over the centuries, desired to reconvert them *en masse* to Hinduism, their original religion. But the Pandits of Benares refused to give their blessings to the Maharaja's wish.[23] This report has been corroborated by Jawaharlal Nehru. The process of conversion to Islam which was a long-drawn affair resulted in 95 per cent of the Hindu population of Kashmir becoming Muslims. In the mid-nineteenth century, Nehru says, "the Hindu ruler of the State found that very large numbers of these people were anxious or willing to return *en bloc* to Hinduism. He sent a deputation to the Pandits of Benares inquiring if this could be done. The Pandits refused to countenance any such change of faith and there the matter ended."[24]

The sale of Kashmir was subject to severe criticism in India and Britain. The Supreme Government was widely blamed for committing a great blunder in preferring the Valley's sale to its retention. According to Cunningham, the transaction which brought the British a paltry sum was unworthy of British name and fame. Deeply regretting the Government's action in wantonly relinquishing all the benefits that accrued to the British from the possession of Kashmir, W. Wakefield wrote: "...the huckstering spirit that so often pervades our national policy and which caused the great Napoleon to apply to us the term of "a nation of shop-keepers" was dominant in this case..."[25] According to Lord Birdwood, the modern Kashmir problem should in a large measure be attributed to this award of "doubtful wisdom and integrity" to a Dogra Chief Minister.

The fact of the whole matter was this: In the first half of the nineteenth century, the British used Kashmir as a "pawn in the subjugation of the Punjab and Afghanistan." After 1846, their sole aim was to weaken the Sikhs who were renowned for their magnificent fighting qualities by reducing the State of Lahore in size. The best way to achieve this was to amputate Kashmir "the easiest limb" by handing it to Gulab Singh as a reward to his service which involved a good deal of cruelty. He would effectively put down the Sikhs if they dared to show signs of gaining power. An additional substantial advantage on which the British counted was the combination of the Dogra Rajputs and the Sikhs which would act as a check upon the Mohammedans of the northwest who constituted a threat to the security of the Indian frontiers on that side.[26]

The saddest part of the entire transaction was that the people of Kashmir hardly counted in it! The Princely States with a few exceptions were noted for absolute autocracy and so, no voice was raised against this transaction within the State.

Gulab Singh proved a tough ruler but the British were greatly drawn to his extraordinary skill in secret diplomacy. With the British assistance, he overcame the Sikh forces in Kashmir and consolidated his territories. During the Great Revolt of 1857, he sided with the British. He died the same year and was succeeded by his son Ranbir Singh who was a marked contrast to his father. He was very popular with both the people and the British. In 1860, he added the northern areas of Gilgit and Punial by conquest to his inheritance and brought the frontier States of Hanza and Nagar and the independent territories Yasni, Kok-Ghizar, Ishkuman, Darely Tangir and Chilas under his suzerainty.

With the closer integration of the State in British India and the final emergence of British Paramountcy, came the realisation of Kashmir's strategic importance. This was of great significance to the British in their imperial and military designs in Central Asia. Thereafter, British India's attitude towards the Maharaja became aggressive. The Government exercised tight control over him especially in respect of Ladakh and Gilgit and also interfered with the administration in order to maintain law and order, prevent disaffection and also carry out rudimentary developmental work like laying of roads that would also serve its military and commercial interests. Two British officers were imposed on the Maharaja. One appointed in 1867 was entrusted with the administration of Gilgit and making annual visits to Ladakh to supervise the affairs of the age-old trade from British India through Srinagar and Leh to Central Asia. The other appointed in 1884 was the permanent Resident Political Agent at Srinagar who would act as the intermediary between the Government of India and the State administration. Thus the British Government's control over the affairs of the State became considerably stiffened.

Ranbir Singh was a large-hearted and considerate ruler but was so close to the British as to help them immeasurably against his own countrymen during the Great Revolt of 1857. He sent to Queen Victoria a pair of Kashmir's *Pashmina* goats as a present and the gracious Queen sent him a return gift of a tank full of tiny trout fingerlings which "flourished so well in Kashmir as to outgrow their ancestors."[27] Paying rich tributes to Ranbir Singh, Francis Younghusband says that his daily public *durbars* were themselves an education of great value to the people who "learn character and hear outside news and it is surprising to see how much more native intelligence, dignity and character men brought up in these conditions have, than the school-bred men of today...Ranbir Singh was a typical ruler of a type that is now almost gone."[28] Blandishments were showered on the Maharaja copiously but in the same breath the British Indian Government aggressively divested him of his legitimate powers.

On Ranbir Singh's death in 1885, his son and successor Pratap Singh continued the same policy towards the British. In fact he was even more friendly with them than his father which prompted Francis Younghusband to dedicate his book on Kashmir to Pratap Singh. By this time the Russian menace had spread widely much upsetting the English. The Czarist Russia, whose greed for territory was as insatiable as that of the British, had emerged as the colonial rival of the British Empire in Central Asia. In 1889, the Russian agents were reported to be active in Kashmir. Thereupon the British occupied Chitral and also established the Gilgit Agency. Two years later, the small states of Hunza and Nagar were also brought under Gilgit, which paid an annual tribute to the Kashmir State. A British Political Agent was stationed at Gilgit and was made responsible to the British Resident in Srinagar. A few days before the partition of India in August 1947, Gilgit was handed back to the Maharaja of Kashmir.

During Pratap Singh's reign, the British Indian Government's intervention in the affairs of the Kashmir administration became ubiquitous. But when rumours implicating Maharaja Pratap Singh in Russian intrigues reached the Government, the latter apparently gave no credence to them. But he was deprived of all authority over his Government which was handed over to a Council of Regency consisting of members hand-picked by the British Indian Government with the Resident as the virtual ruler of Kashmir on the ground of the State's maladministration. In 1889, the Maharaja's resignation was accepted. The motive behind this drama was to annex Kashmir to British India. Col. Pary Nisbet, the British Resident in Kashmir, promulgated to the outside world the edict of the voluntary resignation of the Maharaja. It was anybody's guess that the edict was extracted from the Maharaja. Pratap Singh was forced to sign the draft of an *irsad* which was a declaration of abdication. This drastic act was condemned by many liberal imperialist statesmen who put up a vigorous defence for the Maharaja in the British Parliament. The British statesman William Digby also did his best to prove that there was no misgovernment in Kashmir and that the motive behind the unlawful act was Russophobia.[29] The Maharaja also wrote to the Viceroy of the injustice done him and had the *irsad* withdrawn.

Again in 1903, during his viceroyalty, that consummate Curzon (1899-1905) attempted to annex Kashmir to British India. The rumour of the Maharaja's willingness to voluntarily abdicate his throne and make over Kashmir to the British Government was once again rife in military circles.[30] However, the rumour remained a rumour and thereafter there was no further attempt to annex Kashmir until the British left India.

It must be said in justice to the British that their intervention brought many admirable achievements to the State. Outstanding civil servants like Walter Lawrence "carried out work of truly historic dimensions." A rational system of land settlement, payment of revenue in cash and aboiition of forced labour and beggary to mention but a few were their remarkable feats.[31]

References

1. The name derived from the Greek *Sarakenei* was applied by the Greeks and Romans in very early times to an Arab tribe living in the Sinai Peninsula in Egypt. In the middle ages, it was applied to any person – Arab, Turk or others – who professed the religion of Islam.
2. *Adyar Library Bulletin*, Vol. XXXI – XXXII – 1967-68, *Dr. V. Raghavan Felicitation Volume*, p. 174.
3. *History of Kashmir*, Christian Literature Society for India, p. 9.
4. Ranjit Sitaram Pandit, *Rajatarangini The Saga of the Kings of Kashmir*, p. 126.
5. A.B. Keith, *A History of Sanskrit Literature*, p. 166.
6. Yule and Burnell, *Hobson-Jobson*, p. 169.
7. A. Kaul, *The Kashmiri Pandit*, Calcutta, 1924, p. 44 cited in Henry Sender, *The Kashmiri Pandits – A Study of Cultural Choice in North India*, p. 10.
8. *Annual Report,* Archaeological Survey of India 1915-16, p. 56.
9. Debala Mitra, *Pandrethan, Avantipur and Martand,* p. 14.
10. *Ibid,* pp. 14 & 15.
11. *The Cambridge History of India,* Vol. IV, pp. 124,135,136,143 & 167.
12. Cited in Raghubir Singh, *Kashmir, Garden of Himalayas*, p. 21.
13. *The Cambridge History of India, op. cit, p.* 220.
14. Sir Francis Younghusband, *The History of Kashmir*, p. 159.
15. *Ibid.*, p. 161.
16. Vincent Smith, *The Oxford History of India*, p. 176.
17. Lord Birdwood, *A continent Decides,* pp. 212 & 13.

18. The Rajputs inhabiting Dogra – the hilly region in the Punjab. Settled originally in Oudh or Rajputana, these Rajputs eventually moved to the Punjab.
19. L.A.C. Fry, "History of Jammu and Kashmir State", 16 May 1950, FL/1015/235.
20. John Robinson Ripon was the father of the famous Viceroy of India Samuel Robinson Ripon (1880-84).
21. Hardinge to Ripon, 19 Feb. 1846, DO/196/ 141.
22. "History of Jammu and Kashmir State," *op. cit.*
23. Josef Korbel, *Danger In Kashmir.*
24. Jawaharlal Nehru, *The Discovery of India*, p. 267.
25. M.L. Kapur, *Kashmir Sold and Snatched*, p. 16.
26. *Ibid*, p. 13.
27. Karan Singh, *Heir Apparent An Autobiography*, pp. 15 & 16.
28. *The History of Kashmir, op. cit*, p. 175.
29. Vijay Kumar, *Anglo-American Plot against Kashmir*, pp. 24 – 26.
30. *The Hindu*, 16 July 1903.
31. Jagmohan, *My Frozen Turbulence in Kashmir*, p. 76.

3

The Last Ruler of Kashmir

Pratap Singh, the Hindu Dogra Rajput king, was succeeded by his nephew and Gulab Singh's great grand nephew Lt. General Raj Rajeshwar Maharajadhiraj Maharaja Sri Hari Singh Bahadur. He was the last ruler of Kashmir. Born on 15 September 1895, he was educated by Indian and European instructors until he joined the Mayo College in Ajmer in 1908. Later he received military training at the Imperial Cadet Corps in Dehra Dun. On 23 September 1925, at 30, he ascended the *Gaddi*. His heir apparent was Yuvaraj Shri Karan Singhji Bahadur, who was born on 9 March 1931at Cannes in the south of France.

In 1931, Maharaja Hari Singh represented the Indian Princes at the Second Round Table Conference in London. He delivered at this Conference a patriotic speech exhorting the British to respect the legitimate aspirations of the Indians. The British could not have taken kindly to what he said about freedom and self-rule in the course of his speech. He said that "as Indians and loyal to the land whence they derived their birth and infant nurture, the Princes stood solidly as the rest of their countrymen for India's enjoyment of a position of honour and equality in the British Commonwealth of Nations." During the Second World War (1939-1945) the Maharaja went to England as a Member of the War Cabinet of Winston Churchill. But his relations with the British Indian Government was never cordial as it was putting pressure on him through its Residents in Srinagar with a view to gaining total domination over the State.

When Hari Singh became the ruler, the Pandits constituted a key element in the Government monopolising all crucial appointments. Though they formed only 2 per cent of the total population of the State, they were a powerful segment in the administration. Muslims formed the majority but there were a sizeable number of Hindus and a lesser number of Sikhs, Buddhists and Christians. The valley people in general, though poor spirited and poorly educated, were well off as compared to the inhabitants of the western border regions and the more northerly parts of the State. But the latter were much more virile than their counterparts in the valley. Since these regions were less favoured areas, a major trouble in Kashmir had long been anticipated.

Advent of Sheikh Abdullah

Troubles did arise since the majority community had many grievances. One major discontent was that while the Hindus had to pay a tax of only 8 annas (equivalent to 50 *paise*) for each cow they owned, the Muslims had to pay Rs.5. Communal tensions in the northern parts of British India, especially in the Punjab, gave a fillip to the communal bias in Kashmir. Despite the measures taken to redress the grievances of the Muslims, the disquiet continued.

Agitations and disturbances were not uncommon in Kashmir since Maharaja Hari Singh ascended the throne in 1925. Initially they were engineered by certain Muslim elements from outside the State. And their slogans were "Down with Hindu Raj," "Islam in Danger" etc., which had communal overtones. During the Maharaja's absence in Europe in 1931, the movement against him intensified. There were protest meetings everywhere in the State under the lead of the emerging political leader Sheikh Abdullah whose fierce speeches against the Maharaja attracted a large crowd.

Sheikh Abdullah was born on 5 December 1905 at Soura near Srinagar as the posthumous son of a shawl weaver. His ancestors were Kashmiri Pandits who embraced Islam in 1766 under the influence of Abdur Rashid Baihaqi, a Sufi divine. Abdullah was educated at the Prince of Wales College in Jammu and the Islamia College in Lahore. After securing his M.Sc. Degree in Physics from the Aligarh Muslim University in 1930, Abdullah became a school teacher on a salary of Rs. 60 per month to start with. He was one of the few Kashmiri Muslims to learn English. For one with radical views, pedagogy had no attraction. Politics became Abdullah's forte. During the 1931 agitation, he gained considerable political stature as a staunch opponent of the Maharaja. He organised a series of meetings of Muslims in several mosques where he delivered fiery speeches against the Maharaja's rule and the hardships faced by the people in general and the Muslims in particular. His speeches unfortunately led to tensions between the Muslims and other communities in the State. When the Maharaja returned from Europe with his Maharani and the new born baby boy in May 1931, he was shocked to see the extent of the revolt against his rule. Abdullah who spearheaded the revolt was thrice arrested and released during 1931 and 1932. His incarcerations earned him the nickname *Sher-E-Kashmir* ("Lion of Kashmir").

An inflammatory speech delivered by a Muslim youth in a mosque in Srinagar on 21 June 1931 led to a series of disturbances all over the State. The Government considered the speech seditious and arrested him on that charge. The trial was conducted inside the Srinagar Central Jail. There was a large crowd in front of the jail demanding the withdrawal of the case against the Muslim youth. Soon the demonstration took a violent turn when the people started pelting stones at the police. The police retaliated by opening fire on the people which resulted in the death of twenty-one persons. This tragic incident led to deep resentment amongst the Muslim population and they organised a huge demonstration on 15 July 1931 against the rule of Maharaja Hari Singh. They also demanded an impartial commission of enquiry to investigate into their several grievances. The Government of India also put immense pressure on the Maharaja to order an enquiry into the demands of the Muslim population by an unprejudiced and independent British officer. The Maharaja agreed to this.

In October 1931, there were incursions into Kashmir by a large number of Muslim volunteers from the Punjab to help their Kashmiri co-religionists who were stated to be oppressed by their ruler. The incursions were made through Sialkot and other points in the northwest. There were also threats from the Punjab Muslim Anjuman-Athrai-Ahrai-I-Islam under the lead of Mazhar Ali to the Kashmiri *Durbar* to bring into Kashmir a body of 50,000 Punjabi volunteers. These developments placed the Government of India in a predicament as under Article 9 of the Treaty of 1846 they were bound to protect the Maharaja's "territories from external enemies," and were also under general obligation to protect the Maharaja in the event of a rebellion in the State. The ordinary law of British India had no provision to deal with unarmed persons if they peacefully walked across the frontier. The Government could deal with the Muslim *Jathas* only if they caused a breach of peace in British India. Another difficulty that lay in the way was the loyalty of the Punjabi Muslims to the Punjab Government. Any measure taken against them in their zeal to defend their Kashmiri co-religionists might alienate them besides intensifying communalism in British India. After long consideration, when the situation in the border and inside Kashmir was getting out of control, the British Indian Government despatched troops to bring the situation to normalcy. The Government of India promulgated an Ordinance under which the Punjab Government had to arrest and detain the *Jathas*.[1]

People's Movement: Reforms to Pacify

In November 1931, the Maharaja announced the appointment of a Commission of Enquiry headed by Sir B.J. Glancy of the Foreign and Political Department of the Government of India. The Commission submitted its report to the Maharaja on the grievances of the Muslim population in March 1932. It recommended several measures to provide more educational and employment opportunities to the Muslims. The Maharaja accepted almost all the recommendations and issued a notification to that effect in April 1932.

The Glancy Commission which was also to recommend constitutional reforms for the State submitted its report in April 1932. The report recommended the establishment of a Legislative Assembly and specified its composition, powers and functions. The Maharaja quickly accepted this recommendation also and constituted a Franchise Committee in May 1932. This Committee recommended the establishment of a Legislative Assembly on the model of Minto-Morley Reforms – an assembly with a non-official majority.[2]

The people of the State were not content with these constitutional reforms. They dubbed the Legislative Assembly created on the Minto-Morley Reforms model as a "representative assembly" whereas their demand was for a responsible government answerable to an assembly elected on the basis of adult franchise. To achieve this aim, a political organisation called the Jammu and Kashmir Muslim Conference was formed in Srinagar in October 1932 with Sheikh Abdullah as President and Ghulam Abbas as Secretary.

The Maharaja promulgated a Regulation in 1934 for the establishment of the Praja Sabha consisting of 75 members including 33 elected members – 21 Muslims, 10 Hindus and 2 Sikhs.[3] The franchise was very limited consisting of only about three per cent of State's population. The Maharaja retained all his legislative, executive and judicial powers. Despite their strong feelings over the limited powers of the Praja Sabha, the Jammu and Kashmir Muslim Conference participated in the first ever election held in September 1934 and won 19 of the 21 seats reserved for the Muslims. But they all resigned a year later in protest against the limited powers of the Praja Sabha.

Sheikh Abdullah kept up the momentum of his political activities by continuously holding meetings and rallies throughout the Valley. He organised the Responsible Government Day on 8 May 1936 which proved a great success. Gradually he realised the need to carry with him the non-Muslims also to achieve his aim of gaining responsible government in the State. At the Working Committee meeting of the Jammu and Kashmir Muslim Conference held in June 1938, Sheikh Abdullah moved a resolution proposing a change in the name of the party as Jammu and Kashmir National Conference and amendment of its Constitution to admit the non-Muslims also into the party. Ghulam Abbas was opposed to this move and the proposal was deferred for one year. However, in October 1939, at a special session of the Muslim Conference, the change in the name of the party was approved and its constitution was amended to allow the admission of non-Muslims into the party.[4]

In the very first session of the Jammu and Kashmir National Conference held in October 1939, a resolution was adopted demanding responsible government and a legislature of members elected by adult franchise reserving certain number of seats for the minorities. Sheikh Abdullah was also getting closer to the Indian National Congress and Jawaharlal Nehru with the objective of linking his struggle in Kashmir with the wider struggle of India to gain freedom from the British rule. Nehru visited Kashmir in May 1940. He was all admiration for Sheikh Abdullah and was pleased to see the amount of affection the people of all the communities in Kashmir had for Abdullah. Nehru reckoned him as the "acutest politician" in the State. The National Conference gained considerable strength after the visit of Nehru. In 1941, it affiliated itself with the All-India States' Peoples' Conference – an organisation widely identified with the Indian National Congress. This was resented by Ghulam Abbas which resulted in his parting company with Abdullah and reviving in 1942 the defunct Muslim Conference. Abbas was actually more inclined towards the Indian Muslim League and its charismatic leader Mohammed Ali Jinnah.

Meanwhile, the Maharaja, clearly perceiving the growing demand of the people for more meaningful constitutional reforms, issued a Proclamation on 11 February 1939, by which the number of elected members in the Praja Sabha was increased from 33 to 40 thus providing for the elected majority in that Sabha. Another important provision introduced related to the right of the members to vote on the demand for grants for budget appropriations.[5] The major decision taken by the Maharaja during this year was the promulgation on 7 September 1939 of the Jammu and Kashmir Constitution Act 1939. This Constitution Act, framed by the Maharaja himself and not by any constitutional body, had 78 Sections and 5 Schedules. It dealt with almost all the aspects of governance of a State like the legislature, executive, judiciary, finance and royal prerogatives.[6] Though the Maharaja retained his supremacy in all matters, it was evident that he was keen to involve his people more and more in the administration of his State. But the two main political parties in the State led by Abdullah and Ghulam Abbas were not satisfied with the reforms. They were firm in obtaining a representative government with a fully elected legislature on adult franchise basis and a council of ministers responsible to that legislature.

In July 1943, the Maharaja instituted a Commission of Enquiry to report on the need for further constitutional reforms. This Commission headed by Chief Justice Sir Ganga Nath was called the Royal Commission. It had 22 non-official members including two from the National Conference. The Muslim Conference refused to have anything to do with the Commission and none of its members was nominated to it. The Kashmiri Pandits were equally displeased with their representation. The National Conference also withdrew its association with the Commission. The Chairman submitted his report in October 1944 but no one had any knowledge of its contents or the follow up action.[7] The formation of the Royal Commission proved an exercise in futility.

The National Conference adopted in 1944 a politico-economic manifesto known as *Naya Kashmir* which was considered to be far ahead of its time.

In 1944, during his visit to Kashmir, Jinnah, who was vigorously campaigning for the creation of Pakistan, exhorted the Kashmiri Muslims to organise themselves under one banner and on one platform. But this proved a total failure and to his utter shock and fury, the only public meeting he attended broke up when the Nationalists, who were opposed to his theory, shouted "Go back Jinnah." This bore eloquent testimony to the high esteem in which the people of both communities, barring the members of the Muslim Conference, held the National Conference for its principles of "nationalism, secularism and left-wing socialism."

The year 1945 was significant for the holding of the Sopore session of the National Conference. It was attended by Nehru and Khan Abdul Ghaffar Khan. Nehru's participation in it helped to strengthen Abdullah's ties with him. This session included the meeting of the Standing Committee of the All-India States' Peoples' Conference under the presidency of Nehru. All these were a shot in the arm for Abdullah who was made the President of that All-India body in 1946.

The various reforms of the Maharaja to satisfy the aspirations of the people hardly lessened their discontent with his rule. On the contrary, their displeasure intensified with the return of the soldiers to Kashmir after the

Second World War. The soldiers were much disgruntled since their lot contrasted unfavourably with that of the ex-soldiers of the Punjab. Unfortunately, the Maharaja failed to realise the implications of these developments. He misjudged the situation which left in its trail many disasters.

In May 1946, while the British Cabinet Mission was in New Delhi, Sheikh Abdullah, as President of the National Conference, launched the "Quit Kashmir Movement" against Maharaja Hari Singh. It was stated to be on the lines of Gandhiji's "Quit India Movement" of 1942. While Gandhiji's "Quit India Movement" was against the British, who were aliens, Abdullah's movement was against the Maharaja who was his own countryman. In his speeches, Abdullah criticised vehemently the Treaty of Amritsar which the British entered into with Gulab Singh in 1846 for the sale of Kashmir to him. He demanded not only the abrogation of that Treaty but also the exit of the Maharaja and his clan from Kashmir. He further demanded that the people of the State should be allowed to decide their future by themselves. The Maharaja's Government resorted to ruthless measurers to curb Abdullah's Movement. He and a few other prominent members of the National Conference were arrested and a case of sedition was instituted against them. When Nehru came to Kashmir in June 1946 with a team of lawyers to defend Sheikh Abdullah, he was denied entry into the State. Defying the ban order, Nehru entered Kashmir from the Punjab via the Kohala Bridge. Nehru was taken to Domel where he was detained for two days in a Dak Bungalow. As the case against Abdullah was adjourned to a date in July 1946, Nehru was escorted out of Kashmir. Even people close to the Maharaja were stunned at the treatment meted out to Nehru. In July 1946, when the ban on his entry was lifted, Nehru came to Srinagar to oversee the proceedings in the sessions court. He also interviewed Abdullah in the prison. Abdullah's conviction for agitating for freedom from the Maharaja's rule was a foregone conclusion and he was awarded a nine-year jail sentence.

The Muslim Conference, which was opposed to the "Quit Kashmir Movement," supported the Maharaja who was hitherto its arch enemy. It was in a real dilemma because though opposed to the secularism of the National Conference, it "realised that Sheikh was indispensable to its goal – the integration of Kashmir into Pakistan."[8] Ghulam Abbas appealed to the Maharaja to release Sheikh Abdullah. But the Maharaja, equally crafty and cunning, understood the motive behind the appeal and put all the prominent members of the Muslim Conference behind the bars. On 15 August 1947 – the day of Indian independence – Kashmir found the leaders of both political parties languishing in prison!

Visits of Gandhiji and Mountbatten

The British Cabinet Mission Memorandum of 12 May 1946 declared that when India became independent, His Majesty's Government would cease to exercise the powers of Paramountcy over the Indian States. This meant that thereafter the States would have to fill the void by entering into a federal relationship with the successor Government or Governments or by entering into particular political arrangements. The Indian Independence Act of July 1947, which divided India, did not provide for the future of the Princely states. With its passage on 18 July, the British suzerainty over the Indian States had come to an end and, technically, the States became separate independent entities.

Mountbatten undertook a visit to Kashmir in June 1947 in response to the invitation of the Maharaja "his old friend." During the informal talks for four days between 19 and 23 June with the Maharaja, Mountbatten advised him (i) not to join any Constituent Assembly until Pakistan had set up her Assembly and the situation became clearer; (ii) to make no statement about Kashmir's independence; (iii) to enter into standstill and other agreements with both India and Pakistan; (iv) to eventually send representatives to one Constituent Assembly and join one of the two Dominions for the three central subjects of defence, communications and foreign affairs; and (v) to consult the will of the people and do what the majority thought best.[9] But Mountbatten did not at this stage make consulting the will of the people a condition for accession. It was significant that Mountbatten impressed on the Maharaja that in the existing political situation which was perilous, it was absolutely necessary for him to decide on the accession of Kashmir to India or Pakistan as he had to have the support of one of the two Dominions after 15 August 1947. Guaranteeing that the Government of India would not consider it an unfriendly act if he acceded Kashmir to Pakistan, he said that the States Department would give him an assurance to that effect. Few knew that the States Department made no approach at all to the Maharaja of Kashmir regarding accession. In fact Kashmir was deliberately omitted from the Committee of States representatives called by the pre-independence States Department to discuss the terms of accession while Hyderabad was included.

Both Nehru and Gandhiji were extremely anxious that the Maharaja should make no declaration of independence of Kashmir and were also keen to visit Kashmir. But Mountbatten persuaded Nehru not to visit Kashmir at that stage because of the extreme mutual animosity between Nehru and the Maharaja's administration headed by Prime Minister Ram Chandra Kak. Initially,

Mountbatten was not in favour of Gandhiji also undertaking a trip to Kashmir. As Gandhiji was insistent on his visit to Kashmir, Mountbatten allowed him to go there on condition that he made no political speeches. The Mahatma kept up his promise. On learning that both the Maharaja and the Maharani were anxious to see him, Gandhiji met the royalty. Both admitted that "with the lapse of British Paramountcy, the true Paramountcy of the people of Kashmir would commence... they would have to make the choice in accordance with the wishes of the people."[10]

The visits of neither Mountbatten nor Gandhiji seemed to have made any impact on Maharaja Hari Singh. The widely prevalent view was that every day of his four-day visit to Kashmir, Mountbatten persisted in his advice to the Maharaja to join one of the two Dominions by 14 August at the latest. He reiterated that if Hari Singh decided to accede to the new Dominion of Pakistan, India would not certainly object. If he acceded to India before independence, Pakistan being non-existent could not have interfered. He had to decide one way or the other before 15 August 1947 when British Paramountcy in India would end. But Hari Singh continued to dilly dally. Immediately after the transfer of power on 15 August 1947, Lionel Ismay, Chief of Staff, was sent to Srinagar by Mountbatten but the Maharaja had still not decided which of the two dominions he would accede his State to. He perhaps wanted to choose a course of non-accession to either Dominion. Whatever the precise cause for the delay and whoever was responsible for it, it had the most damaging impact on the sub-continent.

True, both the Maharaja and his Prime Minister Ram Chandra Kak toyed with the idea of independence at one stage. But in this matter, Swami Sant Dev, who had been in Kashmir since the reign of Maharaja Pratap Singh, also had a share. His disastrous advice lured the Maharaja to the independence idea by the prospect of the extension of his Kingdom down to Lahore.[11] But the Maharaja's alternative to independence was definitely accession to India whereas his Prime Minister Kak, who was closer to Pakistan, strongly favoured accession to the latter. Kak's animosity towards the Indian National Congress was proverbial. The Maharaja's delay in arriving at a decision on accession was rightly attributed to the strategic importance of Kashmir and the overwhelming majority of Muslims in it. But there was another factor of greater importance. It was the divergence of opinion among two sections of the Muslim themselves: one section owing allegiance to the National Conference of Abdullah and the other to the Muslim Conference of Ghulam Abbas. These apart, it was also possible that the Maharaja was considering the third option of remaining independent of India and Pakistan to save his subjects from being slaughtered. The massacres in Punjab could have forbidden him to opt for accession to Pakistan as that would have resulted in the massacres and expulsions of Hindus and Sikhs from Kashmir.

Controversy over Mountbatten's Talks with Hari Singh

The talks that transpired between Mountbatten as Crown Representative and the Maharaja during the former's sojourn in Kashmir for four days from 19 to 23 June 1947 became open to doubt. The doubt related to Mountbatten's supposed advice to the Maharaja to decide on the accession of Kashmir to one of the two Dominions before 14 August 1947 at the latest. In his discussions with Nehru on 24 June, Mountbatten had not said anything about his aforesaid advice to the Maharaja.[12] Again in his Personal Report of 27 June, there was no mention of his having given such an advice to the Maharaja.[13] Any mention of such an advice by him was made for the first time by Mountbatten at the meeting of the Defence Committee held on 25 October 1947 when he stated that he had urged the Maharaja and his Prime Minister Kak to take a decision on a permanent accession to either of the two Dominions before 15 August 1947 after ascertaining the will of the people.[14]

When later Mountbatten's attention was drawn to the discrepancy in his two statements – the first of his five points to the Maharaja by which he was "not to join any Constituent Assembly until Pakistan had set up her Assembly and the situation became clearer" and his purported advice to the Maharaja "to decide on the accession of Kashmir to one of the Dominions before 14 August 1947 at the latest" – he admitted there was a "bit of a muddle".[15]

Mountbatten planned his visit to Srinagar only to persuade the Maharaja to join Pakistan. He assured the Maharaja that if he did so, Vallabhbhai Patel would raise no objection to it. It was crystal clear that it was never the Viceroy's intention to drop the "Kashmir apple" into "Patel's basket." Mountbatten accepted to be free India's first Governor General because he "always had a very curious subconscious desire" to hold the "most marvellous job" in a most "marvellous country," as he himself told the journalists and historians Larry Collin and Dominique Lapierre when they interviewed him in the early 1970s.[16]

The inexperienced Viceroy, a former Naval Officer, played a pivotal role in administering the transfer of power from Britain and partitioning the subcontinent. Young James Cameron, the famous newspaper columnist on the BBC, accurately assessed Mountbatten when he said: "Mountbatten did an extraordinary job of political manipulation without knowing anything about politics."[17]

In the light of the above facts, the statement of some renowned authors that the Maharaja avoided seeing Mountbatten before the latter's departure from Kashmir in June 1947 by feigning colic pain does not hold good. He avoided seeing Mountbatten because he did not want to be pressurised into joining Pakistan. There is little doubt that Mountbatten was dissuading the Maharaja from acceding to India by trotting out untenable arguments.

The following evidences and statements would bear out the fears of the Maharaja:

Mehr Chand Mahajan, the Maharaja's last Prime Minister, met Mountbatten in New Delhi in October 1947 before assuming charge in Kashmir. The following is the record of his talk with Mountbatten: "From an hour's talk I had with him, I inferred that he (Mountbatten) felt that there was no option for the Maharaja but to accede to Pakistan in view of the geographical position of the State." Two days after he took over as Prime Minister, Mahajan recorded what he heard from the Maharaja about his conversations with Mountbatten in June: "From the chats in the car and talks in the social functions during these two days, the Maharaja sensed, rightly or wrongly, that the object of his (Mountbatten's) visit was to ask him to accede to Pakistan."[18] This statement is further strengthened by what the Maharaja himself had stated in his memorandum to President Rajendra Prasad. He wrote: "The impression which I gathered from my talks with Lord Mountbatten who explained the situation with plans and maps was that, in his opinion, it was advisable for me to accede to Pakistan."[19] There is yet another corroborative evidence to support the above statements. According to the editor of the *Indian News Chronicle*, J.N. Sahni, both Mountbatten and Ismay met the Maharaja and advised him "to take a firm and early decision in favour of Pakistan." They also said that in making this recommendation "they were only expressing the views of Nehru and Patel."[20]

Mountbatten publicly condemned the Maharaja for "indecision" in his speech to the East India Association in London delivered in June 1948 after his return from India.[21]

Hari Singh's only positive action after the visits of Mountbatten and Gandhiji was to propose telegraphically on 12 August Standstill Agreements with both India and Pakistan. The Pakistan Government sent a reply telegram on 15 August conveying its agreement to the continuance of the existing arrangements "pending settlement of details and formal execution." It is not known whether any formal agreement was ever executed to this effect between the Governments of Kashmir and Pakistan. As regards India, the Government proposed that the Prime Minister or any other Minister of the Government of Kashmir might visit Delhi for negotiations. None came from Kashmir and no Standstill Agreement was signed between the State and the Dominion of India.

The Maharaja felt that Ram Chandra Kak's hatred for the Indian National Congress and advocacy of Kashmir's accession to Pakistan constituted a stumbling block to implement his changed policies in the administration. Infuriated by Kak's activities, the Maharaja dismissed him and "publicly humiliated him." According to British records, he did so under the influence of three men: his Deputy Prime Minister Rai Bahadur Batra, Swami Sant Dev and the Maharani's brother Chand, a "Household Minister" who stood for acceding to India. A Commission was appointed to enquire into the various misdemeanours allegedly committed by Kak during his service in the State first as Minister-in-waiting and later as Prime Minister. Major General Scott who had served under Kak for five years seemed to have made himself unpopular by protesting against the shabby treatment meted out to Kak.[22] He was replaced by Major-General Janak Singh and he, in turn, by Mehr Chand Mahajan.

Kak's dismissal generated unrest in some places particularly in Poonch from where rumblings of revolt among the Muslims were first heard. It was from this area that a large number of men had gone to the Indian army during the Second World War. This area had a long history of opposition to the Maharaja's rule. There was already discontent in this area over the Government's oppressive land tax which led to an agrarian agitation. The demobilised soldiers joined this agitation. The situation was exploited by the new born Pakistan which helped to blow it up into a movement for the State's accession to it. To add to the confusion was a fight about this time between the Hindu and Muslim inhabitants of Poonch and Mirpur which resulted in the Muslim units of the State forces desert the army and the Hindu units to "burn all villages in the three mile wide strip of the State territory bordering Pakistan."[23]

Technically Kashmir was independent on 15 August 1947 as the Maharaja had not decided to join any of the two Dominions. This "anomalous independence" lasted but 68 days!

Why was the Maharaja Indecisive over Accession?

References are aplenty in the British records to the autocratic rule of Hari Singh. But they would have to be taken with a pinch of salt. British prejudices against Maharaja Hari Singh were deep rooted. His speech at the Second Round Table Conference on behalf of the Indian Princes could certainly not have pleased them. It was a clear indication to the British that an assertive monarch like Hari Singh could not be expected to toe their line. Another cause adduced in some quarters was the birth of Yuvaraja Karan Singh which immensely upset them. The British, it was rumoured, were hopeful of annexing the stunningly beautiful Kashmir to British India under the ruthless doctrine of lapse which forbade a ruler without natural heir to adopt a son to succeed him. The birth of a son to the Maharaja on 9 March 1931, at his thirty-sixth year shattered the avowed hope of the British Indian Government to absorb Kashmir into the British Empire and hence the repression against the Maharaja was intensified.[24] A weightier cause than these for the deep dislike of the British for the Maharaja was his persistent demand to abolish the Agency in Gilgit and restore it to him. The British, who had always coveted the Gilgit frontier, had divided its administration into Gilgit Wazarat or settled area directly ruled by the Maharaja and the Political Agency under the control of the Political Agent of the British Indian Government. Ultimately, yielding to the Maharaja's pressure, the Government framed a proposal by which the Political Agent's post was abolished. The Political Officer who would replace him was to be "a lent State servant and not under the orders of the Government of India." But before this could take effect, Kashmir was shaken by a series of revolts against the Maharaja in which the British definitely had a hand. The political turmoil prevailing in Kashmir helped the Government of India to withdraw the proposal. Thereafter, the Maharaja gave up his demand for the restoration of Gilgit and, in 1935, he withdrew his administrative machinery from there and also handed over the Gilgit Wazarat on a "60-year lease."[25] Naturally, under the circumstances which were of the Government of India's own making, the Maharaja's existing defects were exaggerated and new ones invented.

Even granting that the Maharaja was so autocratic as portrayed by the British writings, were there not more arrogant and oppressive rulers in other Princely states? Could Maharaja Hari Singh have been more high-handed or dictatorial than some of the British rulers of India? The Maharaja could not be dismissed as a totally non-benevolent ruler either. Only an enlightened monarch would proclaim on the day he ascended the throne on 23 September 1925: "Justice is my religion and merit alone will be considered the deciding factor for all types of employment. Caste, creed, religion or sex will receive no consideration." And throwing open the temples of his State to the so-called "untouchables" bore eloquent testimony to his benevolence. This major social reform was introduced way back in 1932. Even in his progressive measures relating to land tenure and other administrative reforms, Maharaja Hari Singh was far ahead of many of the rulers of other Princely States.

The British records describe Hari Singh as a "weak" Maharaja who divided his time between "opulent feasts in his winter capital in Jammu and the beautiful flower-choked lagoons of his summer capital in Srinagar, the Venice of the Orient." The British officials often gossiped that the Maharaja spent his time wintering in Jammu and Bombay and moving up to Srinagar just to escape the summer heat. Did not the British Governors General of India and Governors of the Presidencies desert their capitals annually under the system of exodus to hill stations to escape the enervating heat of summer? Those Europeans who exaggerated the perversions and orgies of the Maharaja called him "a Himalayan Borgia." His favourites were said to be the *de facto* rulers of Kashmir despite the existence of a Cabinet and an Assembly (with a nominated majority) whose primary function was to endorse all the measures of the State Administration.

It is certainly not intended to justify the ruler's absence from the State or the pleasures he sought after. But this life style was not peculiar to the ruler of Kashmir. Lavish life style bordering on extravagance was common to royals throughout the world.

The Maharaja did have some drawbacks. He did possess the traits common to the feudal order. He could not trust anyone for long. It was his inability to repose faith in anyone for too long that led to his dispensing with the services of many worthy Prime Ministers in quick succession. This proved his "political undoing." The severity with which he dealt with the erring staff of his Government was evidence of his bad temper which lasted long. Yuvaraja Karan Singh who strongly condemned this trait of the feudal order writes: "As I grew older, these cruel inquisitions began to infuriate me and added to my growing alienation from the order into which I had been born. Here was authority without generosity, power without compassion."[26] The Yuvaraja was completely objective when he stated that his father was "an extremist" and for him "there was no area of grey; a person was either in or out."[27] The Maharaja was conservative to the core. He had a great dislike for Congress socialists like Nehru and radicals like Sheikh Abdullah.

It must be borne in mind that Hari Singh was also assessed by some Englishmen as "an able ruler with ability much above the average of his fellow rulers," who was loved by his subjects who were loyal to him. He might have been severe but he was also humane. He had brilliant administrators noted for their unquestionable integrity and intellectual acumen like N. Gopalaswami Ayyangar, K.N. Haksar, and B.N. Rau to mention but a few, as his Prime Ministers. He welcomed their advice and did take measures to ameliorate the plight of his people and to organise his Government progressively on democratic lines. His reforms especially the enactments in the cause of Muslims uplift did not please the Hindus, but they disturbed the British much more. His pro-Muslim measures only served to intensify the British hostility towards Hari Singh. They delighted in exaggerating minor grievances of the people especially the Muslims. In fact, what was described as the freedom movement in Kashmir was engineered by outside elements at the instigation of the British. Their main concern was that Kashmir should not join India! The stooges of the British, who earlier shouted slogans like "Down with Hindu Raj," "Islam in Danger" etc., landed in plum jobs later in that part of Kashmir forcibly occupied by Pakistan in October 1947.

Many men of consequence – both British and Indian – have highlighted the Maharaja's irresolute nature. This impression is universal. Cryptic words such as "indecisive," "wavering," and "vacillating" have been freely used in portraying the Maharaja. He was accused of persisting in a policy of fence-sitting even after 15 August 1947 which was considered unpardonable. When he did not respond to the pleadings of men in authority to accede his State to one of the two Dominions, he was blamed for dilly-dallying. Immediately after the transfer of power on 15 August 1947, Ismay, who was sent to Srinagar by Mountbatten, found the Maharaja still undecided as to which of the Dominions he would accede his state. He was accused of disregarding the sage counsels of authorities to accede either to India or to Pakistan before 15 August 1947 and planning to choose a course of non-accession to either of the two states in order to make Kashmir an independent sovereign State.

The accusation that the profligate indecisiveness of the Maharaja on the accession issue landed Kashmir in a labyrinth of woes has left an indelible mark on the character of Hari Singh. It is true that owing to procrastination on the question of accession, Kashmir remains a contentious issue to this day. It is also true that it is a tragedy of sub-continental proportions. But why did the Maharaja procrastinate? How many, who accused Hari Singh through speeches and writings day in and day out, have cared to ponder on the implication of the very first advice given to him by no less a person than Mountbatten, the architect of India's partition, that he was not to join any Constituent Assembly until Pakistan set up her own Constituent Assembly?

References

1. P.N.K. Bamzai, *Culture and Political History of Kashmir*, Vol. Three, p. 735.
2. A.S. Anand, *The Constitution of Jammu and Kashmir: Its Developments and Comments*, pp. 35-37.
3. *Culture and Political History of Kashmir, op. cit.*, p. 736.
4. *The Constitution of Jammu and Kashmir, op. cit.*, pp. 41-43.
5. *Ibid*, p. 44.
6. *Ibid*, p. 63.
7. *Ibid*, pp. 67 & 68.
8. Brecher, Michael, *The Struggle for Kashmir*, p. 16, DO/196/141.
9. *Selected Works of Jawaharlal Nehru*, (*SWJN*) Second Series, Vol.3 p. 284.
10. *The Complete Works of Mahatma Gandhi*, Vol. 96, pp. 193 & 94.
11. Karan Singh, *Heir Apparent An Autobiography*, p. 37.
12. *SWJN*, Second Series, Vol. 3, op. cit., pp. 283 – 85.
13. Viceroy's Personal Report No. 10, 27 June 1947, *The Transfer of Power*, Vol. XI, p. 688.
14. Prem Shankar Jha, *The origin of a Dispute, Kashmir 1947*, p. 198.
15. Mountbatten to H.N. Pandit, 3 May 1976, *The Indian Review*, Sep, 1978, p. 10.
16. Larry Collin and Dominique Lapierre, *Mountbatten and the Partition of India, 22 March - 15 August 1947*, p. 7.
17. *Ibid.*
18. M.C. Mahajan, *Looking back*, pp. 266 & 68.
19. Maharaja's Memorandum, Aug. 1952, Appendix, Karan Singh, Jammu and Kashmir 1949-64, p. 312.
20. J.N. Sahni, *The Lid Off: Fifty Years of Indian Politics*, p. 310; H.N. Pandit, "Mountbatten's Role in Kashmir," *Indian Review*, Sep. 1976, pp. 9-15.
21. Moraes, Frank, *Jawaharlal Nehru A Biography*, p. 385.
22. Record of conversation between Major General Scott, late Chief of Staff of the Kashmir State Forces and L.B. Graffley Smith, UK HC to Pakistan, 29 September 1947, Ref. No. 14419/8800/85, File.No.63571.
23. FO to UKD to UN, 30 Dec. 1947, FO/15562/8800/85G, File No.63572.
24. No credence could be given to this theory as on 1 November 1858 itself the Government deliberately and openly renounced the policy of lapse and granted the monarchs *sunnads* or charters empowering them to adopt heirs.
25. *Culture and Political History of Kashmir*, op.cit. - in italics, p. 729.
26. *Heir Apparent An Autobiography, op. cit.*, pp. 12 to 16.
27. *Ibid*, p. 21.

4

India Dismembered

Indisputably, the architect of Pakistan was Mohammad Ali Jinnah though talks of a separate State for Muslims were in the air as early as the first quarter of the twentieth century. The suggestion for the creation of a new State of the Muslim provinces in the northeast and northwest was made as early as 1925 by Lala Lajpat Rai – the "Punjab Lion" – as a palliative for the unending Hindu-Muslim bickerings and jealousies in some provinces.[1] It was generally held that the concept of a separate nation for Muslims was adumbrated when a group of Muslim students in London brought it into prominence during the First Round Table Conference in 1930 and that it received little support from the Muslim leaders of India. A modified proposal of this concept by the Muslim poet and philosopher Mohammad Iqbal for a loose federation of Pakistan comprising one or two Muslim States was also dismissed as a "poetic fancy." In 1933, Choudhary Rahmat Ali, a 40 year-old Punjabi residing in London, provided Mohammad Iqbal's proposal with an ideology and dogma. Writing audaciously on 28 January 1933 in the pamphlet *Now or Never* that the notion that India was a single nation was a "preposterous falsehood,"[2] Rahmat Ali urged for the formation of a Muslim nation called "Pakistan" ("Land of the Pure"). According to Rahmat Ali, the name was the combination of both Persian and Urdu as it was composed of the first letters of **Punjab**, **Afghania** (North West Frontier Province), **Kashmir**, **Iran** (for the vowel **I**) and **Sind** and the last syllable of Baloch**istan**. Rahmat Ali was falsely believed to be a student of the

Cambridge University. He did not seem to have pursued any academic career in any university in London. By what means he found the huge funds he employed to promote his Pakistan movement always remained a mystery.

Britain: Originator of Pakistan Concept

The originators of the concept of Pakistan were not the Muslims but the British. Adepts as the British were in practising the policy of *divide et impera,* they launched the idea of carving out a separate State for Muslims in the northwestern region of India much earlier than 1930. The idea did strike roots in the minds of the Muslim population in that region but belatedly. In fact, the British political leaders regretted that Rahmat Ali had taken a long time to popularise his concept. When and where they located this Rahmat Ali and inspired him with their two-nation theory was never known.

Some British members of the Joint Parliamentary Committee on the Indian Constitutional Reforms cut a very sorry figure when they received little encouragement on the subject of Pakistan from the Indian Muslim delegates who had gone to London to give evidence before the Committee in April 1933. The Muslim leadership in India was dead against the idea of Pakistan. Mischievous questions on the creation of Pakistan were deliberately put persistently by men like Reginald Craddock and Isaac Foot even after all the Muslim delegates had unambiguously expressed their commitment to an all-India Federation. This was a blatant example of the height the British political leaders were prepared to scale to cut India into two pieces. Muslim Indians like Zafrullah Khan, Kalifa Shujauddin and Abdullah Yusuf dismissed the idea of Pakistan as a "Students' Scheme" which was "chimerical and impracticable" and which no respectable person or association had ever considered.[3] That the British politicians were not deterred by this defeat was borne out by the subsequent events.

The contribution of British historians to this most sinister design is no less significant. Clever and tactful, they cautiously drew "the blanket over the stories of their politicians." The Secretary of State for India Samuel Hoare (later Lord Templewood) outdid the historians when he wrote in his *Memoirs (Nine Troubled Years)* that the name Pakistan never occurred at all in any of the questions put by the British to the Indians at the Conference or in the Committees and that "the name Pakistan was practically unknown."[4]

By a quirk of luck, Rahmat Ali, who had been ploughing a lonely furrow in London for six years from 1933, found a weighty recruit to his grand project in 1939. He introduced himself to the Muslim League leader Choudry

Khaliquzzaman, who happened to visit London that year. Rahmat Ali drew very close to him and when the indoctrination was over, took him to Muirhead, Under Secretary of State for India, who received them well. He directed them to Zetland, Secretary of State for India, who was even more cordial and warm to the visitors. Everything worked up to their expectations and Khaliquzzaman was overwhelmed by surprise after surprise. Zetland's sympathy and encouragement for the Muslim cause against the background of Britain's hostility to Hindu India, spurred on the Muslim League leader to preach the message of Pakistan to "a largely uninitiated India." In his book, *Pathway to Pakistan*, Khaliquzzaman frankly stated that the British officials helped the cause of Pakistan in those years.[5] There were of course some Englishmen who inveigled against this unjust concept. For instance, the noted British Indologist, Edward Thompson, when apprised of the move to carve out a separate Muslim nation in India, said: "I was astonished…to find that certain (British) official circles were keen on the Pakistan idea; and still more astonished to find that some of our own British "Left" were beginning to be persuaded into it. There is no surer way of plunging India into eternal civil war."

How did the hideous political concept of Pakistan originate and develop in Jinnah – a most powerful leader in undivided India next only to Gandhiji? He was a man who admired and revered Indian nationalist leaders, who worked day and night in London for Dadabhai Naoroji to help him win the Parliamentary elections and become the first Indian to sit in the House of Commons, who greatly aspired to become a "Muslim Gokhale," and who often spoke of a united India. In fact Jinnah was hailed as the "ambassador of Hindu-Muslim unity." Jinnah publicly declared, "Nobody will welcome an honourable settlement between Hindus and Muslims more than I and nobody will be more ready to help it."[6] Jinnah was in very little sympathy with the Ali brothers' *Khilafat* agitation dismissing it as a "pseudo movement of the Muslim fundamentalists which might lead to a reactionary revivalism."[7] He did his best to bypass the issue first at the Calcutta session of the Muslim League in September 1920 and later at the Nagpur session of the Indian National Congress in December of that year where he remained a lone opponent of it and subsequently resigned from the Congress itself.

For more than a decade and a half after 1920, Jinnah went into political hibernation. But he remained a keen observant of the goings on in the political arena and pursued without fanfare his campaign for the Hindu-Muslim understanding. Even as late as 1937, he did not entertain the idea of a separate nation for Indian Muslims. At a meeting held in Simla (now Shimla) on

18 September 1937, Jinnah said: "There is no difference between the ideals of the Muslim League and those of the Congress...the ideal being complete freedom for India. There could not be any self-respecting Indian, who favoured foreign domination or did not desire complete freedom and self-government for his country."[8] How did such a man choose to allow India, his homeland, to be maimed and crippled? How did he, who loved the Hindus and the Muslims alike, let both harden their hearts against each other forgetting their common heritage and make the sub-continent a fearful arena of slaughter? It was an irony that Jinnah who had never been known to be an austere and hidebound Muslim declared that the dominion he was contemplating should be an Islamic State. And when this dream of his became a reality, he was perhaps more surprised than anybody else at his success. Even during the general elections of 1937 held under the Government of India Act of 1935, both the Indian National Congress and the Muslim League remained friendly and worked unitedly. This unity was especially marked in the United Provinces where there was even an electoral understanding of forming a coalition ministry.

Such cordiality and unity between the two major communities of India suffered a great setback when certain avoidable mistakes were committed. Sparks of misunderstanding that appeared after the elections, snowballed into huge dimensions by the chain of events that followed resulting in sundering a great nation with a hoary past. It marked the beginning of the end of a united India.

Jinnah's Ire

To some extent, the Congress had its own share of the tragedy of partition. It committed a series of grave blunders, unwittingly though, which provoked the anger of the Muslim community. Having secured a clear mandate in the United Provinces in the elections of 1937, the Congress spurned the League's offer of co-operation to form a coalition ministry in that province. The League felt betrayed and construed the act of the Congress as a breach of faith. To quote Nehru's famous biographer Michael Brecher: "Flushed with success, the Congress adopted an imperious attitude to all other political parties, 'a Himalayan blunder' for which it was to pay dearly in the years to come. Nehru himself set the tone with his haughty remark in March 1937: 'There are only two forces in India to-day, British imperialism and Indian nationalism as represented by the Congress.' Jinnah was quick to retort: 'No, there is a third party, the Musalmans.'"[9]

The League's offer of co-operation to the Congress to form a coalition government was a golden opportunity the acceptance of which would have led to its merger in the Congress. But it was arrogantly thrown away by the Congress. It did not realise that by this act it was only giving a fresh lease of life to the League sowing thereby the seeds for Pakistan. A much-distressed Gandhiji confessed when appealed to by Jinnah that he was helpless. "I cry out to God for light," he said.[10] His cry remained unanswered. For the Congress and for India, it was a chance lost for ever. Jinnah quickly grabbed the situation as he knew that a backward community like the Muslim could be easily roused to action by kindling its religious faith. This worked extremely well.

Eight years later, perhaps realising his folly, Nehru wrote: "It is easy to be wise after the event, but I am still inclined to think that politically, and situated as we were then, it was a natural and logical decision for us. Nevertheless, it is true that the consequences of it on the communal question were unfortunate and it led to a feeling of grievance and isolation among many Moslems."[11]

The second time the Congress bungled by failing to avail itself of another opportunity was after the formation of ministries in 1937. Jinnah's Muslim League did not form a ministry in any of the provinces and as such had no voice even in the non-Congress Muslim majority provinces ruled by Muslim Premiers. These Premiers were not in favour of Pakistan. It was the most opportune moment for the Congress to strike a political bargain with these provinces and nip the idea of creating Pakistan in the bud. The Congress's failure to do so provided Jinnah a free hand "to trot ominously on the political horizon and pose a threat a decade later."[12] Sikandar Hyat Khan, Premier of the Punjab, made this prophetic statement in 1938: "Pakistan would be an invitation to the Muslims to cut the throat of every bania...Pakistan would mean a massacre."[13] Thirty years later, referring to the failure of the Congress to evolve the right political strategy when the conditions were favourable, Conrad Corfield of the Indian Civil Service, who served as Political Adviser to the Crown Representative, stated rightly: "Looking back, it seems so clear that the Congress was responsible for creating Pakistan."[14] Congress's unconcern for the Muslim Provinces and overconcern for the Centre suited Jinnah very well. He was most eagerly awaiting an opportune moment which presented itself when the Congress ministries were made to resign by Nehru at the outbreak of the Second World War in 1939. India was declared belligerent by the Government without the consent of the people and without consulting the legislative bodies. The Congress felt that England had taken India for granted and forced on her the war with which India was not concerned directly or indirectly. Of course, many Congress leaders were vexed when the High Command of the Indian National Congress banned attendance of its members at the Simla session of the Central Assembly. Satyamurti, for instance, stoutly opposed the stand and exploded that the ban was "wrong and futile."

Jinnah's Jubilation

The day the Congress Ministries resigned was celebrated as a day of thanksgiving by the Muslim League throughout India. Jinnah jubilantly extended his warm support and assistance to the British Government. This must have certainly made the latter worry about the onerous conditions he would demand as price for the promised Muslim cooperation in the war. Yet having lost the Congress support, Viceroy Linlithgow helped Jinnah to counterbalance the Congress on an all-India basis. Jinnah appealed to the Muslims all over the country to observe 22 December 1939 as a day of deliverance from the Congress regime. Even as late as January 1940 Jinnah did not speak of a separate nation for Muslims. He said that the Hindus and Muslims who formed two separate nations should "share the governance of their common motherland." But within a couple of months, at the Lahore session of the Muslim League he declared that the Muslims should have a separate State called "Pakistan." During the Cripps Mission, the Congress could not count on the support of the Muslim League. Openly repudiating the system of parliamentary democracy as something unsuitable for India, Jinnah declared that separate electorates and safeguards for the minorities could never save the Muslims from the Congress *Raj* at the Centre.[15]

The third time the Congress blundered was in 1942 when it launched the "Quit India Movement" following its rejection of the Cripps Award. It failed to realise at that point of time that this agitation would threaten the country's very integrity from inside. The Government reacted to the Movement very aggressively by clapping up all the Congress leaders from Gandhiji downwards in prisons. They were made to remain behind the bars for three years from August 1942! This unexpected development came as a shot in the arm for Jinnah. He remained alone, unchallenged. He had ample time to go round the country untrammelled and consolidate his position on the issue of Pakistan. In an interview to the *News Chronicle* of London in 1944, Jinnah boldly said: "If the Government announced their intention of setting up of Pakistan and Hindustan, the Congress and Hindus would accept it within three months. In other words, the Government would have called the Congress bluff."[16]

Regrettably certain acts of the Congress leaders even after their release from jail, gave rise to misgivings in many persons about their seriousness in preserving India's unity. For instance, in the 12-point Manifesto of the Congress for the election of 1946 issued on 27 October 1945, there was no mention of a United India. The League's Manifesto, on the other hand, issued four days later, stated clearly: "The elections will give a clear verdict on the issue whether the Muslim India stands for Pakistan or for *Akhand* Hindustan. It is therefore a question of life and death for the Muslims of India."[17] This awakened the Congress whose composite Manifesto of 11 December 1945 which was intended to cover the Central and Provincial elections, implied that the Congress stood for a United India.[18]

The fourth bungling of the Congress was over the Cabinet Mission Scheme. It was generally accepted as the best Scheme since it provided for a United India. Gandhiji said it was a fair solution. Even Jinnah, who was totally against the Scheme initially since it did not recommend the creation of Pakistan, finally veered to the conclusion that nothing better could be had. So, the Muslim League accepted the Scheme. After protracted negotiations of the Scheme, the Congress also accepted it on 7 July 1946 giving the impression that a great political uncertainty had ended. But within three days, this hope was shattered. At the Press Conference of 10 July 1946 in Bombay, Nehru, who had just then taken over as President of the Congress in succession to Maulana Azad, made a very shocking statement. He said emphatically that the Congress had agreed only to participate in the Constituent Assembly and that the party was free to modify the Cabinet Mission Scheme as it liked. Jinnah raged against this statement and interpreted it to mean that the Congress had rejected the Cabinet Mission Scheme. Azad, who proposed Nehru as his successor to the Congress Presidency in the hope that he would carry on the work from where he had left, deeply regretted the "greatest blunder" he had committed in his political life. He said that Nehru had, by his statement done "immense harm to the national cause."[19] In his letter to D.P. Misra on 11 July 1946, Vallabhbhai Patel attributed Nehru's announcement to "emotional insanity."[20]

Bloody Massacres in Bengal and Punjab

The series of blunders enumerated did contribute to blast the Congress goal of making entire India one sovereign State. Chimanlal Setalwad imputed the vivisection of India to the "wobbling and vacillating attitude of one party," meaning the Congress.[21] The Muslim League under Jinnah took full advantage of what it considered the *faux pas* committed by Nehru. Jinnah continued his cry for Pakistan nullifying the genuine efforts of Gandhiji to appease him. Gandhiji's plea that he could be cut to pieces and not India did not move the "rigid, arid and irrevocable" Jinnah.[22] Not losing hope, Gandhiji made another unsuccessful attempt at calling upon Britain to implement the Cabinet Mission's proposals of 16 May 1946 and then quit.[23]

On 8 August 1946, Azad convened a meeting of the Congress Working Committee and reaffirmed the party's decision of 7 July on the Cabinet Mission Scheme making no reference to Nehru's Press statement. But his efforts too bore no fruit. Jinnah maintained that Nehru's statement revealed the true mind of the Congress. Nothing could deflect the "unreligious" Jinnah from his determination to create a separate Islamic State. He wanted Viceroy Wavell to call upon the Muslim League which had accepted the Cabinet Mission Scheme to form the Government. Wavell did not agree to this. On 29 July, an irate Jinnah got the Muslim League reverse its earlier decision, reject the Cabinet Mission Scheme and reiterate the demand for Pakistan. But he did not rescind the resolution accepting the Cabinet Mission Scheme. The failure of both the parties to accept the Cabinet Mission Scheme *in toto* changed completely the course of Indian history.

The Muslim League passed a resolution to launch "Direct Action" on 16 August 1946 against all those who dared to oppose the demand for Pakistan and also to get rid of the British slavery. It was a one-man decision taken at Bombay and it sowed the seed for unprecedented communal riots in India. It was a hate-campaign to foment communal passions. The outbreak of the communal carnage that Calcutta witnessed from 16 to 20 August 1946 beggared all description. The fierce communal conflicts that preceded the halving of India exactly a year later had their beginnings now in the streets of Calcutta. The Hindu community, particularly women and children, were subject to unimaginable indignities. Hundreds were killed and many times that number wounded in the week-long bloodbath. As a leading newspaper bluntly put it "...the more ardent of the League's followers saw in the Direct Action Day not a token demonstration in preparation for the coming struggle but the D-Day itself."[24] After Calcutta, Noakhali and Tipperah became the scenes of massacres. Rajaji, who was disgusted with the Muslim leadership, said that Jinnah was not interested in beginning *Swaraj* in peace "but with ugly demonstrations and conflicts."

On 15 October 1946, the Muslim League entered the Interim Government which Wavell installed in August with Nehru as Vice President. The League joined it not out of a genuine intention to work the Government. Liaquat Ali's budget proposals as Finance Minister clearly proved that it was intended to make the Interim Coalition Government unworkable. It was actually a signal for the outbreak of communal riots in the Punjab. The coercive policy of the League compelled the Unionist Coalition Ministry in the Punjab to resign. Following this, there were widespread disturbances causing heavy loss of life and property in that Province. In the communal tension between the two large communities of India that spilled over, Lahore and Amritsar were the worst affected. The latter in particular became a "veritable inferno." Thus even before the birth of Pakistan, several parts of India plunged into a bloody massacre of thousands of innocent civilians. Neither the army nor the police could stop the killings of the Hindus by the Muslims and vice versa. Many feared that the "shell of freedom" would be "clothed with flesh and blood."[25] These horrendous developments prompted the Congress Working Committee to take a drastic decision on 8 March 1947 by passing a resolution to divide the Punjab into two provinces so that the predominantly Muslim part would be separated from the predominantly non-Muslim part. The "casual manner" in which the partition of the Punjab was proposed to be effected led to much more tragic consequences. The reasons for the hectic haste with which this and many other acts were carried out during this period may never perhaps be known fully.

Following the proposal to partition the Punjab, the Hindu members of the Central Assembly and the Bengal Provincial Congress Committee called for the partition of Bengal also. The members belonging to Muslim League in the Bengal Legislative Assembly did not favour the partition of Bengal. H.S. Suhrawardy, who later became the Prime Minister of Pakistan, made a desperate attempt to stop the partition of Bengal. At a Press Conference in April 1947 he said: "We Bengalis have a common mother tongue and common economic interests. Bengal has very little affinity with the Punjab. Bengal will be an independent State and decide by herself later whether she would link up with Pakistan." It must be remembered that exactly a year before, the same person in a bloodcurdling speech in Delhi threatened the Hindus with dire consequences asserting that the Muslims had absolutely nothing in common with the Hindus![26]

Wavell's Exit

A brief account about the departure of Viceroy Wavell is imperative in this context. He held office during a most momentous period of British India's history. He never "willed, desired or advocated" the partition of India. On the other hand, he did his best to bring about an amicable settlement between the Hindus and the Muslims. In his address to the Central Legislature on 17 February 1944, he declared that India was a natural unit within which the Hindus and the Muslims should learn to live together, emulating countries where communities differing in culture or religion had continued to do so.[27] Stating that no one could alter the geography of a country, he declared unequivocally that from the points of view of defence and internal and external economic problems "India is one unit." But even by the end of his first year of viceroyalty, he was convinced that no progress could be made on the two vital issues of communal tension and political advance. He frankly told the British Prime Minister Attlee that the existing Government of India could not continue for long. He also mentioned *inter alia* that to concede Pakistan would be to encourage the intransigent elements in the Middle East.[28]

In 1946, the political situation in India was highly unstable. The beginning of 1947, witnessed one of the worst crises when the Muslim League boycotted the Constituent Assembly and its Working Committee passed a resolution at its Karachi meeting on 31 January 1947 demanding the immediate dissolution of the Constituent Assembly. An alarmed Wavell informed the Home Government that if the deadlock in the Indian political situation was not broken, the country would drift into a civil war. He suggested that since neither of the parties desired an open breach, the Home Government could make a final attempt at bringing the feuding parties into the Constituent Assembly. He even wired to Pethick Lawrence, Secretary of State for India, the draft of a statement to be made by HMG which "had a chance, though perhaps a slender one, of getting the League, into the Constituent Assembly."[29] But Wavell's advice was not considered.

There was widespread prejudice among the higher echelons in England against the views of Wavell. His observations that the Indian members of the Executive Council who had "a controlling voice" were increasingly aware of their power and that the British Civil Service on which the Government of India rested having become "moribund" would find it difficult to secure the services of good recruits after the war, did not find favour with them. Even as late as 1 January 1947, Ernest Bevin, Foreign Secretary, was against fixing a date for the departure of the British from India. Opposed to Britain's voluntary relinquishment of power in India, he strongly felt that "pessimism" had pervaded the whole Cabinet of Britain. Alluding to the massacres in India, he told Attlee that millions of Indians would surely welcome the continuance of the British Government so as to preserve their safety. Attlee countered this saying that if Britain intended to stay there any longer and put in enough troops to enforce its rule, it would amount to going back on the "pledges that have been given by Governments of every political colour." Bevin was strongly inclined to think that Wavell's apprehensions revealed his "defeatist" attitude. In his purblind passion for the pride and pomp of the British Empire, Bevin shared the view of Winston Churchill "a life-long enemy of Indian freedom." He wrote that "...Field Marshall Wavell is just completely letting us down... With a mind like Wavell's, the demoralisation of the whole Army and the police must be inevitable and I strongly recommend that he be recalled and that you find somebody with courage who, even if he were the last man left there, would come out with dignity and uphold the British Empire and the Commonwealth."[30]

Attlee in reply clarified that Wavell was not "a defeatist but a realist." He said in fairness to Wavell that he had the support of the most experienced civil servants in India.[31] However, the fact that Attlee agreed with the crucial suggestion of Bevin was borne out by his recall of Wavell. Strongly believing that Wavell "had lost his way," Attlee decided to replace him. At the end of his epoch-making declaration of transfer of power to "responsible Indian hands by a date not later than June 1948" made on 20 February 1947, Attlee also announced that Wavell would be succeeded by Louis Mountbatten, the great grandson of Queen Victoria, uncle of Prince Philip, the Duke of Edinburgh and a cousin to the ruling monarch George VI.

In December 1946, Prime Minister Attlee personally conveyed to Mountbatten the happy tidings of his new assignment. This is what Mountbatten said about his meeting with Attlee when he was interviewed by the authors of the celebrated book *Freedom At Midnight*: "On 18 December 1946, Prime Minister Attlee sent for me and absolutely staggered me... Attlee and Stafford Cripps (Chancellor of the Exchequer) went on... explained how they had reached a very murky stalemate... That Wavell had lost contact with Nehru, the Congress Party, with Jinnah, the Sikhs and everybody... This really is going to lead to a major disaster."[32]

Wavell's grief was all the more poignant as the announcement of his recall was made on the day of his daughter's wedding. There was therefore a strong feeling that the Viceroy was "sacked in the curtest and most inconsiderate manner" and that he was sacked "because he (like Gandhi) would not promote the partition of India."[33]

There was one more reason which perhaps was the immediate cause for Wavell's dismissal. It related to the leakage of the Viceroy's letters which were signed on his behalf by his Private Secretary George Abell. These letters revealed a partisan attitude on the part of the Viceroy in the dispute between the Congress and the Muslim League. The story went that an Indian stenographer in the office of the Viceroy's Private Secretary faithfully transmitted to the Congress leaders some of the secret letters. Nehru showed these to Stafford Cripps when he went to London in December 1946 at the invitation of Attlee. He told Cripps that the Congress would not accept Wavell any more as a "neutral Viceroy." In recording this in his *Diary*, Wavell writes that he had warned Abell against trusting Indians in his office.[34]

Arrival of Last Viceroy of India

It was given to Mountbatten, the Supreme Allied Commander of Southern Asia, who had neither administrative experience nor any knowledge of the ground realities of the Indian sub-continent, to preside over the dismantling of the British Empire. He was sworn in as Viceroy on 24 March 1947. Almost immediately after this, he realised that with Jinnah's obstinacy a united policy, which was the goal he was to attain, was not feasible and that partition was inevitable. He described Jinnah as a "psychopathetic case" hell bent on breaking India to pieces.[35]

Towards the end of April 1947, a month after he assumed office, Mountbatten recognised that the partition of India was inevitable. He prepared a plan for the creation of two Dominions and sent Ismay, Chief of his Staff, with the plan to London for the Cabinet to consider it. Noted for his calmness and wisdom, Ismay, who was more than once sent to London to hold critical negotiations, took no pride in the critical act of partition although "he accepted its draconian necessity..."[36] The Cabinet approved the overall objective but made many minor modifications. Mountbatten gave Nehru a preview of the plan prepared by the brilliant V.P. Menon, the Reforms Commissioner, who virtually replaced Conrad Corfield as the Viceroy's Political Adviser. Menon who was entrusted with the drafting of the plan did it in association with the India Office in London. It is relevant to mention here that George Spence, formerly Secretary of the Law Department, who was planning to retire, volunteered to serve as Officer on Special Duty under V.P. Menon who had earlier worked as a clerk under him! This kind of "self-effacing devotion to duty" was characteristic of the best of government servants in India – both British and Indian."[37]

Against this background, Mountbatten's angry denunciation of V.P. Menon several years after 1947 will be viewed with great dismay. That Mountbatten's closeness and association with V.P. Menon in those critical days were just a façade has been exemplified by the graceless remarks he made about the latter. Strongly repudiating the theory that V.P. Menon put up to him the idea of a Dominion Status, Mountbatten accused him of creating the belief that he thought it up, drafted it and presented it to him. "And I cannot allow history," he warned, "to accept the fact that this Dominion Status solution, which at the time was a brainwave, was just V.P. Menon's...the important thing about people like Krishna Menon and V.P. Menon is, that they were not leaders in any sense of the word at all, but they were my links with the leaders."[38] Indeed, a most malicious statement.

Mountbatten felt that the target date of June 1948 announced by Attlee for the hand-over of power to India was too late. So he himself rushed to London on 18 May 1947 to seek the consent of the British Government to the modifications designed to meet Nehru's objections in his plan to create two Dominions and effect the partition of India by 15 August 1947. He chose that date to free India because, to quote Mountbatten: "The date I chose came out of the blue...I was determined to show I was master of the whole event...I went to the 15 August. Why? Because it was the second anniversary of Japan's surrender..."[39] As the Commander of the Eastern Front, he won a decisive battle against Japan. Nehru accepted the date though astrologers said the day was not propitious. He later admitted that he chose the "wrong day."

Where was the need for the irrational advance of the date of transfer of power by ten months – from June 1948 to August 1947? Was it to mutilate India as quickly as possible and then leave her? The consent of the British Government for the uncalled for advance of the date of the transfer of power was given in May 1947.The period of less than three months from this date was too, too short to prepare for the mammoth event of August 1947. The feverish speed with which everything was carried out at the last hour resulted in many errors. Speaking of this unprecedented speed Mountbatten himself said that while it took three years to separate Burma from India, two years to separate Bombay from Sind and two years to separate Orissa from Bihar, it had taken a mere two months and a half to accomplish the partition of India, one of the biggest countries in the world.[40]

To the accusations that he was "too hasty, too quick, a typical sailor, man of action who comes and rushes things," Mountbatten's answer was:

"...this idiotic Indian Government with which I was saddled, which consisted of fifteen members, six (of) Muslim League, six (of) Congress, (and) three others, (sic) the point is, any vote was always 9 - 6 in favour of what the Congress wanted. Therefore, you couldn't govern because the Muslim League would not accept it. I had a brain wave. *I had the idea of breaking the Government up and making two Governments, the Government of the future India and the Government of the future Pakistan*...This kept them busy working on partition and the transfer of assets. But the rumblings were so great that at times we wondered if I had chosen any early enough date..." Mountbatten dismissed the accusation that his "reckless speed" caused all bloodshed as "absolute nonsense." He added "I have not the slightest doubt that any other course would have been a disaster."[41]

This was a most hectic period for every one in power as the time was hardly sufficient to resolve many of the crucial problems before 15 August. The transfer of power was therefore carried out in a most slip-shod manner.

Radcliffe Award: Pakistan's Misconception

The most urgent of all the issues regarding the transfer of power was the delineation of the frontiers of the two Dominions. This factor had got to be addressed by the authorities before 15 August 1947 and the decision should satisfy both the new dominions. Two Boundary Commissions to partition the Punjab and Bengal were appointed by the British Government with the eminent English jurist Cyril Radcliffe acting as independent Chairman of both the Commissions. It was Jinnah who suggested Radcliffe's name. The other members of the Commissions were Mehr Chand Mahajan and Teja Singh from India and Din Mohammad and Mohammad Munir from the yet to be born Pakistan. Since the members of the two countries could not reach an agreement, the final lines between the two Dominions were drawn by the Chairman himself. Hence the report became known as the "Radcliffe Award." The report was ready by the 13 August but it was not published immediately. It was possible that sensing the repercussions of its publication which would mar the Independence Day celebrations, Mountbatten delayed its publication. But a more plausible explanation was that the Award reached Mountbatten on 13 August when he was about to reach Karachi to participate in the Pakistani Independence Day ceremony. So he naturally held it up until 16 August when he would discuss the Award with Nehru and Liaquat.

Though both the countries had solemnly bound themselves to accept the Radcliffe Award, neither India nor Pakistan was pleased with it. In Pakistan it provoked very angry reactions. Jinnah was very confident that the Muslim majority district of Gurdaspur in the Punjab, which was contiguous to Pakistan, would go to the new Dominion. A more important reason was this would deprive India of direct access to Kashmir since the entire usable road from the Indian plains to Kashmir traversed the Gurdaspur district. Consequently, the Maharaja of Kashmir would have no other option than to accede to Pakistan. When the district was included in India giving her thereby a frontier with Jammu and Kashmir, Pakistan was rudely shocked. Jinnah fumed and called the division "perfidious" because the area joined at a point where the only road link between Kashmir and India could be developed. But, in reality, the unit that Radcliffe adopted to divide the Punjab was the *tehsil* (sub-district) and not the district. Accordingly, three of the four *tehsils* of the district, two of which had Muslim majority, formed part of India. This was done considering the security concerns in the Punjab.

Pakistan strongly believed that she received bare justice from Radcliffe. It became an article of faith in Pakistan that Radcliffe was influenced by Mountbatten whose guest he was in New Delhi at the time. There was the allegation of an "understanding" between the U.K. Government and the Congress leaders that the boundaries should be so drawn as to give India direct access to Kashmir. It was alleged that Radcliffe awarded the Gurdaspur district to Pakistan in his original Award which was subsequently changed at the instance of Mountbatten to give India access to Kashmir. In support of this allegation, Pakistan adduced the "mysterious delay" which occurred in the publication of the Award. The alleged exposure of India's "intrigue" by Vallabhbhai Patel "the strong man of the Congress," by some statement in a public speech seemed to have strengthened this erroneous impression. Pakistan was convinced that by including the Muslim majority *tehsils* of Gurdaspur and Batala later in his Award under the influence of Mountbatten, Radcliffe gave India an entry into Kashmir.

When the question regarding the boundary dispute was raised in the British Parliament, the Government denied the allegations. As for the alleged statement of Patel, it was pointed out that there was no record of any reference made by Patel to such an agreement between Mountbatten or the UK Government and the Indian National Congress and that Pakistan never appeared to have quoted "chapter and verse" to prove this. The leading Pakistani paper *Dawn* wrote on 27 April 1948: "With the help of another Briton Radcliffe, he (Mountbatten) lopped off Muslim areas of that district (Gurdaspur) to provide India the argument (sic) as well as the advantage of an artificial contiguity with Kashmir."

The statement of historian Shereen Ilahi that "There is no evidence to imply that anyone gerrymandered the boundary because of its implications for the Princely State," is proof that Pakistan's accusation of a conspiracy against her was baseless.[42]

About two years and a half later, on 3 October 1950, the *Dawn* published the two following questions put by Yusuf Khattack, General Secretary of the Pakistan Muslim League to Cyril Radcliffe: (1) Is it a fact that Radcliffe changed his award to the disadvantage of Pakistan even after it had been communicated to the then Governor of Punjab, E. Jenkins? (2) Is it a fact, as stated by Sardar Vallabhbhai Patel in a speech in Calcutta that it had been agreed beforehand that India would not lose Calcutta? Referring to Nehru's statement that certain charges against Radcliffe were false, Khattack said if false, "let Cyril say so himself."

Radcliffe gave the following replies:

(1) "I made an arbitral award about Indian boundaries over three years ago and I have never taken part in any public discussions since about the details or circumstances of the award."

(2) "I think it is out of place for me to allow myself to start answering questions now such as are raised by the Secretary of the Muslim League in *Dawn*. Whatever I may think of them personally, since I do not think that persons who have filled what was a semi-judicial position can be expected to conduct their affairs in that way."[43]

To put the whole matter in simplest terms: The final draft of the award differed from the first draft only in its treatment of an area in the Ferozepur district and not in that of the Gurdaspur district which remained unchanged. Gurdaspur was shown in East Punjab in the enclosure to a letter of 8 August 1947 from George Abell (then a member of Mountbatten's staff) to the Private Secretary to Evan Jenkins (then Governor of the United Punjab). Mountbatten was extremely careful to dissociate himself from the Boundary Commission's work throughout. As for the alleged "mysterious delay," George Abell in his aforesaid letter of 8 August stated that the Award was expected to be published "within the next 48 hours." But Radcliffe could not complete the Award until 13 August and the Award reached Mountbatten as he was leaving for Karachi. The delay was thus not due to any interference with the Award by Mountbatten. He was in fact anxious not to consider it until he had disclosed it to Nehru and Liaquat.

Radcliffe himself had informed the Commonwealth Secretary that the Award of 13 August 1947 was "the result of his own unfettered judgment" and that at no stage was there any attempt made by the Governor General or any other person to influence his decision.[44]

Twenty four years later in 1971 when Radcliffe was told that the Muslims of Pakistan nurtured against him a grievance that he favoured India in demarcating the borders in his Award, he replied that they (the Pakistani Muslims) should be thankful to him for his having "gone out of the way to give them Lahore which deserved to go to India." Still he said he favoured the Muslims more than the Hindus.[45] It may not be out of place to mention in this context that the Pakistanis had chosen to ignore the fact that the richest land of Lyallpur in the Punjab had gone to them. The districts of Montgomery, Sheikhupara and Lyallpur were the proud creations of the Sikhs. It was also their noble homeland studded with scores of their shrines. Certainly Radcliffe would not have thought even remotely that his award would have such an impact as it did on Kashmir.

Birth of the Two Dominions

On 2 June 1947, the Partition Plan was announced. Mountbatten hastened to carry out the operation to divide India oblivious of the fact that he was sowing the seed for the worst communal catastrophe that was to rock the civilised world. On 9 June, the Muslim League accepted the partition plan "as a compromise."[46] On 15 June, the All-India Congress Committee ratified the decision of the Congress Working Committee to accept the partition. On 9 July, Mountbatten accepted the Governor Generalship of independent India. Some of his own countrymen did not favour this. But King George VI, Churchill and Prime Minister Attlee welcomed it. On 18 July, the King's assent was given to the Indian Independence Bill creating the two Dominions of India and Pakistan. Maulana Azad, who was deeply upset over the drastic decision to cut India, refused to give up his opposition to the final plan.

At the stroke of the midnight hour – on 14 August 1947, India awoke "after long slumber and struggle" to freedom. Paying a tribute to Mahatma Gandhi, Nehru said "not only we but succeeding generations shall never allow that torch of freedom" which he held aloft, "to be blown out, however high the wind, or stormy the tempest."[47]

On 15 August 1947, the Indian Independence Day was celebrated in the capital cities throughout the world particularly in London, New York and Moscow where the tri-colour flag was hoisted.

India gained freedom but at an appalling cost. A great nation which by every test is a unity in diversity had been arbitrarily cut. As Nehru dejectedly remarked: "Division has taken place in the hearts of the people of India." Indeed 14-15 August 1947 was a most fateful day as one ancient country and one ancient people were cut into two unequal parts.

India's independence began with dreadful massacres and migrations of the Hindus and Muslims in the sundered Punjab and Bengal. The bloody sight in these places was much worse than what it was before the transfer of power. They were horrors that lacerated the hearts of all people. There was the unprecedented problem of the refugees both incoming and outgoing. Thanks to the hate campaign generated by the leaders of Pakistan in the wake of the birth of the new Dominion, there was a huge orgy of bloodshed there. Mountbatten was no authentic prophet. His prognosis that in the wake of partition everything would go smooth proved false. Hindus and Muslims, who had hitherto fraternised in an atmosphere of goodwill and cooperation and lived amicably with plurality, were suddenly consumed with such hatred as to bay for each other's blood.

The situation became worse after 15 August. There were ruthless slaughters on both sides. Zafrullah Khan, Chief of the Pakistani Delegation to the UN General Assembly, New York, began his fulminations against India asserting that India had planned the "extermination of a people." He threatened to lodge a formal complaint with the U N "if India failed to end the slaughter of the Muslims." Spewing venom he added that if this did not prove effective, the Government of Pakistan would resort to direct measures. When asked if it meant a civil war, Zafrullah said: "Hardly. It is worse than civil war already."

Accession of the Princely States to the Indian Dominion was another major problem India had to tackle almost from the day of gaining independence. There were as many as 562 Princely States in India and their transformation was not done properly. The Labour Government of Britain failed to formulate an over all policy for the Princes. With the withdrawal of the British from India following the transfer of power, the doctrine of paramountcy automatically lapsed leaving the princes to accede to either of the two Dominions. In response to Vallabhbhai Patel's appeal to their patriotism, one by one, the princes came forward to sign the Instrument of Accession. Junagadh and Hyderabad, whose accession initially proved a tough task for Nehru, finally acceded to the Indian Union in November 1947 and September 1948 respectively. Many problems cropped up in the wake of partition creating bad blood between the two new dominions. But none posed so great a problem as Kashmir which continues to remain a bone of contention between India and Pakistan.

References

1. *Modern Review,* April 1925, p. 489.
2. Larry Collins and Dominique Lapierre, *Freedom At Midnight,* p. 28.
3. H.N. Pandit, "British Inspiration Behind Pakistan Movement," *The Indian Review,* June 1977, p. 10.
4. *Ibid,* p. 9.
5. H.N. Pandit, "The Pakistan Idea: Britain's Hopes and Disillusionment," *The Indian Review*, Aug. 1977, pp. 21 & 22.
6. B. Shiva Rau, *Framing of India's Constitution – A Study,* p. 13.
7. La.Su. Rengarajan, "From a Nationalist to a Secessionist," *The Hindu,* 2 Feb. 1999.
8. *The Indian Annual Register*, July-December 1937, p. 10.
9. Michael Brecher, *Nehru- A Political Biography*, p. 231.
10. Tendulkar, D.G., *Mahatma Life of Mohandas Karamchand Gandhi*, Vol. IV, p. 249.
11. Jawaharlal Nehru, *The Discovery of India,* p. 369.
12. B. Krishna, *Sardar Vallabhbhai Patel India's Iron Man,* p. 200.
13. Penderel Moon, *Divide and Quit,* p. 20.
14. Corfield's answer to B. Krishna's Questionnaire of 13 May 1969, *Corfield Collections.*
15. R. Coupland, *The Constitutional Problem in India,* Part II, P. 199.
16. *The Mail,* 3 March 1944.
17. *Ibid,* 1 Nov. 1945.
18. *Ibid,* 11 Dec .1945.
19. Maulana Abul Kalam Azad, *India Wins Freedom,* p. 170.
20. P.N. Chopra, *The Sardar of India, p.* 109.
21. A.G. Noorani, "India's Partition – Could it have been Avoided?" *The Sunday Standard,* 11 July 1971.
22. Emery Kelen, "Gandhiji at Buckingham Palace," *The Hindu,* 22 June 1964.
23. *Ibid,* 30 May 1946.
24. *A Hundred Years of The Hindu, The Epic Story Of Indian Nationalism,* p. 623.
25. *The Hindu*, 19 July 1947.
26. *A Hundred Years of The Hindu,op. cit.,* p. 649.
27. Penderel Moon, *Wavell: The Viceroy's Journal,* p. 56.

28. *Ibid,* p. 175.
29. *Ibid,* p.418.
30. Bevin to Attlee, 1 Jan. 1947, Ind/47/1.
31. Attlee to Bevin, 2 Jan. 1947, Ind/47/2.
32. Larry Collins and Dominique Lapierre, *Mountbatten and the Partition of India 22 March – 15 August 1947*, p. 8
33. Charles Chenevix Trench, *Viceroy's Agent*, pp. 335 & 36.
34. *Viceroy's Journal, op. cit.*, p. 433.
35. *Freedom at Midnight, op. cit.*, pp. 103-05.
36. *Oxford Dictionary of National Biography*, Vol. 29, p. 440.
37. H.V. Hudson, *The Great Divide: Britain, India and Pakistan*, p. 324.
38. *Mountbatten and Partition of India, op. cit.*, pp. 52 & 54.
39. *Ibid,* p. 49.
40. Andrew Mellor, *India Since Independence*, p. 39.
41. *Mountbatten and Partition of India, op. cit.*, pp. 49 & 50. Emphasis Author's.
42. Cited in Praveen Swami's *India, Pakistan And The Secret Jihad*, p. 20.
43. *Dawn*, 3 Oct. 1950, FL/1015/476; and 9 Oct. 1950, FL /1015/487.
44. CRO to UK HCs to India and Pakistan, 17 April 1948, FL/1015/533.
45. Kuldip Nayar, *Scoop! Inside Stories from the Partition to the Present*, p. 35.
46. *A Hundred Years of The Hindu, op. cit.*, p. 655.
47. *Jawaharlal Nehru's Speeches 1946-1949*, Vol. One, pp. 27 & 28.

5

The First Indo-Pakistan War

Pakistan's invasion of Kashmir which marked the beginning of her unending war with India began on 22 October 1947 – just 69 days after India became independent. Though the estimate of the raiders' strength varied, it easily numbered a few thousands and was composed of four elements:

(i) the Afridi[1] tribesmen from the North West Frontier whose motives were religious sympathy and loot;

(ii) the Muslim League agents as well as elements of the Pakistani army who were on leave and who came across the border to smuggle arms into Kashmir with a view to rousing the Muslim peasantry of the Poonch province;

(iii) elements of population in Kashmir who, being discontented with the rule of Maharaja Hari Singh, raised the Pakistani flag and attacked the Kashmiri officials; and

(iv) the Muslim deserters from the Kashmir forces who had taken their arms with them.

Grisly Happenings: Baramulla under Siege

On 22 October 1947, approximately 300 lorry loads of superbly armed raiders proceeded along the Jhelum Valley to Srinagar. Equipped with up-to-date war weapons like Bren guns, machine guns, mortars and flame throwers, they passed through the Pakistani territory perpetrating absolute mayhem on the way. They looted Domel where the Muslim officers and soldiers of the Kashmir State Forces guarding this frontier under Col. Narain Singh deserted it and joined the raiders after murdering their commander in his office at the Domel Dak Bungalow.[2] The brigands next burnt the key town of Muzaffarabad where the Rawalpindi-Srinagar road crossed the Jhelum. Those killed here included the District Magistrate. They then occupied several towns and massacred a large number of Muslims. By 25 October, they had advanced up the Jhelum Valley to Uri meeting only the weak opposition of the Kashmir State troops. The invaders overran a total of 95 villages, sacked and destroyed many towns including Bhimbar and were soon in possession of a sizeable portion of Poonch on the Pakistani border, northwest of Jammu. It is said that the destruction of many once fair cities and the resultant flight of thousands of panic-stricken people, "could hardly find a parallel unless we go back to the days of Chengiz Khan."[3] The raiders penetrated the southern border of Kashmir in small doses in about ten or fifteen places. The invasion was a well organised affair with the tribesmen carrying out their attacks with unsurpassed savagery. The Kashmir Government was unable to deploy its meagre troops to meet the incursion. It had only 10,000 trained troops of which one-third was Muslim. If the remaining non-Muslim troops were to take positions in Jammu and Kashmir, the border would become vulnerable in many places. This awkward predicament of the State was exploited by the tribal irregulars who poured in from the north as the troops were busy clearing the intruders in the south. Having succeeded in this strategy, the raiders were within 35 miles of Srinagar. Domel and Uri had already fallen to them.

The news of the appalling massacres in Kashmir reached the Government of India only on the night of 24 October 1947. By then, the ruthless tribesmen backed by the Pakistani military advisers in *mufti*, had proceeded through the Abbottabad- Mansara Road (the last outpost on the Pakistani side of Kashmir) down to the Srinagar Road and reached Baramulla, a Muslim majority town. The horrendous experience that Baramulla went through deserves special mention. The most lethal of their deadly attacks was conducted there. The iconoclasts indulged there in rape, murder, arson and loot. The sacrosanct atmosphere of the St. Joseph's Convent did not deter them from defiling it by their molestation of the resident nuns of the Order of St. Francis and eventually murdering them. They thus made the nunnery an utter shambles. Among those murdered were a Lt. Colonel, Mrs. Dykes and the Assistant Mother Superior Teresalina while the Mother Superior of the Convent Aldetrude, who was seriously wounded, later succumbed to it.[4] The few nuns who survived the butchery fled the Convent at dawn. Unsatiated by the carnage already perpetrated on the inmates of the Convent, the brutish invaders rushed to the hospital where the injured nuns were being treated, smashed the x-ray equipments, broke the medicine bottles and indulged in hot-blooded killing. This resulted in the death of two patients, murder of two English tourists and shooting down of two nuns in the Baby Ward.[5] The reign of terror in Baramulla continued for nine days. Even after the air attack of the Indian army, which had left the tribesmen in a nervous condition, they had the audacity to drag out six of the nuns and line them up to be shot. By a quirk of luck, one of these nuns had a gold tooth which was very prominent. As the marauders coveted it, there was a scuffle for the tooth between them but before anyone could snatch it, their chief arrived and ruled out the shooting of the nuns. The nuns were saved.[6]

The murderous tribesmen did not spare even Sheikh Abdullah's co-worker, Mir Maqbool Sherwani, who fervently appealed to the beleaguered Kashmiris to get together irrespective of the communities they belonged to. When he refused to shout "Pakistan *Zindabad*," and "Sher-I-Kashmir *Murdabad*" as ordered by the bandits, they "drove nails through the palms of his hands and pressed on his forehead a sharp piece of tin on which they wrote "The punishment of a traitor is death." Braving the torture, Sherwani yelled "Victory to Hindu-Muslim unity" when fourteen of the thugs shot bullets into his body. Sherwani became known as "*Mujahid* (martyr) Sherwani." To quote a European lady journalist who visited Baramulla soon after it was retrieved from the tribesmen by the Indian troops: "The once lovely town, straddling the Jhelum River at the gateway to the Valley, was as heaped with rubble and blackened with fire as those battered jewels of Italian towns through which many of us moved during the war in Italy."[7] Only 3000 out of the total population of 40,000 survived the arson, rape and massacres in the town. A delegation of students consisting of Hindus, Muslims and Sikhs was sent to clean up the blemished convent and to salvage whatever was left in the library that was pillaged.[8]

The Afridi soldiers in plain clothes and desperados with modern weapons first filtered into the Poonch area, then Sialkot and finally the area adjoining the Hazara district of the State where they indulged in kidnapping, raping, looting and murdering the inhabitants. With the raid going on uninterruptedly, the fate of Kashmir was hanging in the balance.

Brigadier Haight, an American in the Azad Kashmir forces who was responsible for many killings in Kashmir, later made it known that gasoline, a scarce and strictly rationed commodity, was supplied plentifully to the raiders by the Pakistani authorities.[9]

No doubt fear of the seizure of Kashmir by Pakistan was lurking in the minds of the Indian leaders. There were reports from highly reliable sources of the impending danger from Pakistan. On 27 September, Mehr Chand Mahajan, who was on his way to Srinagar to assume charge as Prime Minister, personally met Nehru and Patel in New Delhi, to stress the need for "immediate military aid on any terms," to save Srinagar "at any cost from loot and destruction."[10] In the first week of October, Nehru received a statement from Dewan Shiv Saran Lal, Deputy Commissioner of Dera Ismail Khan in the Frontier highlighting the following: Pakistan was scheming to send armed tribals to the Pakistan-Kashmir border and some tribals had already moved there in transport provided by the Pakistan Government; arms confiscated from non-Muslims were supplied to them; the Wali of Swat had been promised Kashmir; and the States of Dir, Swat and Chitral were preparing to attack Kashmir from the northwest.[11]

Nehru was aware of the perilous situation in Kashmir. His letters to Patel also bore sufficient evidence to his extreme anxiety about the fate of Kashmir. Nehru did write to Mehr Chand Mahajan, the Prime Minister of Kashmir, expressing the fear of a move by Pakistan to capture Kashmir. He said that Pakistan coveted Kashmir as she wanted "to raise capital in America on the strength of Kashmir by giving special privileges, bases etc., for development there to Americans. All their present policy is to get help from America...It will certainly mean the overrunning of Kashmir by adventurers and others. No Kashmiri can welcome this prospect."[12]

It was India's great misfortune that she could do nothing to avert an impending calamity. Still, despite her thrill of uneasiness and fear, India did not expect such a shattering blow to her. She was therefore too rudely shocked by the magnitude of the tribal inroad of October 1947 and the involvement of high Pakistani officials in it. The invaders who called themselves liberators of the Kashmiri Muslims violated and abducted women, massacred children and destroyed the homes of those very Muslims for whose deliverance they proclaimed "they were coming in the name of Islam as friends from Pakistan." Sheikh Abdullah reported that the raiders "even dishonoured the Holy *Quran* and converted mosques into brothels and every Kashmiri loathes the invading tribesmen and their arch inspirers who have been responsible for such horrors in a land which is being peopled by an overwhelming majority of Mussalmans."[13]

It was on 24 October, while Nehru was hosting a dinner to Mountbatten and the Foreign Minister of Siam[14] at his residence in Delhi, Mountbatten took him aside after the guests had left and broke the bad tidings of the tribal infiltration into Kashmir. The next day – 25 October – an official report conveying the terrifying activities of the raiders reached the Government of India from Rob Lockhart, Commander-in-Chief of the Indian Army, who, in turn, had received it from the Pakistani headquarters at Rawalpindi.[15]

Maharaja's Appeal

Rattled by the horrendous deeds of the raiders who were just 35 miles away from Srinagar, Maharaja Hari Singh made a desperate appeal on 24 October to the Government of India for military aid to stem the advance of the invaders and for the accession of Kashmir to the Indian Union. He sent this urgent letter to Mountbatten through his Deputy Prime Minister Ram Lal Batra. He stated therein: "I have no option but to ask help from the Indian union. Naturally they cannot send the help asked for by me without my State acceding to the Dominion of India."[16] He wrote that the alternative to accession "is to leave my State and my people to free booters." This ended the long enforced oscillation of Hari Singh on the question of accession of Kashmir. Hari Singh stated that despite Kashmir's Standstill Agreement with the Government of Pakistan, its local officials had been permitting "a steady and increasing strangulation of supplies like food, salt, petrol, sugar and cloth" which were very vital to the needs of the people. He further stated that Pakistan was also withholding essential services like railways, posts and telegraphs from Kashmir and that the limited number of troops in Kashmir could not face the enemy threatening the State at several points simultaneously. Pakistan's economic blockade of Kashmir was calculated to browbeat Kashmir into acceding to her. Under the leader "Surround Kashmir," the Pakistan journal *Zamindar* suggested that all gates that connected Kashmir with India should be closed. "Let us beleaguer Kashmir" it said and added "let us do it so effectively that it may not be able to get out of our hands and seek refuge beyond the borders of our Dominion. Jammu and Kashmir are parts of Pakistan. Their going out of Muslim domination will badly shatter the prestige of Mussalmans."[17]

Along with his letter of 24 October, Hari Singh also sent two personal letters to Nehru and Patel asking for urgent military help in men, arms and ammunitions. Urgent messages for military aid and appeals to accept the Maharaja's request for Kashmir's accession to India were received also from representatives of the people of Kashmir including Sheikh Abdullah, who had already been released on 29 September from a nine year imprisonment. Among other leaders, Patel had a great hand in advising the Maharaja to release Abdullah and win the people to his side. Abdullah also rose to the occasion by endorsing the Maharaja's decision to accede Kashmir to the Indian Union. He assured the Maharaja his steadfast loyalty regardless of the past happenings and readily allowed several thousands of the volunteers of the Kashmir National Conference to engage themselves in maintaining law and order in Srinagar. This was an event of supreme satisfaction to the non-Muslim population of Kashmir. But with all the precautionary measures, the situation in Kashmir was becoming more and more critical. The invaders' attacks on vital installations included the demolition of the great power house at Mahoba, the supplier of electricity to the entire State of Kashmir. Their destruction plunged the whole area including the palace of Hari Singh into darkness.

In response to the appeals from Maharaja Hari Singh and others, the Government of India convened special meetings of the Defence Committee on 25 and 26 October whereat it was decided to respond positively to the Maharaja's appeals by accepting the accession of Kashmir to India and to send troops for her defence. It was on the testimony of the three British commanding officers of the Indian forces (R.M. Lockhart, Commander-in-Chief, Air Marshal T.W. Elmhirst of Indian Air Force and Rear-Admiral J.T.S. Hall of Indian Navy) that plans were chalked out to send troops to Kashmir by air and road if that became necessary to arrest the tribal incursion. Defence Minister Baldev Singh was ordered to alert the First Sikh Battalion to be ready for combat. While accepting Hari Singh's request for the accession of Kashmir to the Indian Union, Mountbatten clearly stipulated that India's good gesture was subject to two conditions:

(i) Kashmir's accession having become a subject of dispute, it had to be decided in accordance with the wishes of the people of Kashmir after her soil was cleared of the invader and law and order restored; and
(ii) the Maharaja should place the administration in the hands of Sheikh Abdullah.[18]

Since the disturbances continued in Kashmir, the plebiscite could never be held.

At the meeting of 25 October, Mountbatten suggested that V.P. Menon, a seasoned administrator, who played a decisive role in the integration of the Princely States to the Indian Union, fly forthwith to Srinagar with the Instrument of Accession, obtain Hari Singh's signature and fly back to India. Nehru agreed to this though reluctantly because his priority was the defence of

Kashmir. V.P. Menon accompanied by the Indian Army Officer S.F.H.J. Manekshaw flew to Srinagar on 25 October but his mission was a fiasco. He flew back to Delhi the next morning without the Maharaja's signature on the document as the latter, according to Menon, had "gone to pieces completely (and) could come to no decision."[19] While in Srinagar, V.P. Menon as well as the Maharaja's Prime Minister Mehr Chand Mahajan strongly advised the Maharaja to leave Srinagar forthwith to Jammu. Though the rush of events certainly unnerved him, the Maharaja refused to leave the capital at that crucial hour leaving it to the invaders. He was only arranging to send the Maharani and Yuvaraja Karan Singh, who was bed-ridden owing to a fracture of a knee joint, to Jammu. After a good deal of pleading, both Menon and Mahajan finally succeeded in getting the Maharaja agree, though very reluctantly, to leave Srinagar at 2.00 a.m. on 26 October. They told the Maharaja that the situation might demand his personal negotiations with India and in that case it would be more convenient for him if he were in Jammu than in Srinagar. But malicious rumours were afloat that he hurriedly fled to his summer capital adding to the panic of the non-Muslims in Srinagar.

Nehru was getting agitated as any further delay in taking the decision on despatching troops would lead to the fall of Srinagar which would mean the ruin of Kashmir by the brutal raiders. He was against legalities stopping him from saving his ancestral motherland. Though he accepted the recommendation of Mountbatten and Menon that acceptance of Kashmir's accession to the Indian Union must be a prerequisite, he was strongly in favour of rushing immediate help to Srinagar without regard to the question of accession. Nehru's attachment to Kashmir was unique. He once said: "For me Kashmir's future is of the most intimate personal significance. On no account do I want Kashmir to become a kind of colony of foreign interests."[20] Patel also had a major share in rescuing Kashmir. A lot of credit goes to him also for his speedy decision to send the Indian troops into Kashmir.[21]

Here is an interesting account of the exciting happenings on 26 October. It is indeed authentic as it emanates from the pen of Prime Minister Mahajan himself. It was seen that on the morning of 26 October, V.P. Menon returned to Delhi without the signature of the Maharaja in the Instrument of Accession. Mahajan also came to Delhi along with Menon with instructions from the Maharaja to request India to despatch troops forthwith to Srinagar. Mahajan drove straight from the airport to Nehru's residence in York Road where he found him in the company of Patel. He "firmly but respectfully" insisted on the Prime Minister's acceptance of his request to send the troops without further delay to save Srinagar from destruction. Nehru's desire to do so was equally intense. But it was impossible to airlift the army at a moment's notice. Nehru assured Mahajan that it would be done and that, even if before the arrival of the Indian army in Srinagar the tribesmen overran it, the territory could still be retaken. The matter was no doubt very urgent but Mahajan was very impatient. He told Nehru rather "adamantly": "Give us the military force we need. Take accession and give whatever powers you desire to the popular party, but the army must fly to Srinagar this evening or else, I will go to Lahore and negotiate terms with Jinnah as the city must be saved." This was enough provocation for Nehru to lose his temper and shout at Mahajan to go away. Mahajan rose up and when he was about to leave the place, Patel stopped him and whispered into his ears "of course, Mahajan, You are not going to Pakistan." It was then that "something extraordinary" happened. A hurriedly scribbled note was passed over to Nehru by Sheikh Abdullah who was in the adjacent room then as Nehru's guest and heard his altercations with Mahajan. He had left Srinagar for Delhi the previous day. Reading the contents of the note, Nehru's fury vanished instantaneously. Abdullah's timely gesture saved Kashmir from the edge of a precipice.[22]

The Government of India readily accepted the Maharaja's requests for the accession of Kashmir with India and for military aid. V.P. Menon flew to Jammu on the afternoon of 26 October and returned the same day with the Instrument of Accession and the Standstill Agreement duly executed by the Maharaja. On the morning of 27 October, Indian troops were despatched in accordance with the decision taken at the meeting of the Defence Committee to help the Maharaja's own forces to defend his State and to protect the lives, properties and honour of his people.

Before leaving New Delhi, Mahajan requested Nehru to give him in his own hand, the conditions on which he had given military aid to the Maharaja at a very critical juncture. Nehru magnanimously obliged him by writing out briefly the following terms: (i) His Highness should accede Kashmir to India with regard to three subjects – defence, external affairs and communications; (ii) the internal administration of the State should be democratised and a new constitution framed on the lines of the model already set out for the State of Mysore; and (iii) Sheikh Abdullah should be taken in the administration and made responsible for it along with the Prime Minister. When Mahajan protested that having been in a Princely State, he would be a "misfit" in a democratic system, Nehru firmly said: "No, you will have to stay as Prime minister." The next day Nehru confirmed these terms through a formal letter to the Maharaja.

The Maharaja agreed to the terms. Sheikh Abdullah was sworn in as "Head of the Emergency Administration."

Mahajan immediately understood that the Government of India was very keen to make Abdullah a full-fledged Prime Minister. Since that could be done only if he was eased out, he decided to resign. With a heavy heart, the Maharaja relieved him and Mahajan left the State.

Attlee's Deprecatory Response

Soon after receiving the news of the raid and the consequent urgent appeal from the Maharaja for accession and military aid, Nehru sent a message to the British Prime Minister Attlee explaining the perilous military situation in Kashmir. He stressed the dire need to consider such an appeal from any friendly State. Highlighting the fact that Kashmir's northern frontiers ran in common with those of Afghanistan, the USSR, Chinese Turkestan and Tibet and parts of her southern boundary were common to both India and Kashmir, Nehru was emphatic that Kashmir's security was vital to the security of India; and that Kashmir's security depended on her internal tranquillity and a stable government. Nehru called the help extended to Kashmir to defend herself "an obligation of national interest to India" and described the incursion into that State as "a threat of international complications."[23]

Attlee did not react favourably to Nehru's message. In his reply, he cautioned Nehru against responding to the Maharaja's appeal in the form of armed intervention by the Indian forces as that would only aggravate the "communal discord not only in Kashmir but elsewhere." It was a great pity that Britain failed to realise that if India did not respond to the appeals of the Maharaja, Srinagar would have been sacked by the barbaric tribesmen – a catastrophe that would have caused a wave of anti-Muslim feeling throughout India which her Government could not resist. The raiders would take over Kashmir with the probability of Pakistan recognising the resultant provisional Muslim Government and establishing thereby its suzerainty over the State. That Attlee chose to ignore the fact that Pakistan was the aggressor was clear from his statement that armed intervention by India would "tempt the Pakistan Government to intervene also with its own forces if you intervene with yours." He also stated that though the restoration of order was important from every point of view "I do not regard this aspect is so serious as to warrant taking such grave risks in the attempt to quiet immediately the present troubles."[24] This statement and his advice to settle the issue at a meeting of the Prime Ministers of India and Pakistan and the Maharaja of Kashmir bore ample evidence to his disregard of the basic truth that the war was being waged on an Indian territory and that it was the inherent right of the Government of India to drive away the invaders on its land.

Attlee sent a similar message to the Prime Minister of Pakistan also. In his reply Liaquat highlighted the fact that Jinnah's telegram to the Maharaja to send his Prime Minister to Karachi for a friendly discussion of the developments taking place in Kashmir had been ignored. The crux of his reply was that the Government of Pakistan could not recognise the accession of Kashmir to the Indian Union "achieved as it had been by fraud and violence."[25]

There was little doubt that the Governments of Pakistan, West Punjab and North West Frontier Province were responsible for the invasion of Kashmir by *goondas* by sedulously following the "Hitlerian technique" of creating and disseminating panic and hysteria "using improved... big lie techniques." Fortunately, their plan had misfired. Attlee's erroneous advice to Nehru against rescuing Kashmir ignoring the highly critical situation there had already been overtaken by events that followed India's prompt and positive response to the Maharaja's appeal.

Gallantry of Indian Forces

On 27 October, the Government of India forestalled the raiders at Srinagar by flying a very strong brigade of six battalions and an armoured car unit and passing guns over the Banihal Pass. It proved an extremely tough task for the Indian sappers to open the road from Pathankot to Jammu and Srinagar to motor traffic as the assaulters had destroyed some of the bridges there. During the fighting, part of Ladakh had been occupied by the Pakistani raiders. They cut off the main access to the place which was the road from Srinagar to Leh through the Zoji-La pass. The Indian troops did reach Leh but by a most difficult and round about route from Manali in the Kulu Valley over very high mountains. Later, they themselves built the road to Leh. With the onset of winter, they had to overcome many hardships. Their activities were hampered considerably by the rickety line of communications extending for hundreds of miles and the large movement of refugees. Yet the tide turned against the invaders and local rebels were severely beaten by the Indian army at a distance of ten miles from Srinagar, driven out of the Vale of Kashmir itself and chased down the Jhelum Valley Road to the other side of Uri.

Another Indian brigade carried in Dakotas passed into Jammu and Poonch in order to relieve certain garrisons of the Kashmir army which were holding out in isolated areas against tribal attacks. The credit for the splendid results of the airborne operations which were acclaimed as unique went to both the Army and the Royal Indian Air Force (RIAF). On 8 November, the Indian troops retook Baramulla; and on 13 November, Uri was recaptured. Even the Foreign Office of Britain acknowledged that the Indian troops flown into Srinagar definitely saved the town from capture.[26] But for the timely arrival of the Indian Army, none in the Valley would have been spared and Srinagar would have been thoroughly looted and razed to the ground.[27]

Poonch posed a great problem. Two months before the tribal invasion, there was widespread unrest especially in this area where the Mohammadan villagers protested violently against the new taxes levied on them. It was here and the western borderland that the rebellion originated. The mopping operations in this area were slow and proved laborious. Besides these, winter had set in and the large force deployed in Kashmir being widely dispersed made her position vulnerable. India faced great difficulty in bringing about the withdrawal of the tribesmen by means other than force. Nehru who visited Kashmir in November said that the areas might remain in the hands of the invaders as the Indian troops would not be able to drive them out until the snow there melted.

It was seen that Sheikh Abdullah was sworn in as the head of the emergency administration in Kashmir. Himself a Muslim, he enjoyed immense power and popularity in the Kashmir Valley. But the Poonch area, where the rebellion started, refused to recognise his authority. Hence, Abdullah himself was not very keen on the Indian forces retrieving the western areas of the State from the Pakistani troops. Much more serious than all the aforesaid incidents was the formation of a parallel government in the State. Amidst the tribal raids, the rebel Kashmiris established an "Azad Kashmir" (Free Kashmir) Government in the area on 24 October 1947 with Muzaffarabad as the capital. Sardar Mohammad Ibrahim was its President. The Azad Kashmir, which was in fact "Pakistan Occupied Kashmir" (POK), was a Government in exile. Though the constitutional links of the Azad Kashmir Government with Pakistan were not clearly defined, Pakistan exercised effective control over it. According to Pakistan and Azad Kashmir, the new Government would eventually extend its control to the whole of the State of Kashmir. About ten days after its establishment, on 3 November 1947, the Azad Kashmir which was neither a province nor an agency of Pakistan appealed to the heads of many countries including Attlee, Harry Truman, Joseph Stalin and Chiang Kai-Shek through Trygve Lie, Secretary General of the UNO, to recognise its formation and render assistance to the Muslims of Kashmir against the "oppressive and autocratic tyranny of Dogra imperialism."[28]

On 2 November 1947 to cope with the "grave national emergency," Abdullah, as head of the State's emergency Government, appointed ten popular leaders including Bakshi Ghulam Mohammad as honorary heads of the various departments. It must be said to the credit of Abdullah that at a most perilous hour when the enemies were recklessly determined to exploit the fact of the Muslim majority in the State, he and his National Conference were uncompromising in their opposition to communalism and the two-nation theory. Their endeavours to establish total peace and communal harmony in the disturbed areas were indeed praiseworthy. By a Proclamation issued in February 1948, Abdullah took over as Prime Minister on 5 March 1948. Col. Baldev Singh was appointed as Dewan and a member of the Cabinet to represent the Maharaja therein.

Maharaja Exiled

Maharaja Hari Singh's life after he acceded his State to India constitutes a most tragic chapter in the history of Kashmir. It was a fate worse than death. Though at the time of accession, Mahajan as the Maharaja's Prime Minister secured from Nehru and Patel a position similar to that held by the Maharaja of Mysore, the promise was not adhered to. By the Proclamation of February 1948, the Maharaja was reduced to the position of a mere constitutional figurehead. The excuse given for the failure to honour the pledge was that the situation in the State had completely changed since the assurance was given. The dejected Maharaja did not formally abdicate but was exiled from Kashmir. He relinquished control in June 1949 by which time Abdullah had become a very powerful Prime Minister. The Maharaja's son Yuvaraj Karan Singh, eighteen then, did not succeed him but only served as the Head of the State – *Sadr-i-Riyasat* – from 20 June 1949. Karan Singh says that 20 June 1949 was "an important landmark in my life." His father, his staff and servants left by the early morning train for Bombay (now Mumbai) and his mother, uncle and her maid servants left by car for Kasauli soon after. Writes Karan Singh after the departure of his parents, "for half an hour I sat absolutely alone in my hotel room, poised between the weight of the past and burdens of the future. It was one of those critical moments in life that remain for ever in one's memory."[29]

It must be admitted that while Hari Singh was always blamed for the unprecedented and unending problem in Kashmir, his accession of the State to India, though done very belatedly, was a boon to the country. But for his signing the Instrument of Accession in October 1947, India would have lost the most beautiful State of Kashmir to Pakistan.

Accession of Kashmir to India was indisputably "a victory of nationalism and democracy over communalism and totalitarianism." Pakistan's non-acceptance of the accession, though uncharitable, was not unexpected. Jinnah's refusal to accept an event which in his opinion was achieved by "fraudulent" means also was not unanticipated. What caused a most disagreeable surprise to India was the reaction of the British to Kashmir's accession to India. Britain was perhaps more rudely shocked than even Pakistan by this unexpected development in Kashmir. She did not think even remotely that the "vacillating, indolent" Maharaja Hari Singh would ever decide to accede his State to India. Britain was absolutely sanguine about Kashmir's accession to Pakistan. Britain had always held that Kashmir stood apart from other Indian States. Her foreign policy was framed on this firm conviction. Britain found Kashmir an ideal place to stoke up the Indo-Pakistan hostility. In such a context, the unforeseen accession of Kashmir to India upset all calculations of the British Government. Though it did not openly express its opinion of the legality or illegality of the accession, the focus of its foreign policy thereafter was to "undo" the accession [30] by means fair or foul.

General Akbar Khan of the Pakistani armed forces, who later became Chief of Staff of the Pakistani Army and still later jailed for plotting against the Government, took an active role in engineering the infiltration and managing the military operation in Jammu and Kashmir. He later confirmed Pakistan's involvement in the conflict. In his Memoirs titled *Armed Revolt Inside Kashmir*, which elaborated his plan to capture Kashmir, he writes that Kashmir's accession to Pakistan was not a "desirability but an absolute necessity for Pakistan's very existence."[31] His plan was endorsed by Prime Minister Liaquat. The Pakistani authorities had planned for their armed bands to reach Srinagar by 26 October, the day of the *Bakrid*, to form a provisional government which would then announce Kashmir's accession to Pakistan. Jinnah scheduled his visit to Lahore for 27 October in order to coincide with the planned annexation of Kashmir. In accordance with this plan, the raiders entered the Jammu Province from the districts of West Punjab in the beginning of October and subjected the local inhabitants to the most inhuman treatment. But Liaquat alleged that the non-Muslim elements of Kashmir were terrorising the Muslim population there.[32]

The Government of India knew that a brigade of Pakistani troops was kept in readiness nearby to march into Kashmir at the right moment. Explaining the background to the Government of India's quick action in defence of Kashmir, V.P. Menon, Secretary in the Ministry of States,[33] referred to the following four main considerations that prompted India to intervene: (i)Had India not intervened, Srinagar would have fallen; (ii) the tribals would then be in virtual control of Kashmir – a situation in which even Pakistan could not control them; (iii) India had the support of a considerable section of the State population – 50 percent of the Muslims who were with Sheikh Abdullah and his National Conference, the indigenous Hindus and Sikhs and a sizeable number of refugees belonging to all these communities who fled to Kashmir from the Punjab; and (iv) the fear of Russian infiltration through Gilgit.

Notwithstanding her intimate relations with Kashmir geographically, economically and also commercially since the days when the caravan trade routes from Central Asia to India passed through Kashmir, India never desired to have Kashmir acceded to her unless it were a voluntary act on the part of the Maharaja. She had left the question of Kashmir's accession to the Maharaja's option. When the malicious propaganda unleashed by her enemies that India "busily intrigued to inveigle Kashmir into her orbit" was brought to Mountbatten's attention, he said:

> "In my opinion, this is completely untrue. Old Sardar Patel discussed the question of Kashmir with me before the transfer of power and said that India did not wish to have Kashmir accede to them unless it were a voluntary, legal accession. He further authorised me to assure the Maharaja, when I visited him by the end of June 1947, that he was to consider himself entirely free to accede to one Dominion or the other. He further asked me to assure the Maharaja that India would not regard it in any sense an unfriendly act if the decision were to accede to Pakistan. Indeed they hoped to continue friendly relations with Kashmir as with Pakistan after the transfer of power."

Mountbatten also made it known that Nehru had, from the start, been telling that he would accept the accession of Kashmir only if it were afterwards confirmed by a free plebiscite under peaceful conditions.[34]

The Maharaja opted for the accession of his State to India and the Governor General accepted it. The offer of the Maharaja was absolutely unconditional. Consequently Kashmir became an inalienable and integral part of India. The matter ended there. There was no provision for a plebiscite in the Instrument of Accession. The following provision was made in the Government of India Act of 1935 as was adapted in the Indian Independence Act of 1947:

"An Indian State shall be deemed to have acceded to the Dominion if the Governor General has signified his acceptance of instrument of Accession by the ruler thereof."

Both these were the Acts of the British Parliament. Since India, Pakistan and Britain were parties to the agreement, none of them could question the validity of the provision.

Britain's Condemnation

The Defence Committee of the Cabinet took the crucial decision to deny first the whole stretch of the Jhelum Valley Road to tribal ingress and then to replace the Indian army personnel by the State troops and police. Nehru assured that the Government of India would not maintain a single soldier in Kashmir a moment longer than was necessary and that it would not take any offensive action. But he also made it clear that India would never remain static while Pakistani armies remained in the Kashmir State territory. When the State had legally acceded to India, the presence of the Pakistani troops in Kashmir was "aggression" pure and simple. "At the present moment for a variety of reasons it is undesirable for us to indulge in any offensive action. I am not prepared to admit that Pakistan is entitled to attack us or to shell us, simply because our army has taken some minor action somewhere," wrote he to Roy Bucher, Commander-in-Chief of the Indian Army. In his reply to this, Bucher assured him that India would be ready to concentrate on its resources in Jammu and Kashmir so as "to withhold hostile hidden intentions, should these develop offensively."[35]

Acting indifferently to the aforesaid fact, the British officials roundly condemned India's action. They were particularly unhappy with the involvement of Mountbatten, the British Governor General of independent India, in the Kashmir affair. They considered his action most unfortunate because it was bound to upset Pakistan![36] They were also very critical of the despatch of the Sikh troops from Delhi to Srinagar. More importantly, they were deeply disturbed by India's despatch of military aid to Kashmir without consulting Pakistan! In other words, they were only too ready to play down the perilous role of Pakistan whose officials not only connived at the raids but also arranged for assistance from the provincial Government of NWFP and the Government of Pakistan. Bucher wrote that on account of the illegal intervention of Pakistan, it became an almost impossible task for India to rid Kashmir of hostiles. He further stated "I have seen a copy of an appreciation by Douglas Gracey (Commander-in Chief of the Pakistani Army) in which he advocated the use of Pakistani troops to stem any advance by Indian forces."[37] The attitude of the Government of the NWFP coupled with the fact that the British Government did not approve of Indian aid for the defence of Kashmir encouraged the marauders, particularly the Mahsuds and Waziry, to rush into the Jhelum Valley.

The British army officers indulged also in irresponsible utterances. Douglas Gracey, for instance, made a sweeping statement that the Indian forces were to blame for the fleeing of the Kashmiri Muslims from their State. He refused to consider the circumstance under which the Indian forces were despatched. It was true that a large number of Muslims left Kashmir during India's defensive action. But they were chased out not by the Indian army but by the retreating tribal forces whose habit it was to chase away Muslim inhabitants from any place they were retreating. The purpose behind this nasty practice was to show the Indian army as liquidating the Muslim population of the areas which it occupied. Whoever was responsible for this exodus, the presence of a large number of Kashmiri Muslim refugees in Pakistan was no justification for the Pakistani army to enter Kashmir.

It ought to be said in fairness to Ismay that though initially he expressed shock at the despatch of Indian troops to Kashmir, later he urged the Prime Minister to make it clear to Jinnah that his action in conniving at and permitting the tribesmen to pass through his territory was "thoroughly blameworthy" and that HMG would attach considerable responsibility to him for creating such a situation.[38]

Zafrullah gave an interesting twist to the raid more than two years after the catastrophe. Drawing support from a contemporary statement of Sheikh Abdullah that there was a people's movement in Kashmir, he asserted that weeks before the tribal incursion in October 1947, there was a freedom movement in Kashmir and that the tribals invaded Kashmir only to the "rescue of their co-religionists when State troops were used against them."[39] A letter from Winston Churchill to Mountbatten merits mention in this context. Blaming Mountbatten for all the untoward events, Churchill had, by giving credence to wild exaggerations and distortions, accused the Hindus and India in a language that was not in good taste. Churchill wanted to have a debate on this issue. Referring to this, Mountbatten wrote: "How disastrous such a debate would be, since every one of the vitriolic words which Churchill would use on this issue would be reprinted out here as the opinion of a very large section of the British People."[40]

Jinnah's Outrage

Jinnah's anger was unbounded when informed of the turn in the tide of the battle and the safety of Srinagar. On 27 October, Gracey received orders from Jinnah to send troops into Kashmir to seize Baramulla, Srinagar and Banihal Pass and also send troops into the Mirpur district of Jammu. Having learnt of the initial successes of the raiders, he flew from Karachi to Lahore to witness at close quarters the final triumph of Muslim *Jihad.* But the bad tidings of the tribal defeat and Kashmir's accession to India provoked his wrath to such an extent as to issue the order of 27 October. Gracey did not obey the order of the Governor General but informed Auchinleck, the Supreme Commander, of Jinnah's order. The latter accompanied by Gracey met Jinnah then camping at Lahore, explained to him the military weakness of Pakistan and pointed out the incalculable consequences of military violation of what had become a territory of the Indian Union in consequence of its accession to it. Jinnah withdrew the order but was very furious with India for having secured Kashmir's accession.[41] The British papers highlighted that a great tragedy was averted at the eleventh hour only by the Supreme Commander's threat that all British officers in both Pakistani and Indian armies would resign if the Pakistani troops entered Kashmir.[42] A reputed Indian newspaper wrote that Jinnah, who professed to be the Saviour of Islam and appealed for the sympathy of the world and particularly of the Islamic countries,

> "is behaving towards the free Government of India in the same manner as the President of the Muslim League was behaving towards the Indian National Congress before June 3. His faith in the magic effect of the endless repetition of the big lies is undiminished. He has now created the bogey of a 'deeply-laid and well-planned conspiracy executed with utter disregard of the elementary principles of honesty, chivalry and honour.'"[43]

Jinnah however, agreed to the suggestion of Auchinleck that he and his Prime Minister should meet their Indian counterparts at Lahore scheduled for 30 October 1947 to end the Kashmir imbroglio. Later, the meeting was postponed to 1 November owing to Nehru's illness.

The Lahore meeting was a flop. Neither Nehru nor Liaquat turned up for the meeting. Nehru was still ill and no deputy was sent in his place. Mountbatten had made it clear in advance that, as the constitutional Governor General of India, he had no authority to negotiate any settlement.[44] Nehru had every intention to attend the meeting despite his illness but the *communiqué* issued by the Government of Pakistan on 30 October 1947 rendered it impossible for him to do so. The *communiqué* was full of invectives against the Government of India. After repeating the blatantly impudent assertion that Kashmir's accession to India was "based on fraud and violence," it was alleged that since the Pathans were infuriated by the oppression of the Muslims by the Government of Kashmir, the Government of Pakistan could not stop their march through its territory without using its troops which would have led to serious consequences! The fear of a catastrophe, the *Communiqué* averred, impelled the Pakistani authorities to provide the invaders with a large number of lorries and equipments of modern warfare to attack Kashmir. It concluded thus: "If the Indian Government are allowed to act freely unfettered as they please by virtue of having already occupied Kashmir and landed their troops there, then this El Dorado of plebiscite will prove a mirage." Justifying Nehru's decision not to go to Lahore, the UK High Commissioner in India said that "the Indian Cabinet feel too strongly on this matter that if Nehru were to insist on going in the face of this gross defamation, he would undoubtedly be thrown out."[45] The Cabinet decided that India would not be rushed at 24 hours notice into a meeting with the Pakistani authorities on their own ground.[46] The Cabinet grieved that knowing well of the aggressive and unlawful activities of Pakistan on the Indian soil, Britain failed to mete out to India the treatment she deserved.

On 31 October, Ismay asked the Commonwealth Secretary to request the Prime Minister to send a message to Jinnah charging him squarely with responsibility for the Kashmir crisis. The Secretary did not comply with this but instead sent a very innocuous message not to Jinnah but to Liaquat expressing the hope that the 1 November meeting would prove successful! He seemed to have done so to dispel the prevalent feeling in Pakistan that HMG was favouring India.[47] The leadership of Pakistan was highly suspicious and critical not only of India but also of Britain. This was born out of the feeling that Britain was being influenced by Mountbatten who had "abandoned the Muslims to their fate."[48] The *Dawn* credited Mountbatten with "attributes more Indian than the Indian."[49] The irony was that India was equally firm in her conviction that Britain had always been partial to Muslims. All the past events bore ample testimony to this feeling which India had been nurturing since the beginning of the twentieth century when Curzon partitioned Bengal. The belief was strengthened by Britain's tendency to soft-pedal Pakistan's brutalities in Kashmir.

On 1 November 1947 when Mountbatten and Ismay met Jinnah, he proposed that both sides should withdraw from Kashmir at once and simultaneously: "If you do this, I will call the whole thing off." This was a tacit admission that the "tribal raids" were authorised and controlled by the Pakistan Government. Jinnah also objected then to a plebiscite stating that the people of Kashmir would be too frightened to vote for Pakistan.[50]

In his broadcast of 2 November, Nehru protested against the Pakistan Government's characterisation of Kashmir's accession to India as based on "fraud and violence" and also indicted the terror tactics of Pakistan. He said that while actually West Punjab was destroying the villages and towns in Jammu and Poonch, the Pakistani Government was doing its best to paint a dark picture of atrocities against Muslims by the State forces. Nehru also said that India was prepared to have a referendum held under international auspices like the UN when peace, law and order was established.[51] On 4 November, in his broadcast professing to be a reply to Nehru's of 2 November, Liaquat repeated the offending word "fraud". Further, his reference to the Maharaja as a "coward" whose hands were "blood-stained" was unbecoming of his status as the Prime Minister of a country. Liaquat's speeches implied that he rejected the Government of India's suggestion to have the dispute resolved by a plebiscite held under international auspices. He said a referendum would be of no use "after the voters have been driven away from their homes or silenced in death."[52] Deliberately ignoring the role of the ex-members of the Pakistani forces in the invasion of Kashmir and the clear directions of the ex-officers of the army to the raiders, the Pakistan Army Headquarters made a blatant denial of the participation of the Pakistani troops in the invasion.[53]

With Jinnah at the helm, Pakistan refused to recognise Kashmir's accession to India. Referring to the accusations of Jinnah, Liaquat and Zafrullah that Kashmir's accession was obtained by India by fraudulent means and that the Instrument of Accession was signed by a despotic Maharaja, a legal luminary rightly asked: "Are all the rulers of States who acceded to Pakistan paragons of domestic virtue?"[54] Jinnah justified the tribal invasion of Kashmir as an act to avenge the extensive killing of Muslims in East Punjab and Kashmir! This was one of the falsehoods frequently indulged in by Pakistan disregarding the fact that India's Government and her forces had nothing to do with this mutual killing in which Jammu was "powerfully affected."

Fruitless Parleys

In November 1947, Ismay had a long talk with Nehru, V.P. Menon and Mohammad Ali of the Pakistani Ministry of External Affairs when he proposed a draft agreement on Kashmir. Its terms were: Pakistan should use all its power and influence to get the quick withdrawal of the Azad Kashmir forces and the tribesmen and, while this was being done, India should withdraw the bulk of her forces from Kashmir leaving only small contingents at certain crucial points; both the Dominions should approach the UN to conduct under a British officer a plebiscite under the aegis of three persons – one each nominated by the Governments of India and Pakistan and one by the Kashmir Government as observer; and both India and Pakistan should work to bring about a cessation of fighting to enable the Government of Kashmir to make an agreed announcement calculated to create peaceful conditions for a plebiscite. This draft agreement was first discussed by Nehru and Liaquat and later Ismay was invited to join them. Nehru did not agree to the "simultaneous" withdrawal of the forces; nor did he agree to consider the question of plebiscite when Pakistan, the aggressor, had not only not vacated her forces from the occupied portion of Kashmir but also continued the fighting on the Indian soil. In view of the differences that cropped up during the discussion, the two Prime Ministers agreed that there was no question of finalising the agreement.[55]

In his speech at the Constituent Assembly, Nehru said: "It is impossible to escape the conclusion that the raids on Kashmir were carefully planned and well-organised by the Pakistan authorities with the deliberate object of seizing the State by force and then declaring its accession to Pakistan. This was an act of hostility not only to Kashmir but to the Indian Union..." If Ismay's scheme were to succeed, then the Government of India would have been guilty of the betrayal of the people of Kashmir and of grave dereliction of duty to India. It would have a disastrous impact on the communal and political situation all over India. Nehru said that "Kashmir and India have been bound together in many ways from ages past. These last few weeks have forged a new link which no one can sunder."[56] Britain had not an atom of doubt about Nehru's non-communal outlook. She knew that he was strongly opposed to violence of any kind. She also knew that Nehru was no "figurehead – vain, unbalanced and unpractical" as portrayed by Jinnah. On the contrary, Nehru had, since the transfer of power, shown commendable statesmanship of a high order and also moral and physical courage in a marked degree. Even on the Kashmir conflict, he acted most reasonably and the British officers certainly knew it. Roy Bucher, in his letter to Noel-Baker, stated that Nehru was never so adamant over Kashmir as had been thought to be. But he also said: "My firm conviction is that if Patel had lived, much would have been better."[57]

Pakistan expressed her inability to effect the withdrawal of the raiders on the plea that her order would not be obeyed. Her alternative suggestion to stop the fighting was that she would do all in her power to stop the raiders on condition that India agreed to establish before the plebiscite an impartial administration in Kashmir in the place of the Sheikh Abdullah Government which was persecuting all Pakistani supporters in Kashmir and to conduct the plebiscite under international police force.[58]

This was obviously prompted by the conviction that the very existence of Abdullah's administration would ensure victory for India in the plebiscite. India declined the offer expressing her inability to guarantee a coalition administration and force it upon Kashmir where the administration of Abdullah had stopped fighting in the area under its control and knit the people together on non-communal lines.

Any political solution to end the Kashmir tangle depended on a positive approach to it by India and Pakistan. But the chances of any real rapprochement seemed extremely remote. A positive approach was possible only if Pakistan thought more seriously about the presence of her army in the self-styled Azad Kashmir territory. But she refused to agree even to a token withdrawal of her forces from the territory occupied by her in Kashmir although she definitely knew her forces had no business to be there. So, the fighting continued. What began as a raid became a full scale war leaving Kashmir in torment. Bucher wrote that "Reasonableness departed for the nonce...If these two Dominions go to war, every Hindu in the Punjab will be blotted out and every Muslim in Calcutta. 'The Great Calcutta killings' will be far eclipsed."[59]

The British Government which was behind the whole diabolical design could not escape her share of the moral responsibility. She was in a great dilemma as her plan to let Kashmir go to Pakistan had misfired. Her intervention could never go beyond counselling moderation or high level consultations between the feuding parties or acceptance of the *status quo*. They were well aware of the traditional fate of the peace maker – "simultaneous dislike (by) both sides."[60] But they never failed to credit Liaquat with having done much to discourage the growth of the movement for *Jihad* or holy war in Kashmir.

In the view of many British officials, the only man in Pakistan with any degree of statesmanship was Liaquat but he was subject to severe criticism in his own country. These men always roundly condemned Nehru for having "allowed his Kashmiri blood to dull his brain and spoken intemperately of never letting Kashmir go."[61] But they all agreed that the only alternative to a truce was "ultimate chaos and anarchy throughout the sub-continent."[62]

Meanwhile, in pursuance of the messages which Attlee exchanged with Nehru and Liaquat, two meetings were held between the two in Lahore on 27 and 28 November. Once again it looked as if an agreement between the two countries was within reach. But once again it proved false with the situation showing signs of sharp deterioration.

On 8 December, Mountbatten convened a meeting with Nehru and Liaquat in Lahore. He suggested then that the UNO should be asked to send advisers to help solve the Kashmir problem by holding discussions with the two Prime Ministers. While Liaquat agreed to this, Nehru rejected the proposal outright. While rejecting the proposal he asked under what section of the UN Charter any reference could be made to it regarding Kashmir? Nehru also asked bluntly how at all did Pakistan come into the picture. Nehru had all along been insisting on driving out the raiders first from the State. To the shock of Mountbatten, he made the menacing statement that he would "clear Kashmir with the sword," whatever happened. Mountbatten considered this an "extreme" statement.

Anyway at the end of the five-hour meeting, obviously after much persuasion, it was decided that Nehru should examine the UN Charter and see under which provision he could agree to make a reference to the UNO.

The two subsequent meetings held in Delhi on 21 and 22 December between the two Prime Ministers proved equally unproductive. There was no change in the attitude of Pakistan who persisted in linking the Kashmir conflict with every other problem including the splitting up of the financial assets and obligations of the old undivided Government of India which involved payment of Rs.55 crore and transfer of a sizeable portion of military stores to Pakistan. The futility of the talks proved that there was no possibility of an amicable settlement on Kashmir. No sooner had Liaquat returned to Karachi from Delhi than more raiders were encouraged to enter Kashmir and dub the Indian troops there, "the enemy."

Appeal to Security Council

On 28 December, Nehru wired to Attlee that the situation in Kashmir had been worsening and that unless Pakistan stopped all aid to the Muslim forces, the only course for India to face the situation effectively would be to attack Pakistan's bases in her territory. Nehru added that this measure of self-defence would be justified in international law. However, to act in conformity with the Charter of the UNO, his Government proposed to request the Security Council to tell Pakistan to desist from aiding the Muslim forces. He further stated that his request to the Security Council would be made without prejudice to the Indian Government's freedom to take at any time such military action as might be deemed necessary in exercise of its right for self-defence.[63] Attlee, much concerned as he was with the deteriorating situation in Kashmir, felt that India would not be within her rights under International law in moving her forces into Pakistan. Stating in his reply to Nehru that India would be in the wrong in the eyes of the world, he begged Nehru to refrain from doing anything that might lead to war even under extremely provocative circumstance.[64] Again Britain chose to ignore the reality that regular war was being waged in Kashmir from bases in Pakistan. In assessing Nehru's handling of the Kashmir question, Archibald Nye, British High Commissioner in India said very confidently that "India has sinned more than Pakistan that I would have had no difficulty in building up a formidable case against India." According to Nye, Nehru was in the wrong because he was highly emotional and particularly in the case of Kashmir he was the least inclined to see reason since he suspected the British Government of being "pro-Pakistan."[65]

The negative attitude that Pakistan consistently maintained towards India and the baseless charges Britain relentlessly levelled against India, drove Nehru to refer the matter to the Security Council of the UNO, as per the advice of Mountbatten. However before doing so, India made a formal request to the Prime Minister of Pakistan on 22 December 1947 to call upon his nationals to stop participating in the attack on the Jammu and Kashmir State, to deny the tribal invaders access to and use of the Pakistani territory for their operations against Kashmir and also to stop all military aid and other kinds of supplies that might tend to prolong the struggle. Pakistan was also warned that if she failed to comply with the request, India would be compelled to take such action as she might deem necessary to protect her own interests and those of the Government and people of the Jammu and Kashmir State. Pakistan did not care to respond to this as also to the two subsequent reminders of the Government of India. Interestingly, Patrick of the Commonwealth Relations Office described Nehru's letter to Liaquat as an "ultimatum" to Pakistan.[66]

On 30 December 1947, the Government of India appealed to the UNO. Nehru did so at the instance of Mountbatten who firmly believed that the inter-dominion dispute over Kashmir could be settled only by a third party. Invoking Article 35 of the UN Charter, ("situation likely to endanger the maintenance of international peace and security") India protested that in view of Kashmir's accession to India, the aid given to the invading tribesmen by Pakistan was an act of aggression against India. The UN was informed of the critical situation in Kashmir where the maintenance of international peace and security was likely to be endangered. The appeal was purely on the issue of Pakistan's complicity in the attacks of the invaders. Fearing that the appeal to the UN might remain only on paper, Mountbatten requested Nehru to keep Attlee informed of the happenings in Kashmir. This would entitle India to take measures which she deemed necessary for self-defence pending definitive action by the Security Council to restore peace.[67]

Pakistan continued to permit the invaders to transit across the Pakistani territory and also use it as a base for their operations. As for military equipments, training and guidance, they could not have obtained them from any other source than Pakistan. The Government of India requested the Security Council to ask the Pakistan Government to prevent its personnel – civil and military – from participating in or assisting the invasion of Kashmir in any manner that might tend to prolong the invasion.[68] India's reference was thus mild and substantial enough.

On 31 December 1947, India cabled a copy of this reference to the Government of Pakistan. On 1 January 1948, the Government of India received from Pakistan the reply to its first letter of 22 December 1947. It was no surprise that the letter was replete with counterblasts most of them having no relevance to the subject at issue. India was accused of planning to crush, strangle and undo Pakistan, organising genocide of Muslims in India and procuring Kashmir's accession by force and fraudulent means.

Unanswered Question

It is of utmost importance to examine here a very crucial question that has baffled best brains to find an answer. The Indian troops went to Kashmir in response to the Maharaja's appeal and saved Srinagar from the tribesmen. Why did they stop fighting after beating the turbulent tribesmen in that area when their carnage did not abate? The Indian Army got no farther down the Jhelum Valley Road and Uri while Kashmir was sliding into deeper chaos with the marauders launching heavy attacks against Titwal and infiltrating into the whole of Poonch. By 24 November, the various tribal elements along and beyond the North West Frontier combined and motored down the Grand Trunk Road through Lahore and Sialkot and infiltrated into Mirpur and Jammu. It was an unofficial guerrilla type of warfare directed against India. The tribesmen were most dangerous and most impossible to deal with when they continuously played their own elaborate guerrilla game.[69] Their thwarted ambition to occupy the State of Kashmir reinforced their determination to wreak vengeance on India.

The following is an admirable analysis of the British policy towards India during these days by C. Das Gupta of the Indian Foreign Service. In dwelling on Mountbatten's role in the Indo-Pakistani relations over Kashmir, he says Mountbatten was no doubt a friend of India but was never a foe of Pakistan. His "affection for India," he says "never interfered with his pursuit of the British interest. He rendered a great service to Britain and, incidentally also to Pakistan by restraining Indian military initiatives on more than one critical occasion. He made sure that India did not extend military operations up to the Pakistan border in the Poonch and Mirpur districts, going to the extent of sabotaging his Government's plan for creating a *cordon sanitarie* along the border by aerial action. He foiled his Government's instructions for preparing contingency plans for a counter strike across the Pakistani border, while prevailing upon Nehru to take the Kashmir issue to the UN."

Das Gupta refutes the popular belief that Mountbatten influenced Nehru behind the scenes and asserts that the Governor General's success lay in exercising his official powers.[70] Here is an instance that will bear out his contention. During this time there arose a misunderstanding between Nehru and Mountbatten regarding the military measures in Kashmir. Mountbatten was put out when during his absence in London in November 1947 to attend the wedding of Princess Elizabeth (Queen Elizabeth II) with Philip Mountbatten, a change was made in the military programme drawn by him. After the success achieved in Srinagar, the Governor General was concerned only with finding a solution to end the fighting regardless of the activities of the plunderers in other areas.

Nehru was much disturbed by the fact that though the tribals were ejected out of Srinagar, the situation elsewhere in Kashmir was progressively deteriorating. With the enemies more favourably situated than India, Pakistan was giving the tribal incursion the colour of a national war. This drove Nehru to adopt tactics different from what were hitherto followed. Nehru knew that this was urgent if the war was not to go on for months on end and possibly for even a year. Adoption of fresh tactics was vital to arrest Pakistan's training of new armies for invasion and also to prevent her from allowing her territory to be used as a base for new attacks. India had to strike at these concentrations and lines of communications in the Pakistani territory.

Mountbatten's plan was for the army to send columns from Jammu towards Mirpur and Poonch and from Uri to Poonch in order to relieve the garrisons of State forces still holding out. But in his absence, this object was changed by the Government of India. It attempted to impose its military will on the Poonch area which constituted a large majority of the hostile element. Reminding Nehru of his own sentiment that it would be morally unjustifiable to inflict by force of arms India's will on a predominantly Muslim population, Mountbatten asked "how can we escape the charge of using military force against a people who do not want to link their future with India?" Mountbatten was greatly annoyed to hear for the first time that the Government of India was deciding to send forces into Pakistan itself in order to take possession of the "bases" and "nerve centres" from which the raiders were operating because that would mean war between India and Pakistan. Again referring to Nehru's own statement in the Constituent Assembly that the cardinal feature of India's foreign policy was to stand clear of the "mad scramble of power politics and to avoid being caught up in the struggle between rival blocs,"

> Mountbatten wrote that "no single action was more calculated to shatter that aim than to allow India to become involved in a war with Pakistan...India which otherwise enjoys a fair chance of being able to establish a genuinely independent position in the world alignment, would become overnight...actual battlefield in the world struggle...the idea that war between India and Pakistan could be confined to the sub-continent or finished off quickly in favour of India without further complication is to (me) a fatal illusion." Mountbatten ended his letter thus: "you may take it as an indication of my unhappiness at the way events are moving."[71]

It was a clear case where Mountbatten by virtue of his position as the Chairman of the Defence Committee thwarted the plan of Nehru and Patel to launch military operations against Pakistan to bring about Pakistan's withdrawal from Jammu and Kashmir.

While entirely agreeing with Mountbatten's opinion that fighting in Kashmir was most deplorable and expressing his own anxiety to end the fighting, Nehru was not a whit behind in defending India's policy which he termed "a cautious defensive policy." Stating that there was no desire to coerce by force of arms a large section of inhabitants against their will, he emphatically wrote that the very idea of war was hateful to India. She did not start the war and so could not stop it. But any surrender on her part to Pakistan's aggression would amount to a complete degradation of India. It would encourage wild elements in Pakistan and lead to continuing aggression not only in Kashmir but elsewhere in India. He wrote his conclusion was that "we should immediately proceed along two parallel lines of action: (i) Reference to the UNO; (ii) complete military preparations to meet any possible contingency that might arise. If grave danger threatens us in Kashmir as elsewhere on the West Punjab Frontier, then we must not hesitate to march through Pakistan territory towards the bases."[72]

Most amusingly, at the last moment, probably not wanting to refer the Kashmir question to the UN, Mountbatten requested Prime Minister Attlee to fly to India to resolve the issue by "personal mediation." But Attlee did not agree to it.[73]

Mountbatten's letter to Nehru written on the Christmas Day of 1947, which was a top secret document "in a very special degree," was discussed freely by Philip Noel-Baker in a letter to Archibald Nye written two years later. The letter conveyed some more facts and also drastic statements about Nehru and India which did not contain a grain of truth. Admitting that British officers like him were not supposed to have cognizance of it as it was a letter from the Governor General to his Prime Minister, Noel-Baker proceeded to make his inferences from the correspondence. They were: Mountbatten made it plain to Nehru that he was "horrified" by the change in his attitude; he would not have agreed to the sending of troops to Srinagar in October 1947 and would not have accepted the accession of Kashmir to India, had he thought that the Indian troops would push forward into the eastern part of the State. Noel-Baker added that Mountbatten had thought that Nehru's purpose was just to save a massacre at Srinagar so as to make it possible to reach "a quick and peaceful solution by consulting the people's will." Noel-Baker concluded his letter asking Nye to point out to Nehru of the change in his (Nehru's) attitude and advise him against it if he ever reverted to his theme that the Security Council should condemn Pakistan as an aggressor and that the Council was wrong in treating both the parties as "equal."

Noel-Baker was a great friend of Zafrullah Khan. He always favoured Pakistan and even justified the tribal raid on the ground that the root cause of the crisis was the possession by India of a large part of the Kashmir territory which she had "conquered and to which two years ago India made no claim."

Noel-Baker's illogical and false statement was that the original aggressor was not Pakistan but the Maharaja who was oppressing his Muslim subjects. His most unbalanced statement was: "I have never before heard of any Government taking a dispute to an international tribunal as India took the Kashmir business to the Security Council."[74] Noel-Baker had obviously forgotten that Mountbatten had, since the beginning of December 1947, been moving heaven and earth to get India and Pakistan agree to the appointment of the UN intermediaries including the US to settle the Kashmir conflict.[75]

Given Mountbatten's attitude towards India, it was very possible that it was on his advice that Attlee warned Nehru against sending Indian forces to Kashmir in October 1947 to defend the State against the tribal incursion abetted by Pakistan. It was sad that there were occasions when Nehru was more inclined to listen to Mountbatten's counsels than to those advocated by Indian Commanders like Cariappa, Thimayya, and Kulwant Singh. For instance, their advice to Nehru against appealing to the UN to recover the territory of Jammu and Kashmir lost to Pakistan was not heeded by Nehru.

References

1. A Pashtun tribe of uncertain origin. There is no consensus of opinion regarding their identification with the "Aparytae" mentioned by Herodotus as inhabiting the Peshawar area. They fought with the Moghal troops in the sixteenth and seventeenth centuries. In the eighteenth century, Ahmad Shah Durrani employed them in his armies. Their first encounter with the British was during the First Anglo-Afghan War (1839-42). After India became independent, their lands in the North West Frontier Province (NWFP) became a part of Pakistan and it was ruled by a Ministry installed by Jinnah after ousting the previous Congress Ministry.
2. Mehr Chand Mahajan, *Looking Back*, p. 147.
3. *The Hindu*, 14 Jan. 1948.
4. Roy Bucher to Lockhart, 14 Nov. 1947, *Roy Bucher Papers*.
5. Margaret-Bourke-White, *Interview with India*, p. 160.
6. *Ibid*, p. 166.
7. *Ibid*, p. 163.
8. *Ibid*, p. 165.
9. *New York Times*, 29 Jan. 1948.
10. Nehru to Vallabhbhai Patel, 27 Sep. 1947, *fn* No. 3, *Selected Works of Jawaharlal Nehru*, (*SWJN*), Vol. Four, p. 263.
11. *Ibid*, Nehru to Vallabhbhai Patel, 5 Oct. 1947, p. 267.
12. *Ibid*, Nehru to Mahajan, 21 Oct. 1947, pp. 272 & 73.
13. *The Hindu*, 17 Nov. 1947.
14. Siam in South Asia officially renamed itself Thailand in 1949.
15. H.V. Hudson, *The Great Divide*, pp. 445 & 46.
16. Maharaja to Mountbatten, 24 Oct. 1947, M.C. Mahajan, *Looking Back*, p. 150.

17. *Documents on Kashmir Problem*, Editors M.S. Deora and R. Grover, Vol.1, p. 84.
18. Prem Shankar Jha, *The Origins of a Dispute, Kashmir 1947*, Appendix IV.
19. Stanley Wolpert, *Nehru A Tryst with Destiny*, p. 414.
20. Nehru to Sheikh Abdullah, 10 Oct. 1947, *SWJN*, Vol. Four, p. 268.
21. *Y.D. Gundevia Papers*.
22. *Looking Back, op. cit.*, p. 152.
23. Nehru to Attlee, 25 Oct. 1947, Registry No. 13715/8800/85.
24. Attlee to Nehru, 26 Oct. 1947, Registry No. 14419/8800/85.
25. *Ibid*, Liaquat to Attlee, 29 Oct. 1947.
26. FO to UKD to UN, 31 Dec. 1947, FO/63572.
27. Bucher to daughter Elizabeth, Dec 1947, *Roy Bucher Papers*
28. Victoria Schofield, *Kashmir in Conflict – India, Pakistan and the Unending War*, p. 89.
29. *The Earth Has No Corners, Felicitation Volume on the 70th Birthday of Dr. Karan Singh*, p. 61.
30. Prem Shankar Jha, *Kashmir 1947*, p. vii.
31. Cited in J.N. Dixit, *India -Pakistan in War and Peace*, pp.113 & 14.
32. The Pakistan Prime Minister's Allegations, 18 Oct. 1947, File.No.63571.
33. The States Department was created on 5 July 1947 under the stewardship of Vallabhbhai Patel. (It was not a successor of the Political Department and did not enjoy any paramountcy over the States). It was opened in order to have some central machinery in the place of the Political Department to deal with matters of common concern affecting the Princely States after 15 August 1947.
34. Mountbatten to Bucher, 6April 1951, *Roy Bucher Papers*
35. *Ibid*, Bucher to Nehru, 31 Dec. 1947.
36. Peter Murray's Minute, 28 Oct. 1947, F.14419/8800/85.
37. Bucher to Lockhart, 22 Oct.1948, *Roy Bucher Papers*.
38. UK HC (I) to CRO, 31 Oct. 1947, F/14516/8800/85.
39. Zafrullah Khan's speech at the Security Council, 8 Feb. 1950, FL/1015/80.
40. Mountbatten to Ismay, 29 November 1947, Churchill, *The Rt. Hon. W.S., 2–11-1947 to 9-4-1948, India: Viceregal Official Correspondence Files 1947-48*.
41. UK HC (I) to CRO, 28 Oct. 1947, F.14516/8800/85.
42. *The Times and Daily Telegraph*, 30 Oct. 1947.
43. *The Hindustan Times*, 1 Nov. 1947.
44. Para 39, Review of Events in Pakistan from 31 Oct – 6 Nov 1947, File No.63571.

45. UK HC (I) to CRO, 1 Nov. 1947, DO/35/3158.
46. V.P. Menon's talk with Symon & Shellock, 30 Oct. 1947, FO/371/69705.
47. Notings of Peter Murray, 3 Nov. 1947, 14613/8800/85.
48. Minute of Peter Murray, 17 Nov. 1947, F No. 63571.
49. *Dawn*, 31 Oct. 1947.
50. S. Gopal, "The Beginning of the Kashmir Problem," attached to his letter to Vijayalakshmi Pandit, 13 Nov.1961, *Vijayalakshmi Pandit Papers*.
51. *SWJN*, Vol. Four. p. 310.
52. *The Hindustan Times*, 6 Nov. 1947.
53. Peter Murray's Minute, 25 Oct. 1947, Registry No.15305/8800/85.
54. M.C. Chagla, *Kashmir 1947 – 1965*, p. 23.
55. UK HC (I) to CRO, 30 Nov. 1947, DO/35/3158.
56. Nehru's Statement in the Constituent Assembly, 25 Nov. 1947.
57. Bucher to Noel-Baker, 1 Dec. 1951, *Roy Bucher Papers*.
58. FO to UKD to UN, 30 Dec. 1947, F.No. 63572.
59. Bucher to Rob Lockhart, 6 Dec.1947, *Roy Bucher Papers*.
60. Minute of Peter Murray, 25 Nov. 1947, Registry No.15305/8800/85.
61. Note of Peter Murray, 13 Dec. 1947, F.16016/8800/2/85.
62. Personal Note of Lord Ismay, 5 Oct. 1947, CAB 21/3/38.
63. FO to UKD to UN, 30 Dec. 1947, F. No. 63572.
64. *Ibid.*
65. Nye to Noel-Baker, 28 Dec. 1948, DO/121/17.
66. US Charge in UK (Gallman) to US S of S, 29 Dec. 1947, *FRUS* 1947, vol. III, pp. 185-87.
67. Minute by T.S. Tull, 5 Jan. 1948, FO/371/69705.
68. India's Complaint, F/371/69707.
69. Bucher to Minister of Defence, 17 Nov. 1947, *Roy Bucher Papers*
70. Das Gupta, *War and Diplomacy in Kashmir*, pp.200 & 01.
71. Mountbatten to Nehru, 25 Dec.1947, DO/142/490.
72. *Ibid*, Nehru to Mountbatten, 26 Dec. 1947.
73. *SWJN*, Vol. Four, P. 410, fn 2.
74. Philip Noel-Baker to Archibald Nye, 2 Jan. 1950, DO/121/76.
75. Foreign Relations of the United States (FRUS), 1947, Vol. III, pp. 184-85.

6

At The Security Council

The Pakistan-sponsored war on India in 1947 brought forth a vital change in India's policy towards the Princely State of Kashmir. According to Mountbatten, prior to the partition of India, both Nehru and Patel were generous enough to welcome Kashmir's accession to Pakistan. The veracity of Mountbatten's oft-repeated statements relating to this factor was open to question. But it was also a fact that the Government of India never forced the ruler to accede Kashmir to India. Even when the State was threatened by the surprise onslaught of the tribal hordes aided by gangsters from Pakistan, Nehru was more anxious to rescue Kashmir from the marauders than to insist on accession first. The accession was accepted only in response to the Maharaja's request. The accession was done legally. Kashmir became an Indian territory. There was nothing strange or unusual about this, given the pervasive influence of the genius of the valley, which had from time immemorial taken the pride of place as the centre of Indian culture.

Even after the Government of India lodged its complaint with the UN Security Council, the fighting continued with the massing of armed raiders on the Kashmir border. The situation in Kashmir continued to be the same as it was in the last months of 1947. The occurrence of events since then confirmed the genuine fear that a divided India would bid farewell to peace and also easily become a menace to the peace of Asia. The role of the perpetrators of heinous crimes in Jammu and Kashmir stemmed from the politically motivated expression *Kashmir Banayya Pakistan* ("Kashmir will be part of Pakistan"). The Pakistanis, who gloated over the destruction wrought by the tribesmen in many areas of Jammu and Kashmir, joyfully hoisted the Pakistani flag atop Gilgit – the northern outpost of the Indian sub-continent on 3 November 1947 when it fell to them. When Baltistan fell, even in the biting cold, the Pakistanis managed to circulate thousands of posters and pamphlets loaded with anti-India sentiments among the people of the frontier region. Jinnah was alive to hear the "happy tidings" of the fall of Baltistan. He was at Ziarat in Baltistan and the news was conveyed to him by his sister Fatima. Jinnah had full knowledge of the course of action planned in the remote area of Baltistan. He knew that many Pakistani dignitaries including the Chief Minister of NWFP, the Health Minister of Sind and Major General Akbar Khan of the Pakistani Army had a lion's share in planning the fall of Baltistan.[1] Jinnah died after its capture, having lived as a Pakistani for 393 days. It was a clear case of Britain soft-pedalling Pakistan's sinister role in the catastrophe. And there cannot be a stronger admission of the guilt than the following confirmation of Shaukat Hyat Khan, a Senior Minister of the West Punjab Government, about the role of Jinnah's Pakistan in this havoc. In a BBC television programme on Jinnah in 1997 (produced and directed by John Das) Shaukat Hyat Khan replied when asked, "Did Jinnah actually say to you 'invade Kashmir?' Hyat Khan replied: of course; no one could move, not a leaf could move, in those days without Jinnah's blessings."[2]

Opening of Kashmir Issue

The Security Council was seized of the Kashmir conflict on 1 January 1948 apropos of India's complaint to it on 30 December 1947. India went to the UN not to seek a verdict on Kashmir's accession to India which was a *fait accompli*. She approached that international body only to ask it to call upon Pakistan to withdraw her forces from the Indian territory. It was to avoid a recrudescence of fighting and bloodshed that India sought the help of the UN.

Even on 5 January 1948 – on the eve of the Security Council taking up the question of tribal incursion into Kashmir – there were armed tribesmen at various points along the Pakistan-Jammu border. With Pakistan's support and supply of arms and other sinews of war, the tribals were accumulating every day. The Council opened the debate on 6 January but immediately adjourned to meet again not later than 15 January so as to enable Zafrullah to be present there.

Before the Council began its deliberations, Philip Noel-Baker and Ismay met Lovett of the US delegation at Washington to impress upon him the indispensable role America had to play in putting forward constructive proposals during the discussions at the Security Council. But they drew a blank when Lovett did not respond well and broke up the meeting with no promise of any constructive suggestion.[3]

It would be amusing to know that a couple of days before the Council opened the debate on Kashmir, the Prime Minister of Pakistan chose to describe the murderous raiders as peaceful "Pawindah shepherds" from Afghanistan which prompted journalist Douglas Brown to repudiate it with the remark that "the lorry-loads of armed men whom I have seen day and night driving through that city (Rawalpindi) to Kashmir do not bear any particular resemblance to shepherds."[4]

The Security Council commenced discussions on Kashmir on 15 January 1948. N. Gopalaswami Ayyangar, Minister without Portfolio in the Government of India and a former Prime Minister of Kashmir and Mohammad Zafrullah Khan, Foreign Minister of Pakistan, were the leaders of the Indian and Pakistani delegations respectively to the Security Council. Gopalaswami Ayyangar emphasised that the immediate issue before the Council was to end aggression in Kashmir and restore peace to the people. India had a moral responsibility to protect the people of Kashmir which she would not shirk as long as even a single raider was on Kashmir's soil, he said.

In his reply to India's complaint, Zafrullah harped on Pakistan's record being guiltless – a story he was to keep up for long. He maintained that far from abetting the tribal movement, his Government used all means short of war to discourage it and vehemently denied that Pakistanis were assisting the "Azad Kashmir" Government in its struggle against the autocratic rule of the Maharaja of Kashmir. Then he began haranguing India for genocide and forcible occupation of Junagadh. He even went to such extreme as to suggest that India intended to destroy Pakistan. Zaffrullah raised all sort of other matters which had little to do with Kashmir. He wanted the Security Council to appoint a commission to investigate into all these.

After hearing both the representatives, the Security Council passed a resolution on 17 January 1948 by which they were to take all measures within their power to improve the situation in Kashmir and to refrain from making any statement or permitting any act that might aggravate the situation. They were further asked to inform the Council forthwith any material change in the situation that might occur while the matter was under consideration by the Council and consult the latter thereon.

On 20 January, obviously actuated by a sense of urgency, the Security Council presented to India and Pakistan a draft resolution proposing the appointment of a three-member UN Commission to investigate the Kashmir dispute on the spot. This was accepted by both India and Pakistan.

On 24 January 1948, the President of the Security Council invited the suggestion of both the parties on a resolution he informally put to them. It was to the effect that a plebiscite should be "organised, held and supervised under the authority of the Security Council." The Indian Paper on it submitted on 28 January laid down the action to be undertaken by Pakistan to secure the withdrawal of the raiders from Kashmir and prevent their further incursions into it. After the hostilities had ended, it envisaged a period of six months for pacification. Thereafter, the Indian forces in decreasing numbers should remain to safeguard law and order until the completion of a plebiscite. The paper also stated that the Maharaja and his Government would convene a National Assembly to constitute a National Government which would conduct the plebiscite "under the advice and observation of persons appointed by the UN." On the same date, Pakistan submitted a draft resolution requesting the Council to arrange for an interim administration in Kashmir, withdrawal of Indian forces, invaders and interlopers, return of the refugees to their homes and holding a plebiscite.[5]

India was most unhappy over the Council's failure to condemn Pakistan's aggression in Kashmir in its resolutions. Her complaint was neither recognised nor placed in the forefront. The Council's resolution did not take into account India's key charge against Pakistan which should have been dealt with first. The cardinal point that Pakistan was the transgressor was left out at the instance of Zafrullah who was backed by Noel-Baker. Instead, plebiscite was given precedence over it. Attlee justified this gross omission on the plea that it would not be a "hopeful way" to begin the process by "an initial casting of blame on Pakistan" whose co-operation would be forthcoming only if they were "convinced of the impartiality of the Security Council."[6] Did impartiality lie in protecting the aggressor?

Britain succeeded in spreading the wrong notion that she could not control the actions of the Security Council. The truth was, as Gopalaswami Ayyangar rightly spelt out, Noel-Baker "towered intellectually" above most of the members of the Security Council who practically followed his lead.[7]

The following lines from Mountbatten to Prime Minister Attlee testify to the former's deep depression over the deplorable attitude of the British Government towards India:

"I am at a loss to understand why India who has been brought to her present predominant position in Asia largely through British efforts in the past and which is the only country now likely to give a lead in the Far East, is being treated in this way. The policy which you have initiated and which I have endeavoured to carry out during the past year is now being compromised by this leaning towards Pakistan's cause and Noel-Baker's obvious antagonism to India...the continuation of this attitude and an adverse decision in the Security Council towards India can only result in the plebiscite which we all wish to see hold being put further and further into the future...I wish to assure you that I am not all unhopeful about the future if British policy can avoid giving the Indians the impression of unfair prejudice against them for the sake of conciliating Arab opinion."[8]

It was palpably clear that India's faith in the UN would be eroded unless the British Government convinced her that Pakistan would not be favoured at India's expense and also assured its support to India's legitimate claim that her complaint should be considered first. But this was not done.

Dr. Tingfu Tsiang's Resolution and After

Until March 1948, the Security Council made no move worth the name to find a solution to the knotty problem of Kashmir. Zafrullah continued to sidetrack the issue both in New York and in London repeatedly raising the bogey that the Indian troops were sent to support the Maharaja's autocracy and that "the tribesmen are really a secondary question."[9]

On 15 March, in a broadcast interview from the New York City Radio Station, Gopalaswami Ayyangar was critical of the Council's sluggishness in the case of Kashmir. He complained that though two months and a half had elapsed since the complaint was brought to it, the Council had not been able to get Pakistan do the right thing.

On 18 March, Tsiang, representative of Nationalist China, presented a draft resolution before the Security Council to resolve the Kashmir issue. It was a twelve-point plan under which Pakistan would undertake to give no aid to the tribesmen and call on them to cease fighting, while India would undertake to withdraw gradually as many troops as were not required for the defence and security of Kashmir. India would establish a special plebiscite administration which would include six UN officers and ensure that no pressure was put on the voters. Refugees from Kashmir would be guaranteed safe return to their State and the Government of Kashmir under Sheikh Abdullah would be expanded to include all major political groups.

After Tsiang submitted his draft resolution, the Council was adjourned for a month during which the draft resolution was successively revised.

India called Tsiang's draft resolution a "valiant attempt at a just compromise," though certain amendments were considered necessary before accepting the resolution in its entirety. In fact, India straightaway accepted the draft in substance since it did not commit her to depart from her fundamentals. Later, the Government of India endorsed Ayyangar's acceptance of the substance of the draft and authorised him to repeat it to the Council. But the Azad Kashmir Government categorically rejected it calling it a "preposterous idea."[10] This was a profound disappointment to India. The President of the Council Alfonso Lopez of Colombia regretted much that the Indian and the Pakistani points of view could not be reconciled.

On 17 April, when the Security Council met exactly a month after Tsiang's resolution was introduced, a new resolution was jointly submitted by the representatives of Belgium, Canada, China, Colombia, Britain and the United States. In the informal conference held amongst the sponsors of the fresh resolution, Tsiang's draft was changed beyond recognition. India found that the original resolution was "twisted out of shape in its essential particulars." Every amendment to the original draft of Tsiang was in a sense adverse to India. Even the "anaemic" reference to Pakistan's responsibility found in the preamble to the original draft resolution had been deleted and replaced with a mere request to Pakistan to do her best to secure the removal of the tribesmen.

Speaking at the Security Council, Ayyangar said that the approach of the original resolution of China was so altered in many respects as to make it "a definite worsening of our position and constitutes a breach, in some cases a violent one, into our fundamentals." In the new resolution before the Council, the original Chinese resolution had been "so attenuated that it is not possible for us to agree to the resolution,"[11] he declared. The provisions in the new resolution were so designed as to safeguard the advantageous positions gained by the invaders in Kashmir. The provision relating to the composition of a new Government in Kashmir was vitiated by the unreasonable desire to place the aggressor and the aggressed on the same footing. It was really unheard of for a good government functioning smoothly to be changed into a new coalition government to satisfy all parties to a dispute.

Ayyangar blamed the UN in rather strong words for hurting India by "cold-shouldering" her main complaint and "tarring" the accused and the victim with the same brush in the new "niggardly" resolution. This invited a mild rebuke from Lopez but Ayyangar firmly told that political elements played a greater role than principles of international law in the Security Council. He further warned that if the new resolution which replaced that of Tsiang were to be carried disregarding India's objections, "it will be for my Government to decide what the course of action will be to end the fighting."

In answer to the UK representative's repeated reference to the Indian army in Kashmir as an "army of occupation," Ayyangar said that the Indian army was in Kashmir by virtue of its legal position of India and that to call it an "army of occupation" was unjust to both the Government and the army of India. Ayyangar also made it clear that Kashmir's accession to India was not temporary. Since it was entirely legal, it would remain after the withdrawal of the tribesmen and cessation of fighting. It would continue to remain so unless the plebiscite had gone against it, he affirmed.

Ayyangar's rejection of the resolution was wholeheartedly endorsed by the Government of India. The final resolution did not meet with the approval of the Pakistan Government either. Pakistan's grievance was that though originally the Council appeared to sympathise with her grievances, later it turned against her giving much importance to the position that India had already gained in Kashmir.

On 21 April 1948, the aforesaid jointly sponsored resolution which by-passed the really crucial issue – the fact of aggression by Pakistan in the guise of raiders – was adopted by the Security Council. Its main provisions were an increase in the membership of the proposed UN Commission envisaged in the Council's resolution of 20 January from 3 to 5 and its immediate visit to the Indian sub-continent to help the feuding parties to stop fighting and create an atmosphere conducive to hold a plebiscite. It certainly passed one's comprehension as to why the Security Council chose to link Pakistan's blatant complicity in the tribal invasion with the holding of a plebiscite to decide the future of Kashmir!

India, however, made it known that even after knowing her strong objections to the resolution which she had publicly expressed, if the Security Council decided to send the Commission, she would gladly confer with it.

Fresh Proposals for Kashmir

Quite a few interesting developments relating to the Kashmir question were taking place alongside the vehement debates and discussions within and outside the Security Council. In January 1948, Kearney, Canadian High Commissioner to India, suggested the independence of Kashmir as a possible solution to end the Kashmir dispute. Oddly enough, Jinnah himself had made a similar proposal for a return of the control over Kashmir to the Maharaja but attaching the condition that India cancelled Kashmir's accession to her.

According to Kearney's proposal, instead of accession to one of the two Dominions, the plebiscite should be confined to the question whether Kashmir should be independent under the joint protection of India and Pakistan. However, if the people did not opt for independence, he suggested a second plebiscite on their preference to join one of the two Dominions. In substantiating his independence proposal, Kearney said that foreign relations of independent Kashmir with the rest of the world should be on the model of Luxembourg whose economy was tied to Belgium while political representation was handled by Holland. Similar division of Kashmir's interests could be worked out between India and Pakistan, he said. Nehru reacted favourably to the proposal as he believed it would remove a great deal of the controversial matters inherent in a plebiscite on accession and would further bring India and Pakistan into closer harmony in other fields. Patrick Gordon Walker, Parliamentary Under Secratary in the CRO, who was prepared to accept the proposal remarked that there was no clarity of the essential issue as to whether the Indian troops would remain in Kashmir or be rejected by Pakistan. Certain others also were in favour of the proposal. Sheikh Abdullah felt that the sharing of a common interest in Kashmir would serve to unite and link the two Dominions. In general it was agreed that the heat wave in the sub-continent would be considerably reduced by this solution. But Liaquat opposed it on the plea that it would solve nothing and leave Kashmir a hotbed of inter-Dominion intrigue. America also did not welcome the proposal seeing little merit in it. She felt that it would provide fresh scope for friction between India and Pakistan and that the establishment of a non-viable independent State in an exposed position would be an invitation for Russian intrigues.

As for Britain, it was a known fact that any proposal not agreeable to Pakistan was anathema to her. She did not think it worthwhile to consider the suggestion of Kearney. After obtaining the approval of Noel-Baker to disapprove the suggestion of independence for Kashmir, Britain conveyed her opinion to her High Commissioner in New Delhi and also telegraphed to Ottawa directing her High Commissioner there to instruct the Canadian Government "to discourage Mr. Kearney from crossing the lines by his activities at New Delhi and in particular from pursuing his proposal for an independent kingdom of Kashmir." Attlee approved the action of the Foreign Office.[12] This was Britain's reception to a well-meaning suggestion put forth in all good faith simply because the Prime Minister of Pakistan was against it.

Another solution presented in all seriousness to resolve the Kashmir issue emerged from the Commonwealth Relations Office itself. It was a proposal to partition Kashmir by conceding outright certain areas in the southeast of Kashmir to India and certain other areas to Pakistan and conducting the plebiscite only in the remaining areas of the State. Though Britain considered this a laudable suggestion, she was afraid of the unpleasantness it would cause if the parties came to know that this step was devised by Britain to promote a solution on these lines. Hence it was decided that the UN Commission proposed in the Council's resolution of 21 April 1948 should take the initiative by proposing this measure in its report.[13] Although some of the devices came from Britain, the latter scrupulously avoided giving India the impression that they emanated from Britain. Again, towards the end of 1949, the move to give up the idea of a plebiscite and reach instead a settlement by the partition of the State on the basis of the existing truce line was gathering momentum.[14] But the attempt proved abortive.

Britain's one and only worry in this context was not to provoke Pakistan even in the remotest sense. Nothing could upset Britain more than losing the confidence of the Government and the people of Pakistan. Nothing could be more fatal to her than the apprehension that Pakistan was doubting her sincerity.

Majority of the British officials had not really tuned in to India's genuine grievance. There was no realistic assessment on Britain's part of the grave situation created by Pakistan in Kashmir. She did not make even once a reference to Pakistan's unprovoked aggression against India. Undeniably, Britain was partial. When Pakistan denied she had a hand in the invasion of Kashmir, Britain accepted her denial. The history of UN's role in settling the Kashmir dispute would show that the Security Council which was under the strong influence of the Western powers made more demands on India as if she was the aggressor and guilty party. After carefully watching the goings on at the Security Council for months on end, Nehru had little doubt that the UK representatives at the UN were consistently hostile to India. He also said "the whole show on the military side in Pakistan is run by British officers who are more intractable and hostile to us than the Pakistanis."[15]

Britain's Extreme Bias for Pakistan

When India lodged her complaint with the Security Council, the British CRO strongly felt that its Secretary, Philip Noel-Baker, should proceed to New York to represent the UK during the discussions in the Security Council. Though Attlee consented to this, there were objections to the proposal from some higher echelons, like Ernest Bevin, Foreign Secretary and Denning, Parliamentary Under Secretary. Their objection related to a Cabinet Member representing the UK in the Security Council. Bevin also warned the Prime Minister of the "obvious dangers of allowing ourselves to be manoeuvred by Nehru into siding against (sic) or appearing to side Pakistan. With the Palestine position so critical we simply could not afford to put Pakistan against us and so have the whole of Islam against us." Attlee who was much more anxious than his colleagues to maintain good relations with Pakistan wanted at all costs to avoid giving her the impression that Britain was siding with India against her.

It would be well to remember that during his stay in New York in January-February 1948 to participate in the proceedings in the Security Council on the Kashmir issue, Noel-Baker met members of several delegations including those of India and Pakistan. Earlier he met the officials of the US State Department on 10 January 1948. Among the several proposals he outlined to them to solve the Kashmir issue, one was to evolve a complex plan to stop the fighting and place Kashmir under the UN control pending the holding of a plebiscite. Aside this, he told Sheikh Abdullah, that on the strength of his own sources of information, he was satisfied that Pakistan had no hand at all in the invasion of Kashmir and so she was blameless!

There was another act of the British army officers which came as a disagreeable surprise to many in India. At a time when the Pakistani aggression was getting intensified, the Indian army, then under the command of British officers, had been faithfully sending to Pakistan train loads of the latter's share of the division of the spoils of partition. The Pakistani army, also under the command of the British officers, was using the weapons to shoot back at the Indian army in Kashmir. Later, under Nehru's stern orders, these dangerous despatches were stopped.

On 8 May 1948, it was reliably learnt from the US Ambassador in Karachi that three battalions of the Pakistani army were in Kashmir near Uri, Poonch and Mirpur which presaged open war between India and Pakistan.[16] The Ambassador got the information from his military attaché. But Noel-Baker, on the other hand, complained of the advances of the Indian forces in Mirpur and Poonch in contravention of the Council's resolution of 17 January which called on both the parties to refrain from any action. He warned that if the flow of refugees from Kashmir to Pakistan, which had already begun, developed on a larger scale, it would disrupt the Pakistani economy and greatly weaken the pro-Pakistan element in Kashmir.[17] Obviously, Noel-Baker had been lending his ears to the falsehoods spread by the Azad Kashmir Radio as also the concoctions of Zafrullah at the Security Council. For, about the same time – May 1948, Indira Gandhi complained to Nehru that there was a woeful lack of political propaganda on behalf of the Kashmir Government. While the Azad Kashmir Radio "was blaring out the most brazen lies night and day, there is nothing to counteract them...Every day there is a fresh crop of rumours," she said and suggested that only the All India Radio could "reach into the byways of Srinagar and give authentic news and contradict the ridiculous stories spread by the Azad Kashmir Radio."[18]

Nehru's wire to Liaquat in June to confirm or contradict the information he got that the Pakistan-fighter aircraft might be used in a sudden attack to shoot the Indian air force on its airfields in Kashmir elicited no response from him. What Pakistan contemplated was an act of aggression and constituted a violation of the pledge given in the House of Commons on 30 October 1947 that Britain should not be a party to the use of its armed personnel in a combatant capacity on either side in the Kashmir dispute. The pledge was given in reply to a supplementary question put by Winston Churchill. As per the pledge, on receipt of the codeword "Stand Down," every British officer of any rank "shall cease forthwith to take any further part in his command or administration of the armed forces of India and Pakistan."

Britain was very anxious to prevent a situation in which the British officers would come into physical conflict with one another. About ten British technical officers serving with the Pakistani army did volunteer for service in Azad Kashmir without the knowledge of the British Government. Nehru warned that if the British officers in the Pakistani army assumed any role, it would be impossible for him to hold Indian public opinion and hence an open conflict between India and Pakistan was imminent. In July 1948, one of the ten technical officers was killed in Kashmir by a mine. This prompted Attlee to send an immediate but friendly warning to Liaquat on 7 July 1948 that any such occurrence as reported by India threatening the general peace of the sub-continent would "place my government in a position in which they would certainly have to apply the Stand-Down arrangements and withdraw all British officers from both the Indian and Pakistani forces. I want to leave you in no doubt," and added that this would be the immediate and inevitable result of the outbreak of an open war. A copy of this letter was sent to Nehru. Attlee's message was significant as it was the first of its kind from the Government of the UK to a Dominion Government explaining the circumstances in which the "Stand Down" would be applied. In his telegram of 14 July sent to Liaquat but

not to Nehru, Attlee explained that the step to withdraw British officers would be taken only with the greatest reluctance in order to prevent a situation in which the British officers would be fighting with one another. In his third telegram sent on 23 July again only to Liaquat, Attlee said: "The position is that the withdrawal of British officers from India or Pakistan alone on the ground that one or other was the aggressive State is a step which we could not contemplate unless it were in pursuance of some decision of the Security Council."[19]

Regarding India, H.A.F. Rumbold minuted on 15 July 1948 that "it is common knowledge that British officers a ; withdrawn from the Indian units sent to Kashmir." Two British Generals of the Indian army visited Kashmir in a non-combatant capacity but only after obtaining the approval of the British authorities. Roy Bucher, the British Commander-in-Chief of the Indian army, gave the British an assurance that except for the visit by the two Generals, no other British officer or personnel serving in the Indian army had visited Kashmir and that there was no intention to use such officers in Kashmir. [20]

It was a matter of great regret that British officers of the stature of Secretaries of State gave room to suspect that they were carrying on some kind of an intense activity against India. When the Government of India was gravely disturbed at the prospect of a fresh outbreak of hostilities between India and Pakistan and apprised Britain of it, the latter's response indicated a callous disregard for the perilous situation faced by India. Pakistan was engaged in buying air-craft and arms from various sources and there was the threat of a sudden unprovoked attack at any time on the Indian airfields. V.K. Krishna Menon pointed out that the Pakistani troops ostensibly on leave were still operating in Kashmir and arms were being flown into Hyderabad by a British subject by name F.C. Cotton. Menon stressed the urgency for the British military staff to withdraw immediately from both sides if hostilities should occur. The Commonwealth Secretary was sceptical of India's apprehensions. While he agreed that Pakistan was obtaining arms from Italy and Switzerland, he exaggerated her weak military position. He said that Pakistan's own war potential was "slight" when compared with that of India – a most insensible and ridiculous argument which Britain was never tired of adducing to defend Pakistan. It was as if Pakistan's smaller forces than India's had nothing to do with Pakistan's territorial smallness. The Secretary further stated that all the best efforts of the Commonwealth Relations Office to stop F.C. Cotton from gun running had proved to be of no avail.[21]

About this time, Rajkumari Amrit Kaur raised an alarm on the rumour of the withdrawal of British forces from India alone. Following this, the decision regarding "Stand Down" was reiterated by Britain if the situation turned to one of overt war.[22] But Pakistan as usual, stoutly denied the rumours asserting that she would never turn an aggressor and that all her doings were only in self-defence. Paradoxically, in response to this "Stand Down" decision, Jinnah conveyed a categorical assurance to HMG that no UK personnel would be employed in the Pakistani Government forces in Kashmir and if any such personnel were present in Kashmir even casually, they would be withdrawn immediately.[23]

In August 1948, when the presence of the units of the Pakistani army in Kashmir became publicly known, India wanted that all British personnel in that army should be officially withdrawn. She further stated that since Pakistan was at fault, the withdrawal would not apply to the Indian army. Attlee sent a personal reply to Nehru on 23 August to the effect that it would be a mistake for the UK Government to take any "precipitate unilateral action" while the UN Commission was arranging for a ceasefire and a plebiscite in Kashmir. Stating that it would cut across the existing negotiations, he stressed that the withdrawal of British officers "would not, in our view, conduce to the observance of the conditions of the cease-fire arrangements."

Nehru was not satisfied with the reply of Attlee. Alluding to the Pakistani bombardment of December 1947, in which the Beripattam Bridge on the main supply route of the Indian forces in southwest Kashmir was destroyed, he bluntly wrote that such operations meant that the British officers including the Commander-in-Chief were engaged in planning and carrying out this offensive against India. India took the strongest exception to this carefully planned operation of Pakistan against her and more especially to the role of the British officers in it. India found it hard to believe that the British Government had chosen to adopt so hostile an attitude to her as to allow high ranking British officers to take full part in these operations. "The Government of India view this development with grave concern and they must ask His Majesty's Government in the United Kingdom to withdraw such British officers," wrote Nehru to Attlee. In his reply, after reiterating the points of his previous letter, Attlee rejected the suggestion that the "progressive deterioration" in the condition of Kashmir should be attributed to the services rendered by the British officers to Pakistan. He added that the British officers could not be withdrawn from one side only except "in pursuance of some decision of the Security Council."[24]

Nehru was right in his stand that the UK Government should in justice have applied the "Stand Down" order to the Pakistani forces in October 1947 itself considering the role assumed by the British officers under General Gracey. Nehru was also justified in resenting Britain's conduct in treating India and Pakistan as equal partners in the conflict. Men of Archibald Nye's ilk, who were heartless to the misery caused to the public of Kashmir by Pakistan criticised Nehru's attitude as "highly legalistic."

Discussing the crisis proportions, which a "Stand Down" of the British officers in the Indian and Pakistani forces would assume, Britain felt that it would affect Pakistan more than India. V.K. Krishna Menon was held responsible for approaching higher dignitaries like the Chancellor and the Commonwealth Secretary to induce the Government to order the "Stand Down." The British Government's pro-Pakistan stance was palpably evident when it said that whereas the Indian army and Indian Air Force would scratch along even if there was a "Stand Down," the Pakistani Army and Air Force would disintegrate as a result of the removal of British officers from their units. Britain knew that she would be ill-advised to resort to such a course for other reasons as well. Disintegration of the Pakistani armed forces was not in the interests of Britain as Pakistan stood as a barrier to Soviet penetration into the Indian sub-continent. There would be immediate trouble in the North West Frontier in the wake of such disintegration which would present an excellent opportunity for Afghanistan and Russia to make capital out of it. It would also lead to further deterioration in Britain's relations with the Arab world. "The result in Pakistan itself," recorded Denning, "hardly bears contemplation and I should be very surprised indeed if the Pakistanis did not become our bitterest enemies."[25]

It was significant that Britain was so circumspect as to advise her delegation at the UN in New York as early as June 1948 to avoid any discussion in the Security Council on the presence of the Pakistani troops in Kashmir![26]

UNCIP in the Sub-Continent

The five-member UN Commission for India and Pakistan (UNCIP) for which provision was made in the Security Council's resolution of 21 April 1948 consisted of Ricardo de Labougle of Argentina (Pakistan's nominee), Joseph Korbel of Czechoslovakia (India's nominee), Alberto Gonzales of Columbia and Egbert Graeffe of Belgium (both nominated by the President of the Security Council) and Jerome K. Huddle of the United States, also nominated by the President since the two parties could not agree upon the jointly nominated Member which the UN Commission should contain. Joseph Korbel was the Chairman of the Commission. The UNCIP had no British member. It had its first formal meeting at Geneva on 16 June 1948. All the subsequent meetings held in Geneva were devoted mainly to the purposes and plans to be adopted by it. A few days before the landing of the Commission in the sub-continent, Noel-Baker, while expressing the hope that the Commission would be a good, united and fairly resolute team also stated that its members

> "are not at first sight heavy weights, they may not realise how important it is to stand up to Indian intransigence. If Nehru and company start by being hostile and uncooperative, by far the safest (way) will be for them to stand up for themselves with great firmness. This is the way to make the Indians respect you and to bring them round to a responsible state of mind...India will certainly pull a fast one and fake the plebiscite, at least in the Valley of Srinagar, if not elsewhere."[27]

India had already stated that if after her rejection of the ill-conceived resolution of 21 April, the Council insisted on sending a Commission, she would certainly extend courtesy to the visiting representatives of that Commission. So, the statement in the British official circles that when the Commission arrived in the sub-continent, the reception in both the countries lacked even a "semblance of goodwill and good faith," was a travesty of truth. The Delhi papers announced that India would offer the Commission only "a conditional co-operation." As for Pakistan, she had warned the Commission even before its arrival in Karachi that it would be received by a display of black flags. The atmosphere there was thus unfriendly and cold. The Commission was thus in an awkward position, as it had to abide by the Security Council's resolution of the 21 April which had been turned down by both the parties. Added to this were the incessant massive raids on Kashmir abetted by Pakistan. There was irrefutable evidence that, apart from individual soldiers and arms, whole units of Pakistani army were participating in the fighting in Kashmir. Under these most unfavourable conditions, the Commission, with its limited powers, began its work with great caution and tact.

The UNCIP first proceeded to Pakistan on 7 July and called on Jinnah, who was suffering from advanced TB – a fatal illness which he kept a secret till his very end on 11 September 1948. The Commission stayed in Karachi till 9 July. It met Prime Minister Liaquat Ali and Foreign Minister Zafrullah Khan. It quickly found out that, in the fighting going on then, there was irrefutable evidence of the participation not only of individual soldiers and arms but the whole units of the Pakistani army. Finding himself in an awkward predicament, Zafrullah admitted to the role of the Pakistani army in the invasion. He told the Commission that three Pakistani brigades had been on the Kashmir territory since May but explained the measure as an act of self-defence. Zafrullah's admission of Pakistan's guilt was the "first bombshell" to the Commission.[28] It did not express its opinion openly but merely asked whether the Pakistan Government had informed the Security Council of its army's action. Zafrullah replied in the negative. Only eight months earlier, on 15 January 1948, he vehemently denied in the Security Council all the three charges of India: that Pakistan was privy to the invasion of Kashmir; that she was aiding the invaders substantially; and that her action was "unfriendly in the juridical sense." On this firm denial of Zafrullah, India's appeal to the Council that Pakistan should be asked to desist from abetting the raiders was ignored.

The Council's resolution of 21 April 1948 by-passed the crucial issue of the Indian complaint on the complicity of Pakistan in the invasion of Kashmir. This amounted to putting a premium on aggression. This situation had drastically changed with the admission of Pakistan though grudgingly of her unlawful acts which the UNCIP had gathered on the spot. It was also established that British officers in the Pakistani army were actively involved in it. Involvement of the British officers was in total violation of the original understanding by which in the event of war between the two Dominions they would be withdrawn. In its discussions with Pakistan, the UNCIP elicited the further admission that all the forces fighting on the Azad Kashmir front were under the overall command of the Pakistani army. This revelation "confronted the Commission with an unforeseen and entirely new situation."

It took Zafrullah two months to admit of the illegal entry in May 1948 of the Pakistani troops into the Indian territory knowing well that it was in violation of the pledge to report material changes to the Security Council. Even, while admitting the troops' entry into Kashmir, he said they did so only in certain defensive positions in Kashmir! None could beat Zafrullah in his logic of "defensive positions" in a foreign country.

The UNCIP then proceeded to Delhi. The Indian newspapers reported its visit in "calmer tones" than those of Pakistan. India however offered only a "conditional cooperation." The Commission had its audience with the Governor General C. Rajagopalachari, who it described as "quiet, gentle, almost ethereal." It met Nehru and was all admiration for him. Surprisingly, there was no word about Kashmir in the first couple of days of its stay. It was only on 13 July Girija Shankar Bajpai, Secretary General, Ministry of External Affairs, placed the case of Kashmir before the Commission. Speaking of his exemplary presentation, the Chairman of the Commission, writes "...with the English of Shakespeare and himself the quintessence of ancient Indian culture and Oxford schooling...(Bajpai) was a great diplomat of the English school..." Referring to the great change that had occurred in the situation in the State since the passage of the Council's resolution of 21 April, Bajpai told the Commission that the Indian troops were fighting the regular armed forces of Pakistan on all fronts in and around Jammu and Kashmir. He deplored the Security Council for its failure to declare Pakistan's guilt which was the moral aspect of the issue. He concluded stating that "the sands of time are running short; if the problem is not resolved by reason, the sword will find the solution." During its informal talks with Nehru, Gopalaswami Ayyangar and Bajpai, the Commission found that their attitudes were identical: the displeasure over the failure of the Security Council to condemn Pakistan's aggression in Kashmir and the determination that, unless this was done, India would not consider the implementation of the Council's resolution.[29]

The UNCIP was in a quandary. It was incumbent on it to adhere to the directives of the Security Council embodied in its resolution of 21 April which wantonly imposed an embargo against any pronouncement of judgment regarding the guilt or the juridical validity of the accession.[30]

One highly commendable outcome of the visit of the UNCIP was that it accepted the sovereignty of the State of Jammu and Kashmir as a fact. It never discussed the legality or otherwise of the act of accession and this meant that it recognised the *de facto* sovereignty of India over Kashmir. As a corollary to it was the Commission's non-acceptance of the legality of the presence of Pakistan's troops in Kashmir, an Indian territory. It thus became clear why the UNCIP wanted the total withdrawal of the Pakistani forces and only a part of the withdrawal of the Indian forces to maintain internal order and peace.

During its stay in Delhi, the UNCIP had frequent personal discussions with the members of the Indian Cabinet, other responsible officials and the Prime Minister to ascertain their views on the question of a cease-fire. The principal points submitted by the Indian representatives were: (i) the Pakistani regular forces should be withdrawn from the State of Jammu and Kashmir; (ii) the Indian forces should remain along fixed lines and occupy certain advanced strategic positions; and (iii) the evacuated territories situated outside the fixed line should be provisionally administered by the existing local authorities who could be designated and supervised by the observers of the Commission but remain under the sovereignty of the State of Jammu and Kashmir until the final settlement of the dispute was reached. Nehru said that nothing would give him greater joy than that "the UN Commission should work the miracle of persuading the invaders to withdraw and thereby shorten the stay of the Indian troops in the State territory."

On 31 July, the Commission left Delhi for Karachi where six formal meetings were held to ascertain Pakistan's attitude to cease-fire. Zafrullah pointed out among other things that if the Radcliffe Award had followed the terms of reference under which the Boundary Commission operated and included all Muslim majority areas in West Punjab, the Pakistan boundary would have been much farther to the east and India would then have had no direct access to Kashmir. Allusion to the award was certainly not relevant in this context.

Resolution of 13 August 1948

At its fortieth meeting held on 13 August 1948, the UNCIP unanimously adopted the following three-part resolution. Part I related to a cease-fire order which was to apply to all forces under the control of both the Governments in Kashmir. The High Commands of the two Governments were to decide on a date when the cease-fire order would come into effect under the supervision of the UN military observers. Part II related to a truce agreement under which Pakistan would secure the withdrawal of the Pathan tribesmen and the Pakistani nationals who were not normally resident there but entered it for the purpose of fighting. Pending final solution, the territory evacuated by the Pakistani troops would be administered by local authorities under the surveillance of the UNCIP. The withdrawal of the above elements would terminate the situation which was represented by the Government of India to the Security Council. When the Pakistani forces withdrew from Kashmir, the Government of India should remove a bulk of its forces in stages to be agreed upon by the UNCIP leaving the minimum requirements to safeguard peace, law and order and guarantee all human and political rights. Part III related to plebiscite under which both the Governments should reaffirm their agreement that the future status of Kashmir would be determined in accordance with the will of her people.

For more than a month after the above resolution was communicated to India and Pakistan, there was no response from both. P.F. Grey, Head of the South East Asian Department in the British Foreign Office, was much frustrated over this. Though he did admit it was no easy task to make both the Dominions see sense, he was most unreasonably inclined to blame only India and not

Pakistan. He said that India as a bigger partner who committed the "fundamental error of going to Kashmir must somehow be brought to see that they are fiddling while Rome is burning... While the shadow of Bolshevism is falling more and more over South East Asia, they are fighting with a sister Dominion without whose cooperation they are likely to be overwhelmed."[31]

Grey ignored the fact that Nehru wrote to Liaquat on 27 September 1948 inviting the latter's attention to the aforesaid resolution which unequivocally confirmed that Pakistani troops were in Kashmir in considerable numbers and there was therefore an act of aggression against the Indian Union which might lead to a conflict. He urged him to take early steps to withdraw all Pakistani troops from Kashmir.[32] There was no reply to this letter from Liaquat. Thereupon India communicated her acceptance of the resolution of 13 August on certain conditions: the sovereignty of Jammu and Kashmir should not be brought into question; no recognition would be accorded to the Azad Kashmir Government; the territory occupied by the Pakistani troops would not be consolidated to the disadvantage of the State; there would be a large scale disarming and disbanding of the Azad forces; and the question of the northern areas would be considered in the implementation of the UNCIP's proposal. India's primary objective was that Kashmir should be saved from being overrun and becoming a vassal State. It was in this spirit of accommodation that she accepted the resolution of the UNCIP. But Pakistan rejected it in September creating thereby a very serious situation. The rejection by Pakistan of the cease-fire proposals especially after the UNCIP had elicited from her the admission of the presence of her troops on the Kashmir front constituted a "material change" since the passage of the Security Council resolution of 21 April. The UNCIP reported to the Security Council its failure to bring about the cessation of hostilities and published its correspondence with India and Pakistan in this regard. The Commission's report showed that Pakistan had, without informing the Security Council, acquired control over the northern areas after August 1948. Her "naked aggression" of building up of the "Azad Kashmir" forces into 32 battalions which was an obstacle to cease-fire, materially altered the situation that existed when India agreed to the UNCIP's resolution of 13 August. The Commission's revelations caused a stir in India who demanded in vain the Security Council to take action.

Pakistan's concealment of her act in letting her army fight in Kashmir did no serious damage to her though Nehru pointed out "these admissions knocked the bottom out of Pakistan's case before the Security Council."[33]

Pakistan's rejection of the resolution was born out of the fear that if the fighting stopped, India who possessed the coveted portion of Kashmir would agree to a *de facto* partition of the State and obstruct a free plebiscite. By way of elucidation, the UNCIP prepared a supplementary proposal to the resolution of 13 August particularly to allay the fears of Pakistan. This proposal provided for (i) the nomination of a Plebiscite Administrator defining his powers; (ii) a final disposal of the Indian and Azad forces after the implementation of the Truce agreement; and (iii) elaborate conditions to ensure free and fair plebiscite. There arose a problem again. While India wanted the appointment of the Plebiscite Administrator to be deferred until the truce agreement was implemented, Pakistan insisted on his immediate appointment. Pakistan's refusal to accept the cease-fire proposals of the UNCIP revealed her intention to gain her ends by force. This attitude, which aimed at avoiding a plebiscite coupled with her policy of threats and blockades to coerce Kashmir into joining Pakistan, drove the Kashmiris to demonstrate to the world their complete faith in India and to express their desire to join the Indian union. This had great significance.

In October 1948, a few days after Nehru's visit to Kashmir, the Working Committee of the National Conference of Kashmir confirmed the State's accession to the Indian Union. After mature consideration, it was felt that a people with advanced outlook on fundamental issues would never be able to find a proper place in Pakistan with her basis on the two nation theory, persistence in religious distinctions and an outlook that was the very negation of social justice. The Working Committee also passed a resolution that urged the convening of a Constituent Assembly on the basis of adult franchise to frame a democratic constitution for Kashmir that would fulfil the aspirations of the people. The resolution was ratified by an extraordinary convention of the National Conference on 12 October 1948.

Linking the passage of the resolution of the Working Committee of the National Conference with Nehru's visit to Kashmir in October, Britain presumed that Sheikh Abdullah would go ahead with his plan of the Constituent Assembly without waiting for a settlement of the Kashmir question. She feared that this would enable the Assembly to vote for Kashmir's accession to India and thus eliminate the necessity for a plebiscite "without too blatant a *volte face* on the part of India." It was concluded that unless the Commonwealth Conference produced a solution, India would easily absorb Kashmir.

UN Under Fire

Pakistan's intractable attitude and the UNCIP's inability to act quickly, prompted Vallabhbhai Patel to remark that "The Security Council has so far not solved any problem, be it Palestine's or anything else that came before it...In fact it would be more appropriate to call it *Insecurity Council* disturbing the peace of the world."[34] Again criticising the UN for the prolonged course it had taken to settle the Kashmir dispute which was submitted by India for speedy solution, Patel said: "We (India) shall not fail to arm ourselves to the requisite extent. The UN is not able to do anything...If the Security Council releases us from that embarrassment, we shall perform the Kashmir operation also as in the case of Hyderabad, with the least amount of danger."[35] Britain retorted that Patel's success in Hyderabad had made him "more chauvinistic than ever and since foreign affairs were Nehru's domain and not his, he was emboldened to make a public speech of this nature."[36]

As early as January 1948, Canada fired the UN for its inefficiency. She said that while the founders of the UN conceived it as an impartial body which would strive to make the world safe for democracy, under the tutelage of certain powerful western nations, the UN machine was only aggravating rather than allaying the difficulties of the international situation. The Prime Minister of Canada, Mackenzie King remarked in January 1948 that the UN was "creating more problems than it was solving." He also said that "dangerously explosive problems" could never be solved through the passage of resolutions without any means to implement them. The manner of its functioning had brought the UN into disrepute and also undermined its members' confidence in it. These angry remarks came in a torrent from the Canadian Prime Minister when the UK High Commissioner to Canada approached him at the instance of his Government to put to him the constructive role that Canada was expected to play both in the Security Council itself and behind the scenes in resolving the Indo-Pakistan dispute. But the Prime Minister expressed sternly though politely his disinclination to acquiesce in any request from Attlee or Noel-Baker. He further said that Canada would never agree to involve herself in any way in the Indo-Pakistan dispute.

In October 1948, Bevin told Nehru while a cease-fire could come into effect immediately, the withdrawal of the Pakistani forces should not be insisted upon at that moment. Nehru gave no definite answer to this. But he did say that his Government had been considering whether they should stop where they were, defend that position and hold an election in the rest of the territory.[37] The subsequent one or two informal *in camera* meetings held between Nehru and Liaquat in the presence of Attlee and Bevin in London produced no concrete result.

The fact that there was no fighting since the arrival of the UNCIP in the sub-continent in July 1948 and that there was no immediate danger of a collision did not mean that Pakistan had stopped building up her armed forces and preparations for war. High-level propaganda was afoot in Pakistan favouring Kashmir's accession to her. In Britain, behind the scene, Messervy, a former British Commander of the Pakistani army, played a key role in this ominous move by elaborating the absurd thesis that geographically, culturally and economically, Kashmir belonged to Pakistan. But the British officialdom was excessively worried about the outbreak of a war. If a war did break out between India and Pakistan, Britain would face very serious problems. A "Stand Down" from both sides would result in the withdrawal of both nations from the British Commonwealth. It was also open to question whether they would be allowed to remain in the Commonwealth in the event of an open war.

During a discussion with Liaquat in October 1948, Nehru again broached the Kashmir issue and put before him two alternative bases: unreserved acceptance of the UNCIP's resolution of 13 August or partition of Kashmir between India and Pakistan in accordance with the areas then held by the Indian and the Azad Forces. Liaquat rejected both the options and firmly said that only if India handed over Kashmir to Pakistan there would be fruitful cooperation in all spheres between the two Dominions. Nehru dismissed such a gesture on India's part as impracticable.[38]

Meanwhile the UNCIP, which left Srinagar for Geneva, prepared its First Interim Report which was presented to the President of the Security Council on 22 December 1948. It was notified therein that while the Government of India signified its acceptance of the 13 August resolution as a whole, the Government of Pakistan attached to its acceptance certain conditions. These stipulations went beyond the compass of the resolution, making an immediate cease-fire and fruitful negotiations for a final settlement impossible.[39] India, on the other hand, wanted to support the UN notwithstanding its weaknesses because it was the only hope of the world and therefore could not be abandoned.

With the UNCIP's proposals having reached a deadlock, the situation in Kashmir was going from bad to worse. Britain was much concerned about the spread of communism in South East Asia which was posing a great threat to the already dangerous situation. Unless India and Pakistan stood together, there would be internal disorder in both countries through communist influence. The communist successes in China had clearly shown the great urgency to stabilise the situation in South East Asia. Britain strongly felt that the Council should demand an immediate and unconditional cease-fire and address itself to the appointment of a mediator to be designated as "Plebiscite Administrator" who would derive his power from the Government of Jammu and Kashmir. Since he should be a figure of international importance, the name of even General Eisenhower was suggested by many despite knowing that he would be very reluctant to take the job. The US Government as a matter of policy was unwilling to play a leading role in this dispute. The US also ruled out the appointment of Eisenhower as Plebiscite Administrator as he wanted to devote himself to his new job at the Columbia University which he had just taken over. Since the Kashmir dispute was a Commonwealth problem, America was reluctant to rush in where angels feared to tread. Alexander Cadogan, Chief of the UK Delegation to the UN, stated that while the American delegation's anxiety to cooperate with Britain could never be called to question, "when it comes to our asking them to take the job over from us they are inclined to retort: "well, who started the British Empire?"[40]

Towards the end of December 1948, when the bulk of the Pakistani army was in Kashmir or just across the border, Attlee sent a telegram not to Pakistan but to the Government of India requesting it not to advance. An irate Krishna Menon, India's High Commissioner to the UK, immediately wrote to Stafford Cripps making a reference to this letter, the contents and phraseology of which he much regretted. He said: "We are faced with a major offensive, the cutting off of our communications and heavy shellings. Are we expected to sacrifice our troops and allow the offensive to creep nearer while we sit with folded hands"?[41]

A Dramatic End

The year 1948 which was marked throughout by misunderstandings and mutual recriminations between the two parties blocking thereby the way to a meaningful relationship, ended with a dramatic climax. Good tidings emerged from the Inter-Dominion Conference held in Delhi in December 1948 when both the Dominions mutually agreed to an immediate cease-fire in Kashmir.[42]

The fourteen-month old hostilities between India and Pakistan appeared to have been brought to an end by the most welcome decision of both to accept the "Cease-Fire" proposal of the UNCIP. On 11 December, on the basis of the understanding reached during conversations in New Delhi and Karachi between the representatives of the two Governments and Minister Lozano of Columbia, both the Governments signified their acceptance of the UNCIP's proposal. As a first step, the cease-fire was ordered on the mid-night of 1 January 1949. Both the countries signed the Cease-Fire Agreement under the UN's supervision. By this agreement, of Kashmir's original area of 2,22,236 square kilometres, 83,294 square kilometres remained under the occupation of Pakistan. Pakistan was to have the areas to the west and north of the Cease-Fire Line (CFL) which included the western sections of the Provinces of Jammu, Poonch and Kashmir and also the northern territories of Gilgit and Baltistan. India was to have a larger share of Jammu and Kashmir (including Srinagar and the Valley) as well as Ladakh, east of the Pir Panjal mountains. A resolution to this effect incorporating the resolution of 13 August 1948 and the supplementary proposal to it prepared by the UNCIP was passed unanimously on 5 January 1949 at Lake Success. The CFL was monitored by a small force of the UN Military Observer Group of India and Pakistan (UNMOGIP). Lieutenant General R.H. Nimmo, an Australian, was appointed as the Chief Military Observer.

The decision was universally welcomed as a wise move on the part of the affected parties. India took the initiative in hastening the ordering of the cease-fire so that it might come into operation on the New Year Day. India was most concerned about putting an end to the toll of human life and waste of resources which war would definitely entail. Of course, she knew it was only a necessary first step, and many more obstacles would have to be surmounted before reaching a final settlement.

Meanwhile, a crucial change had taken place in the highest position of the Indian army. General Roy Bucher had long been advising the Government of India to replace him as Commander-in-Chief by an officer of the Indian army. In response to his advice, in December 1948, Lt. Gl. Cariappa was appointed as the Commander-in-Chief of the Indian Army. But Bucher was not consulted about the choice of his successor. High Commissioner Nye, who was unsparing in his criticism of Indian leaders and high profile officers, made the sweeping statement that "there was no officer of the Indian Army fit to be Commander-in-Chief but there are some probably better qualified than Cariappa. He is vain, superficial, impetuous, lacking in stability, moral courage and military judgement." He said that despite his acquaintance with Cariappa for many years, he would be very cautious in offering advice gratuitously. Grieving over the vanishing of the British way in the military circles in India, he said, "our influence in military circles will therefore diminish and may disappear altogether...his (Cariappa's) appointment makes the finding of a potential situation in the Kashmir problem even more urgent."[43]

The cash balance settlement between the two Governments on which Zafrullah was always harping at the Security Council during debates on Kashmir merits mention here. The Arbitral Tribunal allocated a sum of Rs. 75 Crore to Pakistan. Though the amount was considered too generous, India sincerely felt that this would have "reciprocal response." India also paid to Pakistan an initial amount of Rs. 20 crore out of the Rs. 75 crore. It was made clear then by Vallabhbhai Patel that this financial deal was linked with the overall settlement of all outstanding issues between the two Governments. In the meantime, in October 1947 Pakistan waged an undeclared war on India in Kashmir. Fearing that the balance of Rs. 55 crore would be utilised against India in Kashmir, India withheld payment of it. But when this led to extreme bitterness between the two countries, Mahatma Gandhi began a fast unto death on 13 January 1948. This was his last fast and it was an appeal to India to abjure "ill-will, prejudice and passion which poisoned the relations between India and Pakistan." The Indian Government agreed to transfer the balance amount of Rs. 55 crore to Pakistan.[44] On 18 January, the Mahatma terminated his fast. Later, Zafrullah confirmed that the Government of India had paid Pakistan Rs. 500,000,000 of the balance of Rs. 550,000,000 due to Pakistan and assured that he would not trouble the Council over the remaining amount of Rs. 50,000,000.[45]

References

1. B.L. Kak, *The Fall of Gilgit, The Untold Story of Indo-Pakistan Affairs from Jinnah to Bhutto 1947-1977*, p. 17.
2. C. Das Gupta, *War and Diplomacy in Kashmir*, 1947-48, pp.39 &219.
3. UKD to UN to FO, 13 Jan. 1948, FO/371/69706.
4. *The Hindu*, 14 Jan. 1948.
5. Memorandum by the Commonwealth Secretary, 28 Feb. 1948, CAB/134/55.
6. Attlee to Nehru, 15 Feb. 1948, DO/142/496.
7. Mountbatten to Attlee, 17 Feb. 1948, FO/371/69710.
8. Mountbatten to Attlee, 24 Feb. 1948, FO/371/69711.
9. His statement in London on 3 March 1948, *The Hindu*,8 March 1948.
10. *Ibid*, 24 March 1948.
11. *Ibid,21 April 1948.*
12. Notings of Rumbold, 10 & 15 March 1948; FO to UKD to UN, 19 March 1948, DO/142/504.
13. *Ibid, Aide Memoir* by CRO.
14. *The Times*, 13 Dec. 1949.

15. Nehru to Stafford Cripps, 17 Dec. 1948, CAB/127/143.
16. US Ambassador to FO, 10 May 1948, FO/371/69717.
17. *Ibid,* Noel-Baker's Note to Attlee, 11 May 1948.
18. Katherine Frank, *Life of Indira Nehru Gandhi*, p. 221.
19. Memorandum on the Policy to withdraw British Officers from the Armed Forces of India and Pakistan in the event of armed conflict between India and Pakistan, DO/142/535.
20. UK HC (I) to CRO, 22 July 1948, DO/35/3153.
21. Note by Secretary to the Cabinet, 6 July 1948, CAB/134/55.
22. Attlee to Chancellor of Exchequer, 22 July 1948, Premier 8/801, E.1845.
23. *Ibid,* UK HC (P) to HC (I), 17 July 1948.
24. *Ibid.*
25. Denning to SOS, 9 Aug. 1948, FO/371/69721.
26. FO to UKD to UN, 8 June 1948, FO/371/69719.
27. Noel-Baker to Alexander Cadogan, 3 July 1948, FO/371/169720.
28. Josef Korbel, *Danger In Kashmir*, p. 121.
29. *Ibid*, pp. 122–24.
30. *Ibid*, p. 125.
31. P.F. Grey's Note, 28 Sep. 1948, FO/371/69721.
32. *Ibid*, Nehru to Liaquat, 27 Sep. 1948.
33. *The Hindu,* 24 Nov. 1948.
34. Reuters India and Pakistan Services, 1 Oct. 1948, FO/371/69722.
35. *Ibid,* Patel's speech to the officers of the Royal Indian Air force, 1 Oct. 1948.
36. *Ibid,* Note of the FO on Patel's speech, 1 Oct. 1948.
37. *Ibid,* Record of Bevin's meeting with Nehru in Paris, 27 Oct. 1948.
38. *Ibid,* UKD to UN to FO, 1 Nov. 1948.
39. UNCIP's presentation of its Interim Report to the SC, 23 Nov. 1948, FO/371/69724.
40. *Ibid*, UKD to UN to FO, 26 Nov. 1948.
41. Attlee to Nehru, 27 Dec. 1948; VKK Menon to Cripps, 28 Dec.1948, CAB/127/143.
42. UK HC (I) to CRO, 12 Jan. 1949, FO/1447/10112/85.
43. UK HC (I) to CRO, 6 Dec 1948, FO/371/69725.
44. Nehru's Statement, 15 Jan. 1948, *Jawaharlal Nehru's Speeches*, 1946-49, p. 172.
45. Zafullah to FO, 7 May 1948, FO/317/69717.

7

Cease-Fire In The Doldrums

Between July 1948, when the UNCIP arrived in the sub-continent, and 1 January 1949, when a cease-fire was called, the UNCIP did a commendable job. But later, when the problem became more and more complicated, the Commission was unable to cope with the challenging task ahead. Its hitherto positive approach to the dispute was given up setting at naught its several months of sincere efforts to bring in a reconciliation between the parties. The Commission's desire to placate not only the Big Powers which held sway over the UN but also Pakistan despite her unseemly means to gobble entire Kashmir, distorted its vision. Steadfastly following in the footsteps of Britain in particular, it resorted to faulting India regardless of the justice or otherwise of her actions. The Commission's mistakes, which were serious, paved the way to its unpopularity.

The cease-fire took effect from one minute before the midnight of 1 January 1949. By this the forces on both sides were to remain behind the actual fighting line with such adjustments as the two Commanders-in-Chief might agree on. But the cease-fire was short-lived as there were serious violations of it. As early as 4 January, Nehru wrote to Attlee:

> "We confess we are entirely unable to follow justice or logic or position taken by the UK Government in regard to Kashmir and employment of British officers there in these operations. Even the UNCIP's finding that Pakistani armies were in Kashmir had made no

difference. So India could not but conclude that this general unfriendly attitude towards India in regard to Kashmir had nothing to do with justice or equity but is apparently based on some other reasons which we are unable to understand."[1]

Meanwhile, the UNCIP was preparing the Second Interim Report covering its activities during the period from the date of its return to Geneva from the sub-continent on 25 September 1948 to the date of the adoption of the resolution of 5 January 1949. This resolution embodied the basic needs for a plebiscite in the State of Jammu and Kashmir. The report adopted unanimously by the Commission on 8 January at Lake Success was submitted to the Security Council on 10 January 1949.

For a little while the fighting in the State of Jammu and Kashmir did cease. The High Commands of both the armies held on their own initiative a conference in New Delhi on 15 January in the presence of the Military Adviser of the UNCIP. It was decided that the cease-fire should be advanced from an informal to a formal basis. A line of demarcation was considered essential to further the implementation of Part I of the 13 August resolution and also to establish the position of the forces in order to avoid violations of the cease-fire. Both the Commanders-in-Chief also agreed on certain proposals regarding the truce which formed Part II of the 13 August resolution of the UNCIP. These proposals were referred to the respective Governments for their approval. All these appeared to be an encouraging sign. But they were all an illusion. The High Commands' proposals of 15 January were rendered inoperative as they were not endorsed by their Governments.[2]

To put the whole matter in a nutshell: A fairly detailed plan to bring about a truce and to hold a fair and impartial plebiscite in Kashmir under the auspices of the UN was contained in the two resolutions of 13 August 1948 and 5 January 1949. It was agreed to by India and Pakistan. These resolutions gave Pakistan no right to retain her troops, regular or irregular or tribesmen or her nationals in the State. Pakistan, the aggressor, was denied any voice in questions relating to the conduct of the plebiscite which was the concern of the Government of India and the Government of Jammu and Kashmir on the one hand and the UNCIP and the Plebiscite Administrator on the other. The resolutions recognised India's responsibility for the defence of the State which had acceded to India and the lawful character of the Government of Jammu and Kashmir and its sovereignty over the State. Thus, the fundamental principles laid down by the resolutions to settle the dispute were considered fair and just by all the parties which accepted them.

Unedifying Negotiations

The UNCIP returned to the subcontinent on 4 February 1949, landing in Karachi first. Trouble began when the Pakistan Government submitted that a plan should be prepared by which the withdrawal of the Pakistani forces and the "bulk" of the Indian forces would be synchronised. One should not miss Pakistan's claim to "synchronise" and not to "precede" the withdrawal of her forces. There was no such plan of a synchronised withdrawal even under the 13 August resolution which was accepted by both India and Pakistan. When the Commission arrived in New Delhi, Bajpai, representative of the Government of India, said that before the implementation of the truce could be elaborated, the scope and meaning of the resolutions of 13 August 1948 and 5 January 1949 should be clearly understood. He was particular that the expressions "local authorities" and "surveillance" in Part II of the 13 August resolution should be well explained so as to leave no doubt. He also said that the disbanding and disarming of the Azad forces on a large scale was an essential condition to be fulfilled before a truce and plebiscite could be arranged.[3]

Failure of repeated attempts to negotiate a settlement led the UNCIP to conclude that the two parties could no longer be expected to agree independent of the Commission on the implementation of truce proposals. On 2 March, the Commission sent letters to both the Governments inviting them to send their civil and military representatives to meet under the auspices of the Commission's Truce Sub-Committee. Both accepted the invitation and the meetings began in New Delhi on 9 March. The Pakistani delegate submitted a comprehensive scheme for implementing Part III of the 13 August resolution. India did not agree with the very premise on which the scheme was based. She expressed her inability to respond until a basis for agreement was reached. During the Truce negotiations when Pakistan repeatedly made a demand for synchronised withdrawal of both forces, the Commission stated that "the Pakistan Government could not in reason expect, nor could the Commission have granted synchronisation, which would have been incompatible with the terms of August 13 resolution." Since no understanding was reached, the meetings were adjourned.[4]

When the UNCIP met after adjournment, there followed a series of conversations and exchanges of correspondence between it and the two Governments. These were conducted along parallel lines in each capital. Though these conversations did not lead to accepting the formula the Commission had in mind, it was felt it provided a basis for the formulation of a plan. The Commission took the initiative in drafting the truce proposals and presented them to the parties on 15 April 1949 for their acceptance. But neither of them accepted the proposals. India rejected the truce proposals but Pakistan dodged the issue with no firm answer one way or the other while the political atmosphere was deteriorating. India claimed her right to post garrisons in the northern area, reverse local administration in these areas to the Kashmir Government, and reduce forces in Azad Kashmir to civil armed force of 4000 men of which half should be unarmed and 12 percent non-Muslims. Pakistan, as she had repeatedly stated, never wanted any discussion on the disbandment of the Azad Kashmir forces or their conversion into civil armed force until the truce agreement was signed and plans for synchronised withdrawal of Indian and Pakistani troops published.[5] Pakistan's theory of a balance in the time-tables for the withdrawal of Pakistani and Indian forces and for the disposal of Azad Kashmir and Kashmir State forces was unreasonable. It created a great problem. Even Britain was not sure whether a strict interpretation of the relevant passages in the UNCIP's resolutions of 13 August 1948 and 5 January 1949 would support Pakistan's thesis.[6]

The cease-fire that became operative from 1 January 1949 did not in the least upset the Pakistani army. One could multiply instances of Pakistan's defiance of the agreement. To cite but one instance: it was after this agreement that the Pakistani army launched a concerted drive to establish itself firmly in the Baltistan and Gilgit territories. Pakistan's blatant disregard of the cease-fire agreement took the form of propaganda campaigns such as accusing India of bad faith, issuance of warnings of revival of armed conflict and igniting the tempers of religious fanatics. Right from day one of the agreement on ceasefire, Pakistan had been "consistently, repeatedly, continuously and uninterruptedly" violating the agreement. The hymn of hate poured out by the Pakistani Press particularly the vernacular papers against a neighbouring country, her people and her leaders showed the depths to which they would descend to rouse the communal passions of the Muslims in Pakistan. In short, they were acts which were not normal in a civilised society.

Pakistan was out to cause death and create confusion to destabilise India. The fighting quality of the so-called Azad Kashmir forces numbering 32 battalions was substantially improved under the control of the Pakistani military headquarters. This was not calculated to facilitate the large scale disbanding and disarming of these forces. The constant shelling from across the border coupled with the psychological climate in Pakistan heralded a renewed wave of war. The Indian Government feared that its troops would be forced to face an arduous winter for a second time.

Pakistan's attempts to stoke the religious sentiments and infuse hatred into her countrymen against the "infidels" unmindful of their potential to cause immense harm to India were completely out of tune with the "Objectives Resolution" moved by Prime Minister Liaquat at the Constituent Assembly on 7 March 1949. The resolution envisaged a "Sovereign Independent State" in which power could be exercised through the chosen representatives of the people and the Islamic principles of democracy, freedom, equality, tolerance and social justice would be fully observed.[7]

Not disheartened by the rejection of its Truce proposals of 15 April, the UNCIP revised the proposals and transmitted them to the parties on 28 April. In its view, the revised proposals under the designation of "Truce Terms," represented a fair compromise. In its accompanying letters to both parties, the Commission stressed the urgency it attached to the withdrawal of armed forces from the State of Jammu and Kashmir as until then no fruitful results would be obtained from further discussions. It also requested of both the Governments their "unreserved acceptance" of the Truce Terms suggested. The terms were divided into three parts: (i) Cease-fire Line; (ii) Withdrawal of troops; and (iii) General Provisions. The Commission established the schedules of withdrawal of the Pakistani troops and the bulk of the Indian forces.[8]

The Government of India sent its reply to the UNCIP on 18 May and subsequently sent two more letters on 17 and 19 June. The Government of Pakistan sent its reply on 30 May. Neither of the responses constituted an acceptance of the truce terms. They however brought out clearly the great differences of opinion that still existed between the two parties. Following this, the UNCIP sent a mission to New Delhi to ascertain on what conditions the Government of India would accept the truce terms. A similar mission was sent to Karachi also. The reports of both missions were significant and valuable as they revealed that the main obstacles to the implementation of Part II of the 13 August resolution still remained. In all its three letters to the Commission (18 May, 17 and 19 June), the main issue raised by the Government of India was its concern about the disbanding and disarming of the Azad Kashmir forces and its relations with the withdrawal of the bulk of the Indian forces and the treatment of the sparsely populated areas of the northern region.[9] The Government of Pakistan which conveyed its non-acceptance of the revised truce proposals on 30 May subsequently reconfirmed it when the Commission's mission visited Karachi.

On 7 June 1949, at a Press Conference in Lake Success to discuss India's conditions to accept the proposals on the Kashmir issue, B.N. Rau,

India's permanent delegate to the UN, explained how the existing situation created by Pakistan would militate against a free and fair verdict by the *bona fide* inhabitants of Kashmir. He said India could not accept the proposals for two reasons: (1) with the existence of about 32,000 armed and equipped Azad Kashmir troops on the Pakistani side of the proposed truce line, a free and impartial plebiscite was totally out of question; and (2) the sparsely populated northern parts of the State, with an area of 155,400 square kilometres had been plundered by the "irregulars" who were trespassers. As per the truce proposal, the Azad troops had to go back restoring the place to the position that existed prior to the invasion in 1947. Once that was done, the Government of India could assume responsibility for the defence of those areas and the Government of Kashmir for their internal administration until a plebiscite was held.[10] It was thus made clear that India would never surrender her right to defend her territory, and that her sovereignty over Kashmir would never be abandoned.

On 4 July, the UNCIP sent letters to both the Governments to send their military representatives to a joint meeting under the auspices of the Commission's Truce Sub-Committee to demarcate the CFL on the ground. Both accepted the invitation and joint meetings of military representatives were held from 18 to 27 July. Both parties conceded certain important adjustments in the factual positions which had until then been presenting serious problems. On 27 July both the delegations signed an agreement stating that as a complement to the suspension of hostilities in the State of Jammu and Kashmir on 1 January 1949, "a Cease-Fire Line (was) established." It was also stated that "both sides (should) be free to adjust their defensive positions behind the cease-fire line...(and that) there (should) be no increase in forces or defences." There was the stipulation that the Commission would station observers where it deemed necessary. It was decided that the delegations would refer the agreement to their respective Governments for ratification and deposit the ratified documents with the Commission not later than 31 July 1949. Both the Governments ratified the agreement and the instruments of ratification were deposited with the UNCIP.[11]

During this period between the actual cessation of fighting and the drawing up of the CFL, there were only minor incidents and no breach of the cease-fire. This appeared to be a definite sign that the contending parties had realised the folly of reopening hostilities. But again it was an illusion.

Pakistan had no intention to withdraw her troops and vacate aggression. So far as the cease-fire was concerned, Pakistan was "in sin." This was the fact. But Zafrullah, who refused to accept realism, tirelessly raged against

India as if she was the aggressor and he the owner of Kashmir! Well-known for the stridency of his utterances, he once asked Krishna Menon in the Security Council if he wanted Kashmir to be handed to him on a golden platter. Such a caustic locution was obviously born out of Zafrullah's penchant for besmirching a millennia old country of which Kashmir was a part.

Indeed Zafrullah had no match in uttering blatanties even at the international forum. He had the audacity to make a cryptic statement during a speech at the Security Council in July 1949 which clearly suggested that the UN intervention was no longer needed except for holding a plebiscite because Pakistan had withdrawn the tribesmen from Kashmir as demanded by the Government of India and as he promised to the Security Council in 1948. In truth, Pakistan had not only not withdrawn the tribes from Kashmir but also had, since making the "promise" to the Security Council, publicly thrown the Pakistani army into the battlefield on the side of the invaders. His whole speech was thus a barefaced lie. It was an open secret that the Pakistan Government officered, equipped and even manned the Azad army which rose to a formidable strength of 32 battalions within a very short time. The UNCIP failed to understand the significance of this development. So, it did not attempt to tackle the situation. Nor did it report the fact to the Security Council.[12]

Blindly Partisan

Even her worst detractors knew only too well that India had never intended to launch the offensive and never made preparations to start hostilities against Pakistan even under extreme provocations. But she made it plain that if Pakistan launched an offensive against the Indian forces in Kashmir, India would definitely resort to such counter measures as were intended to protect her troops in Kashmir. India's counter measures though in essence defensive might involve extension of the area of hostilities and open conflict between India and Pakistan. As a member of the Commonwealth, India had every right to be informed of two things: (1) what was Britain's plan to prevent action against the Indian forces by the Pakistani troops and other troops under Pakistan's control; and (2) how she proposed to stop the continued employment of British officers in the Pakistani army. In fact, the British High Commissioner in India also stressed this point to HMG.[13]

India's hardships were no concern of Britain. More so, if they related to the unmitigated violence of Pakistan against her. Getting wind of the news that the Pakistani army was preparing to attack the Indian lines of communication in Kashmir, the Indian Government planned to send Girija

Shankar Bajpai and an Indian General to London to discuss the situation with Attlee. The latter on being informed of this said that Britain's intervention at that juncture would amount to by passing the machinery of the UNCIP and the UN. He added however that if India was very keen to have discussions in London, his Government would welcome the representatives provided the discussions were "informal, completely without prejudice to whatever the Commission of the Security Council might decide to do," and more importantly Pakistan also agreed to send representatives at the same time.[14] Could there be a more classic evidence of Britain's overconcern and anxiety to avoid anything that might cause umbrage to Pakistan? Indignant at this response, which betrayed Britain's detestable indifference to India, the Government of India decided not to depute anyone to London for conversations. In conveying the decision to Attlee, Krishna Menon wrote candidly that his Government was still receiving a clear answer from HMG to its query to indicate Britain's views on the employment of British personnel in the Pakistani army which only helped to escalate the hostilities between India and Pakistan. The entire Pakistani army implicitly obeyed the ruling mind represented by the British army chief serving there. The high-ranking British officers were responsible for all the steps that were being taken in Kashmir by the Pakistani armies. Instances can be cited galore to prove the intimate connection of the British Commander-in-Chief of Pakistan and his Chief of Staff with the operations in Kashmir.

Condemning the blindly partisan attitude of Britain to always toe the line of Pakistan and consider her assurances sacrosanct, Krishna Menon warned that unfriendly attitude towards India was not in the interest of good Indo-British relations.[15] Voicing his concern about this, Nehru also stated that a feeling of animosity towards India on the Kashmir issue was strongly marked in some of the senior British officers – both civil and military. This unhealthy attitude contributed substantially to nullify all efforts to reach a settlement on Kashmir and thwart genuine attempts to develop cordial relations between India and Britain.

Once, in a public speech, Mushtaq Ahmed Gurmani, Pakistan's roving Ambassador and Minister of Kashmir Affairs, appealed to the people of Pakistan to close their ranks and give unqualified support for their struggle in Kashmir. He observed "If, however, you find that someone among the leaders is sabotaging the Kashmir effort, his punishment is not verbal criticism, but through Ku Klux Klan method."[16] This insinuation was intended to inflame the worst passion of the Muslims. Krishna Menon handed an extract of this speech to Attlee. As usual, Britain was disinclined to treat it seriously.

UNCIP'S Fresh Efforts

Undeterred by its successive failures to bring the feuding parties together to sign the truce agreement, the UNCIP continued its attempts. On 9 August 1949, it invited both the Governments for joint meetings at ministerial level under the auspices of the Commission in New Delhi. To this letter, a provisional agenda was attached. Both agreed to the meeting but had strong reservations about the provisional agenda. Pakistan objected to the discussion of the following two issues at the meeting: (i) the question of withdrawal of the tribesmen and all Pakistani nationals who had entered Kashmir for the purpose of fighting; and (ii) the whole question of the Northern Region which was not only beyond the scope but also contrary to the Resolution of 13 August. But India insisted on the inclusion of the two items proposed by the Commission in the agenda.[17] The 13 August resolution did contemplate the restoration of local authority in those areas, after the withdrawal of the tribesmen. Thus both the Commission and India agreed on this point. But Pakistan demanded most unreasonably that the Azad Kashmir should be regarded as the local authority mentioned in the resolution. She was an obdurate defender of her stand not to allow the Azad forces to be disbanded, disarmed or repatriated. She was insistent that the meeting should confine itself strictly to the 13 August resolution by not raising "Related Questions" by which she meant the exclusion of the question of the Azad Kashmir force. India's consistent stand on this issue was based on the ground that both the internal and external security of Kashmir and freedom of voting during the plebiscite demanded the withdrawal of such a large body of armed men from the State. If they remained in the State, the inhabitants of the evacuated territories, who did not fully subscribe to the political views of Pakistan, would not dare to re-enter their territories.

The discouraging developments caused by Pakistan's uncompromising attitude drove the UNCIP to conclude that it could play no useful role in furthering the negotiations which were foredoomed to failure at the very outset. Since Pakistan refused to allow the question of Azad forces to be discussed there, the Commission dropped the joint conference proposal. It was unfortunate that the three-cornered correspondence ultimately resulted in the cancellation of the Indo-Pakistan joint talks to implement the truce part of the Commission's original plan. The Commission abandoned the idea of bringing India and Pakistan together and having exhausted its power to mediate under limitations, thought in terms of an arbitrator in the person of Admiral Chester W. Nimitz, who had been appointed as Plebiscite Administrator in March 1949.

A memorandum on arbitration outlining the course of action to be taken was handed by the Chairman of the Commission and its Principal Secretary first to Zafrullah at Karachi on 29 August and then to Nehru at New Delhi on 30 August. The feeling of both the recipients of the memorandum was the same. The cancellation of the joint meeting by the Commission on its own responsibility was an unpleasant surprise to both.[18] It was a serious mistake as both parties consented to the joint political conference to be convened on 22 August 1949.

On 7 September, Pakistan expressed her acceptance of the Commission's arbitration proposal. Her readiness to accept an arbitrator was on condition that his task should be confined to the implementation of the UN resolutions. This gesture was meant to show that she was very anxious to reach a settlement. But the real motive behind the condition was to reserve the right to put her own interpretation on them and repudiate the clarifications of the resolutions given to India by the UNCIP from time to time. On 8 September, India expressed her inability to accept the arbitration proposal.[19] She had repeatedly insisted on the State being cleared of the tribal invaders and their uniformed supporters out of the genuine concern to end the prolonged deadlock. Strangely enough, moves were also made by President Truman and Premier Attlee simultaneously to appeal to the parties to accept the UNCIP's arbitration proposal. This intervention deepened India's suspicion that the real intention was to impose arbitration on her. The two western powers did not seem to consider that any proposal in this case should concern not only India and Pakistan but also the political future of the people of Kashmir. The Indian public was amused since the two statesmen had neither the time nor the material to fully acquaint themselves with the Kashmir developments up-to-date to favour the Commission's proposal. India was opposed to arbitration because the people of Kashmir, who had to decide their future, could do so only if the large bands of armed partisans roaming certain areas were withdrawn. Hence it was that Nehru made the disbanding and disarming of the Azad forces a *sine qua non* of any truce agreement. He said: "If what we say is in accordance with facts, the whole world ought to appreciate that our stand is justified. If we are in the wrong, we should be plainly told so. But it is not right to side-track the basic cause of the conflict. Such a situation obviously makes us restless and uneasy."[20]

The Indian Government's opposition to both the arbitration proposal of the UNCIP and the Truman-Attlee intervention foiled only the immediate tactics of the Anglo-American powers for installing Nimitz as arbitrator in Kashmir. The opposition was not therefore total. As a result, the opportunities for foreign intervention at a later stage were allowed to remain open. This enabled the big powers to pursue their attempts to achieve their end by other methods and devices.

Meanwhile the All-Jammu and Kashmir National Conference at its session held in the last week of September 1949 passed a comprehensive resolution which contained Kashmir's sharp reaction to the UNCIP proposal for arbitration. Viewing the proposal with great alarm, it rightly said that it was yet another device to deny justice to Kashmir and appease Pakistan, the aggressor. Speaking of the creation of Pakistan as an imperialist manoeuvre to weaken the liberation movement surging in the Indian sub-continent and to undermine the anti-imperialist forces in Asia by the partition of India, the resolution said: "...as custodians of the destiny of four million people of Jammu and Kashmir, the National Conference wishes to state emphatically that in no circumstances whatsoever can it surrender the right of the people to take a free decision about the future of our country."[21]

India's Displeasure with UNCIP

India blamed the UNCIP for overstepping its authority in suggesting arbitration which was beyond its terms of reference. *The Hindu* in its leader titled *ultra vires* questioned the Commission's right to delegate its functions wholly or partly to a third party. While recognising that the UNCIP was actuated by the best of intentions, the paper observed that what it suggested amounted to a "desperate attempt to find a way out of the impossible situation into which it had been placed by the inconsistent impositions and commitments" made by the past Presidents of the Council "rather than a practical road over the obstacles to the conversion of the cease-fire into a truce."[22]

Nehru had no high opinion of the UNCIP which according to him was composed of "third rate men" and whose personnel were constantly changing. He was getting disgusted with the proposals presented by the UNCIP which India had to reject. From his experience, Nehru found that acceptance of vague formulae which were capable of different interpretations might prove dangerous. Interestingly, Pakistan also held the same view about the Commission. Mohammad Ali, who later became the Prime Minister of Pakistan and who was very outspoken, told a member of the UK Delegation to the UN General Assembly in Paris that the whole Commission was "a bunch of political idiots quite unsuited for the task entrusted to them."[23] Nehru was also unhappy over the appointment of Nimitz as Plebiscite Administrator. He wrote that "the US had got themselves into a muddle by hurrying Nimitz's appointment although the function of the Plebiscite Administrator did not arise until many other matters had been settled."[24] Nehru would have mediation by some outstanding independent personality but this must be **mediation** and **not arbitration**. Unfortunately, there was confusion about the two functions of mediation and arbitration. If what the Security Council meant was mediation between the two countries, it would be impossible for a single person to succeed where a Commission of five members had failed. If the real intention of the Commission was arbitration, it could not take a major decision unilaterally without consulting the disputants. Such a measure had of course a place in the UN Charter but it had not been tried out. Nehru said that India was prepared for arbitration on other matters like water rights but maintained that the Kashmir dispute was not justiciable. Nehru conveyed these to the British Prime Minister and the Chancellor of the Exchequer during his long talk with them at London on his way to the US in October 1949.[25]

strangely enough, it became a habit with Attlee after any meeting with Nehru to advise his High Commissioner to Pakistan to pass on the contents of their conversations to Liaquat. In these messages of Attlee, Nehru would invariably be charged with hardening his attitude towards the Kashmir issue thus making it impossible to reach an understanding with Pakistan. Attlee was really worried over Pakistan's reactions to Nehru's objection to arbitration. If the arbitration proposal was abandoned by the UNCIP, the Pakistan Government and public opinion in Pakistan would attribute it to Anglo-US surrender to Indian pressure. This, according to Britain, would be an unfortunate development coinciding with Liaquat's visit to Moscow in November 1949.[26]

It was some relief to Britain when Nehru was inclined to think of mediation outside the UN. In his talks with the Canadian Prime Minister Louis St. Laurent and his Secretary of State for External Affairs Lester Pearson, Nehru frankly said that it would be wiser to appoint a mediator not connected with the Kashmir dispute than one from the UN. But Britain's worry was this would mean separating the functions of the mediator from those of the Plebiscite Administrator, the position held by Admiral Nimitz.[27] Referring to this conversation that Nehru had with the Canadian dignitaries, Philip Noel-

Baker, then in Ottawa, said: "I am rather worried that Nehru seems to have succeeded in pulling the wool over their eyes a little...Nehru is, after all, a most persuasive talker."[28]

Since its proposal for arbitration did not carry conviction, the UNCIP withdrew to Geneva to prepare its final report.

UNCIP's Final Reports

On 12 December 1949, the UNCIP presented two reports to the Security Council. The majority report signed by the US, Belgium, Colombia and Argentina highlighted the following points on which the attitudes of the two Governments had been irreconcilable:

(i) the legality of the Maharaja's accession of Kashmir to the Indian Union;
(ii) the disposal of Azad Kashmir forces;
(iii) the withdrawal of troops; and
(iv) the northern areas of the State which had acquired a significance out of proportion to their real importance.

The report signified that there was little prospect of a final settlement of the Kashmir dispute on the lines laid down by the Security Council. Since the Commission had exhausted all possibilities of mediation open to it, it frankly suggested that future negotiations had to be conducted by a single person. While the cease-fire was to its credit, the major objective of a plebiscite had receded.

Despite conducting a series of arduous negotiations and doing a good deal of paper work, the UNCIP failed to achieve a positive result.

The report which had exhaustively discussed the respective positions of the Governments of India and Pakistan in respect of the four problems; had kept mum on the contradictory promises and mutually exclusive assurances which the Commission gave the two Governments. On the question of demilitarisation, the four members had concluded that the problem should be treated *de novo* "eliminating all distinctions and comprising all questions concerning the final disposal of all armed forces in the State of Jammu and Kashmir." On the question of northern areas, their conclusion was that "the situation in the Northern Area today is such that the posting of garrisons of the Indian Army at points beyond those which are now held by it would result in an extension of military activities by the Government of India..."

The minority report was submitted by Dr. Chyle of Czechoslovakia. He exhaustively exposed the unlawful activities of the UNCIP especially the cancellation of the Joint Indo-Pakistan Political Conference, unauthorised proposal for arbitration, disclosure of the secret memorandum on arbitration to the Governments of the UK and the US before being presented to India and Pakistan and failure to mention in the 13 August Resolution of the Azad Kashmir forces which ere long grew into 32 disciplined and fully armed battalions. Chyle further revealed that the secret arbitration memorandum was in the hands of the UK High Commissioners in New Delhi and Karachi at the same time or even earlier than it was presented to the Government of India. Two days after the memorandum was placed before the two Governments, in a synchronised action, both Truman and Attlee wrote to Nehru and Liaquat urging their immediate and unreserved acceptance of it. Speaking of their motive behind this action, the *Time and Tide*, London wrote: "Four main trade routes to Central Asia pass through Kashmir. A few miles beyond the northern border lies the Soviet Union...Both Great Britain and the US are aware of this situation and that explains the Truman-Attlee demarche."[29]

The UNCIP recommended to the Security Council the abolition of the five-member body and its replacement by a "single person enjoying a broad authority." The intention was to eliminate the voice of Czechoslovakia which was relentless in its fight against imperialist schemes in the Commission. Chyle's minority report unmasked the villainous acts and conspiracies of the UNCIP which aimed at countenancing the Anglo-American schemes against Kashmir. Dissociating himself from the Commission's finding that its mission had failed because of the intransigence of both India and Pakistan, Chyle stated tersely that the real causes for its failure "must be looked for in the activities of the Commission *per se*, with a proper light thrown on the substance of the whole problem of Kashmir." He blamed the Commission for judging its task largely "only from the technical angle, without a capacity for seeing and drawing its conclusions from the whole political background of the Kashmir problem." This was responsible not only for its inability to contribute a positive solution to the whole problem but also for undermining its mediatory role, he stressed.

No one could deny that the UNCIP often found itself in an awkward predicament. Being often confronted with new and startling facts, it was extremely difficult for it to keep pace with the ever-changing scene in the sub-continent. The plebiscite issue was a classic example. It was India who first offered plebiscite in Kashmir but **under favourable conditions**. Both Governor General Jinnah and Prime Minister Liaquat of Pakistan ridiculed the idea then. Yet, when the situation was too chaotic to hold a fair plebiscite, Pakistan had the temerity to charge India with reneging on her word regarding plebiscite.

Encompassed by limits which it could not exceed, the UNCIP had to toe the line of the UN which was under the strong influence of the Western powers. Its genuine efforts to bring about a quick cease-fire were always frustrated by Pakistan who was interested not in defusing but escalating the crisis. The Commission was most unhappy that its reputation for finding a solution to the Kashmir dispute had sunk to the lowest point. But, these hardships which the Commission faced, could not absolve it of its wrong appraisal of India's role in the conflict. It discriminated unfairly against India in its final report of December 1949 by its deliberate omission of certain crucial facts and also by levelling false charges against India by twisting facts. In fact, its final report ran counter to its own earlier interim reports of November 1948 and January 1949. After taking an inordinately long time to make up its mind regarding the drafting of the final report to be presented to the Security Council, the UNCIP rushed matters in December 1949 at the fag end of the UN sitting when the delegates were leaving for their respective countries. The final report was flown to Lake Success with its copies being simultaneously sent to Karachi and New Delhi.

Suffice it to give just one blatant omission or two in the UNCIP's final report. The Commission knew the truth about Pakistan's active role in the invasion of Kashmir as it was an eye-witness to it. Her aggression was proved to its complete satisfaction on the spot. It was also recorded in the interim report that the presence of the Pakistani troops was a clear act of aggression. But in the final report, the Commission had discreetly omitted Pakistan's vigorous role in the invasion of Kashmir. Instead of reaffirming the facts recorded in the earlier reports, the final one stated that while Pakistan readily accepted an "unconditional cease-fire, India was reluctant to consider the CFL prior to the withdrawal of the Pakistani troops from Kashmir." Again it was a known fact that the tone of Zafrullah's reply to the UNCIP's letter of 9 August 1949 to which was attached a provisional agenda, was totally devoid of cordiality. It revealed Pakistan's obstinate refusal to allow the question of the Azad forces even to be raised under the head "related questions." India on the other hand, emphasised the importance of the provisional agenda. Yet, in its last report, the UNCIP had no compunction about stating that both the Governments were equally intransigent causing the cancellation of the Joint Conference. The report was premised notably on faulting India to placate Britain and omitting Pakistan's aggression so as not to give umbrage to the western bloc. It was therefore little wonder that the Commission chose to downplay all the demoralising activities of Pakistan.

The UNCIP committed another mistake in not conveying to Nimitz the verbatim text of the notification of the Government of India of 18 March 1949 acquainting the Commission with its consent to Nimitz's designation as Plebiscite Administrator. Alluding to this lapse of the Commission, the delegate of Czechoslovakia recorded in his minority report that the Commission "therefore bears itself the responsibility for lack of moderation on the part of the designated Plebiscite Administrator."[30]

Obviously, when it came to enforcing its own views, the UNCIP developed cold feet. It could not muster courage to do so because it did not want to antagonise Pakistan. It was rightly said that the UNCIP's final report was "an essay in glossing over its own weaknesses in handling situations created by Pakistan."[31]

The only redeeming feature of the Commission's final report was its admission that Pakistan had no *locus standi* at all in the northern area from the beginning.

There is need to point out that the Security Council was also to blame for the happenings over the Kashmir dispute. Pakistan and her supporters glibly attributed the Kashmir impasse to India's "obstructive tactics" while the real causes were the Council's indecision and vacillation. Even after India's original complaint about Pakistan's complicity in the tribal invasion was proved, the Council did nothing about it. Pakistan was allowed to violate the understanding that she would not consolidate her occupied territory in Kashmir to the disadvantage of the State or increase her military potential and build up the Azad forces in the northern area. Even if by November 1948, the Security Council had effected the withdrawal of the Pakistani forces, a lot of mischief would have been averted. But the Council merely asked the UNCIP to pursue its efforts at finding a solution. The Chairman of the Commission superbly summed up the position in one line: "Resolutions of the Security Council are static, but solutions must be dynamic."[32] The Commission felt that it had outlived its usefulness and requested dissolution.

McNaughton's Proposals: India's Rejection

On 17 December 1949, the Security Council entrusted the functions of the UNCIP to General McNaughton, President of the Council for that month. He was made an informal mediator to plan a solution for the Kashmir deadlock. He held discussions with both the Governments but held private talks only with the Pakistani delegation. He met Zafrullah quite a few times privately including the one on 21 December at the Canadian Delegation Office in New York. This was said to be the fourth or fifth meeting with him since the UNCIP's report reached Lake Success. But McNaughton held no meeting on that date or before with any member of the Indian delegation.

On 22 December, McNaughton put forward his proposals which ran thus: Both the parties should (a) confirm the continued and unconditional inviolability of the CFL; (b) reach an agreement in New York on the basic principles of a programme of demilitarisation, which would include the withdrawal from Kashmir of Pakistani regular forces, and the reduction of Indian and State Forces and militia on the one side and of Azad Kashmir forces on the other to the minimum compatible with the maintenance of local law and order; and (c) agree to the appointment of a UN representative by the Secretary General in consultation with the two Governments to supervise the demilitarisation and prepare generally the way for a plebiscite.

India rejected the McNaughton plan as it did not seek to improve the situation. It proposed an equal withdrawal of both forces according to a synchronised plan. Not merely this. It provided for the bulk of the Azad forces to remain in the State to maintain law and order in the "evacuated territory" and also related the disbandment of the balance of those forces to the withdrawal of the Indian army. In fine, it was nothing more than what the UNCIP proposed in April 1949 deleting certain portions favourable to India and adding certain provisions favourable to Pakistan. Speaking in favour of McNaughton's proposal for demilitarisation on a synchronised plan, the *New York Times* wrote that India rejected it because it ran counter to her "adamantly held position that all Pakistani and Azad forces must be out of the State before the Indian army there is reduced."[33] Votaries of Pakistan failed to see that in rejecting the McNaughton plan, India was not legalistic and that if she claimed a superior right as against Pakistan, it was for two reasons: (i) the State's accession to her; and (ii) Pakistan's aggression which was first vehemently denied by her at the Security Council but later impassively admitted before the UNCIP.

Pakistan substantially accepted the McNaughton proposals because they had virtually conceded all her demands. India on the other hand proposed amendments which brought the negotiations back to the point at which it was broken in August 1949. Underlying the proposed amendments of India were the following: Pakistan who was the aggressor could not be treated as an equal to India in the dispute; and the responsibility for the administration of the Northern area then under the control of the local authorities who were the creation of Pakistan must vest in India. This area was captured by Pakistan during the interval that elapsed between the acceptance of the 13 August resolution by India in September and by Pakistan in December 1948. In India's view, the mediator had to be sent out with broad and undefined terms of reference on the aforesaid two points of McNaughton. In other words, the mediator should start with a clean slate.

Criticising the undue haste with which the British delegation pre-judged the outcome of McNaughton's plan, a renowned Indian journalist wrote from New York that the new plan "may for all practical purposes be deemed as dead as the dodo and to Alexander Cadogan, Chief of the UK Delegation, who rushed to pronounce prior judgment over it and give to it his Government's blessings in the Security Council yesterday may well go the credit for sounding its last post..." The journalist added that it was the Soviet delegate's timely warning that the final judges of the formula were the concerned parties and not the Council Members and also the American representative's hint that there might be alternative proposals which might provide a fairer solution that "ultimately broke the chain of patting McNaughton unreservedly on the back..."[34]

In his extremely friendly talk with Pearson at Colombo on 13 January 1950 for more than an hour and a half, Nehru reiterated his argument about the disbandment of the Azad Kashmir forces. Pearson felt there was force in India's criticisms of McNaughton's proposals. He was inclined to agree that the Azad Kashmir forces should not be treated on the same basis as the regulars and that the former should be demilitarised first. This gave the jitters to Britain who described the talk as most unfortunate "since Pearson has played right into Indian hands...it looks as though we may be stymied until the Security Council meets again in a regular away." It was reported that Pearson had "adopted the defeatist attitude." When Pearson told Nehru that McNaughton would abandon his efforts and withdraw as soon as he could from his position in the negotiations, the latter did not demure to this. This was interpreted that Nehru regarded it as "reasonable and inevitable."[35] Pearson later dismissed McNaughton from his role as mediator.

In Britain's view, India's delay to accept a public debate on McNaughton's formula was unreasonable given that a majority of the members of the Security Council supported it. Nehru was squarely blamed for his "delaying tactics." Nehru was always against military persons dealing with the Kashmir issue. In fact after its rejection of the McNaughton formula, the position of the Government of India in the Security Council toughened because of the Western countries' impatience to have it accepted by India. The proposal that both parties should come to a settlement before 31 January 1950, was intended to hustle India into an agreement. It was clear that this deadline was set at the suggestion of Pakistan who was anxious to fulfil her pledges to her public that the dispute would be settled and plebiscite held soon. Already the public morale in Pakistan and in that part of Kashmir occupied by her was running low. American papers wrote that "if India is in good faith she will accept UN mediation." From Kashmir, Bakshi Ghulam Mohammad and Mirza Mohammad Afzal warned India against bowing down to Anglo-American pressure and accepting McNaughton's proposals which equated the aggressor and the aggressed.

As for public debate on his formula, McNaughton was doubtful about India modifying her attitude if the matter went public. So, he wanted to avoid a public debate when there was a ray of hope that India might be moved by pressure exerted privately. He wanted that the future strategy should be formulated in the light of the outcome of discussions on Kashmir at the Colombo Conference to be held. It was expected that the American Government might adopt direct Anglo-American mediation in the Kashmir dispute. Decision on this would await the results of the Colombo meeting at which Canada was expected to propose such a procedure. But this did not materialise as the UK Delegation warned from Colombo against committing the grave mistake of letting either India or Pakistan think that the Kashmir question could be transferred from the Security Council to Colombo.

Though the McNaughton plan as such was dead, its ghost was still walking. The British High Commissioner in India suggested to HMG that Pearson could be persuaded to meet Nehru and tell him in a friendly way that the world opinion was turning against India over the Kashmir dispute and that "if the case came out into the open, India, the apostle of non-violence, would come out very badly in the eyes of the world."[36] But this cut no ice. Pearson frankly told that he himself would not broach the subject with Nehru. While in India, he could not meet Nehru who was very busy with the celebrations of the First Republic Day of India on 26 January 1950. On this date, India became a Federal Republic in the Commonwealth. Pearson discussed Kashmir only with Patel and Bajpai and both strongly justified India's case. There was no prospect of India accepting the McNaughton proposals and the idea of a plebiscite seemed totally out of question. The talks proved desultory. Since Pearson could not detect any weakening in the stand which India had already taken up, he made no effort to dissuade them from their attitude.

Nehru had stated clearly and unambiguously that there should be a "New Start," of the Kashmir question. B.N. Rau also favoured the recommendation that the whole issue had to be considered *de novo.* He suggested the appointment of a three-member mediatory body and also outlined informally India's idea on the partition of the State. But Pakistan was not prepared either for a partition or for the restriction of the plebiscite to the valley.[37]

A brief mention of the clarification made by V.P. Menon to arrest the subtle attempts of Pakistan to link up the canal water dispute with the Kashmir issue is a desideratum. Pakistan's argument that the Jammu and Kashmir State should go to her was based on the wrong premise that three important rivers providing vital water supply to her were flowing from Kashmir into Pakistan. If the State went to India, the latter would divert these waters for her own benefit causing thereby an irreparable loss to Pakistan economically. Having made a deep study of the hydrology of the Indus River and her tributaries, Menon revealed that Pakistan was deliberately misrepresenting facts in order to prejudice world opinion in her favour. Only the River Indus and her tributary Jhelum flowed through Kashmir. These two waters together carried two-thirds of the entire supplies in the Indus basin both in summer and winter. With the remaining four tributaries of the Indus – Beas, Chenab, Ravi and Sutlej – which rose in the Punjab and the Himachal Pradesh and carried the remaining one-third of the Indus water, Kashmir had no connection. Only the Indus and Jhelum rose in and had their upper reaches in the province of Jammu and Kashmir. Kashmir used only a negligible fraction of these waters before they left the State. Besides, the physiography of the region was such that diversion of any supplies from these two rivers for utilisation in India was not at all possible. Since the rivers passed through mountainous tracts and flowed into Pakistan at a level of about 5,000 feet, it was physically impossible to stop their flow into Pakistan. Menon emphasised that unless Pakistan intended to deny Kashmir her inherent right to use the insignificant quantity of water passing through the State, it was beyond anyone's comprehension as to "how the upper reaches of these two rivers lying in Kashmir can adversely affect the interests of Pakistan and be linked with the Kashmir issue."[38]

Maelstrom over Trivial Remarks

Around this time Britain ever on the alert for statements by India that did not suit her, had an opportunity to revile her. She made much ado about some statements made by Vallabhbhai Patel in a speech in Bombay on

4 January 1950. The statements, which were couched in the mildest language and were not untrue, were coloured and circulated. The essence of the talk was that when India was eager to cultivate the friendship of Pakistan through love, the latter spurned it and talked of war. If Pakistan wanted war, he said, "We are prepared for it...We will not allow India's integrity to be placed in jeopardy." Stating that contrary to India's hope that they were parting as sisters and brothers and hence would live in amity and peace, the events that followed partition took a different course. "Until the position which we envisaged is attained, we must be on our guard. We would be guilty of criminal neglect if we are not vigilant and alert. After all, we have to remember that Pakistan has to bear a proportionately higher burden for her defence. Even then, some of them indulge in loose talks of planting their flag on the Red Fort," he said.

Referring to the trade deadlock in consequence of the devaluation of her rupee by India, he said:

> "We felt that if we could not pay the price which they (Pakistan) asked of us, we would rather stop our mills than suffer economic ruins. At the same time, we have planned to avoid that catastrophe. We shall not be a victim of coercion... Our Prime Minister has been inviting them to settle our disputes by peaceful means, but they resort to other methods. They are turning out Sindhi Hindus by robbing them of their property. This is not the way of peace."

This speech was relayed to the nation through the All India Radio.

Britain regarded these statements as deplorable. Deliberately ignoring Patel's criticism of the Hindu Mahasabha for its inclusion of Pakistan in India in its party programme, Britain described his talk as "sabre-rattling." Rebutting this accusation, Patel clarified that his object was merely to make clear to Pakistan that the Government of India was not impressed by the "sabre-rattling" on the other side of the frontier.[39]

Britain's sympathies with Pakistan for the difficulties she had to face in the wake of partition and blowing out of proportions the refugee problem irritated India whose problems were much greater than those of Pakistan. The insinuation was that India's delay to solve the Kashmir issue was responsible for Pakistan's position which was "one of life and death." Patel said emphatically that there would be no plebiscite in Kashmir as long as the Azad Kashmir authorities were in effective control of that area and the northern territories. Bajpai also said that plebiscite was out of question at that time as it was outdated by developments in the military and political situation in Kashmir.

Smarting from India's rejection of the proposals of McNaughton, Britain said that if a deadlock ensued on account of India's "intransigence," the US would feel bound to support any action of the Security Council intended to overcome the deadlock. But this hope of Britain was shattered by the message of Dean Acheson to the British Foreign Secretary Bevin sent through Warren Austin, US Ambassador to the UN. This message was described as "unfriendly in tone and substance" by Britain as it put her in the wrong. Supporting the genuine desire of the Government of India to find a settlement to the Kashmir dispute, Acheson's message blamed Britain whose approach to the problem had led to a further deterioration of the Indo-Pakistan relations and to the eventual prolongation of the conflict in Kashmir. His message openly said that the McNaughton proposals and similar ones "showed disregard for the security and safety of the homes and persons of the people of Kashmir who had suffered so much already at the hands of the invaders." The message contained the categorical statement that the Government of India would be false to its moral and legal obligations resting on it if it left these people exposed to a repetition of the violence and danger from which they had just been recovered. Stating that India always shunned war as an instrument of settlement of any dispute with Pakistan, Acheson made it known that India would readily accept mediation but could never "submit to such mediation being on the basis of a determination beforehand of vital issues." The message appreciated India's genuine feeling that further negotiations at Lake Success would not bear fruit. The leader of the UK delegation at the UN, who was much upset, considered Acheson's message a matter of great personal regret to him. He was very unhappy that "Acheson should have sent us a message of this kind."[40] Very funnily, Britain chose to blame only India for this message!

But one ought to remember that America's relations with India had never been firm and steadfast. The attitude of Dean Acheson especially to the Kashmir issue was mercurial. Only a few days earlier on 9 January during his interview with Bajpai and Vijayalakshmi Pandit at New York, Acheson expressed the growing concern in the States Department at the deteriorating situation in Kashmir and the grievous failure to reach a settlement. The motive behind these statements was to make India reconsider her decision on McNaughton's proposals. Half way through the interview, Acheson brought the interview to an abrupt end. Anyway, in what he did a week later through the message to the British Foreign Secretary discussed above, Acheson had more than atoned for his earlier conduct.

Britain felt India's object in rejecting McNaughton's proposals was to gain time and work for a solution other than a plebiscite. The Security Council met many times to consider the Kashmir issue in the light of the infructuous McNaughton plan but brought forth nothing. Before its meeting on 7 February 1950, Cadogan was telegraphically instructed to stand firm on McNaughton's proposals as India could be influenced only by the force of opinion in the Security Council.

Zafrullah's Damaging Disclosures

During his speech at the Security Council in February 1950, Zafrullah said that the "possession" of Kashmir was vital for Pakistan. When Rau pointed out that Pakistan was no longer content with the "accession" of Kashmir but desired "possession," Zafrullah hastened to explain that he used the word "possession" inadvertently. That it was not unintentional but showed the workings of his Government's mind was transparent. During this period of discussions on the McNaughton plan at the Security Council, Zafrullah made lengthy speeches. On 8 February, continuing his four-hour speech in the two previous sittings, he raked up one controversy or other, reviled India on many counts and attributed certain statements to Rau and Setalwad which they had never made.

The most devastating speech of Zafrullah was the one delivered on 12 February when he committed a grave act of betrayal which stunned many and certainly gave the severest blow to the British. Perhaps not realising the enormity of his *faux pas*, he admitted that it was upon the recommendation of Commander-in-Chief Douglas Gracey of the Pakistani army that regular units of the Pakistani forces were sent into Kashmir in 1948. As a matter of fact, this treacherous act of Gracey was known in certain quarters in 1948 itself. Mohammad Ali divulged to Curzon, Member of the British Delegation to the UN, that Gracey warned the Pakistan Government in April 1948 that if it wished Pakistan to survive, it had no option but to send its troops into Kashmir and that Pakistan followed his (Gracey's) advice to safeguard its vital interests.[41] Therefore, what happened on 12 February 1950 was a damaging disclosure publicly in the Security Council by which Zafrullah put Gracey on the spot. It did not escape the notice of the illustrious jurist B.N. Rau. He explained the dire implications of Zafrullah's disclosure, which, if true, would make Gracey liable to trial for treason. Gracey had violated the British Foreign Enlistment Act which barred any Briton from engaging in any act of war against a country which was on friendly terms with Britain. A much graver charge than this was his sending troops into Kashmir, a part of India after accession, which amounted to waging a war against the King who headed the Indian Dominion. Rau pointed that India had a strong case for pressing for Gracey's trial and demanding reparations from Britain. He further said that India would be fully justified in asking reparations from the US also for the irresponsible activities of Haight, the American General, who, as the "Brigadier General" of the Azad forces, helped to organise the forces. This was also an offence under the Foreign Enlistment Act, he said. Rau made it public that Haight who also belonged to a country at peace with India, once took immense pride in recounting his exploits in Kashmir where he killed many Hindus with his own hands!

This Haight later denounced the Azad Kashmir forces. During his clandestine interview at Lahore with Robert Turnbull, Correspondent of the *New York Times* in India, on 17 January 1948, he confessed that three attempts were made on his life in Pakistan which was none too safe for him to stay, that the Pakistani army was running the Azad Kashmir Radio Station and that the Provisional Government of Azad Kashmir headed by Sardar Mohammad Ibrahim Khan was a "Pakistani Puppet."[42]

Strongly condemning Gracey's advice to send units of the Pakistani army into Kashmir, the *Hindustan Times* in a leading article headed "Aggression in Kashmir" wrote that "the least that HMG can do in the face of this astonishing revelation is to recall not merely General Gracey but all British Officers serving in the Pakistani army."[43]

Constant charges, most of them untrue, levelled against Nehru and India on the Kashmir issue irritated Rau so much as to impel him to put forward a very inconvenient question to Britain regarding her policy on Cyprus.[44] At the meeting of 3 March, Rau embarrassed Britain by citing a rough parallel between Cyprus and Kashmir. He wanted to know what would be the situation, if Greece moved an army into Cyprus, occupied half the island for several years and then said that the future of the colony must be decided by holding a plebiscite with half of it under local Greek authorities with the British security forces removed and its administration supplanted. Would the UK Government, he asked, allow the Greek authorities to control the civilian administration of the Greek occupied area of the Crown Colony? The dumbfounded members of the British Delegation could make no reply to this most timely and relevant question.

Discussions in the Security Council had no impact on the tension between India and Pakistan. The latter's hostility towards India and her greed to get Kashmir had been growing in virulence. In India, Nehru was under pressure to take a strong line with Pakistan. There were serious talks in some quarters on waging a war against Pakistan. If only the UN could publicly brand Pakistan as the aggressor, which she really was, it would go a long way towards solving the problem. But Britain would never allow the UN to do so. Nehru and others including the President of India and Patel, had shown much irritation over Cadogan's speech at the Security Council dismissing India's demand for a judgement on the issue of aggression by tribesmen from Pakistan as "irrelevant to the present issue."[45]

Krishna Menon was particularly critical of the speeches and activities of Cadogan. During a conversation with Gordon Walker on 28 February 1950, Menon said relations between India and Britain had never been worse since independence.

Time Limit for Demilitarisation

At its meeting on 14 March 1950, the Security Council passed a resolution sponsored by the US, Britain, Norway and Cuba which called both the Governments to prepare and execute within five months a programme for demilitarisation of Kashmir. It also provided for the appointment of a UN representative to assist the parties over demilitarization, to offer any suggestion that would contribute to "the expeditious and enduring" solution of the dispute and to arrange at the appropriate stage of demilitarization for the Plebiscite Administrator to take over the functions already allotted to him. The resolution was adopted by 8 votes in favour, none against with two abstentions, namely India and Yugoslavia. The Security Council had apparently secured the acceptance of India albeit with reservations. If India who refused to compromise on the objectionable implications of the demilitarisation plan of McNaughton at three consecutive meetings finally accepted the Council's resolution, it was because the clarifications given by Terence Shone, Deputy to Permanent Representative of United Kingdom at the United Nations, on the specific points raised by her were found to be encouraging.

Two comments were made in this context by the British officialdom. One was that Nehru, though born in Allahabad in the then United Provinces (now Uttar Pradesh), descended from a minority "highest caste" of the Hindus which long dominated the Valley of Kashmir. The other was the fact that his "idealist emotions" were profoundly stirred by the tribesmen's outrages in the peaceful Valley. It was concluded that both the factors caused him virtually to dictate India's policy towards Kashmir throughout the dispute. In Prof.

George Catlin's assessment of Nehru's role *vis-à-vis* the State of Kashmir, matters like his family's Kashmiri connections, sharing of river waters etc., etc., were only of secondary importance for him. Nehru's real fear according to him was that if India lost in the plebiscite, a flood of refugees would descend on Delhi and start an agitation which would "overthrow the Nehru-Patel administration with unknown consequences." Hence Nehru's strategy for dealing with the situation was to "delay," he said. The solution to this according to Catlin was to put the disputed area under an international commission of control comparable to that of Saar[46] for a strictly limited period of ten years prior to the holding of a plebiscite.[47] But nothing could deflect Nehru from his conviction that since Jammu and Kashmir had acceded to India, only the Government of Sheikh Abdullah, the State forces and militia and the Indian army had the right to exercise control over the whole State of Jammu and Kashmir. He would never recognise the *locus standi* of not only Pakistan but also of the Azad Kashmir authorities and forces.

There were discussions and discussions some very lengthy on Kashmir but none satisfying both the parties. At one stage it was suggested that Ralph Blunche, a Black-American, should go to Kashmir as the UN representative to assist Admiral Nimitz who had already been appointed as the Plebiscite Administrator to oversee the preparatory work. Blunche was considered capable for the job and he could not be accused of "White imperialism." More importantly, he was believed to enjoy the goodwill of Nehru who "displayed exceptional attraction towards him during his American tour." It was said he would be acceptable to Pakistan also. But India was unwilling to accept the combination of Nimitz and Blunche. India had already said she was prepared to accept a single mediator who should not however be Nimitz. Pakistan suggested General Marshall but that too was dropped. There was another suggestion to the effect that Nehru and Liaquat should meet and Addison, Member of the House of Lords, should be sent to assist them. Nehru rejected the proposal considering Addison's age and state of health. L.A.C. Fry said that if a first class man was chosen as the UN representative, whatever the Indian reservations might be, he would at least "advance a solution if not produce one."[48]

Pakistan said that the UN was always brow-beaten by Nehru. Zafrullah complained that throughout the history of the dispute, the UN had tended to make one concession after another to India. The leadership of Pakistan was highly suspicious and critical not only of India but also of Britain. It was firm in its conviction that Britain was influenced by Mountbatten who had left India precipitately, abandoning the Muslims to their fate.[49] As V.P. Menon rightly put it, "clearly the UK was suspect on both sides."

The situation in Kashmir remained fluid until April 1950. The Security Council under the influence of Britain was determined not to raise the point of Pakistan's aggression. It did not even choose to warn Pakistan against abetting the tribal aggression in Kashmir. Nehru's repeated insistence that the Council should pronounce judgment on what he regarded as a moral issue went unheeded. The Council's argument that it had done nothing of the kind before and that such action would not promote settlement, annoyed him. At one stage, in a ruminative mood, Nehru doubted if he was at all right in having taken the dispute to the Security Council, disregarding the advice of many well-wishers including higher echelons of the Military and Civil Service around him. It was a belated realisation. As he himself said in a different context, illuminating wisdom always came after the event.

Nehru's unbending attitude over Kashmir provoked the British so much as to irresponsibly carp at him. Anything he said about Kashmir in Press Conferences was interpreted as creating a "lamentable impression" of India on foreign correspondents. There were gossips that even the officials in India were feeling very uneasy about his views on Kashmir. Britain's undue emphasis on the solid opposition of the major powers to the Indian attitude to the Kashmir dispute was intended to spread the distorted story that Nehru's popularity was dipping precipitously.

References

1. Nehru to Attlee, 4 Jan. 1949, DO/35/3168.
2. *Documents on Kashmir Problem*, Editors: M.S. Deora and R. Grover, Vol.10, pp. 257, 58 & 62.
3. *Ibid*, p. 259.
4. *Ibid*, p. 262.
5. CRO to UK HCs (I and P), 14 April 1949, DO/142/529.
6. J.J.S. Garner to Grafftey-Smith, 13 July 1949, DO/142/530.
7. UK HC (P) to CRO, 7 March 1949, 5546/10112/85.
8. *Documents on Kashmir Problem*, *op. cit.*, pp 263 & 64.
9. *Ibid*, p. 265.
10. B.N. Rau on India's Conditions for Kashmir Truce, DO/142/530.
11. *Documents on Kashmir, op .cit.* p. 261.

12. *The Hindu*, 15 Dec. 1949.
13. UK HC (I) to CRO, 3 July 1949, DO/142/530.
14. Attlee to Krishna Menon, 4 July 1949, DO/142/535.
15. *Ibid*, Krishna Menon to Attlee, 11 July 1949.
16. There were two American secret terrorist organisations of Whites of this name which committed heinous crimes. The original Ku Klux Klan (KKK) was started at Tennessee in 1865 by a number of young men under the leadership of a Tennessee cavalry man by name N.B. Forest. It held secret meetings and its members wore white cloaks with hooded caps which hid all but their eyes. The KKK rode by night, striking terror into the ex-slaves and the "Carpet bagger politicians" from the North. The Congress legislated against it and by 1871, it became practically non-existent.

    The Second KKK was founded in Atlanta in Georgia in 1915 by W.J. Simmons. It soon became a power in politics. Like the first KKK, it also opposed the Negroes. It stood for White Protestant domination in politics and business. But its lawless acts and internecine quarrels led to the deposition of Simmons in 1922 and to the official dissolution of the organisation in 1944.

    The nomenclature KKK appeared to have been derived from the Greek Word KYKLOS from which comes the English "circle." Klan was added for the sake of alliteration.
17. *Documents on Kashmir Problem, op. cit.*, Vol.10, pp. 266 & 67.
18. *Ibid*, p. 320.
19. UNCIP's Statement, 20 Sep. 1949, DO/142/537; *Documents on Kashmir, op. cit*, p. 268.
20. *The Hindu*, 6 Sep. 1949.
21. *Ibid*, 29 Sep. 1949.
22. *Ibid.*
23. Curzon to Rumbold, 30 Oct. 1948, DO/142/521.
24. Nehru's letters to Vijayalakshmi Pandit, 17 May & 11 July 1949, *Vijayalakshmi Pandit Papers.*
25. PM's Personal Minute, 10 Oct. 1949, DO/142/537.
26. *Ibid*, FO to Washington, 18 Oct. 1949.
27. UK HC (Canada) to CRO, 27 Oct. 1949, DO/142/538.
28. *Ibid*, Noel-Baker to Percevale, 31 Oct. 1949.
29. *Time and Tide*, London, 17 Sep. 1949.
30. *Documents on Kashmir, op. cit.*, p. 321.
31. *The Hindu*, 15 Dec. 1949.
32. *Ibid*, 18 Feb. 1957.

33. *New York Times*, 28 Dec. 1949.
34. K. Balaraman, "The Kashmir Dispute," *The Hindu*, 1 Jan. 1950.
35. R.H. Scott's Note, 17 Jan. 1950, FL/1015/23.
36. UK HC (I) to FO, 23 Jan. 1950, FL/1015/43.
37. Robert's talk with V.P. Menon, 18 Jan.1950, FL/1015/27.
38. UK HC (I) to FO, 16 Jan. 1950, FL/1015/27.
39. Patel to American Ambassador, 12 Jan. 1950, FL/1015/26.
40. UKD to UN to FO, 16 Jan. 1950, FL/1015/24.
41. Curzon to Rumbold, 30 Oct. 1948, DO/142/521.
42. *New York Times*, 29 Jan. 1948.
43. *The Hindustan Times*, 13 Feb. 1950.
44. The third largest island in the Mediterranean. An independent republic belonging to the British Commonwealth. More than three millennia ago, was colonised by the Greeks who brought with them the Greek language and culture. Suffered political vicissitudes for several centuries. In 1571, Turks conquered the island. In 1878, the Turkish Sultan ceded to Britain the island's administration but not its sovereignty. In 1914, Britain annexed it which the Turks recognised by the Treaty of Lausanne in 1923. In 1925, it was made a crown colony. In 1960, it became an independent republic. But the agitation for the island's union with Greece (ENOSIS) continued.
45. UK HC (I) to CRO, FL/1015/145.
46. Saarland in West Germany was administered by the League of Nations from 1919 to 1935 when she was returned to Germany after a plebiscite.
47. Catlin to Stafford Cripps, 16 Feb. 1950, FL/1015/158.
48. L.A.C. Fry's Note, 20 March 1950, FL/1015/167.
49. *Review of events in Pakistan from 31 Oct. to 6 Nov. 1947*, F.NO.63571.

8

The Dixon Mission

The period from 1950 to 1957 proved a most disturbing septennium in the sub-continent witnessing the unsuccessful mediatory efforts undertaken by as many as three men – Owen Dixon in 1950, Frank Porter Graham from 1951 to 1953 and again in 1957 and Gunnar Jarring in 1957 – to resolve the Kashmir crisis. This septennium was marked by a welter of political disturbances robbing India of peace and tranquillity. Even with the painstaking endeavours of the three stalwarts, there was not the remotest sign of the conflict weakening.

The Security Council's resolution of 14 March 1950 called upon India and Pakistan to effect within a period of five months the demilitarisation of Kashmir on the lines proposed by McNaughton. The resolution also authorised the appointment of a UN representative to India and Pakistan to take over the powers of the UNCIP. Many names for appointment to this position were proposed and rejected until finally the name of Owen Dixon, an Australian jurist of eminence, was approved.

Before Dixon commenced his work in May 1950, there were two meetings between Nehru and Liaquat in New Delhi and Karachi. While the proceedings of the first meeting gave the hope of the beginning of a new era in the Indo-Pakistan understanding, those of the second completely falsified it. Agreements on certain disputes, particularly the refugee influx from East Pakistan, reached at the end of the New Delhi meeting really appeared to augur well for the future relations of India and Pakistan. Liaquat's categorical repudiation of the theory of the religious State raised the hope that Pakistan would whole-heartedly work for a free and fair plebiscite and that if she came for some working arrangement with the Government of India, even the appointment of a mediator would become superfluous. It must be remembered that the Kashmir question was not discussed at this New Delhi meeting. The happenings at the Karachi meeting between the two dignitaries clearly went against the earlier Nehru-Liaquat Agreement. It did not eschew fanatical propaganda. Zafrullah, as was his wont, launched a tirade of charges against India on the Kashmir issue knowing well that what he said did not represent the whole truth about India's stand in the matter. Liaquat's subsequent address delivered on 9 May at the American Council of Commerce in New York and his utterances at Press meets also showed no sign of any improved relations between the two neighbours.[1]

Dixon's Visit to Sub-Continent

Though at the time of the adoption of the 14 March 1950 resolution, B.N. Rau said that India would not favour any attempt of the Security Council to thrust a representative "down India's throat," India welcomed Dixon as UN representative. According to Nehru, Dixon was a man of "high reputation for independence, integrity and ability."[2] Bajpai knew Dixon as they were both envoys in Washington from 1942 to 1944. Dixon's primary task was to bring about a speedy demilitarisation of the State so as to ensure a free and fair plebiscite. The Council's resolution also invested him with the power to suggest alternatives to the agreed objective if a situation arose calling for it.

Dixon first met Nehru on 27 May 1950. Nehru straightaway emphasised that the confirmation of the accession of Kashmir to India was to be done through the Constituent Assembly of Kashmir which would be elected in 1951. Dixon then went to Kashmir where he met Maulana Abul Kalam Azad who also endorsed Nehru's view about the confirmation of the accession of the State. He recommended partition of the State with a vote only in the disputed areas as this would minimise any migration of the refugees besides avoiding the need for demilitarisation. Maulana Azad was also equally emphatic that the Azad Kashmir forces must be withdrawn. Dixon, who stayed in Kashmir from 7 June to 11 July 1950, was unimpressed with the Vale which he felt had lost all its old charm and beauty. He described Sheikh Abdullah's Government as "Police *Raj*." Getting back to New Delhi, he proposed to Nehru a summit with Liaquat to which both agreed. It was held in Delhi from 20 to 24 July without aids under the aegis of Dixon. Nehru took 10 of the 18 hour discussion. Liaquat's speech was marked by "intermittent protests against Nehru's statements." Dixon remained a silent listener.

Dixon's visit did not brighten the situation in the sub-continent. The proposal he designed for the settlement of the dispute was "starkly unrealistic." It put the Kashmir Government "in commission" by which the regular constitutional administrators would be replaced with the UN appointed persons. The Ministers who would continue to hold office would be relieved of their responsibilities. A renowned constitutional lawyer and columnist wrote: "No Indian Prime Minister could possibly have accepted that. It went beyond the terms for plebiscite in the UNCIP's Resolution of 5 January 1949. This was to prove fatal, eventually, on the limited plebiscite...'The Government in Commission' was a concept for which the great jurist would have found hardly any precedent."[3]

Dixon's attempts to obtain an agreement on demilitarisation proved a fiasco. He attributed this failure solely to Nehru's insistence on the recognition of Sheikh Abdullah's Government as the legitimate Government of the whole State. This implied that the Pakistani or Azad Kashmir authorities had no right to participate in the arrangements necessary for the security of the State. Nehru also objected to the degree of international supervision over the functioning of the Government of Kashmir which in Dixon's view was necessary. All these were so twisted by the Pakistani Press as to assert that India was responsible for hindering any progress of the Kashmir question. It wanted Dixon to declare this publicly in unambiguous language. Dixon felt that Nehru was evasive and that Patel who was more eager for an agreement should have been present at the talk. He also wanted Ghulam Mohammad to the Conference table and keep Zafrullah away although he knew well this would be very difficult.[4]

In view of the bottlenecks he faced, Dixon put forward a proposal by which the feuding parties should be allotted certain areas of the State and plebiscite held in the remaining area which was very likely to be the Vale. His objection to an over-all plebiscite stemmed from his conviction that the State of Jammu and Kashmir was "not a unit geographically, demographically or economically. It is an agglomeration of territories brought under the political power of one Maharaja. That is the unity it possesses." In substantiating his theory, he said that if an over-all plebiscite went in favour of India, there would be a large scale migration of Muslims resulting in another refugee problem for Pakistan. If the plebiscite favoured merger with Pakistan, there would be a refugee problem for India also, though of a lesser dimension, because of the movement of Hindus and Sikhs. The only course open to avoid a recurrence of the huge refugee problem was to partition Kashmir.

Great areas in the State were unequivocally Muslim, other areas were predominantly Hindu and a further area was Buddhist. If another refugee problem were to be averted, wisdom lay in adopting partition and abandoning over-all plebiscite. Region-wise plebiscite would narrow the problem down to the Kashmir valley – the real bone of contention. He warned that sound judgment was very necessary to draw the line of partition.

Both parties agreed that if there was to be a limited plebiscite it was to be held in the area roughly described as the Vale of Kashmir. Initially Pakistan rejected it on the ground that both the Governments were committed to an over-all plebiscite but Dixon managed to get her approval to a plan involving partition and a partial plebiscite which he would himself prepare. Pakistan accepted this proposal on the condition that India should first accept practical measures to ensure the freedom and fairness of the plebiscite. This meant the virtual supersession of the existing Kashmir Government. India was not prepared to agree to it leading to the failure of Dixon's mission. It was clear by experience that the Security Council could not decide a course of action that would satisfy both India and Pakistan. Almost all its efforts since January 1948 having failed, there remained to the Council's credit just two agreed documents – the resolutions of 13 August 1948 and 5 January 1949 of the UNCIP – which formed the basis for further steps. The only one hopeful element was the cease-fire which had held for 17 months. But that was an uneasy truce which was "precariously perched between two armies facing each other in a state of preparedness."

Dixon was impressed by the Indian argument about the Chenab waters. He felt there was considerable force in its statement that any diversion of the Chenab waters away from Pakistan would be a major and most expensive engineering undertaking on which India would not embark. Apart from this, Nehru also gave Dixon the most formal and effective guarantee against the use of the Chenab waters in any way prejudicial to Pakistani interests.[5]

Failure of the Mission

Dixon continued to stay in the sub-continent even after 14 August – the time limit fixed by the Security Council for him to reach an agreement on demilitarisation in Kashmir as a prelude to a plebiscite. The mediator could not persuade the parties to agree to a common plan. To a question if he would go back by 14 August after failing in his mission, his answer was that the obligation placed on both India and Pakistan by the Security Council did not end on that date. He further said, "They still have to settle and I still have to assist them."

He continued to stay in Karachi having meetings with Liaquat and communicating with Nehru from there.[6] But there was no understanding in sight. Sheikh Abdullah said that if Pakistan had any new idea and put it through the mediator, India would certainly consider it on condition that Pakistan first committed herself definitely to its acceptance. But Dixon who "came within a few feet, if not inches, of solving the Kashmir dispute and bagging the Nobel Prize for Peace...gave up impatiently, impetuously rather, and left on August 23, 1950, vowing never to return to the region."[7]

Having stayed in the sub-continent for three months, Dixon arrived in London on 26 August 1950 "tired and faded." He had talks with both Foreign Secretary Ernest Bevin and Prime Minister Attlee. To Bevin he said that while India adhered to her pledge, she "haggled over" the question of what constituted a fair plebiscite in order to ensure that Sheikh Abdullah's Government would run the plebiscite in such a manner as to make the territory go to India. To Attlee he specifically stated that if the troops withdrew from Kashmir, the problem would fall into its place with other issues like the sharing of river waters, refugee resettlement etc. There was still scope for an effective solution if Britain managed to bring the parties together through their High Commissioners rather than leaving it to the UN. Dixon was firm in his stand to avoid a general open discussion of the whole question in the UN.[8]

Even before Dixon held these talks with Bevin and Attlee, the idea that he should be persuaded to embody in his report that the plebiscite proposal was dead was gaining momentum. When the subject was broached to Dixon, he was naturally disillusioned because he was toying with the idea that if the Security Council washed its hands off the Kashmir dispute, the feuding parties would be driven to further their negotiations in a more reasonable frame of mind; and in the meantime, it would be possible to retain the Security Council's observer machinery in Kashmir. Of course, Dixon was not without misgivings about the justification of his hope on either ground.

Dixon contemplated submitting a report which, though factual, would carry the clear implication that the responsibility for the failure to break the deadlock over Kashmir rested with India. He could not be said to have taken a broad view of the issue. His assessment of Nehru was not balanced. He dismissed him as "fundamentally anti-British" which was considered by some British officials as an "over simplified conception."[9] Opinion leaders in India felt that just because India could not accept some of his proposals, Dixon had allowed himself to "stray slightly beyond the province of a mediator" by pronouncing a verdict on India's stand which appeared to support Pakistan's charge that India was trying to "jump the plebiscite." He did not view objectively

India's policy on issues other than Kashmir. It was doubted whether he made a judicious appraisal of the Indo-Pakistan relations in its totality apart from the Kashmir crisis. Dixon was least inclined to include any specific recommendation in his report. He was anxious to get back to Australia with no intention to prolong his stay at Lake Success after submitting the report. As Dixon enjoyed the confidence of both India and Pakistan, Britain was most eager to persuade him to stay back and conduct the proposed negotiations at Lake Success. Britain was even more anxious to ensure that Dixon did not include in his report any recommendation unacceptable to her, for instance, the recommendation that the Security Council should divest itself of the Kashmir question and leave the two countries to settle it by direct negotiation.[10]

While the plebiscite proposal was buried and Britain also had admitted it, Pakistan persisted in harping on an over-all plebiscite. This disgusted the British Prime Minister so much that he advised Pakistan through his High Commissioner there against expecting anything more from him until he had considered the report of Dixon.[11] Chaudri Ghulam Abbas, Supreme Head of the Azad Kashmir Government, declared by the end of August 1950 that the stage for mediation and conciliation was over. He criticised the UN for its "vague directives and nebulous plans" which were no longer of any value. The *Dawn* of Pakistan published a signed article by Agha Shaukat Ali, an Azad Kashmir notable, which declared that Pakistan's problem was not Kashmir alone but "India's greed and lust for power."[12]

These unwarranted statements were made at a time when the situation in Pakistan was assuming alarming proportions. There was large scale insurrection in Poonch, Bagh and Palandari in the Azad Kashmir territory. There were rival groups and parallel administrations in many places. Demonstrations were organised against the Abbas group which was being helped by the Pakistani forces. Unmindful of the internal squabbles in the POK, the Governor General Ghulam Mohammad encouraged what he persisted in stating as the struggle for freedom in Kashmir and reminded the people of the Gilgit Agency and adjoining territories that they were not to rest until the whole State of Jammu and Kashmir had been liberated. He repeated *ad nauseum* that Kashmir being an "integral part of Pakistan," would one day be united to it.[13]

Error of Judgment

Britain for her part never ceased to believe that Nehru's policy on Kashmir was the major stumbling block to finding a solution to the dispute. A rumour was set afloat that Nehru was the sole director of the Kashmir policy and that the higher echelons in the Indian administration – civil and military – were totally disenchanted with his role. However, the statements of some of the seasoned Indian leaders gave the lie to such irresponsible talks in Britain. When the buzz of discussion was high on the Kashmir issue after Dixon's mission had failed, the UK High Commissioner picked out C. Rajagopalachari (Rajaji) for a private talk on the subject as the latter was well-known for his friendly approach to Pakistan. Contrary to the British officer's expectations, Rajaji in a moderate language but with "considerable intensity," identified himself totally with Nehru's policy on Kashmir and justified his rejection of Dixon's proposal to put Sheikh Abdullah's Government into commission for the plebiscite period. While certainly expressing his desire for an early settlement of the Kashmir dispute, Rajaji was positive that Dixon's proposal was indefensible. He had a strong feeling that Dixon's proposal had the blessings of Pakistan. Noted for his sharp sense, Rajaji had from the start grave doubts about Dixon's genuine interest in securing demilitarisation. He said candidly that if the Security Council were to base its future recommendations on Dixon's proposals, there was no hope for further progress. According to him, the best course in the existing situation would be to abandon the idea of a plebiscite and leave the entire problem as it was until an election took place in Kashmir in the normal way. The election would give the people's verdict to support or not the Abdullah Government. Based on the verdict, their preference to accede to India or Pakistan would be decided. In this way, the future of Kashmir could be decided without any plebiscite. To the question whether the solution meant the prolongation of the tension, he replied "Five Years." India favoured an early reduction in her armed forces and was prepared to reduce her own forces unilaterally without waiting for further progress in the negotiations on Kashmir. Rajaji categorically stated that India had no "aggressive intentions" towards Pakistan and that she did not also believe that Pakistan would be so foolish as to attack India in Kashmir or elsewhere.[14]

Even Patel, who was definitely anxious to have the Kashmir question resolved at the earliest, minced no words when the British officers approached him also for his views on the crisis. He firmly said that he would not interfere with the foreign policy of India which was the Prime Minister's domain. Implied in his statement was his agreement with Nehru's action at that point of time. Nehru was resolutely opposed to any deviation from Abdullah's sovereignty in the Vale as part of the plebiscite arrangement as that would unsettle the population there. He feared it might cause a mass exodus of the minorities.

Dixon formally handed over his report to the Security Council on 6 September 1950. Some pronounced it "an admirable document and completely objective." One reputed Indian journalist said in 2001 that Dixon's report "is a classic; unexcelled for its elegant style, incisive analysis and transparent honesty. No UN mediator received a warmer welcome. No mediator before or since came so close to success." It must be said in fairness to Dixon that unlike his predecessors from Lake Success, he spelt out in definite terms the types of problem that stood in the way of resolving the issue on the basis of the plan that had until then held the field. He even went further to explore alternative proposals which had failed because the parties could not be brought to accept them.

Zafrullah was not anxious to discuss the Dixon report. India gave no indication to think differently. The publication of the report deepened the crisis as some news agencies gave mutilated and inadequate summaries of the report. The *Reuters,* for instance, ignored portions of Dixon's Report which were adverse to India and Nehru. This was naturally pronounced as a "serious lapse" by India's enemies. Dixon's conclusion that the Security Council should give up its efforts at settlement greatly annoyed Pakistan since it would leave India in possession of most of Kashmir. Britain's efforts to stop Dixon from including such a recommendation in his report failed. Zafrullah thundered: "The Security Council must act. It cannot stultify itself."[15] In retaliation for the unkind words heaped on Dixon, an article in the *Civil and military Gazette* stated that Dixon had fulfilled his mission with the "highest integrity and capacity" and that a study of the whole report "makes it abundantly clear that the eminent jurist has been grossly misjudged in Pakistan."[16] The *United American Press (UAP)* published much that was omitted by the *Reuters.* Its version was also different from that of the *Reuters.* Though there was no damage on account of the *Reuters* news, it did cause much offence to Pakistan. The general feeling was that until Pakistan was made independent of the *Reuter Indian Service* and the transference of control completed, incidents like this would always be magnified out of all proportion for propaganda purposes. Britain was much worried about the outburst of anger reflecting public feeling in Pakistan as it would render Zafrullah's work in New York very difficult. He was expected to adopt a moderate attitude in the Security Council to any proposals like partition and abandonment of over-all plebiscite.[17] Another factor that worried Britain much more than this was the deleterious consequences that the Government of Pakistan would have to face if Britain succeeded in her efforts to reach settlements in Korea and Formosa (now

Taiwan), and secure the admissions of China and Indonesia to the UN leaving only the Kashmir crisis unsettled.

At a Press Conference held on 1 October 1950 to discuss Dixon's report, Nehru made it unambiguously clear that India's stand on Kashmir had not changed and could not change until the fundamental principles of her stand were understood and appreciated. India could not accept the two main points in his report namely (i) Dixon's insistence on denuding the Indian side of the State troops; and (ii) removal of the lawful Government of Abdullah. Again, if India agreed to consider partition of the State in spite of her "deep-seated" objection to any surrender to aggression, it was not because she approved of Pakistan's claim to any part of Kashmir but solely in the interests of peace, he said. Nehru stressed that the concession could not be used to make India agree that Pakistan should have the same status as India in the plebiscite area. He further disclosed that discussions on a "No War Declaration" had been renewed by India.

In October 1950, it was reported to Nehru that Britain was planning to propose to the Security Council to form a committee of its non-permanent members, excluding India, to consider the best way of conducting an impartial plebiscite in Kashmir and submit its report before the end of 1950. But Nehru did not view the proposal with favour as, in his opinion, it was bad for India to "get tied up with the committee that is proposed."[18]

Unhealthy Nexus

On 24 October 1950, Azad Kashmir celebrated the third anniversary of its birth. Its President Col. Shah stated in Muzaffarabad that partition of the State was unacceptable to them. The former President Sardar Ibrahim declared in Rawalpindi that Pakistan would warn the UN that Azad Kashmir would be free to resume its war of liberation if India failed to act on the plebiscite proposals forthwith. Speeches of the same tenor were made in Karachi also. In view of these disturbing developments, the Pakistani delegation urged Britain for a resolution of the Security Council on Kashmir. It was keen on some action before the American Presidency of the Security Council terminated by the end of October 1950. In November, it would be passed to Yugoslavia and in December to China. In January 1951, it would most probably be Brazil and in February China would be back. The prospects were therefore not very favourable to Pakistan. The UK Government was advised by its High Commissioner in India not to make any approach to Nehru in regard to Kashmir at that point of time but wait for a better atmosphere for negotiations as and when the rupee revaluation dispute was settled and trade relations between the parties resumed.

The British Government which was anxious to propitiate Pakistan by a resolution was in no mood to listen to its High Commissioner's counsel. The UK Delegation in New York was accordingly advised to draft a resolution. The resultant resolution met the same fate as many others before it. But what made it worthy of being reviewed was the unhealthy nexus between Britain and Pakistan in the drafting and redrafting of it, keeping the Indian Delegation in the dark. On 27 October 1950, the UK Delegation showed the draft resolution to Zafrullah who felt much beholden to Britain for having given the Pakistan Government a chance to express its views of the resolution at the preliminary stage. The Pakistani Delegation preferred to risk the possibility of the still-birth of the resolution owing to Indian objections to any compromise on Pakistan's stand on the over-all plebiscite. The UK Delegation incorporated in the resolution the amendments suggested by Pakistan during the secret meeting. When the Indian Delegation enquired about the resolution, it was told that it was in a "tentative form." Later a copy of the draft resolution was sent to the Indian Delegation which was told that a copy of the same was being sent to the Pakistani Delegation! The UK Delegation however warned Zafrullah of the difficulty in getting the Indian acceptance of the revised resolution. He was also told it would be embarrassing if the Indians came to know that Britain had preliminary discussions of the draft with the Pakistani Delegation.[19]

On 4 November, Rau confirmed India's rejection of the proposed resolution of 27 October at the Security Council and put forward counter proposals that the Council should accept Dixon's advice and leave India and Pakistan to work out a solution together. Alternatively, the Council should face the issue of Pakistani "aggression" and should not consider any further proposals for a settlement until the question had been determined. The Indian Delegation also restated the proposal of the President of the Security Council that two members of the Council would work out in private negotiation with India and Pakistan a solution agreeable to both. The Indian Delegation emphasised that the two members should be the US and the UK.[20] The UK Delegation, which did not favour this, observed that India's proposals aimed at ratifying the accession of Jammu and Kashmir to India by the proposed Constituent Assembly and then proclaiming it as the fulfilment of her obligation to consult the will of the people.

On 27 October, when Britain presented the draft resolution in the Security Council to appease Pakistan, the General Council of the National Conference in Kashmir also passed unanimously a resolution for convening a Constituent Assembly based on adult franchise to determine the State's future. Criticising the UN's handling of the Kashmir case which condemned its people to a "life of agonising uncertainty," the resolution said that it was high time the initiative was "regained by the people to put an end to this indeterminate state of drift and indecision." Nehru who was in Kashmir to address the National Conference welcomed the resolution as the convening of a Constituent Assembly would enable the State to ascertain the wish of the people. Anticipating opposition to the holding of elections when the case was still before the UN, he declared that Kashmir was part of India and that eventually, through the elected Constituent Assembly, the Kashmiris would ratify the formal accession of their State to India. Expressing his appreciation that Kashmir was progressing on right lines, Nehru regretted that "nowhere in the world was the Kashmir dispute viewed on its merit, but it had become pawn in world politics." He also said if some big powers failed to appreciate India's stand on Kashmir and instead lent support to Pakistan, it was because India was following an independent policy in world affairs while Pakistan toed their line.

In his interview with the *Reuters*, Nehru said that the resolution of the National Conference did not conflict with the UN's attempt to settle the Kashmir dispute. More than two years earlier, the Kashmir Government planned to convene a Constituent Assembly to decide among other things the framing of a Constitution for Kashmir, her political future and the real attitude of her people regarding accession of their State to the Indian Union. It was the legitimate right of the people of Kashmir to restore some normality in the State so as to rebuild a stable Kashmir. They had long waited and were determined to end the state of uncertainty. Nehru admitted that in view of Pakistan's aggression and occupation of parts of Kashmir, the proposed elections would be held only in areas under the Government of Sheikh Abdullah. He also agreed with the Government's claim that since it was the legal and continuing Government of the whole of Kashmir, the "resolution should treat elections as valid for the whole State of Jammu and Kashmir."[21]

Fresh Outburst of Pakistani Fury

With the passing of the resolution to convene a Constituent Assembly in Kashmir, accusations against India intensified in Pakistan. Even the first visit of Rajendra Prasad, the first President of India, to Kashmir to deliver the convocation address at the Kashmir University was viewed suspiciously. The speech had no special political significance and the President hardly made any pronouncement on the Kashmir conflict. Rahimtoola, Pakistan's High Commissioner to the UK, interpreted the activities of the National Conference as a manoeuvre by Nehru and Abdullah to prejudice the discussion in the Security Council. Influenced by such misrepresentations, Pakistan wantonly ignored the three real factors: that the initiative for elections came from Sheikh Abdullah; that such elections were long overdue; and that unless and until the Constituent Assembly was convened, many crucial questions including the fate of the Maharaja and other matters could not be decided. There were two alternatives open to the Kashmir Government: either wage a war and clear the entire territory of Kashmir of aggressors; or call a Constituent Assembly leaving out the territories on the other side of the CFL. The Kashmir Government chose the second alternative as the best way to stabilise its position.

The statement of the Government of India that the proposed Assembly would take no action on the accession issue did not allay the fears of Pakistan. She wanted a public statement to that effect but India's relations with Sheikh Abdullah precluded her from doing so.

Pakistan was equally unhappy with Britain's methods of handling the Kashmir issue which reflected the desire of both Britain and America to avoid offending Nehru at any cost.[22] A 1555 yard long scroll of cloth, bearing a million signatures obtained from Muslims all over the world under a Kashmir Liberation Pledge, was presented to the UN Secretary General Trygve Lie by Imanullah Khan of the World Muslim Conference. The scroll mounted on a roller stand demanded of the UN "not to be swayed by considerations other than those of justice, take determined action in the case of Kashmir and do justice by Kashmir and Kashmiris, not only in the interest of that unfortunate land but also in the interest of world peace, even as the UN has, by taking prompt action in Korea, upheld the cause of peace."[23]

On 18 November 1950, S.G.H. Shah, President, Muslim League Branch in Great Britain, sent a representation in the form of a resolution to James Chuter Ede, British Home Secretary. The resolution gave a catalogue of the "fearful hardships" suffered by the 3,000,000 Kashmiri Muslims because of the presence there of Indian armed forces and observed that their salvation lay only in the more forceful intervention by the British Government. Chuter Ede sent it to Bevin for answer and the essence of the latter's answer was that Shah's matter was receiving attention.[24] This made the Pakistani public bluntly voice its opinion that both the power blocs were Godless and that where the Kashmir issue was concerned, the anti-communists had rejected God's commandments by "preferring expediency to truth and narrow self-interest to universal justice." Even more damaging was the statement that while Truman was airing his fears of communism, a more serious threat to morality and spirituality than communism emanated from the triumph of "militant Hinduism."[25]

The Pakistani Press was no longer inclined to give any credence to the statements of her own representatives at the UN commending the sincerity of the Security Council in trying to formulate a proposal on Kashmir acceptable to both India and Pakistan. The *Dawn* wrote; "The real issue is plain and simple. Can the US and Britain persuade India to give up Kashmir?...They dare not...because they are leaning heavily on Nehru to get them out of their own scrapes."[26] Pakistan very often spoke of a holy war refusing to concede that the Kashmir issue was no religious problem and that regarding it so would bring in all the disasters that led to partition in 1947.

Around this time, in December 1950, Dixon suggested that Kashmir was more accessible to militant threat from Sinkiang (Kashgar-Khotan area) than from Tibet. From the latter the most that might be expected would be infiltration by small bands. One of the routes of possible approach was through Kashgar-Kargil-Leh and thence to west to Kargil, Zoji La and Srinagar (i.e. through India's Kashmir). In the Kargil area, India had just about two battalions – partly regulars and partly State forces. Dixon justified India's claim to maintain forces on approximately the existing scale in the Kargil-Zoji La areas after demilitarisation, and pending plebiscite, to guard against the possibility of infiltration of small bands from Sinkiang or Tibet.[27] This related to the repercussions on the Indian borders of communist China's occupation of Tibet in 1950. The shocking situation prompted Bevin to suggest making a new approach to Nehru, linking the question of Kashmir with the whole problem of defence against communist menace as India was "an essential part of the defence of the West." India being very exposed to attack from China, he was keen that she should be brought to realise that a new situation had arisen by the threatening advance of communism.[28]

Disregarding the deplorable condition in the continent, Pakistan was very insistent on an urgent consideration by the Security Council of the burning question of Kashmir which was agitating the mind of every Pakistani. But there was little scope for further negotiations in the shocking context of the militant aggressiveness of Red China which had completely altered the world situation. In view of the tone of the Pakistani Press and frequent Pakistani threats of a *Jihad* in Kashmir, India felt that the atmosphere for a resumption of negotiations on Kashmir simply did not exist. Bajpai strongly put it that the Kashmir question could be taken up by the Security Council only after the Commonwealth Prime Ministers' Conference which was to open in London on 6 January 1951.[29] Pakistan chose to impute the decision to postpone the reopening of the question of Kashmir to Britain's anxiety "to present a smiling and united front" at the Commonwealth Conference so as to avoid any action that might be "unpalatable to India before them."[30]

The growing anti-UK and anti-US feeling in Pakistan was so agonising to the two powers as to drive the US to find someone sponsor a resolution which would allay Pakistani anxiety without unduly annoying India and also deterring Sheikh Abdullah from taking any further step towards calling the proposed Constituent Assembly. Accordingly, Britain informed Nehru and Liaquat that Prime Minister Attlee would raise the issue at the January Commonwealth Conference against the background of the deteriorating international situation and the course of events in Asia. The theme of the meeting was the need for cooperation among the democratic countries against the menace from Soviet Russia and China. To lessen America's anxiety against the growth of wrong opinion gaining momentum among the public and the Press in Pakistan, its Government was asked to do all it could to mute the anti-US and anti-UK campaign.[31] India was against transferring the Kashmir controversy from the UN to a Commonwealth level. Nehru considered the inclusion of the Kashmir issue in the discussions at the Commonwealth Prime Ministers' Conference an injudicious approach to the problem. Even so, he was willing to go a long way to meet Liaquat's wishes provided there was no proposal for all the Prime Ministers to sit at a given time in a conclave to discuss the issue because it would not certainly promote a settlement.[32] He wanted the discussion to be informal and held outside the Conference with the Prime Ministers of India, Pakistan, Britain and a few others. Britain also was against placing the Kashmir question on the agenda of the Commonwealth Conference. Liaquat also made it known that Pakistan would not try to put India in the dock and hold the Commonwealth to ransom. But he was clearly in an awkward predicament as he could not tell his people about his trip to London unless he was sure of the fulfilment of Pakistan's condition.

Liaquat's intention was to canvass support at the Commonwealth Conference for Pakistan's contention that not only the Indian troops should withdraw from Kashmir but the Kashmir Government under Sheikh Abdullah also should go before the plebiscite was held. He went so far as to state that he might not attend the Conference unless the Kashmir question was put on the agenda. But it was an unwritten rule of the Commonwealth that disputes between its members were not discussed in the formal sessions of the Conference since they would be construed as interference in their policies. However, to please Pakistan, it was decided that it could be the subject of informal talks between the leaders concerned.

The informal discussions at the Commonwealth Prime Ministers' Conference on 9 January 1951 got nowhere. The Australian Prime Minister Robert Gordon Menzies's proposal to withdraw the Indian troops and place a Commonwealth brigade to hold the CFL during the plebiscite in the valley was rejected by India. The general feeling also was that this should be discouraged. However, two new suggestions emerged from these discussions. One was stationing a neutral force in the State to safeguard its security during the period from the withdrawal of the Indian and Pakistani troops to the announcement of the result of the plebiscite; the other was to conduct the actual voting by the areas as this would pave the way for the eventual partition of Kashmir that was agreed and for close local supervision of the plebiscite without overt interference with the functioning of the Abdullah Government. But attempts to reach an agreement on a resolution of the Security Council based on the aforesaid suggestions failed. Britain blamed Nehru for his insistence that only the Indian Government possessed the legal right to station troops in the State.

India had consistently maintained that she could never agree to any proposal which "infringes or in any way limits the sovereignty of the Kashmiri Government or endangers the security of the State." Pakistan's diametrically opposite attitude did not offer any meeting ground. The Commonwealth Conference afforded Liaquat an opportunity to indulge in his poisonous anti-India propaganda before the western statesmen.

References

1. *The Hindu*, 13 May 1950.
2. Nehru to Sheikh Abdullah, 6 April 1950, *SWJN*, Vol. 14, Part I, p. 205.
3. A.G. Noorani, "The Dixon Plan," *Front Line*, 25 Oct. 2002.
4. UK HC (I) to CRO, 14 Aug. 1950, FL/1015/537.
5. F.K. Roberts of UK HC (I) to Maclennan, 12 Aug. 1950, FL/1015/344.
6. *The Hindu*, 19 Aug. 1950.

7. A.G Noorani, "Justice Dixon – Mediator and Judge," Review Article, *Frontline*, Vol.20, Issue 14, July 05 – 18, 2003.
8. Conversations with the Foreign Secretary, 31 Aug. 1950, FL/1015/400 and Prime Minister on 1 Sep. 1950, FL/1015/398.
9. Frank to Garner, 15 Sep. 1950, FL/1015/405.
10. Cabinet Paper prepared by Denning, 30 Aug. 1950, FL/1015/403.
11. Ogmore's Minute, 29 Aug. 1950, FL/1015/404.
12. *Dawn*, 31 Aug. 1950.
13. Ag. HC (P) to CRO, 18 Sep. 1950, FL/1015/432.
14. UK HC (I) talk with Rajaji, 6 Sep. 1950, FL/1015/4110.
15. UK HC (P), 27 Sep. 1950, FL/1015/454.
16. *Civil and Military Gazette,* 10 Oct. 1950, FL/1015/463.
17. Minute of S.J.L. Olver, 26 Sep. 1950, FL/1015/443.
18. Nehru to Bajpai, 27 Oct. 1950, *SWJN,* Vol. 15, Part II, pp. 261 & 62.
19. UKD to UN to FO, 27 Oct. 1950, FL/1015/514.
20. UK HC (I) to CRO, 29 and 30 Oct. 1950, FL/1015/517.
21. UKD to UN to FO, 4 Nov. 1950, FL/1015/530.
22. UK HC (P) to CRO, 21 Nov. 1950, FL/1015/554.
23. UN (New York) Press Release, 16 Nov. 1950, FL/1015/557.
24. James Chuter Ede to Bevin, 20 Nov. 1950, FL/1015/561.
25. UK HC (P) to CRO, 7 Dec. 1950, FL/1015/571.
26. *Dawn,* 7 Dec. 1950.
27. F.E. Cunning-Bruce to Maclennan, 20 Nov. 1950, FL/1015/561.
28. Bevin's discussions with Gordon Walker, 8 Dec. 1950, FL/1015/579.
29. UK HC (I) to CRO, 14 Dec. 1950, FL/1015/587.
30. UK HC (P) to CRO, 15 Dec.1950, FL/1015/591.
31. FO to Washington, 18 Dec. 1950, FL/1015/596.
32. UK HC (I) to CRO, 31 Dec. 1950, FL/1015/7.

9

The Graham Mission

It was seen that Nehru rejected outright the proposal made at the Commonwealth Prime Ministers' Conference in London in January 1951 to station a commonwealth brigade in Kashmir. India's reaction to this was clear and unambiguous: she would not accept the entry of foreign troops in Kashmir or in any other part of India.

Meanwhile, consequent upon the failure of the Dixon mission, resentment in Pakistan against the interminable delay in resolving the Kashmir issue was mounting. Its Government was hard put particularly to check the opposition to its membership in the Commonwealth which was characterised as "nothing but a huge fraud, serving only the interests of the Anglo-American imperialists." There were also references aplenty to India's "accession plot" not to speak of the innumerable false and baseless charges, insinuations and talks of *Jihad* against her with a view to stoking the people's communal passions and religious bigotry. These developments made Britain furious not at Pakistan but at India who was accused of deepening the Kashmir crisis. In Britain's view, while Liaquat was reasonable and anxious to reach a settlement, Nehru was not genuinely interested in ending the impasse.

An Impolitic Resolution

To assuage the fears of the Pakistan Government, which was being tormented by a hostile public and Press over the Kashmir tangle, Britain and America embarked on an unwise course. In January 1951, they secretly prepared a draft resolution whose five main features were: (i) censure of the National Conference for its plan to convene a Constituent Assembly to determine Kashmir's future in violation of the principle that the final disposition of Kashmir should be a free plebiscite under the UN auspices; (ii) demilitarisation; (iii) stationing of Commonwealth troops in Kashmir; (iv) a State-wide plebiscite which provided for districts with a substantial majority to adjust their boundaries in favour of the party with minority votes; and (v) enumeration of the duties of the UN representative (with no mention of the person to be appointed), who should report back to the Security Council within five months.

It should be noted that this draft resolution was another instance where transparency was conspicuous by its absence. Its text was secretly shown to the Pakistani delegation in New York and a messenger was sent to Karachi inviting modifications in it. Pakistan wanted omission of the provision dealing with the possibility of boundary adjustments. But the British Ministers could not agree to any such omission fearing the leakage to the Indian side of any message sent to Karachi. India would then have a very legitimate grievance against the UK for "ganging up" with the Pakistanis and any hope of their cooperation on the Kashmir question would be lost. India did have a suspicion about the goings on between Britain and the Pakistan delegation. It was very probable that Bajpai got some hint of it from Nehru who was much upset when informed by Krishna Menon telegraphically that he believed that the draft resolution was being discussed in London with Rahimtoola. The telegram also stated that the British Prime Minister received only Rahimtoola and not Krishna Menon. All these clandestine activities came to the fore when the British High Commissioner to India asked the CRO what explanation he (the High Commissioner) was to give to Bajpai, who was bombarding him for the particulars of the draft resolution, if Britain's failure to treat both parties alike came to light.[1]

Pakistan was unhappy over the draft resolution. She was perturbed to find that while stressing over-all plebiscite, the Anglo-American resolution also provided for an adjustment of boundaries in favour of the party with minority votes in the State-wide plebiscite. This was taken by Pakistan as favouring the minority Hindus. Since the omission suggested by Pakistan was not carried out, her animus was directed against Britain, "the principal culprit."

An amended Anglo-American resolution was moved in the Security Council on 21 February 1951, by the British delegate Gladwyn Jebb. It contained the following features: i) appointment of a UN representative to effect demilitarisation and prepare an agreed scheme to hold a plebiscite in consultation with the Governments of India and Pakistan; ii) Supervision of the functioning of the Kashmir Government; iii) and forces for facilitating demilitarisation and holding of Plebiscite to be provided either by the UN or raised locally. In his opening speech, instead of elaborating the new plan set out for resolving the Kashmir deadlock, Jebb resorted to a wholesale condemnation of the proposed election to the Constituent Assembly in Jammu and Kashmir. There was no reference either in the resolution or in his speech to the perennial fanatical propaganda in Pakistan urging a *Jihad* against India.

Nehru was most indignant about the resolution and questioned the motives and good faith of the sponsors. According to British records, Nehru had sharp exchanges with Rau and also Bajpai who advised that India should take as modest a line as possible at Lake Success. These exchanges were grossly exaggerated by the British officialdom in its correspondence. According to it, Nehru instructed Rau to reject the resolution summarily and make no constructive counter proposals. Nehru's anger was attributed to his unflinching loyalty to Sheikh Abdullah and his personal commitment to the Constituent Assembly solution to Kashmir against the view of his official advisers. It was further reported that Rau did not want to have the responsibility of arguing the Indian case at all and that he personally disagreed with the line he had been instructed to take.[2]

Nehru sent telegrams to all Indian missions abroad instructing them to put the Indian case in their respective countries and to make it clear that under no circumstance would India accept the UK-US sponsored resolution. Had the normal procedure of consulting both the parties to the dispute in advance on the terms of the draft resolution been adhered to, much of the bitterness would have been averted. In voicing this officially and not privately, Bajpai said that though such consultations would not have achieved any tangible result, the fact that such consultations had taken place would have removed some of the bitterness from Nehru's criticisms. In Britain's view, this statement of Bajpai confirmed that India's outlook on the Kashmir issue was "extremely unpromising."

On 1 March 1951, while speaking at the Security Council, Rau clarified that India was not intransigent in rejecting the draft resolution which was introduced on 21 February but that she only reflected the public opinion. India was against arbitration on any matter that might affect unfavourably the internal security of Kashmir. He pointed out that the Government of India had agreed with the UNCIP on a programme of demilitarisation as well as arrangements for supervising the plebiscite. He said India had already reduced her forces in Kashmir by 20 to 25 per cent without waiting for any corresponding reduction by Pakistan. But Pakistan maintained that after the "so-called reductions," India had four divisions in Kashmir totalling about 65,000 men in addition to the State forces of 21 battalions and a cavalry regiment. Rau also said that India would not object to the appointment of a UN representative if his functions were entirely advisory. He concluded stating that the passage of the resolution would amount to repudiation of the UNCIP's decisions agreed to by both the parties and also of the Commission's assurances to India.

Though India did favour bilateral negotiations to reach an agreement on Kashmir, she now said there was no room for it against the background of Pakistan's talks of a *Jihad* and charges of a deep conspiracy on the part of India to devour Kashmir. Also contrary to the earlier agreement, Pakistan demanded the withdrawal of all Indian forces from Kashmir. Pakistan's friend the *Daily Telegraph*, the Tory paper of Britain, which always delighted in having a dig at India, because of its anger over India's daring to free herself from the yoke of British imperialism; squarely blamed Nehru for everything. His intransigence over Kashmir, it said, fuelled the flames of discontent in Pakistan. The paper wrote: "Every hope that his (Nehru's) self-assumed role of conciliator over Korea might make conciliation more acceptable to him on his own frontiers has disappeared and so has a large part of the prestige which India was beginning to win for herself at Lake Success."[3]

On 21 March 1951, after circulating a revised Anglo-American resolution, the Security Council adjourned till 29 March. The revised draft differed very little from the original proposal. The main point boiled down to a transfer of the initiative to arbitration by a UN representative if the parties failed to reach an agreement within three months. The persistent demand of Washington and London to submit the dispute to arbitration left no doubt about the imperialist designs. Their fear of communism urged them to find a barrier against it. The strategic importance of Kashmir with her nearness to the Soviet Union and her border with the People's Republic of China drove the Anglo-American bloc to plan to convert this area into a military base and a centre of espionage.

India reiterated her earlier stand that to accept the resolution would be dishonourable to India. The National Conference organised demonstrations in Srinagar to protest against the resolution. Sheikh Abdullah declared that the imperialist proposal of demilitarisation of Kashmir and supervision of plebiscite by a UN representative betrayed its real motive which was to transform Kashmir into "a base for Anglo-American aggression." The Deputy Prime Minister of Kashmir declared that accession being a domestic issue, the State Government would go ahead with the Constituent Assembly plan regardless of its acceptability or not to the Anglo-US bloc. Nehru strongly deprecated the attitude of the British and American representatives at the Security Council as the tone and contents of their speeches displayed "an astonishing ignorance of the entire problem." The speeches of Gladwyn Jebb, for instance, were replete with sharp thrusts. In his speech on 21 March, he took the Indian delegates to task for their attitude to arbitration. His speech on 30 March was also not free from invectives against India. There were in it expressions of alarm at Abdullah's statements about the functions of the proposed Constituent Assembly. Jebb rebuked the Indian representative for implying that the Kashmir question was already settled.[4] These broadsides drove Nehru to declare more emphatically than before that Kashmir was an integral and inalienable part of India and was subject to the Indian Constitution. Still, when the Indian Parliament during a discussion proposed that India should consider leaving the UN if the Security Council persisted in its anti-Indian policy on Kashmir, Nehru strictly repudiated the suggestion. His firmness on this matter was well received by the House.[5]

New Mediator's Arrival

Indian protests against the entry of foreign troops into Kashmir coupled with the criticisms of some of the member nations like the Soviet Union which characterised the UK-US proposal as a "crude intervention," forced the sponsors to drop their proposal for the entry of foreign troops into Kashmir. Their next move was to appoint a UN representative in the place of Dixon.

For several days, there were discussions regarding the person to be appointed as UN representative for Kashmir in succession to Dixon. Many names were recommended, considered and dropped including that of Adlai Ewing Stevenson, Governor of Illinois. Even on 30 March 1951 when the Security Council debated the fresh resolution on the Kashmir question, it was not decided who should succeed Dixon. The Preamble to this resolution called attention to the declared intention of Sheikh Abdullah's Government to convene a Constituent Assembly and announced that any declaration relating to the State's accession made by the Constituent Assembly would be regarded by the Security Council as having no validity. The resolution also said that the new UN representative to be appointed was to bring about the demilitarisation of Kashmir in accordance with the two resolutions of the

UNCIP (13 August 1948 and 5 January 1949) within three months of reaching the Indian sub-continent. Points on which he failed to reach an agreement would be referred to arbitration by a panel appointed by the President of the International Court of Justice after consulting the Governments of India and Pakistan. Pakistan accepted the resolution but India rejected it taking exception both to the provision for arbitration and the references to the Kashmir Constituent Assembly. When put to vote, the resolution was adopted with 8 in favour and 3 abstentions (India, Yugoslavia and the Soviet Union). Rau abstained from voting in accordance with Article 27(3) of the UN Charter.

At its meeting on 30 April 1951, the Security Council announced the appointment of Frank Porter Graham of North Carolina, a former Professor of History and Democratic Senator as the UN representative for India and Pakistan to settle the Kashmir dispute. A resolution to this effect was adopted by 7 votes to none with four abstentions (India, Netherlands, USSR and Yugoslavia). Some in the British circles felt that Graham, who was Pentagon's representative, was little known even in the States' Department except through what was given in the "Who is who in America." Some commented on his strong opposition to colonialism. But such comments were scotched on the ground that when Britain herself did not put up a candidate, it was unfair to cavil at the American choice.[6] Britain was sure that Graham would not be unacceptable to India given his record in Indonesia as a member of the Good Offices Committee of the Security Council on Indonesia and adviser to the Secretary of State on Indonesian affairs in 1948. He backed the Indonesians against the Dutch on anti-colonial grounds. But vexed as India was at the UK-US resolution, there was the fear that she might be inclined to prove troublesome over the selection of a US representative. There was also the comment that not being a man of strong character, Graham would be "a putty in Nehru's hands."[7]

Graham was in the sub-continent with his entourage of secretaries, political and military advisers and administrative assistants from 30 June to 9 September 1951. He was in Karachi from 30 June to 1 July and arrived in New Delhi on 2 July. Notwithstanding her rejection of the Security Council's resolution of 30 March which related to the appointment of the UN representative, India welcomed Graham and accorded him the consideration due to a distinguished citizen of another country desirous to make a friendly effort to solve the Kashmir problem. Moreover India had already definitely stated that she would be prepared to have consultations with Graham only if he came as an adviser and mediator. In the absence of Nehru, who was then in

Kashmir, Graham first met President Rajendra Prasad. Pakistan's reaction to Graham's Mission was unfavourable. Bowing to the growing criticism in the country that the Pakistan Government had already wasted three vital years by basing her Kashmir policy on the UN and the British and American action, Pakistan insisted on a fresh resolution to "overcome Nehru's resistance to a settlement." Britain ruled out any consideration of her demand until Graham had submitted his report.[8]

It was Graham's misfortune that his visit to the sub-continent synchronised with a sudden flare up of raids across the CFL, after a period of uneasy calm. Nimmo, the UN Chief Military Observer, was put to immense hardship shuttling between the two armies. Liaquat's Pakistan had planned well for a renewal of the fanatical campaign of "Save Kashmir" to incite the people of Pakistan and the tribal belt to get ready for a *Jihad.* The same Pakistani Government, which created the impression in the UN circles that it would always abide by the UN decisions and would abjure force to settle the Kashmir question, vigorously protested against the convening of the Constituent Assembly in Kashmir by the people of that State. Pakistan knew that the Security Council would come to her rescue whenever she erred egregiously. These developments posed a new problem to Graham in addition to the main task for which he was sent to the sub-continent by the Security Council.

There was widespread speculation that Graham had formulated his proposals, submitted them to Nehru and would be presenting them to Liaquat at Karachi. The story went further to say that Graham intended to revisit Delhi which meant that Nehru had not come out with his views on Graham's proposals. Nehru promptly scotched these speculations and reaffirmed India's stand on Kashmir and on Graham's mission. When a question was raised on demilitarisation at a Press Conference on 28 August, he made a candid statement that his discussions with Graham were informal covering the past history of the dispute and the implications of UN's resolutions on Kashmir. By this he meant that there was no discussion on the resolution of 30 March in pursuance of which Graham had been sent and which India had already rejected. Nehru also informed that he had no formal communication from Graham about demilitarisation or any other subject. Asked whether he had any suggestion to avert the renewal of hostilities, he said that a perfect gentleman that Graham was, he never even referred to them though he had been supplied with the copies of the letters exchanged between him and Liaquat. Nehru also denied the rumours that Graham requested the postponement of elections to the Constituent Assembly as the subject was never mooted. These must have caused a bitter disappointment to the Pakistani authorities as their fond hope that the UN representative's presence in the sub-continent would torpedo the entire plan of the Constituent Assembly had been shattered.

The general talk in India was that though Graham would not bring about an agreement on disarmament, the points of disagreements would be so narrowed down as to pursue the path of peaceful negotiations. This related to the many concessions that India had been making to Pakistan over Kashmir. While she stood firm on her refusal to grant parity of status to Pakistan, who was the aggressor and to dissolve the lawful Government of Jammu and Kashmir in the name of demilitarisation, she had continuously and unilaterally been reducing the strength of her armed forces in Kashmir. Consistent with this policy, she went more than half way to meet Graham's proposal of demilitarisation by agreeing to withdraw far more than the bulk of her forces as stipulated in the UNCIP resolutions. In fact, this minimum agreed to by India was insufficient for any major operation if Kashmir was to face another invasion. Still India took the risk on the assumption that Pakistan would not allow a repetition of the horrific raids of 1947. Addressing a Press Conference, Nehru said if the situation improved 100 per cent "We would remove our forces 100 percent."

Statements of the above genre inflamed some parties in India as well as some persons of consequence, who were opposed to the Indian Government's handling of the Kashmir imbroglio. Opponents like Shyama Prasad Mookherjee and parties like the Jan Sangh and the Rashtriya Swayam Sevak Sangh[9] went to the extent of alleging that there was a secret pact between India and Pakistan on Kashmir. They were all against Nehru's overconfidence in Sheikh Abdullah. Since the Maharaja's legal position was unassailable, his supporters were bent upon bringing the royal family back to Kashmir. Possibly egged on by his loyalists, the Maharaja seemed to have made a move by refusing to sign the relevant documents needed to hold the elections to the Constituent Assembly. He did not want to sign away his last remaining vestige of authority. Indisputably, it was his accession of Kashmir to India that really provided the one and only legal justification for the presence of Indian troops in Kashmir. It was further rumoured that exploiting the disquieting situation in Kashmir, Hari Singh, much disheartened at the "raw deal" he got from the Indian Government, was contemplating a revocation of the accession of Kashmir to India. But all these proved a false alarm. It was common knowledge that he could never stand up to pressure from the Indian Government. When a reference was made to the vexation of the exiled Maharaja, Nehru ruled out, during his speech in Jammu on 3 April 1951, the question of the Maharaja's return to Kashmir. He bluntly reminded those who pleaded for his return of the harm his administration had done in the past to the "true interest of Kashmir."

As announced by Sheikh Abdullah, the Constituent Assembly was convened by Hari Singh's son Yuvaraj Karan Singh who became the Regent and Head of the State after his father Maharaja Hari Singh left Jammu for Bombay on 20 June 1949. Sheikh Abdullah's action ignored the Security Council's resolution of 30 March 1951 passed before the convening of the Constituent Assembly. Graham carried his work under such most difficult circumstances.

Failure of the Mission

Not unexpectedly, Graham failed to bring about an amicable settlement of the dispute. Even before Graham set about his work in conjunction with his military adviser Jacob L. Devers, the query "If Graham's mission failed," was on the lip of many a British Officer. It was of course a foregone conclusion that his mission also would meet with the same fate as that of Dixon, since the problem was proving the hardest nut to crack. On 7 September 1951 – about a week before the conclusion of his visit to the sub-continent, Graham submitted to the Governments of India and Pakistan twelve proposals for a plan of demilitarisation of the State of Jammu and Kashmir. Though there were points of difference between the parties on certain issues like making demilitarisation a continuous process, fixation of 15 July 1952 as the date for the completion of demilitarisation, the appointment of Plebiscite Administrator by that date etc, it was the crucial proposal number 7 relating to the number of troops to be left on each side of the CFL that proved most irksome. Both the parties differed fundamentally on this point. Graham's recommendation of a proportionate reduction of troops proceeded from the wrong notion that the two countries should be treated as equals. This decision was entirely unacceptable to India who had, right from the inception of UN's operations, been demanding that the aggressor and the aggressed should not be equated. Pronouncing its verdict in favour of Pakistan, the *Times* accused Nehru for rejecting Graham's conciliation proposals.[10]

Graham presented his first report to the Security Council on 15 October 1951. It contained nothing new. On 17 January 1952, he submitted his second report to the Security Council which contained an admission of his failure to reach an agreement on the core issues. Actually, Graham could not make any progress since he first reported to the Security Council in October 1951. One important factor for his failure that had to be reckoned with was the most inconvenient time of his visit to India. Entire India was in the throes of a general election campaign. Ismay the then Commonwealth Secretary wisely felt the need to postpone the launching of any resolution on Graham's report until the completion of the Indian elections although he certainly knew this would entail a lot of pains to persuade Pakistan to accept this slight delay. To his credit, the Secretary also rightly appraised it would be disastrous if Pakistan thought that she "could sit back and expect all concessions to come from India" and that there could never be a successful settlement "unless both sides are ready to make concessions to the point of view of the other." This point was stressed to Zafrullah many times especially in relation to the problems of the number of troops on both sides of the CFL. Both Zafrullah and Mohammad Ali were clearly told that "whatever happens on Graham's last lap, there can be no possible question of sanctions."[11]

The Infamous Devers Plan

In September 1951 – about a couple of months after India's rejection of proposal 7 of Graham, there were encouraging signs on both sides of some relaxation of rigidity about the quantum of regular troops to be left behind after demilitarisation. It was hinted that India who had hitherto remained firm on 21,000 on the Indian side and 4000 on the Pakistani side would agree to reduce her forces. India sought the expert advice of Devers on this vital question and he held talks separately with both parties. A new device called the "Devers Plan" was drawn on 29 November 1951 which envisaged the stationing of 21,000 Indian troops, inclusive of 6,000 members of State militia on the Indian side and 7,600 troops including both regular Pakistani troops and the civilian armed forces, on the Pakistani side of the border. There was no mention of the Gilgit Scouts in the plan. The "Devers Plan" was communicated to both the Governments and it was widely believed that India had accepted its substance. On 21 January 1952, the UN Secretariat published a paper containing the "Devers Plan" which very nearly wrecked the Graham Mission. This was a different form of the demilitarisation plan – an enlarged and varied one – purported to be the original Devers Plan of 29 November 1951 which was agreed upon by the parties. The new plan provided for the (i) stationing of 10,000 troops on the Pakistani side and 14,000 on the Indian side; (ii) presence of Gilgit Scouts on the Pakistani side of which there was no mention in the earlier plan; and (iii) completion of demilitarisation by 15 July 1952 and the induction into office of the Plebiscite Administrator on that day. India was taken by surprise since the plan discussed with and communicated to her was not the one published which conceded to Pakistan near-parity with India in the matter of the strength and quality of the armed forces to be left on both sides of the CFL during the plebiscite. India stoutly denied that she had ever received these proposals for consideration. Both Rau who was in Delhi then and Thimayya, Military Adviser to India, confirmed they had never seen these portions. This signalled highly critical press comments and there was a warning that if a satisfactory explanation for the difference between the two versions of the Devers Plans submitted to India and Pakistan was not given immediately, "doubts would be cast on the tactics and behaviour of the Graham Mission as a whole." But at this stage the Indian authorities decided against playing up this incident any further, and refrained from giving any more guidance to the Press thus saving the mission from an ignominious exit.

Meanwhile, Pakistan suffered the sudden and shattering blow of the assassination of Liaquat Ali Khan – the first Prime Minister of Pakistan. On 16 October 1951, when he was about to make an important announcement at a public meeting in Rawalpindi, he was shot dead. The security forces immediately shot the assassin erasing thereby all clues to the identity of the real culprit behind the killing. The assassin was later identified as Saad Akbar. It was to the credit of Liaquat that during the first four years of the new born Pakistan, he successfully weathered many a storm.

Graham's Return to Sub-Continent

On 25 January 1952, Ismay, Commonwealth Secretary, in his oral statement to the Cabinet said that on the number and proportion of troops to be left on each side of the CFL, there were indications that India might be ready for a compromise. He also said that in view of this the best course would be to give the parties a further chance to reach an agreement by negotiation between themselves with "Graham's assistance, without the Security Council expressing a view."

Around this time there was a strong rumour in the British officialdom that Bajpai conveyed to Chester Bowles the desire of Nehru and the Indian Government for Graham to return to the sub-continent and continue his mission. There were also talks of Nehru telling Chester Bowles personally in London that he would like Graham to revisit the sub-continent at the earliest. Though this was welcome news to Britain, she was inclined to conclude that it was a trick of the "astute but untrustworthy" diplomat Bajpai in order to gain time.[12]

Britain was wrong in her misgiving given the uneasy situation prevailing in India during these months and the genuine desire of the Government to end the impasse. On 31 January 1952, at the Security Council meeting held in Paris, Setalwad, Attorney General of India, represented India along with Bajpai as his adviser when Kashmir was discussed. At the very outset describing his speech as "no language of convention but the free expression of a deep and sincere sentiment," Setalwad expressed the hope that the Council would continue the negotiations under the auspices of Graham to settle the differences between India and Pakistan that still divided the two over certain parts of his plan. He assured the cooperation of India in the pursuit of peace and progress.

On 12 February 1952, in the Indian Parliament, Shyama Prasad Mookherjee went so far as to suggest that since the POK could not be liberated through the machinery of the Security Council, it was time India withdrew the case from the Council and settle it with Pakistan. Repudiating the suggestion, Nehru explained that since he went to the UN respecting the world organisation, the case had to remain there although certain things that India disliked did happen there. He also reiterated that although in law, sovereignty over the POK was vested in the existing Government of Kashmir, India did not resort to military measures to recover it, because she always stood for peace. But if others intervened militarily to grab more Indian territories, India would meet them whatever the consequences. Nehru expressed the hope that the Security Council would pursue the matter. It was evident that this statement of Nehru implied his desire to get Graham return to the sub-continent. Zafrullah, who initially ruled out any revisit of Graham to the sub-continent to continue his mission without the authority of a second resolution of the Security Council, also changed his earlier stance. He told the American Ambassador in Karachi that he was keen on Graham's early return for renewed negotiations. He also stressed the importance of making further negotiations part of a continuing process and not dependent on any further formal action by the Security Council. He was impelled to make this suggestion as otherwise it would be difficult to hold public opinion in Pakistan which was already very vexed over the delay in finding a settlement.

These developments led the Security Council to decide that Graham should resume his negotiations in the sub-continent and report to the Council by 31 March 1952.

Graham proceeded to the sub-continent in the last week of February 1952. India welcomed his revisit. Zafrullah also did so. Graham held discussions with the parties separately in New Delhi and Karachi and then left for Geneva on 25 March to prepare his third report without having secured an accord between the two parties on the most pressing point namely the number of troops that should remain on each side of the CFL. Before he submitted his third report in April 1952, he told Rau in New York that he had come to the inevitable conclusion that there was not sufficient prospect of an agreement between the two parties to entitle him to complete his mission satisfactorily. He had no intention to apportion any praise or blame between the parties since he was encouraged to find that he could reach an agreement on at least eight of the twelve points listed in his original proposals.

Graham's departure from the sub-continent without achieving an accord led to an outburst of anger in Pakistan. But her fury over his impromptu departure from the sub-continent did not move Graham to deviate from his schedule. He did not wish to leave Geneva for the sub-continent once again to hold discussions with the parties before submitting his report. But he proposed to have discussions with the representatives of the two countries in New York before completing his report and he did see them in New York. It was very significant that India made two definite moves now: (i) she was ready to agree to the automatic appointment of the Plebiscite Administrator as part of the process of demilitarisation; and (ii) she privately informed Britain and also Pakistan that arrangements were in train for a bulk withdrawal of her forces from the advance positions they took up in the Punjab in July 1951 which Pakistan viewed as a direct menace to her.

Graham's third report was published on 22 April 1952. Not willing to notify his failure, he pointed out that only two points remained unsettled. One was withdrawal of troops. While India decided to withdraw her troops from the Pakistani border near Amritsar varying from 70 to 450 miles, Pakistan contended that the Indian forces had been only relieved and not withdrawn. The other related to the timing of the arrival of the Plebiscite Administrator. India objected to calling Chester Nimitz at that stage into discussions with the representatives of India and Pakistan on the immediate issues of the dispute. In India's view to designate him as Plebiscite Administrator at that point of time, would place him in a false position *vis-à-vis* both Governments later on. The British Government could not understand the logic of this.[13] Pakistan was anxious that nothing should be done in pursuance of Graham's latest proposal which would in any way disqualify Nimitz for his real work as Plebiscite Administrator. Graham's report further suggested that he should continue to negotiate with the parties in order to reach an agreement on the outstanding issues. There were criticisms of his incurable optimism.

In his fourth report presented to the Security Council in September 1952, Graham himself had clearly described the functions and responsibility of both forces to be left on either side of the CFL. According to these proposals, on the Pakistani side there should be the minimum number of forces needed to maintain law and order and the cease-fire agreement, "with due regard to the freedom of the plebiscite" and on the Indian side there should be the minimum number of Indian forces and State armed forces needed to maintain law and order and the cease-fire agreement "with due regard to the security of the State and the freedom of the plebiscite." The message was clear and definite that unlike Pakistan, India should have the right to maintain her armed forces because the security of the State was her and only her responsibility. India was happy that the proposals were "conceived in the right spirit." But Pakistan demanded the deletion of the phrase "with due regard to the security of the State." Since Graham was not prepared to oblige Pakistan, he reported that no agreement could be reached on his draft proposals.

The subsequent Anglo-American resolution on Kashmir presented to the Security Council in November 1952 did not stop with recording the progress made by Graham. It chose to circumscribe the scope of the negotiations. Apart from stipulating limits to the strength of the armed forces on both sides of the CFL, it also stated that troops on both sides should be concerned with the maintenance of the security of the State, as distinct from the maintenance of law and order during the plebiscite. It went further to prescribe a time limit of one month for the negotiations.

Gladwyn Jebb, who was widely believed to be the author of this resolution, yielded to the demand of Pakistan in laying down the time-limit in his speech on the resolution. By the passage of this resolution which deliberately ignored the facts of the problem, the Security Council stultified itself by going back on its own resolutions, on the conclusions reached by Graham and also on whatever good work was done by the UNCIP to narrow the differences between the parties. This was a wanton attempt on the part of Britain, America and the British Delegate Jebb "to destroy solemn agreements reached in the past few years...its effect will not be to promote a settlement on the Kashmir dispute, but to aggravate the situation and encourage fanatical elements in Pakistan to raise once again the ugly cry of *Jihad*."[14]

Throughout this period, possibly to maintain the tempo of hatred against India and to pacify the rebellious public of Pakistan, Zafrullah continued his never-ceasing India-bashing. At the Pakistani legislature, Zafrullah did not shrink from hinting at the possibility of settling the Kashmir issue by "other than peaceful means." The Pakistan Prime Minister Khwaja Nazimuddin declared in his public address on Pakistan's Independence Day on 14 August 1952: "We have not accepted the accession of Kashmir to India and notwithstanding anything that Mr. Nehru may say, we will never accept it." Utterances of this type did disturb Britain also because such remarks made in summer 1951 led to a crescendo of war talks by all and sundry in Pakistan. The troop movements as a precautionary measure in the wake of Zafrullah's statements were marked by a period of "extremely acute tension."

Geneva Negotiations of 1953

On 23 December 1952, the Security Council had before it an Anglo-American resolution which called on India and Pakistan to start negotiations forthwith in New York to settle the elusive point dealing with the quantum and composition of forces to be left behind after the withdrawal of the main forces. In putting forward the figures of the troops, the resolution specified that India's forces should be reduced to a number between 12,000 and 18,000. India rejected the resolution. Nehru who was then in Trivandrum reiterated at a Press Conference on 28 December India's rejection of the resolution and refusal "to act under its compulsion." He was most unhappy about the "cavalier treatment" India received despite her loyal cooperation with the Security Council and the UNCIP in the matter of Kashmir. When N.R. Pillai, Secretary General, Ministry of External Affairs, approached the UK High Commissioner to discuss the resolution, he was told that it did not seek to impose a solution but only called for further negotiations and that it was supported by all the members of the Security Council except Russia.[15]

In her opening speech in the debate on the resolution, Vijayalakshmi Pandit drew the attention of the Council to the resolution passed by the Punjab Muslim League under the presidency of the Prime Minister of Pakistan. It exhorted the several lakhs of people attending the session to take "direct action" for the liberation of the Kashmiris if the UN persisted in its "dilatory tactics." She sincerely hoped that the British delegate Gladwyn Jebb who had earlier expressed his "deep satisfaction" over the points of agreement reached by India and Pakistan on Graham's proposals would also indicate his deep disappointment over the Muslim League's resolution. This hope was blighted when in his speech Jebb completely ignored the basic fact of Pakistan's aggression which was an admitted fact and advised the other members to do likewise. The portents were clear and all that Mrs. Pandit could do was to warn the Council against ignoring them.[16]

Meanwhile, on 12 January 1953, the British Foreign Secretary learnt from the US Embassy in the UK that Graham had resumed negotiations with the parties at Geneva. He had already expressed a desire to transfer the venue for future talks from the UN headquarters to some other place like Geneva and to hold talks with representatives of Cabinet Minister's rank to be nominated by the two Governments.[17] The Geneva meeting was held under the auspices of the UN representative in the European office of the UN at Geneva from 14 February. India was represented by G.S. Bajpai, who was then the Governor of Bombay, along with his advisers D.P. Dhar, V. Shankar and J. Kidwai and Pakistan by Zafrullah with his military advisers K.H. Shak and Mohammad Iqbal Khan. Both the countries reached a broad agreement on 11 out of the 12 main points which Graham put forward in his first plan. It was again the proposal which related to the strength and composition of the forces to remain on each side of the CFL when demilitarisation had reached its final stage that defied agreement. The Anglo-American resolution suggesting compromise figures for the forces on each side which was later adopted by the Security Council was rejected by India. She stood firm on her decision not to tolerate a plan, however reasonable it might appear to the outside world, which admitted the right of either Pakistan or the POK to keep armed forces on the Kashmir territory while the plebiscite was being held.

Immediately after the Geneva negotiations which unmistakably indicated Graham's failure and the nature of the impasse, the US wanted the UN representative to exercise more caution. Graham was advised not to give any conclusions and recommendations in the report he was preparing but just to indicate in his covering letter to the President of the Security Council that his conclusions and recommendations would follow. Even if Graham should be pressured into submitting his conclusions, he was urged to refrain from making recommendations relating to the specific numbers of armed forces to be retained. In fine, America was anxious to avoid any discussion of the Kashmir question in the Security Council in March and April when Pakistan and the Soviet Union would have the presidency."[18]

In his private conversations with the UK delegation in New York, Graham made the forthright statement that while India's rejection of the report on the ground it did not provide for a total disbandment of the Azad Kashmir forces was expected, that of Pakistan on the plea that the proposal gave 3000 more troops to India than what the Security Council's resolution had suggested was most unwise. He suggested that Britain should, in conjunction with America, advise Pakistan to change her attitude and accept reasonable proposals regardless of India's decision. Britain accepted that Pakistan had nothing to lose by agreeing to this. But she also realised that Pakistan was very likely to feel that acceptance of the proposals by her would encourage India to demand further concessions on the Azad Kashmir forces. In view of these snags, Graham imposed the condition that his proposals had to be accepted or rejected as a whole and that Pakistan must be "usefully reminded of this."[19]

The party that was worst affected by this perennial conflict was the people of Kashmir. They were very bitter as their State had been broken to pieces. Their sufferings were legion: in the Dogra Jammu, there was a violent reaction against the Sheikh Abdullah Government, which, while stating that the accession of Kashmir to India was complete, had also been claiming that the State's autonomy would continue unimpaired; the Praja Parishad demanded that Jammu should be cut off from the State and integrated with India where their interests would be better taken care of; the Ladakhis were discontented with the Kashmiri rule and their Buddhist leaders were turning to Tibet which had come under the control of Communist China; the former Gilgit Agency and Baltistan had already thrown in their lot with Pakistan; even in the Kashmir Valley, notwithstanding its pull to India, there was disaffection; and in the Pakistan occupied Kashmir territory, "friction was endemic."[20]

Graham's Final Report

Graham submitted his fifth and final report comprising in all five parts to the Security Council on 27 March 1953. It reviewed the suggestions put forth to end the differences over the number and the character of the forces to be left on both sides of the CFL after demilitarisation; pointed out the benefits of the induction of the Plebiscite Administrator into office at an early date; referred to the assurances and elucidations of the UN Commission's resolutions of 13 August 1948 and 5 January 1949; summarised the negotiations since the meeting of the Security Council on 23 December 1952; and emphasised the importance of an agreement over Kashmir to the peoples of Kashmir, Pakistan, India and the world.

The report, which was "completely factual," did not say either in the text or in the covering letter to the President of the Security Council that the UN representative proposed to table a further report containing his recommendations. After its publication on 1 April 1953, the Press which studied it closely concluded that Graham was not contemplating any further move. Describing the report as "a homily by Dr. Graham," the British Government pointed out an important anomaly in it. Though described as "a mere recital of facts and negotiations," the report had drawn statements from the elucidations and conclusions of the UNCIP which constituted "a slight strengthening of India's position" in Kashmir. This fact had since been acknowledged in the subsequent proposals of the Security Council. On the strength of this report, India could credibly argue that her special position was recognised to a further degree in the Security Council's negotiations. But Graham had not come to any conclusion regarding the validity of India's claim.[21]

Zafrullah called the report a "disappointing document" as it had failed to recommend the number to which the armed forces on each side of the CFL should be reduced. He also objected to Graham's proposal at the Geneva talks that on the Indian side the force should be fixed at 21,000 whereas the Security Council's resolution of23 December 1952 indicated a reduction between 12000 and 18000. He wanted the Council to call on the parties to reduce their forces to specified numbers. Zafrullah had forgotten that the figure 21,000 was suggested by Britain. Graham's fifth report conveyed the truth that his negotiations with India and Pakistan having proved "sterile," it was unwisdom to pursue discussions on demilitarisation. If it was imperative to continue the UN efforts, then the only course open was to take the issue to the General Assembly.

It may be recalled that India rejected the Security Council resolution of 23 December 1952 and refused to resume negotiations on that basis. However, later she agreed to do so under the aegis of Graham on the understanding that the latter would not allow himself to be bound by the Security Council resolution but freely resume the negotiations from where he left off in his fourth report. Unfortunately, Graham could not dissociate himself from the Council's approach. He found himself unable to uphold his own views which were just and favourable to India. Anxious to bring a parity of status between the two forces without regard to the fundamental differences between their respective functions, Graham proposed the denial of armour and artillery to both parties. How did he expect the Indian forces to meet external aggression without armour and artillery?

When the prospects of a settlement appeared bleak after the debacle of the UNCIP and the two missions of Dixon and Graham, the ire of some British officials unreasonably turned against India. R.W.D. Fowler, for instance, who had a reputation for his deep dislike for India, said with full confidence that if Graham had pressed the Indians to quote "chapter and verse" their claims for disarming and disbanding the Azad forces, he would have called their bluff.[22]

Fowler, who had no thorough knowledge of the workings of the UNCIP and the talks between the Commission and representatives of India, asserted that "there was no authority for their claims either in the resolutions or in the statements, made from time to time by the Commission to the Government of India." Another statement, which was not impolite but perhaps desperate, came from J.J.S. Garner. He said :

> "I personally regard it as axiomatic that Nehru will never willingly give up the Vale...far too much is involved...his own emotions, his passionate love for Kashmir, his prestige, his ideal of the secular State (and) his personal loyalty to Sheikh Abdullah. That being so, no amount of external pressure (short of military and economic sanctions which have always been ruled out), will move him."[23]

To keep the UN mediation going it was suggested by America that Graham should revisit the sub-continent on a fact finding mission the motive behind it being to break away from the plebiscite settlement agreed to by the two Governments in the two resolutions of the UNCIP and switch to negotiations towards some form of partition of Kashmir. Some like P. Liesching felt that America's suggestion would mean abandoning Britain's support to Pakistan and that this would not bring the settlement any nearer. Liesching was so disgusted with the suggestions of the US that he said voicing his grievance: "It is unfortunate we should have to carry the State Department along with us in anything we wish to do in the UN on the Kashmir question." But he immediately consoled himself with the truth that unless Britain supported America's suggestions, she would not get the seven votes necessary for the adoption of a Security Council resolution and that "without America's support we should be powerless to do anything effective in the Security Council."[24]

References

1. UK HC (I) to CRO, 16 Feb. 1951, FL/1015/116.
2. UK HC (I) to CRO, 16 March 1951, FL/1015/229.
3. India had no part or lot in the Korean War. As a member of the Security Council then. India voted its resolution condemning North Korea's aggression on South Korea in 1950, although it went against the Communist Bloc. She also accepted the second resolution of the Council calling upon its members to help South Korea but this did not involve any departure from her foreign policy or keeping aloof from rival group of nations. When the War ended on 27 July 1953, India was made the Chairman of the Neutral Nations Repatriation Commission. India sent 5500 men of all ranks to Korea to complete the task assigned to them.

4. Note of W.J. Smith, 17 Nov. 1952, DO/35/6592.
5. UK HC (I) to CRO, 28 March 1951, FL/1015/253.
6. Note of R.H. Scott, 4 April 1951, FL/1015/264.
7. UK HC (I) to CRO, 7 April 1951, FL/1015/282.
8. Note of R.W.D. Fowler, 11 April 1951, FL/1015/296.
9. Now called Rashtriya Sevak Sangh (RSS).
10. *Times*, 7 Sep. 1951.
11. CRO to Gilbert Laithwaite, 19 Feb. 1952, 1052/1/11252.
12. *Ibid*, R.H. Belcher to G.P. Hampshire (CRO), 19 Feb. 1952.
13. *Ibid*, Laithwaite to Salisbury, 14 March 1952.
14. *The Hindu*, 14 Nov. 1952.
15. G.P. Hampshire's Minute, 11 Jan. 1953, DO/35/6605.
16. *The Hindu*, 1 Jan. 1953.
17. *Ibid*, 24 July 1952.
18. Note left with FO by Arthur Ringwalf of the US Embassy, 27 Feb. 1953, DO/35/6606.
19. *Ibid*, Gladwyn Jebb to FO, 25 Feb. 1953.
20. *Times*, 14 Feb. 1953.
21. Notes of W.J. Smith (CRO), 8 April and R.W.D. Fowler, 9 April 1953, DO/35/6607.
22. *Ibid*, Fowler's Note on Kashmir, 9 April 1953.
23. *Ibid*, Garner's Note, 25 April 1953.
24.s *Ibid*, P. Liesching to CRO, 17 April 1953.

10

Road Blocks to Demilitarisation

For more than five years since 1947, when the Government of India referred the Kashmir issue to the UN, there was no improvement in the Indo-Pakistan relations. The British friends of Pakistan were most unhappy about keeping the dispute simmering. The only consoling feature that emerged out of the various discussions and debates on the subject was the decision to leave the whole question to be settled bilaterally between India and Pakistan. This paved the way for the conduct of meetings and exchange of correspondence between the two Prime Ministers.

Bilateral Talks Go Awry

It was agreed that Nehru and Prime Minister Khwaja Nazimuddin of Pakistan should first meet in London where they were expected to be in June 1953 to attend the Coronation of Queen Elizabeth II. The political climate also seemed to be shaping towards an early meeting between the two Prime Ministers. But before the event took place, there was a sudden and sweeping change in the Government of Pakistan. The Cabinet of Khwaja Nazimuddin, the elected leader of the Pakistan Muslim League, which had a predominant majority in the Legislature, was dismissed and Mohammad Ali Bogra, also of the same party, was chosen to form a new ministry. What was most intriguing was the testimony of a British official spokesman that the dramatic dismissal of the Cabinet was constitutionally correct! The meetings arranged between Nehru and Mohammad Ali Bogra continued intermittently. After the London meeting, the two Prime Ministers met first in Karachi in July and then in New Delhi in August. The New Delhi meeting took place after the summary replacement of Sheikh Abdullah's Government in Kashmir which has been discussed elsewhere in this chapter. In fact, the Delhi meeting was held at the urgent request of Mohammad Ali Bogra who was driven to do so by the furore caused by certain anti-Indian elements in Pakistan over some incidents in Kashmir in the wake of the dismissal of the Sheikh Abdullah Government. Mohammad Ali Bogra declared that he was convinced that India had no role in any untoward happening in Kashmir. But the Pakistani Press persisted in making wild allegations about the changes wrought by what in its opinion was a *coup* in Kashmir.

Discussions were held at some length during the Delhi meetings giving a ray of hope initially that they would make real progress towards the holding of the plebiscite to which both the parties were committed by accepting the two resolutions of the UNCIP. At the end of the Delhi meeting, a joint *communiqué* was issued on 30 August comprising the following two points: (i) the Plebiscite Administrator should be appointed before the end of April 1954; and (ii) before his appointment, joint committees of experts should be set up to deal with certain preliminary issues which needed to be settled before holding the plebiscite. These were regarded as considerable advance in the Indo-Pakistan relations on Kashmir. The general impression was that since Nehru's difficulties with Sheikh Abdullah had been overcome, he was relatively more forthcoming at the Delhi Conference. Britain said that Nehru was anxious to reach a solution on Kashmir acceptable to him with his own fame as "an apostle of peace and a leader of Asia." Britain was also certain that for this reason Nehru would ratify the 1947 accession of Kashmir to India by a plebiscite "as soon as he is satisfied its result will be satisfactory." Britain praised Mohammad Ali Bogra also for his "exemplary restraint and patently sincere efforts" to forge a new relationship with India. It was even believed that the old demilitarisation problem had been diminished.[1] But these were all imagination running riot.

After the Delhi meet, Nehru put forward two proposals to solve the Kashmir problem. One was that plebiscite had to be held by regions instead of an overall one for the whole State as one unit. The other proposal was that Admiral Nimitz who was appointed as Plebiscite Administrator should be replaced by some one from South East Asia or from one of the smaller West European countries. Nehru put this proposal for two reasons: to isolate the Kashmir question from big power politics and to avoid troubling the big powers to supply a representative as Plebiscite Administrator. There were instances when the US was in no position to spare the services of the veteran statesmen suggested by the UN at the instance of the UK. Nehru rightly felt that there were many countries in Asia and Europe which, though small, could supply a proper man of distinction.

Pakistan was not happy about the proposals put forward by Nehru. She would accept regional plebiscite only if the regions were so divided as to give her the Chenab Valley with the Muslim areas of northwest and not with the Hindu areas of southeast. The replacement of Nimitz was also ruled out. Finding a solution acceptable to both countries proved an immense task. Pakistan's insistence on Nimitz's retention was incomprehensible as he was appointed in March 1949 by the UN on the assumption that the Security Council would surely succeed in creating conditions needed for conducting an impartial plebiscite. Since all these efforts had failed, Nimitz's appointment ought to have been considered as lapsed. Moreover, Nimitz himself had asked the Secretary General of the UN to accept his resignation but the latter could take no decision without consulting Pakistan's Zafrullah![2]

A new disconcerting factor that cropped up at this juncture was Premier Mohammad Ali Bogra's reversal of his earlier statement of India's role in the change of Government in Kashmir. It was astounding that he publicly contradicted his own earlier declaration and pronounced as "facts" the wild allegations by the Pakistani Press that the Government of India was suppressing, through the authorities in Kashmir, expression of opinion in favour of Pakistan. So, the hopes of a settlement entertained only in August at the Delhi meeting were belied. The only achievement was the convening of a meeting of the officials of the two Governments by the India and Pakistan Committee of Official Experts set up in accordance with a decision taken at the Delhi meeting in August. This Committee was to advise the two Governments on preliminary issues. The Committee examined the issues in considerable detail at nine sessions from 21 to 29 December 1953. Though these meetings were held in a cordial atmosphere, there was no agreement on the all-important issue of demilitarisation. About the same time, the two Prime Ministers also met to discuss the possibilities of a solution by regional plebiscites leading to some form of partition of Kashmir. But nothing positive came out of this also. There was no more meeting of the two Prime Ministers. The road ahead for a settlement on Kashmir appeared most formidable.

In November 1953, a fundamental change took place in the name of Pakistan. Its Constituent Assembly named Pakistan as "The Islamic Republic of Pakistan." This was a major deviation from the promise made by Jinnah in 1947 that the new nation of Pakistan would be a national modern State where Muslims and non-Muslims would have perfect equality. Having by then given up the two-nation theory, Jinnah categorically stated that the Hindus and the Muslims did not constitute two different nations. But, the new name now given was based on the supposition that Pakistan was founded on the two-nation theory and hence the Hindus should be treated as members of a different nationality. It was clear that by the decision of the Constituent Assembly, the non-Muslims in Pakistan would have only a second class citizenship.

Dismissal of Abdullah: A Regrettable Necessity

Two events occurred in 1953 which blocked further parleys between the two Prime Ministers. Of course, whether any such parleys would have helped to find a settlement even without these impediments was extremely doubtful. One of these was the dismissal of Sheikh Abdullah's Government in Kashmir for which Pakistan held Nehru directly responsible. The other and the more important development was the US decision to extend military aid to Pakistan.

The two winning qualities that attracted Abdullah to Nehru were his concern for secularism and disapproval of Pakistan's two-nation theory. In the early days of Abdullah's regime, the way in which he handled the delicate situation in Kashmir strengthened Nehru's trust in him. It was sincerely believed that Abdullah was showing a spirit of cordiality in his relations with India, but, in truth, he was not. Since he was totally dependent on India's support, the opinion gained ground that he was very loyal to India, especially in encouraging the Kashmiris to think of permanent association with her. But very soon, this impression proved deceptive.

True, Abdullah was not a Muslim fanatic, but he was an uncompromising political opportunist. Though at the time of the transfer of power, he was against the State's union with Pakistan, he did cherish the idea that with American support he could carve out an independent Kashmir, "a sort of Switzerland of the East."[3] As early as 28 January 1948, he met Austin, US Representative at the UN in New York, and discussed with him the need to make Kashmir independent. He was "overly anxious" that Kashmir should not become a bone of contention between India and Pakistan but should remain independent and hence sought American and British aid for her development.[4]

In September 1948, Abdullah said in his broadcast message on the *Id* festival that Kashmir had freed herself from the autocratic rule of the Maharaja and that having achieved this, she would call upon her people to exercise their opinion freely whether the "betterment of the State lay in accession to India or Pakistan or in maintaining friendly relations with both by remaining independent." Thus Abdullah was wedded to the concept of an independent Kashmir right from the start. As the Prime Minster of Kashmir, which was an integral part of India, he openly voiced this view in the public. During an interview with Michael Davidson, Correspondent, *Scotsman*, in April 1949, he declared that "accession to either side cannot bring peace...an independent Kashmir must be guaranteed not only by India and Pakistan but also by Britain, the US and other members of the United Nations." Nehru who was much taken aback by this statement, which did create some sensation among the political circles in London, wrote to Abdullah " I wish you had not given that interview, because this kind of thing leads to wrong interpretations...I am afraid the suggestion you made will have a bad effect on the UN Commission. We are passing through a delicate stage in this business and the less we say the better."[5]

Around this time, Nehru complained to his sister Vijayalakshmi of his two headaches. One of course was Kashmir. The other related to the activities of the Maharaja and Abdullah in contrary directions. He wrote, "On the whole, Sheikh Abdullah has recently been more irresponsible of the two..." Two months later he wrote again that "Abdullah was behaving very badly in Kashmir in regard to domestic affairs...He appears to be bent on seeking a conflict with us. He has gone into wrong hands there and is being misled."[6]

Abdullah's Revenue Minister went one further when he said that Kashmir would be made an autonomous republic with its own President, its own National Assembly and its own judicial set-up within the Indian Union. He justified the decision of the Kashmir Constituent Assembly to withhold compensation for the land expropriated from the large land owners under the Big Landed Estates Abolition Act of October 1950 which affected 10,000 landowners who were left with 22¾ acres each. Anticipating India's intervention as the decision was in contravention of the Indian Constitution, Abdullah said audaciously during a debate in the Constituent Assembly :

> "We are one hundred per cent a Sovereign body. No country, neither India nor Pakistan, can put any spoke in the wheels of our progress...to tell us that the sovereignty rests with the Indian Parliament is to challenge the very basic principles on which we have already set to work. Ours is a sovereign body with undisputed power to decide the future of even a hundred year old royal dynasty not to speak of a few big Zamindars."[7]

There were occasions when Abdullah's speeches were self-contradictory. While his speeches throughout 1952 were marked by growing disaffection with India, in January 1953 addressing a public meeting at the Congress House in Madras (now Chennai), he categorically said there was no question of reneging on the constitutional arrangements entered into between Kashmir and the Government of India. Stating that Kashmir was closely associated with India's freedom movement, he observed:

> "For India the issue in Kashmir is not one concerning territory but high principle and ideology. Kashmir is the only place to resist the two-nation theory and, in spite of being predominantly Muslim, the people resisted the influence of the Muslim League and its ideology...They did so, not because of ill-will to those who formed Pakistan, but because they honestly believed that the Muslims League's ways were fraught with danger for them as well as for the country as a whole."

Sheikh Abdullah became notoriously unpredictable.

The founder of the National Conference had no qualms about adopting the flag of his party as the State flag! How did he expect India of which Kashmir was a part to recognise the party flag as the State flag? Did he not know that these considerations were responsible for India's decision not to adopt the Congress Charka Flag as the National Flag of India?

Abdullah's irresponsible speeches and unwarranted speed shown in regard to matters which were not so very urgent were a definite indication of his manoeuvres to reverse his basic policies to implement which the Government he was leading came into being. In a speech at Ranbirsingpura delivered in May 1952, he said without the least hesitation that there was need to reconsider Kashmir's accession to India. The accession to India, he stressed, had to be of a restricted nature as long as communalism had a foothold in India. He did not hesitate to say that many Kashmiris were worried about their future after Nehru![8] But later, he explained it away stating he was wrongly reported. On 23 July 1952 while addressing the members of the Congress Party in the Parliament, Abdullah devoted a major portion of it to dispel the doubts and fears the people entertained. He said the struggle which India and Kashmir jointly carried out for twenty years was not so "brittle" as to be easily broken by one speech which was misquoted. In another speech at Ganderbal, he attributed his disillusionment with India to "Indian Communalism." This time, he did not care to question the veracity of the newspaper reports.[9]

Abdullah's unseemly haste to retire the Maharaja came under sharp criticism. In June 1952, The Jammu-Kashmir Constituent Assembly decided to terminate hereditary monarchy in tne State and to have instead an elected head, who would be removable by the people as in all republican countries. The Assembly also decided that Kashmir's future Constitution should be "wholly democratic." On 14 June, while addressing the Constituent Assembly, Abdullah insisted on the Maharaja retiring and the Yuvaraja functioning as a constitutional ruler. It was certainly open to a sovereign people to decide upon the type of government that best suited them. However, since Kashmir had still many pressing problems to solve, it was generally felt that a decision on this important but not an urgent issue could have been delayed.

Abdullah's repeated harp on the special and distinct position recognised and conceded to Kashmir by the Indian Constitution annoyed not a few. The Government of India did confer on the State certain privileges including the designation of the Prime Minister. It did provide, in the form of Article 370, a constitutional guarantee to the people of Kashmir that their distinct identity would be protected and steps taken to fulfil their aspirations. But Abdullah refused to recognise that these privileges were conferred on the State of Kashmir, which was treated differently from other Princely States, out of consideration of the brutal tribal incursions and other untoward happenings in Kashmir. All the other Indian States had, subsequent to their accession to India, become integrated into the Indian Union. Abdullah failed to realise that the specially favoured position enjoyed by Kashmir was but transitory. In the event of the people of Kashmir deciding to join the Indian Union through a fair plebiscite the existing relations would change. A meeting between Abdullah and Nehru was arranged in August in New Delhi to smooth out the difficulties and clear the doubts entertained over the relations between India and Kashmir in future. An understanding appeared to have been reached then. The need for such a meeting arose owing to the irresponsible speeches made by the leaders of the National Conference and the wrong decisions taken by the State Constituent Assembly. The decisions of the Assembly in matters like the institution of the Rajpramukh, land reforms and a separate State Flag were out of tune with the provisions of the Indian Constitution. Abdullah's denial of any inconsistencies in his attitude should again be attributed to his theory of the special status conferred on Kashmir by the Indian Constitution which granted "a full measure of freedom of initiative and action in regard to all matters of the State."

Nehru exercised remarkable patience where Abdullah was concerned despite the latter's uncalled for comments with a marked anti-India tone and revival of his advocacy for an independent Kashmir. During his visit to Kashmir in May 1953, Nehru witnessed the rapidly deteriorating political and economic plight of the State which caused no concern to Abdullah. Nehru expressed his grave concern over this situation. The land reform which was no doubt good was not properly implemented and much injustice was done to one section of the people. There was political instability as the Government was not functioning properly owing to internal squabbles. Nehru was displeased to find serious differences between Premier Abdullah and the majority of his Cabinet colleagues over the Government's indifference to the distress and discontent among the people. After his return from Europe, Nehru invited Abdullah many times to Delhi to talk to him about his misguided policy towards the State but he never responded to them. He was clearly drifting away from India. Still, Nehru was inclined to give weightage to his adherence to secularism and principle of communal amity rather than his failings and errors. He still characterised Abdullah as "an excellent man and a very effective popular leader." Even while addressing public meetings, Nehru tended to defend Abdullah. He chose to say that the activities of the Jammu Praja Parishad to create dissensions among the Kashmiris and to undo the work of Abdullah forced the latter to say "something which might have been appropriate in the context of the situation in Jammu where the speech was delivered, but out of place anywhere else." But Abdullah's explosive speeches and actions against India were rapidly going beyond the bounds of justice and fair play. When his activities became completely at variance with his past behaviour affording the Pakistani Press a chance to write that Hindu India's real intention was to gobble up Kashmir, action against him became imminent.

Two months before action was taken against him, in May 1953, Adlai Stevenson came to Kashmir. His visit was linked by the public to the widespread news of America's move for an "independent" Kashmir. Stevenson had meetings with Abdullah for three days from 1 May and the last meeting on 3 May lasted for seven hours. It was held *in camera* and so nothing was disclosed to the Pressmen from New Delhi. There was speculation that Stevenson had come to propagate the idea of an independent Kashmir. It was also rumoured that American military interests in Pakistan were related to air bases in Gilgit and that in the event of a conflict with Soviet Russia, Gilgit and Kashmir would assume strategic importance. But these were stoutly denied.

More than three months after Stevenson's visit, the *Manchester Guardian* wrote that Stevenson "seems to have listened to suggestions that the best status for Kashmir could be independence both from India and Pakistan. He mentioned this on returning to Delhi and this perhaps led some people in India to be afraid that Sheikh Abdullah might be planning to enter on his own into relations with Washington."[10] After Stevenson's departure, at the Working Committee of the National Conference held on 18 May, Abdullah surprised his colleagues by placing before them the plan of an "independent" Kashmir and pressed them to "accept it unreservedly." But his attempt was defeated on account of the overwhelming refusal to accept his plan. Undeterred by this defeat, Abdullah tried to rouse the sentiments of the people against the continued accession of Kashmir to India. In his *Id-ul-Fitre* broadcast on 14 June, he went so far as to place three alternatives before his people: accession to India; accession to Pakistan; independence and friendly relations with both.

Meanwhile, Abdullah's differences with his deputy Bakshi Ghulam Mohammad and other members of the Cabinet became so acute as to lead to a split both in the Cabinet and in the National Conference. It was also fairly well established that Abdullah was in secret correspondence with the Government of Pakistan and that Nehru had received the information that he was angling for some promise of autonomy for Kashmir as a *quid pro quo* for its accession to Pakistan.[11]

Abdullah's unbridled personal ambitions were his undoing. On 8 August 1953, his Government was dismissed by Karan Singh, the constitutional head of Kashmir. Bakshi Ghulam Mohammad, the outgoing Deputy Prime Minister, was invited to form a new Government. There were demonstrations in the Vale by Abdullah's supporters resulting in some casualties although the Pakistani Press blew these incidents out of proportions by its reports on wholesale shooting by the army and police. Pakistan chose to interpret the change of Government as an "Indian instigated *coup* by Hindu communalists against the Kashmir Muslims" which exposed Nehru's "determination to retain possession of Kashmir against the wishes of the inhabitants." Since Karan Singh and Bakshi Ghulam Mohammad could not have dismissed Abdullah's Government, Pakistan wanted to fish in troubled waters by rousing public sentiment. But she also feared that if the Muslims in Kashmir were oppressed, it would cause a new influx of refugees into Pakistan. This, coupled with permanent accession of the State to India under the new Government, would place Pakistan in a most difficult position of restraining the tribals who offered support to the Kashmiri Muslims. So Pakistan also was in a distinctly pessimistic mood.

According to S. Gopal, Nehru's biographer, the dismissal took place "by stealth of night" and Nehru's consent had been neither sought nor given for the arrest of Abdullah. Nevertheless, in the coming years Nehru's "ultimate responsibility for the detention of Sheikh Abdullah gnawed persistently at his whole sense of public values" and also surely, the trust implicit in private friendship.[12]

The vote of confidence secured by the new Government of Kashmir headed by Bakshi Ghulam Mohammad at the Convention of the National Conference, gave the lie to the allegation of *coup* in Kashmir made by the Pakistani Press. The confidence vote sponsored by fifty of the eighty members of the Constituent Assembly ensured that the new Premier would gain a similar vote of confidence in the Kashmir Legislature also.[13]

While Abdullah was in power, Bakshi, who held the home portfolio, led the section that favoured closer ties with India. Bakshi was a shrewd leader though the British records painted him as "an arch priest of unscrupulousness" and charged him with using the police and security apparatus ruthlessly for political ends. As the head of the new Government, Bakshi charged Abdullah with "apostasy" and dubbed the UN observer corps as agents of foreign powers.

J.J.S. Garner's portrayal of the dissimilarities between Sheikh Abdullah and Bakshi Ghulam Mohammad reproduced below, exposes his delight in running down Indian leaders:

> "We have simply changed one rogue for another. But Abdullah and Bakshi are very different types of rogues. Bakshi is a bully where Abdullah is subtle. Bakshi is a realist, Abdullah an idealist. Both are unscrupulous – Bakshi for material gains, Abdullah more in the realm of ideas. Bakshi is ruthless and efficient, Abdullah is not. Bakshi is feared, Abdullah revered...Bakshi has nothing of the communist about him. He would probably make use of any means to gain his own ends, but he certainly has nothing to complain of about a capitalist society. All this means that the Vale is likely to be more effectively administered in future than it has in the past, that Bakshi sees the material benefits of Indian association without bothering about its ideological drawbacks, and that, even if he does not inspire a large following, he has other means of ensuring his popularity and satisfying himself that his will is carried out. In a word, I do not think

that Abdullah wanted to persuade Kashmiris to vote for India: I believe that Bakshi does and will."[14]

Bakshi's first act after assuming power was to announce that Kashmir was an integral part of India. Later, he announced his Government's intention to seek the approval of the Constituent Assembly when it met in October 1953, for the immediate ratification of Kashmir's accession to India. Pakistan feared that these developments in Kashmir would mar the prospects of a settlement resulting from the Delhi Agreement the two Prime Ministers reached in August 1953.[15]

Towards the end of January 1954, there were talks between the Government of India and the representatives of the Kashmir Government on the full implementation of the Delhi Agreement of July 1952 between Nehru and Abdullah. It was decided to extend the jurisdiction of the Supreme Court to Jammu and Kashmir subject to the proviso that the Kashmir Government's land reform legislation would not be repugnant to the terms of the Indian Constitution. The other important decisions taken were: (i) In return for its surrender of Income Tax and Customs dues to the Central Government and early removal of the States Customs' barrier, the Central Government should make an annual grant of Rs 2 crore to the Kashmir Government; (ii) the Government of Kashmir should surrender the power to legislate on certain (unspecified) subjects not covered by the Instrument of Accession to the Union Parliament; and (iii) Application to Kashmir the emergency provisions of Article 352 of the Indian Constitution (Declaration of Emergency by the President) in case of internal disturbance "at the request of or with the concurrence of the Government of the State." The Press reports added to these that the Delhi Agreement would be submitted to the Constituent Assembly for its ratification during its session commencing from 3 February 1954. With the decision of the leaders of the National Conference to throw in their lot with India in accordance with the abiding interest of the people of Jammu and Kashmir, permanent accession to India was considered a certainty. It was expected to be made clear by a formal resolution of the Constituent Assembly.[16]

US Arms Aid to Pakistan: India's Reaction

Towards the end of 1953, Pakistan decided to negotiate a military aid agreement with the US and a treaty with Turkey in this regard. There was absolutely no urgent need for such an agreement. In concocting stories to justify the arms aid, none could excel the "quidnuncs" of Pakistan's capital.

They and the foreign correspondents in Karachi lost no time in flashing round the world a new story that the Pakistan Intelligence Department had unearthed the existence of a secret pact which India had with Communist China and Soviet Russia to help her in the event of a general outbreak of war. And the story went further to say that this report of the Pakistan Secret Services drove Pakistan to accept American aid.[17] Whatever the cause, the decision was a highly disturbing factor to India. Even Britain was not at all in favour of the aid. The British political circles entertained serious doubts about the wisdom of this step to fortify Pakistan at a time when international relations were smooth. Britain was unhappy that the US had planned everything without a word to her first. The idea was conveyed to her only in January 1954. Britain was aware that the direct linking of the US aid with a Middle East defence arrangements would arouse the worst suspicions of India and aggravate her reactions. India would view it as primarily intended to strengthen Pakistan against her.[18] Britain entered a caveat against massive American arms commitments but, on second thought, did not push her misgivings to the point of opposition. Pakistan's stout denials in this regard also drove Britain to conclude "nothing very much was afoot."

There was another crucial factor that prevented Britain from raising any objection. If Pakistan were to get 25,000,000 dollars worth of aid from the US to buy military equipments, she would definitely like Pakistan to use the aid for the off-shore purchase of British equipment which would preserve the uniformity of military equipment in the Pakistani forces. Britain knew India would certainly protest against this transaction but her argument was that she could not refuse arms supply to Pakistan and it was in her own interest to supply them.[19] Krishna Menon told the British Foreign Secretary that if the British Government participated in the transaction by supplying any part of the armaments in the form of "off-shore purchases," it would create the worst possible impression in India.[20]

Mohammad Ali Bogra, who had all along been using a language that was mild and moderate, with no show of hostility towards India, changed it into a strong one of accusations against her after deciding to accept the US military aid. His speeches on the effects of Pakistani rearmament on the Kashmir dispute revealed his unwillingness to sign a "No War" pact with India. This was a clear proof of Pakistan's intention to keep alive the Kashmir crisis and shut the door to a final settlement with India on it.

What distressed India most on this issue were the unconvincing explanations of John Foster Dulles to justify America's ill-considered move.

Dulles told the Indian Ambassador in Washington that military aid had to be extended to a strategically placed country that could be relied upon to use the arms and equipment to fight communism. Communist menace thus came in very handy to the American. Stating that India would do well not to construe American strengthening of Pakistan militarily to fight communism as an act of unfriendliness towards her, Dulles made an illogical statement: America had cut off the supply of arms to Israel and the Arab States because of the likelihood of their being used against each other but "this consideration did not however apply to Pakistan who had only a fraction of the area and population of India, and was so much weaker than India in every way that there could be no likelihood of any arms supplied by the US being used against India." Evidently, his memory was too short to remember the event of 1947.

Dulles told the Indian Ambassador bluntly that in the painful context of a solution to the Kashmir problem appearing very remote, America could not halt her general policy of "a military build up in a vital area" in immediate danger of communist threat. N.R. Pillai, in talking to the British High Commissioner about this, appreciated the awkward predicament Britain was in where the military aid was concerned. She could not openly oppose it in view of her special relations with both the US and Pakistan. But Pillai clearly warned him of the consequences of this move throughout South East Asia and also Middle East not to speak of the vehement reactions to it in India. He wanted India's apprehension to be conveyed to the British Prime Minister.[21]

But the British Government's response to India's concern was totally devoid of warmth and sympathy. It said that if the Security Council reopened discussion on the Kashmir crisis which then remained suspended and found there was no progress on account of the US military aid, the UK Government would not countenance India's case. It was an admonition to India to beware of losing the sympathy of a majority of the Security Council. Britain asked her High Commissioner in India to "inject" this into Pillai.[22]

The US military aid to Pakistan and the associated scheme for promoting closer links between Pakistan and Turkey by some kind of military collaboration were intended to provide a basis for the collective organisation of the Middle East Defence. The possibility of basing Middle East defence upon the "Northern tier" countries extending from Turkey to Pakistan was actually adumbrated by Dulles at an Anglo-American bi-partite meeting on Middle East Affairs. It was held in Washington about July 1953. But he did take into account the difficulty of implementing it in view of the difficult situation in Kashmir.[23] In October 1953, the Pakistani Commander-in-Chief succeeded in convincing the US authorities in confidential confabulations that there was a strong case for them to grant Pakistan a moderate sum of about 25 million dollars of military aid. All this was a closely guarded secret. Even HMG advised the authorities on the need for secrecy. However, despite all the warnings, the programme became public knowledge.[24] This created strong resentment in India where the military aid was viewed as calamitous involving the Indian sub-continent in the cold war. Military assistance to the neighbouring Pakistan with whom India was not on best of terms would make Pakistan more aggressive "wielding a big stick with respect to Kashmir." There was the further complication of India's role in world affairs which was variously described as the concept of "No War Area" or "Neutral Group" or "Neutral Bloc." The fear that the military aid to Pakistan would destroy the "neutrality" of the sub-continent and bring the cold war to India's borders greatly agitated India. Against the possibility of such a catastrophe India bitterly protested. Her apprehension was intensified by rumours that Pakistan would give America bases and also form an alliance in return for the aid though Pakistan and western powers dismissed them as groundless.

There was much force in India's contention that there was a clear distinction between military supplies purchased from a country's own resources and military supplies given to it or purchased from the funds given to it by another country. The former carried no obligation of any kind in relation to the purchasing country's external policy. But the latter even if no strings were attached carried at least a moral obligation on the part of the receiving country which limited its freedom of action. But the US Government did nothing to reassure India on this point.[25]

Meanwhile, the US President sent a personal message to Nehru in January 1954 through his Ambassador to India George V. Allen. It was an assurance to the Indian Prime Minister that the US military aid to Pakistan did not in any way affect the friendship between the two countries. The message stated that the contemplated accord between Pakistan and Turkey and the US military aid to the former were intended to attain the goal of peace. The American President categorically declared that if there was any misuse of the aid by a move directed against India, he would "undertake immediate action inside and outside the UN to thwart such measures."[26] While replying to questions about the US military aid to Pakistan and also referring to the message of the US President to him, Nehru said in the Indian Parliament that the US military aid posed a danger as much to Asia as to India and that in the existing situation the most India could do was to express her point of view to her friends without exerting pressure.[27]

On 1 March 1954, Nehru made a statement at the House of People wherein referring to the American military aid, he openly said that this new development had to be considered in the light of Pakistan's repeated refusal of India's offer of a "No War" pact. More importantly, he said that in the context of the American military aid to Pakistan, one of the parties to the Kashmir dispute, the US members of the Kashmir observers team could no longer be treated as neutral.[28] By way of substantiating his statement he said that the American members of the team could no longer be treated as neutrals since the US military aid was a form of intervention in the dispute between India and Pakistan. As such "their presence appears to us to be improper," he expressed. At the end of 1953, out of about 100 observers on the cease-fire team representing nine countries, 14 belonged to the US. Nehru demanded that the US observers should get off the team in Kashmir. The Parliament cheered him when he made a caustic comment on Eisenhower's personal message to him explaining the US decision to grant military aid to Pakistan for defence purposes and offering the same treatment to India also. He remarked "the President has done less than justice to us or to himself. If we object to military aid being given to Pakistan, we would be hypocrites and unprincipled opportunists to accept it ourselves."[29]

The UN Secretary General Dag Hammarskjöld was provoked by Nehru's statement about the position of the American members of the Kashmir observers team in the context of the US arms aid to Pakistan. He took objection to Nehru's questioning the propriety of the US personnel to serve as neutral observers in Kashmir. In the first place, the demand for their withdrawal did not arise at that point of time. Secondly, there was no complaint that they did not remain neutral. The crux of the whole argument of Nehru was that the American observers themselves would be in an embarrassing position as thereafter they would have to equip and train the Pakistani army – a situation which the US itself would be keen to avoid. One important remark of the Secretary General was his description of the US personnel as "denationalised." Actually, they were not "denationalised" as they continued to belong to the US Government. Because, the representatives of the various member countries serving in the UN would not cut their moorings completely. In fact, it was not expected of them. Besides, though the officers selected as observers by the UN would be paid their local expenses by the latter, they would receive their salaries only from the mother countries whose nationals they were. America herself had claimed in another context that the Americans serving in the UN Secretariat did not become "denationalised" on that account.[30]

Kashmir's Accession Ratified

On 3 February 1954, the new Constituent Assembly of Kashmir elected on the basis of adult franchise met. It took up for consideration the reports submitted by the Basic Principles Committee and the Citizenship and Fundamental Rights Committee. During the debate on the reports, a speaker expressed his disagreement with certain aspects of the report particularly Rau's assurance in the Security Council in 1951 that the Constituent Assembly could only express an opinion but not take any decision on accession. Notwithstanding the member's dissent, the Assembly accepted the reports unanimously through a resolution on 6 February 1954. Bakshi said, perhaps in reply to those who pointed out that the Constitution deprived Kashmir of the right to secede from the Indian Union, "We irrevocably acceded to India more than six years ago and to-day we are only fulfilling the formalities to our unbreakable bonds with India." The general opinion in the State was that the beneficiaries of a plebiscite being the people of Kashmir it was for them to decide whether a plebiscite was at all necessary. As such India could not force a plebiscite against their wishes to honour an earlier commitment. One school of thought opined that although Kashmir's political future had been a closed chapter, it did not in any way "affect India's position in the UN as regards the Kashmir question. A free plebiscite is certain to bring back the area now under foreign occupation."[31]

Kashmir's accession to India that took place on 26 October 1947 was ratified rendering thereby the oft-emphasised plebiscite null and void. Kashmir had, during the six years, registered many constructive achievements including the abolition of monarchy and *jagirdari*, and free election of the Head of the State. These developments were too much for Pakistan to stomach. Reference has already been made to the change of Mohammad Ali's attitude towards India for the worse. This should be ascribed to the lure of the American military aid and Zafrullah's speeches replete with threats of renewed aggression in Kashmir and open declaration for the use of US military aid presaging the revival of the cry for a war against India.

Mohammad Ali complained to the CRO on 9 February about the resolution of the Kashmir Constituent Assembly to ratify the accession of Kashmir to India which was violative of his agreement with Nehru and an insult to the UN. He expressed the hope that Nehru would repudiate the

Assembly's resolution. But Nehru said in the Council of States in February 1954 that it would be completely wrong for him to repudiate the decisions of the elected Assembly of Kashmir which was perfectly justified to declare and decide what it chose to do. He also admitted that India had to stand and had always stood by her commitments whether international or otherwise "subject to such changes as might come about by other events. We do not propose to denounce or change any assurance or commitments we have made internationally. But we have to consider them in the new context of events." By this he meant the US military aid to Pakistan.

On 25 February 1954, Mohammad Ali officially announced that the Government of the US had agreed to give military aid to Pakistan under the US Mutual Security Legislation. On 2 April, Pakistan signed the Turko-Pakistan pact aimed at friendly cooperation with Turkey which was ratified at Ankara on 12 June. On 19 May, the Governments of the US and Pakistan signed a Mutual Defence Assistance Agreement under which the US Government would provide military equipment and training assistance to the Pakistani Armed Forces. This agreement was in response to the Pakistan Government's request for military aid. President Eisenhower wholeheartedly extended the help on the ground that Pakistan was eligible to such a grant under the provisions of the Mutual Security Act of 1951.

The US Government came under severe fire for the agreement signed with Pakistan from Senator Fulbright, Democrat from Arkansas and Member of the Senate Foreign Relations Committee (SFRC). He went so explicitly on record as opposing the US military aid to Pakistan which was given over his objection. He urged that the Congressional Record should show very clearly his disapproval "because in the future, when the results of this policy are evident to all, I want it to be clear where the responsibility rests." He said this "unwise and improvident" decision was to a large extent promoted by the members of the SFRC who were highly critical of Nehru's neutralism. It was dangerous to alienate either India or Pakistan when tension was already at its height between the two he said and added forcefully: "When the investigating committees or historians of the future are trying to ascertain why we lost the friendship of India, I want it to be perfectly clear where the responsibility is to be placed."[32]

Puffed up with the prospect of US military aid, Mohammad Ali made a tour of America after signing the agreement on the deal. During his sojourn there, he did not lose a single opportunity to tell the American public that there was absolutely no chance of Pakistan reaching an understanding with

India on the Kashmir question and also on the canal waters through direct negotiations. However, with the World Bank circles being thoroughly convinced of the reasonableness of India's stand, he was compelled to resume discussions on the latter problem. But he refused to budge on the Kashmir issue though he dropped his threat of taking it back to the Security Council.

Mohammad Ali was forced to cut short his American tour and return hurriedly to Pakistan to quell the disturbance that was brewing there in his absence. Of course, he chose to dismiss it as a passing phase of "constitutional bickering." But these constitutional developments had certainly impelled Mohammad Ali to adopt a more realistic attitude towards the Indo-Pakistan relations.

Demilitarisation in Kashmir as a condition to precede a plebiscite was the only issue that remained to be settled when the talks that began in August 1953 broke off on account of US military aid to Pakistan. Nehru justly pointed out that there could be no real demilitarisation in the new context of American military aid to one of the two parties "within easy striking distance of the demilitarised zone." Though there was no change in India's stand on this, Nehru accepted to resume the parleys in keeping with his policy of not rejecting an invitation to settle differences peacefully.

Dubious Western Pacts in Asia

Apart from the American military aid, which gave a fillip to Pakistan's calumny against India, another opportunity presented itself to her to carry her hate propaganda to a larger audience. It was the formation of anti-Communist bastions by America and Britain in Asia. Pakistan was inducted as a member of two of these fora and she exploited this position to raise out of context the Kashmir question against India.

The world situation changed in the early 1950s with three events – the election of Dwight Eisenhower with resounding victory to the American Presidency in November 1952, the death of Prime Minister Joseph Stalin of USSR in March 1953 and the emergence of Communist China as a third world power. The sequel was, from mid-1954, both America and Britain were actively engaged in setting up security zones to fight communism in Asia. Serious talks were held between the British Prime Minister Anthony Eden and the American Secretary of State John Foster Dulles on 14 August 1954. The upshot of these talks was the birth of the South East Asian Treaty Organisation (SEATO). Britain announced her agreement with like-minded nations to establish a collective security arrangement in South East Asia in accordance with the purposes and principles of the UN Charter "to strengthen the fabric of peace in the general area of South East Asia and South West Pacific." Accordingly, the delegates of Australia, France, New Zealand, Pakistan, The Philippine Republic, Thailand, the UK and the US met at Manila on 8 September 1954 and signed on 9 September the South East Asia Collective Defence Treaty (SEACDT). It arose as a pact for military cooperation against the external pressure of communists and revolutionary subversion. Communist China's occupation of Tibet and the invasion of South Korea by North Korea in 1950 without a formal declaration of war were cited as grave reminders of this danger to South East Asia which lacked industrial and military resources to fight the communist forces. Later, the SEACDT, whose original objective was military cooperation, was expanded to include the technical, economic and cultural fields. It thus allowed itself to intrude into the problems of underdeveloped countries. The organisation was keen to stabilise its position in South East Asia after the Geneva Conference of April-July 1954, which was convened to settle the future of Korea and Indo-China. Though nothing was achieved in the case of Korea at this Conference, an armistice ending the Indo-China War was signed on 21 July 1954. The British policy at this time of the Geneva Conference on Indo-China and thereafter was marked by the twin objectives of achieving a peaceful political settlement on Indo-China "without appeasing the communists" and securing an effective defence organisation in South East Asia "without offending Asian, and especially Indian opinion." The new organisation was regarded by the UN as the logical corollary to the Geneva Agreement of 1954. Britain and other Western powers did not expect India with her non-alignment policy to join the Treaty. In fact, all the five Colombo Powers (Burma, Ceylon (now Sri Lanka), India, Indonesia and Pakistan), with the exception of Pakistan, decided against participation in the Manila Conference and the SEACDT.

On 19 February 1955, at the first meeting held at Bangkok, the Treaty came into force. It was here that the member countries agreed that the term SEATO should be used in preference to SEACDT, since the former was already in popular use and was easily pronounceable.

For Pakistan, the SEATO was primarily an instrument to strengthen herself against India not to speak of the additional economic aid she would receive from the US. But Britain said she was firm that her policy should be to "restrain the Pakistanis from seeking to impart an anti-Indian slant to SEATO."

There arose another defensive and economic organisation – the Baghdad Pact – so called because it was first signed at Baghdad between

Turkey and Iraq in February 1955. Later, during the same year, Britain, Pakistan and Iran also signed the Pact. It was actually evolved by Britain to maintain treaty relations and air bases in Iraq notwithstanding the opposition from Iraqi nationalists. Though the Pact contributed to bring in some stability in the Middle East, its existence aroused the hostility of the more militant members of the Arab League. This apart, the attempts to secure Jordan's adherence resulted in riots in Amman which presaged the decline of British influence there. The Anglo-French attack on Egypt dealt a mortal blow to the Baghdad Pact. When Pakistan called a meeting of the Pact in January 1957, Iraq refused to participate in any meeting that included Britain. America did not want to take the place of Britain in the Pact. This caused great disappointment to Turkey, Iran and Pakistan. After Iraq left it in 1958 when King Faisal II was assassinated and the country became a republic, the Pact was renamed the Central Treaty Organisation (CENTO) and its headquarters shifted to Ankara.

To dispel Nehru's anxieties over Pakistani membership in the Pact and its implications on Indo-Pakistan relations, Prime Minister Anthony Eden said: "I cannot see that Pakistan's military position has been strengthened through membership of the Pact in such a way as could cause alarm in India. No military supplies have been sent from the UK to Pakistan in consequence of the Pact."[33]

But Pakistan's sole reason for joining the regional Pacts was to earn the sympathy and support of the countries of the Western bloc in her disputes with India. She was confident that her membership would enable her to use their platforms to pour out her venom on India.

India's Distrust of Military Pacts

Nehru's intense hatred for western colonialism and racial discrimination was too well-known to Britain to ignore. In fact this attitude moulded the lives of Nehru and many other contemporary Indian statesmen. Their sensitivity to the SEATO and the Baghdad Pact was natural. Nehru proved the stern foe of these alliances as he believed them to be symptomatic of an indirect return of western imperialism to its erstwhile colonies. He viewed the pacts or military alliances as "a symbol of disturbance, insecurity, disunity and trouble." Though no one would challenge SEATO's genuine object to stop aggression and secure peace, in reality "it increases the insecurity in people's minds... if we want peace we must avoid doing things which create an atmosphere of war," he said.[34] Nehru considered all collective defence treaties as tending to divide the world into two hostile blocs. His inflexible objection to the SEATO in particular was that having only three Asian members – Pakistan, Philippines and Thailand – it was not representative of Asian opinion in general. To be more precise, it was "unsupported" by several countries in the danger zone. And this amounted to European interference in Asian affairs which would doubtless provoke communist reactions. Embarrassed by some of Nehru's comments, Britain said in support of SEATO that it was purely defensive; that its signatories had a perfect right in conformity with the Charter of the UN to organise themselves for their own defence against potential aggression; that the idea of a war between the two Commonwealth countries of India and Pakistan was unthinkable; and that when communist China had, by her words and deeds, cast them for the role of defence, one could not fault the parties to Treaty on this. But Nehru refused to accept these arguments in defence of the SEATO. In view of India's opposition to the SEATO, Britain rejected the proposal to hold the second meeting of the organisation at Lahore stating that it might be regarded an "unnecessary provocative step."

India's deep distrust of military pacts was shared by Listowel who was the Secretary of State for India in August 1947. He doubted their efficacy to curb communism in Asia. He was frank in admitting that the SEATO had done more harm than good to India. During a debate in the House of Lords, he said: "I fear that in these days, taking into account the strong feelings of nationalism in Asia, any alliance which is predominantly non-Asian in character, will antagonise the very people whose freedom we want to preserve."[35]

The collective defence treaties and pacts were said to have been born out of the concern of the UK and some other European powers and the US to contain communism and to defend South East Asia against any external aggression. There was a very strong doubt whether the angst of the great powers was genuine. Had it been so, it was not reflected in their attitude to and dealings with Pakistan who was the aggressor in the 1947 undeclared war on Kashmir. Pakistan was not only never blamed by the UK or the UN for her abetment and unstinted help extended to the crude, turbulent and monstrous tribesmen in their incursions into Kashmir but was rewarded by being made a member of pacts to fight territorial aggressions in the South East Asian region!

References

1. J.J.S. Garner to Fowler, 1 Sep. 1953, DO/35/6646.
2. *Ibid*, UK HC (I) to CRO, 20 Aug. 1953.

3. *The Hindu*, 3 Aug. 2008.
4. FRUS, 1948, Vol. V, Part I, pp. 291-94.
5. Nehru to Abdullah, 10 May 1949, *SWJN*, Vol. 11, p. 115.
6. Nehru to Vijayalakshmi Pandit, 17 May & 18 July 1949, *Vijayalakshmi Pandit Papers*.
7. *Ibid.*
8. UK HC (I) to CRO, 16 April 1952, DO/35/6631.
9. *The Hindu*, 11 August 1953.
10. *Manchester Guardian*, 17 Aug. 1953.
11. R.W.D. Fowler's Note, 31 Aug. 1953, DO/35/6646.
12. Cited in Katherine Frank, *Life of Indira Nehru Gandhi*, p. 234.
13. *The Hindu*, 19 Sep. 1953.
14. J.J.S. Garner to Fowler, 1 Sep. 1953, DO/35/6646.
15. *Ibid*, CRO to all UK High Commissioners, 2 Sep. 1953.
16. UK HC (I) to CRO, 2 Feb. 1954, FO/371/112308.
17. *The Hindu*, 2 Jan. 1954.
18. Minute submitted to the Secretary of State, 4 Jan. 1954, FO/371/112314.
19. Selwyn Lloyd's Brief, 15 Jan. 1954, FO/371/112315.
20. *Ibid*, Menon's Statement, 21Jan. 1954.
21. UK HC (I) to CRO, 30 Nov. 1953, DO/35/6646.
22. CRO to HC (I), 25 Jan. 1954, FO/371/112308.
23. W.D. Allen's Note, 5 Jan. 1954, FO/371/112314.
24. Memorandum by the Foreign Secretary, 5 Jan. 1954, PREM/11/1520.
25. UK HC (I) to CRO, 2 Jan. 1954, FO/371/112314.
26. Eisenhower to Nehru, 19 Jan. 1954, FO/371/112318.
27. *Ibid*, UK HC (I) to CRO, 20 Feb. 1954.
28. *Ibid*, UK HC (I) to CRO, 1 March 1954.
29. *Washington Post*, 2 March 1954.
30. *The Hindu*, 13 March 1954.
31. UK HC (I) to CRO, 14 Feb. 1954, FO/371/112308.
32. *Congressional Record - Senate*, 2 March 1954, pp. 2351-52, FO/371/ 112319.
33. Anthony Eden to Nehru (date not given), DO/35/6578.
34. SEATO Document, UK Government Overseas Information Services, DO/35/ 8870.
35. Extract from *Hansard* (House of Lords), 30 Nov. 1955, p. 988.

11

Two More Unsuccessful UN Missions

Pakistan's acceptance of the American military aid and her tie up with Western and Middle Eastern military blocs had changed the international scenario. The impact of these developments on India and more importantly on Kashmir was substantial. Pakistan was not unaware of this. With Mohammad Ali Bogra as the Prime Minister, the Indo-Pakistan relations showed some vague signs of improvement. On 28 January 1955, Governor General Ghulam Mohammad of Pakistan himself came to Delhi to meet Nehru and hand him a four-point proposal for a plebiscite in, and partition of, Kashmir. In his reply to it on 27 February, Nehru expressed his appreciation of Ghulam Mohammad's welcome approach to the problem by keeping out third party intervention and relying on mutual trust to settle the problem. However, Nehru, who stood for the *status quo*, conveyed to Ghulam Mohammad his "mixed reactions" to his proposal. While he welcomed Ghulam Mohammad's "approach of mutual trust," he was against any "upset in the Jammu and Kashmir State."

The matter was pursued and Bogra met Nehru again on 14, 15 and 16 May along with Iskander Mirza, Pakistan Minister of the Interior. On the Indian side, Govind Ballabh Pant, Minister for Home Affairs was present. They reached an agreement to reduce the number of border forces to minimise the clashes between the two armed forces. But there was no understanding worth the name on Kashmir. Both Bogra and Mirza pointed out that the people of Pakistan would accept no solution that completely ignored their wishes and demands. They were very keen that something had to be done "to make them feel that they had gained something." The leaders also said that they had come to Delhi because their Governor General had given them "to understand that there was a broad acceptance of a new base for negotiations." In view of this expectation, they did not want to break the talks but "part amicably."

On 17 May, the visitors from Pakistan met Nehru again and showed their map marking the partition of Kashmir on a communal basis. Nehru could not accept this. Maulana Azad who was present intervened and offered to add "a bit of Mirpur" to Poonch in the transfer. Thereupon, a conciliatory Joint *Communiqué* was issued on 18 May which covered a wide range of subjects of common concern. About Kashmir, it stated that the subject had been discussed "fully in all its aspects" and that it had been decided "to continue the talks at a later stage."[1] Bogra chose to "picturesquely but cryptically" call the *Communiqué* "The 1955 Approach."[2] This was the best part of the whole show.

Pakistan's Active Role in Pacts

In August 1955, there was again a change of Government in Pakistan. And as usual, it was accompanied by a renewed outburst of hostility against India. Chaudhri Mohammad Ali's assumption of office as Prime Minister in the place of Bogra was no exception to this rule. In fact this time the anti-India campaigns were more virulent than on previous occasions. The Pakistanis indulged in violent demonstrations, slogan shouting and picketing of the offices of the Indian High Commission in Karachi, Lahore and Dacca. The Pakistani Press was not a whit behind the public in publishing immoderately worded demands. There was a strong feeling in many quarters that the eruption of violence was Government inspired. Whether this was true or not, the Government certainly gained by these unlawful activities. The Pakistani leaders had long found the slogan "War over Kashmir" very convenient to divert public attention from the internal problems. In the present context they were worried about the drastic consequences of the delay in framing a constitution for Pakistan.

Situation in Azad Kashmir was even worse than in Pakistan. Popular discontent was boiling up against the tyranny of the officials of the Pakistan Ministry for Kashmir Affairs which was a "hot-bed of intrigue, corruption, misappropriation of funds and maladministration." When the unrest assumed serious dimensions, the Prime Minister had to rush to Muzafarrabad where a memorandum demanding among other things elections for a popular legislature was presented to him. With such stark facts staring the Pakistani administration in the face, it was indeed puzzling that Prime Minister Chaudhri Mohammad Ali could not see the incongruity of the wild allegation about the "tyranny of Bharati rule" in Kashmir![3]

After the release of the Joint *Communiqué* of the two Prime ministers in May 1955, the Kashmir question was left in abeyance. Pakistan was much perturbed about this, unnecessarily, as she was already in the grip of many internal problems. As usual, she started urging Britain that the Kashmir problem should be taken up again by the Security Council. Pakistan's anxiety was aggravated by the visit of the Russian dignitaries – Marshal Bulganin and Nikita Khrushchev – to India in November 1955. She was extremely indignant over the gestures of friendship displayed by the Russian leaders, the statement of Khrushchev in Srinagar and the Joint Statement signed by Nehru and the Soviet leaders. Khrushchev's statement was that the people of Kashmir, who had already given the verdict that Kashmir was one of the States of India, did not want to become a toy in the hands of imperialist powers. But this was what exactly some imperial powers were trying to do under the pretext of supporting the Pakistani case on the Kashmir question. He also exposed an unfriendly act of Pakistan in making a suggestion to the Soviet leaders not to visit Kashmir and Afghanistan. He chose to call this an unprecedented interference in other people's affairs.[4] The Joint Statement said that peace had never been furthered by military alliances and regional blocs which only "widen the frontiers of cold-war, cause instability, fear and tension and hamper peaceful development..."[5] These events led Pakistan to conclude that the visit of the Soviet statesmen had done grave disservice to Indo-Pakistan relations. Feeling that whatever hope was there earlier of an agreement on Kashmir was lost, Pakistan was bent upon bringing the dispute to the attention of the Security Council.

Sensing that some countries had become jittery about the visit of the Soviet leaders to India, Nehru reiterated at a public meeting in Calcutta that the basic policy of India was not to join any camp or alliance and that friendship with the Soviet Union was not aimed against anyone. Highlighting India's choice to follow an independent foreign policy, he said that she "could not do otherwise unless she was false to herself and to all she stood for."

Despite Pakistan's insistence on reopening the Kashmir question, Britain was determined to avoid it for some time as, in her view, it would definitely anger the Indians and make them more inclined to listen to "Russian blandishments." Britain was well aware of India's sensitivity to her (Britain's) alliance with Pakistan in the Baghdad Pact. The British Prime Minister's assurance that the Pact was not aggressive in character and that it was designed, under Article 51 of the UN Charter, to provide an effective machinery to meet the threat of international communism to the Middle East hardly convinced Nehru.

India's resentment at the possibility of Britain's military aid to Pakistan was deepened by America's announcement that she would have military and political liaison with the members of the Baghdad Pact and would spend 20 million dollars immediately on improving air fields and other installations in Pakistan. Added to these were the reports in the Karachi newspapers that Pakistan, as member of the Baghdad Pact, intended to ask additional arms from both the UK and the US. Against these disquieting factors, Britain summoned courage to stress the need to retain Indian goodwill and avoid raking up the Kashmir issue in the Security Council at that juncture.

India knew only too well that these alliances of which the UK and the US were powerful members provided Pakistan a further opportunity to continue at international levels her campaigns of hate and holy war against India which she had been doing since 1948. As usual, Britain chose to downplay it maintaining that such alliances were perfectly consistent with the UN Charter. Before long, Britain reneged on her assurances and promises to India. In its final *Communiqué* issued on 8 March 1956, the SEATO Council meeting held at Karachi reaffirmed Pakistan's western frontier along the Durand Line[6] and emphasised from that forum the need for an early settlement of the Kashmir problem. At a meeting of the National Assembly, the Pakistan Foreign Minister Hamidul Huq Choudhury openly said that as far as Pakistan was concerned, "the most notable achievement of the SEATO is the joint reaffirmation by its members of our stand on Kashmir." The Baghdad Pact meeting held at Teheran in April 1956 included the Kashmir question in the stated purposes of the Pact besides referring to it in the final *Communiqué* of 19 April. The text of India's protest against these breaches which was handed by Foreign Secretary M.J. Desai to the UK Deputy High Commissioner stated:

> "The Government of India wholly reject the competence of the Baghdad Pact and its Council to pronounce on the question of Kashmir irrespective of the contents of any such pronouncements. Further, they would like to point out to the Government of the UK that Kashmir is one of the States in the Indian Union. The discussion of Kashmir or the inclusion of it in pronouncements without the consent of the Government of India is not consistent with the respect of the sovereignty of the Union of India which the Government of India have the right to expect from the United Kingdom Government.

> "... They deplore more particularly the UK's participation in this matter having regard to the known views and feelings of India and the protests the Government of India have made to them in respect of a similar occurrence at the SEATO conference..."[7]

Britain was unhappy over the developments at the meetings of the SEATO and the Baghdad Pact for which Chaudhri Mohammad Ali was responsible. The latter was bent upon making a reference to Kashmir at the meeting of the SEATO Council. Britain could not effectively resist Pakistan at this meeting as it was held on the soil of Pakistan – Karachi. Britain found two more factors in favour of Pakistan: (i) the fact that Kashmir was not under discussion in any other forum at that time had emboldened Pakistan to do what she did at the meetings of SEATO and Baghdad Pact; and (ii) the more important factor was that Pakistan keenly felt that the statements of the Soviet leaders during their visit to India required a rebuttal from Pakistan's allies. Under the circumstances, all that Britain could do was to warn Pakistan that Chaudhri Mohammad Ali's insistence on a reference to Kashmir disregarding Britain's advice, would get her nowhere as Pakistan was going farther from the objective she had held before the SEATO Conference and that public reference to Kashmir would ruin any chance of Britain influencing Nehru at the Prime Ministers' Conference in June.

Britain failed to convince India by her assertions that the merits of the case of Kashmir were not discussed at the meetings and that Britain did not take sides.

Apart from joining regional pacts, Pakistan demonstrated her hatred of India through an excessive show of friendliness to Portugal. When India's dispute with Portugal took the form of an economic boycott of Goa and the snapping off of diplomatic relations with the latter, Pakistan proceeded with indecent haste to afford facilities to Portugal to keep her hold on her Indian pockets. She allowed her Press to indulge in anti-Indian and pro-Portuguese comments on the Goa question. Pakistan used such phrases as the "war-mongering lust of Bharat" being directed towards independent Portuguese territories in India![8] She also allowed an air-link to be established between Goa and Karachi to enable Portugal to continue her supply line for her troops in Goa, Daman and Diu. Suhrawardy, who was made Prime Minister on 12 September 1956, took a trip to Lisbon under the pretext of meeting the Premier and the Foreign Minister of Portugal but really to start a campaign to defame and denigrate India in that European capital.

The SEATO *Communiqué* of March 1956 was enough provocation for a fresh strong reaction in India. As a corollary of this Indian reaction came the demand from Pakistan to reopen the Kashmir question for public debate though such debates served only to harden the attitudes of both the countries. Although initially Britain found it very hard to persuade Pakistan to desist from referring the dispute back to the Security Council, ultimately she succeeded in convincing her of the futility of such a move at that time. There was some hesitation on the part of Pakistan also to make a move. This led Britain to infer that Pakistan had given up the idea of a fresh reference to Kashmir at the Security Council.

But as ill-luck would have it, the UN's role in the Suez crisis at the end of 1956, buoyed up Pakistan to follow suit. She insisted on a similar treatment for the Kashmir issue also. Britain referred the Suez crisis to the UN because she received no support from America who took a pro-Egypt stand. In the circumstance, Britain could not prevent Pakistan from reopening the Kashmir question at the UN. India interpreted the line taken by the UK as extending support to Pakistan on the Kashmir case mainly to seek revenge for her criticism of Britain's policy on the Suez crisis. In the Suez case, India was angry over the Anglo-French assault on Suez, which according to her amounted to a revival of western imperialism on non-whites. The Suez crisis and the subsequent debates in the Security Council on Kashmir in 1957 witnessed the low watermark in Indo-British relations. There were certain other factors which also reinforced India's firm belief that where Kashmir was concerned, Britain would not abandon her traditional policy of partiality to Pakistan. The belief was strengthened by Suhrawardy's fulsome praise of Britain in public for her support to Pakistan in the Security Council and his assertions that in the event of a war between India and Pakistan, the latter could count on support and assistance from her SEATO and Baghdad Pact allies.[9]

Two Ill-fated Resolutions

Pakistan's one and only intention was to get the UN censure India on the ground that she was responsible for the deadlock over demilitarisation. Her delegates in New York were busily engaged in lobbying the Western powers to achieve this goal. In January 1957, when there were unmistakable signs of peace and prosperity in Kashmir, the Government of Pakistan sent a note to the Security Council to revive the discussion on Kashmir which was stated to be facing a grave threat to peace. Zafrullah even spoke of a "reign of terror" in Kashmir. All these were a crude attempt to stir up anti-India feeling in Kashmir. Yielding to Pakistan's misrepresentations, the Security Council which had a "closed mind on the subject" carried on a "rambling debate" over Kashmir although there was not even a vestige of justification for such a debate at that point of time.

Hitherto, the pro-Pakistan Western bloc which reigned supreme in Lake Success closed its mind to the legitimate case of India in all its proposals to end the Kashmir imbroglio created by Pakistan. In January 1957, it openly showed its unwillingness to give India even a full hearing. Two resolutions on Kashmir were tabled in the Security Council. The first one was passed on 24 January in undue haste even before the leader of the Indian delegation V.K. Krishna Menon completed his speech in reply to the tirade of Pakistan's Feroz Khan Noon against India.

This resolution sponsored by America, Britain, Australia, Colombia and Cuba was to the effect that the framing of a Constitution for Kashmir by the Kashmir Constituent Assembly was not a final disposition of the State in accordance with the principles for such a disposition which had been laid down by the Security Council. There was no crisis discernible anywhere in Kashmir to justify this special notice of the Council. The motion contained nothing new but merely reaffirmed the past resolutions of the Council, which were unworkable and totally unrelated to the existing conditions in Kashmir. It merely sought to stop the process of constitution making by the people of Kashmir on a free and democratic basis. But Kashmir wanted to integrate constitutionally with Inda. The Constituent Assembly did this and thus set the seal of voluntary, democratic approval of the integration of Kashmir with India which was the instantaneous result of Pakistan's unprovoked attack on Kashmir. If the people of Kashmir engaged themselves gainfully with constructive activities like constitution making and other related matters, how could anyone question the propriety of such acts? If the intention of the sponsors of the resolution was to question in 1957, the validity of Kashmir's accession that took place in 1947, alas, it was one decade too late. This injudicious resolution left the situation in Kashmir the same as it was prior to its passage. But the five sponsors of the resolution wanted to do exactly what was imprudent at the instigation of Pakistan. Hence their declaration that the decision of the Constituent Assembly of Kashmir would not constitute "a final disposition of the State."

The second resolution sponsored by Britain, America, Australia and Cuba referred in more specific terms to a proposal for sending a UN force to Kashmir. It became known from available sources of information that like most of the previous resolutions of the Security Council this would also go against India. The resolution read as if the Council was expecting an explosive situation in Kashmir. Before its introduction in the Council, the members held many private talks on the next step to be taken. Krishna Menon's brilliant arguments on India's case fell on deaf ears in the Council. In his speech on 8 February, Menon eloquently summarised in eight points the assurances given by Alfred Lozano, Representative of the Secretary General in the UNCIP, to India before the latter accepted the two resolutions of the UNCIP. They were:

1. Responsibility for Kashmir's security rested with India.
2. The sovereignty of the Jammu and Kashmir Government over the entire territory of the State should not be called to question.
3. Plebiscite proposals should not be binding on India if Pakistan failed to implement Parts I and II of the resolution of 13 August 1948.
4. There should be no recognition of the so-called "Azad Kashmir Government."
5. The territory occupied by Pakistan should not be consolidated.
6. Reversion of the administration of the evacuated territory in the north to the Government of Kashmir and its defence to the Government of India to maintain garrisons for preventing the incursion of tribesmen and to guard the main trade routes.
7. The Azad Kashmir forces should be disbanded and disarmed.
8. Exclusion of Pakistan from all affairs of Jammu and Kashmir.

The points enumerated were unequivocally recognised by the UNCIP. It made a clear distinction between the two forces in the State when it ruled out simultaneous withdrawal of forces and insisted on the instant withdrawal of the Pakistani forces from the State. It was only after that India would withdraw the "bulk" but not the whole of her army from Kashmir. India was also given the right to station enough forces in Kashmir to safeguard the State from external aggression. The UNCIP categorically affirmed the sovereignty and responsibility of the Kashmir Government to maintain law and order and the civil liberties of the people during the plebiscite. There was no question at all of depriving Kashmir of its armed strength required to undertake these responsibilities. Clearly Pakistan's efforts to get a resolution passed by the Security Council aimed at introducing a UN force into Kashmir were intended to nullify the findings of the UNCIP.

The resolution under review did not consider the assurances given to India. The majority of the Council members who were pro-Pakistan were determined to concentrate only on the means of bringing about a plebiscite in

Kashmir. The British delegation which was out and out anti-India played a principal role in getting the Council draft a resolution that would reject India's contention that a plebiscite was no longer feasible and advocate indirectly Pakistan's demand to despatch a UN force to Kashmir to expedite a plebiscite. Needless to say that Pakistan had a lion's share in all these. She had been lobbying the Council members for a resolution that would put down in clear terms a programme for demilitarisation of all forces – Indian, Pakistani and local – and their replacement by a UN force. The idea was to make such demilitarisation serve as a prelude to a plebiscite. For over nine years, Pakistan had been strenuously working to achieve this through a resolution of the Security Council. This would put Pakistan, the aggressor, on par with India, the defender, and earn Pakistan UN's recognition of a parity of status with India. But India was firm on her stand not to compromise on this issue. She was equally firm on her stand regarding the withdrawal of the Pakistani forces from the areas illegally occupied by her before deciding the question of a plebiscite. Peace and order, she maintained, had to be restored in the territory where disquiet, disorder and distress prevailed.

The sponsors of the resolution deliberately ignored the realities of the situation in Kashmir which was not at all critical to warrant the stationing of a UN emergency force there. Nehru who was amazed at this development cautioned the members of the Council "not to fall victims to Pakistan's propaganda or take self-stultifying decisions based on individual prejudices and preconceived notions not relevant to the real issues involved."[10]

The resolution to send a UN force to Kashmir was tabled on 15 February by Britain and her allies despite the outright rejection of it by India and the Kashmir Government – the two vitally interested parties. Though there were many meetings, some lengthy ones, between Vijayalakshmi Pandit and the British Prime Minister Macmillan and Commonwealth Relations Secretary Douglas-Home for more than two weeks, there was no common ground between the two sides.

During the debate on 18 February, Francisco Urrutia, Colombian representative in the UN, made a candid statement that India had been more sinned against than sinning. It was a very unusual pronouncement especially when the US was co-sponsor of the resolution he was objecting to. The amendments Urrutia suggested would cut out all special emphasis the resolution put on demilitarisation and stationing of the UN forces. This must have been most unpalatable to the sponsors of the resolution. His amendments took all members by surprise and the Council was adjourned till 20 February.

Feroz Khan Noon also backed out of his offer to let the UN force take over Azad Kashmir and said that Pakistan would agree to it only if India also did likewise.[11]

On 21 February, when the resolution was put to vote, it was vetoed by Russia. The Soviet delegate cast his vote against the Anglo-American resolution not only because India had objected to the proposal of stationing of foreign troops on her soil, but because it violated the UN Charter which did not provide for the use of its forces to forcibly hold a plebiscite in Kashmir. The use of UN forces, he said, "would be a flagrant contradiction of the purposes of the Charter and an offence to the Kashmir people." Even during the debate on the resolution, the Russian delegate said that since Kashmir's accession was settled by its people, all the hullabaloo made by the Security Council was aimed at "sharpening the existing differences." Declaring that the Indian territory included Kashmir the legality of whose accession to India had not been questioned by anyone except Pakistan, Krishna Menon bluntly warned that it was India's duty under the Charter to resist the invasion of Kashmir. The "invasion of any part of India was an invasion of the whole country," he added. This statement was made on account of the massing of men and arms by Pakistan in that part of Kashmir which she grabbed during her original aggression in 1947 to use it as a base for attacking Indian territory.

Jarring Mission

Immediately following the Russian veto of the February 1957 resolution, a compromise resolution was adopted by the Security Council. It requested the President of the Security Council, Gunnar V. Jarring, the representative of Sweden, "to examine with the Governments of India and Pakistan any proposals which, in his opinion, are likely to contribute towards the settlement of the dispute, having regard to the previous resolutions of the Security Council and of the UNCIP, to visit the sub-continent for this purpose and to report to the Security Council not later than 15 April 1957." The clause in the resolution authorising Jarring to make proposals "which are likely to contribute towards a settlement of the dispute," suggested the willingness of the Security Council to find new and practical ways of settlement without disrupting the administration of the State. The parties were requested to cooperate with Jarring in performing his duties. For India it was the most inconvenient time. It was extremely doubtful whether Nehru, who would be pre-occupied with India's second general election, would spare any time for Jarring before the 15 April which was the dead-line the resolution had set for the mission.

Jarring went first to India and held talks with Nehru in New Delhi on 26 and 27 March. When he referred to India's acceptance of the two resolutions of August 1948 and January 1949 of the UNCIP, Nehru pointed out that though what Jarring said was very true, India could honour them only if Pakistan gave effect to the first two parts of the August resolution. Nehru stressed the need to get this preliminary hurdle cleared. After his discussions with Suhrawardy in Karachi, Jarring had talks with Nehru again on 6 and 8 April. He then proposed to Nehru arbitration over the question of Part 1 of the resolution which he said was agreeable to Suhrawardy. Nehru's immediate reaction was that the proposal was odd since it was isolated from other matters. Nehru emphatically said: "No sovereign Government would agree to refer the question of its sovereignty to arbitration."

In his report submitted to the Security Council on 29 April 1957, Jarring admitted his failure to bridge the differences between the two sides on the procedure to implement the UN resolutions. All the same, he stated that despite the deadlock, both the parties were desirous of finding a solution to the problem which had been hanging fire for about a decade. About India's acceptance of a plebiscite, "once the necessary conditions were established," he stated there would never come a time when it would be positively declared that the "necessary conditions had been established." However since both had accepted a plebiscite, the Kashmir question could never become an "acute crisis," he said.

Jarring made no concrete proposals or recommendations but gave an account of his proposal to both the parties for arbitration on Part I of the 13 August 1948 resolution of the UNCIP which dealt with the conditions of the cease-fire. Pakistan accepted the Jarring proposal but India rejected it on two grounds: (i) arbitration would be inconsistent with the sovereignty of Jammu and Kashmir and the rights and obligations of the Union of India in respect of this State; and (ii) the apprehension that arbitration even on isolated parts of the resolutions might be interpreted as indicating that Pakistan had a *locus standi* in the question. In Britain's opinion, the real reason for India's refusal to accept arbitration was her fear that once committing herself to arbitration on part I of the resolution, she might find herself in a weak position to refuse to accept arbitration on other parts of it and also on the UNCIP's resolution of 5 January 1949.

Jarring's brief report reflected the basic truth that in the nine years that elapsed since India brought the Kashmir issue before the UN in 1948, many crucial changes had taken place making the problem more complex than it was in the beginning. Changes had taken place not only in the life of the Kashmiris but also in the political condition of that part of Asia. Given these realities, it would be "unrealistic" to be guided by the proposals and recommendations advanced on the Kashmir question nearly a decade earlier.

It is worth reviewing a specific statement or two made by Jarring in his report as they were valuable and practical. He said that on exploring the question of plebiscite he became aware of the "great problems that might arise in connection with and as a result of a plebiscite." He appreciated the anxiety expressed over the changing political, economic and strategic factors surrounding the whole of the Kashmir question which were related to the changing pattern of power relations in West and South Asia. Jarring further stated that "the Council will be aware of the fact that the implementation of international agreements of an *ad hoc* character, which has not been achieved fairly speedily, may become progressively more difficult." This implied plebiscite. These statements did not commit Jarring to any partisan view but they were likely to make the Pakistanis slightly more cautions in their approach.

Jarring's report stated in no uncertain language that India stuck to her guns and was emphatic that Pakistan had no *locus standi* in Kashmir. For that reason, she would not even accept the proposal for arbitration to determine whether Pakistan had implemented Part I of the UNCIP's resolution of 13 August 1948. India would not budge an inch on her demand that the Council should pronounce on Pakistan's aggression and that, until the latter vacated that aggression, she could do nothing regarding her commitments in the matter.

What next? Pakistan, ever busy on the Kashmir question, did not refrain from reactivating it. As usual, she started with accusations against India. She wrote to the President of the Security Council charging India with taking steps towards unilateral integration of the State into the Union of India by making it a member of the Northern Zonal Council. Pakistan warned that this would bring in a grave situation. Neither Britain nor America appeared to have responded satisfactorily to this. It was possible that they were against rekindling passions in the sub-continent.

On 21 March 1957, the British Prime Minister Harold Macmillan and American President Eisenhower met at Bermuda, a self-governing British colony in the western North Atlantic Ocean, to discuss the Kashmir issue and persuade India to make some constructive move towards reaching a settlement. Referring to his talk with Nehru during the latter's visit to the US, Eisenhower said that Nehru would not accept a plebiscite in Kashmir wholly or partially and might accept partition on the basis of the armistice line but definitely never on a religious basis as that would start again a holy war. A vexed British Prime Minister blamed India for the failure to solve the problem even after nearly a decade. Pakistan, he maintained, could not be held to obloquy as she accepted the UN resolutions, the proposals of Dixon, most of those of Graham and submission of the problem of demilitarisation to arbitration while India rejected them all. Macmillan said there was no way out to solve the problem unless the Pakistanis gained some material advantages like the Indus waters in exchange for a concession on Kashmir and said that this was the line that both Nehru and Krishna Menon took.[12]

In July 1957, Macmillan held secret private talks with Nehru and Suhrawardy. Nehru stated that under the UN resolution of 13 August 1948, Pakistani forces had to be withdrawn but not the Indian. Suhrawardy refused to accept this. But both were willing to approach the canal waters issue cordially and if any progress was registered, both would be willing in the resultant improved atmosphere to let the Kashmir problem "tick over" for a while. Both were prepared in private to admit that the Kashmir issue could be resolved only by direct negotiation between them and that the settlement would be some sort of partition.[13]

Again Graham

The report of Jarring came up for discussion at the Security Council in September 1957 which lasted up to 2 December. Earlier, during the visit of Suhrawardy to the US in July, the representatives of America and Pakistan had agreed on a resolution which the US promised to support at the Council with some changes in the wordings. Britain was against the introduction of any resolution until the discussions on the Jarring report were over.

On 22 November, a resolution jointly sponsored by Australia, Colombia, The Philippines, the UK and the US was introduced in the Council. It called upon Graham to make any recommendations to the Council based on his previous reports, the UNCIP resolutions and the Jarring report so as to reach an agreement on the reduction of forces to a specific number on each side of the CFL. As there was no consensus of opinion among the members, on 27 November, Jarring proposed some amendments to the five power resolution which included a request to Graham as envisaged in the original resolution. This was adopted on 2 December 1957. The very fact that the five sponsors had abandoned their original resolution which favoured Pakistan's contention and accepted the compromise formula of the Swedish representative showed that the Security Council had rejected Pakistan's claim that she had fully implemented Part I of UNCIP's 13 August 1948 resolution. By the resolution of 2 December, Graham was to go again to the sub-continent and reopen talks with India and Pakistan.

The suggestion that Graham should be sent again to the Indian sub-continent was made in the Council by Pierson Dixon, the British Delegate to the UN, but the idea originated from Feroz Khan Noon. Dixon did not subscribe to the view that there were "insuperable obstacles" to progress on the withdrawal of troops starting from the Pakistani side. He opined that Graham, whose earlier mission which came very near to making progress on demilitarisation but reached no agreement on the number of troops to remain on either side of the CFL, could again play a useful role.

The decision to send Graham again to the sub-continent astonished many. In passing a resolution to this effect, the Security Council had ignored Graham's own view expressed unequivocally in his fifth and final report in 1953 that the concerned parties should settle their problem by direct negotiation. Based on this, Nehru extended his offer of a "No War" pact with Pakistan for a second time although Pakistan never reciprocated this gesture. Instead, she used the interval of four years to strengthen her military potential through the acceptance of American military aid and step-up her anti-India propaganda both at home and overseas. Graham described this process most appositely as "attrition of years."

Pakistan accepted the resolution on Graham. India rejected it but agreed to offer the traditional hospitality to Graham. Krishna Menon said India would always welcome the UN representative to her soil but she would not discuss anything other than the vacation of Pakistan's aggression in Kashmir. Declaring that the Government of India had authorised him to say that India would not accept the amended five power resolution, he said: "we have accepted no resolutions except the resolutions of 17 January 1948, 13 August 1948 and 5 January 1949." As on previous occasions, this time also, there was no question of India's acceptance of or acquiescence in what had been put in the resolution. The policy based on the two UNCIP'S resolutions of 1948 and 1949, which were hitherto followed, was no longer regarded by India as a neutral line since her own policy had now changed to consider a plebiscite no longer practicable. As for demilitarisation, while India insisted on the vacation of the Pakistani forces on the Indian territory, Pakistan refused to accept the validity of Kashmir's accession to India and India's charge of aggression. She accused India of frustrating her attempts to implement the UN resolutions.

At the end of the proceedings of the Council, Pierson Dixon advanced some cogent arguments highlighting the certain failure of the Graham mission and the definite refusal of Pakistan to surrender to the Indian policy of forcing a partition on the ceasefire line. Finding herself in a very invidious position, Britain decided that the wisest course for her was to "preserve the appearance of impartiality," which she normally adopted towards an intra-Commonwealth dispute. She hoped that Nehru or Noon might "unexpectedly display" a flexible attitude leading to a settlement though she did know this was wishful thinking.[14]

Having remitted the Kashmir problem to Graham and despatched him on his mission to the sub-continent, his report had to be considered by the Council at some stage. Under the existing situation Britain could see no choice but to appear to be doing something and continue to act until the day when the situation was ripe for a settlement. There would be no problem to enact this drama as the members of the Council would not recommend to push the matter. As for India, she would only be too glad to welcome an indefinite postponement of the question. But Pakistan who had to mollify her turbulent public would press strongly for a debate on the report before the Council's off season in July and August. But Britain was hopeful that Pakistan could be persuaded to accept a September debate when the General Assembly would also be in session and until then convince the public that negotiations were continuing in some other more hopeful way! It would be easier then to transfer the case to the General Assembly which would be advantageous to her in her election campaign. Britain was thinking along these and many other ways but almost every approach seemed ultimately to exacerbate rather than improve the situation.

The one crucial event that took place in Kashmir on the eve of Graham's visit to the Indian sub-continent was the release on 8 January 1958 of Sheikh Abdullah from the Kud Hill station where he was detained in a special bungalow for 53 months. He was arrested on 9 August 1953.

On 28 March 1958, Graham presented his latest report which, as expected, brought no cheers. This mission also failed like its predecessors. The main complaint was that it had failed to take account of the basic facts. This was because over a decade many events had become totally out of date. One example would suffice to prove this. The resolution of 13 August 1948 laid down that the territory evacuated by the Pakistani troops would be administered by "local authorities" under UN "surveillance." But conditions in that area had gone through many changes during the ten years of illegal occupation by Pakistan that to determine who the original "local authorities" were was no easy task at all. In the circumstance, Graham committed the same blunder of equating the aggressor and the aggressed. Graham said he had made five recommendations to the parties with the object of making progress towards demilitarisation and a plebiscite and also proposed a meeting of the two Prime Ministers under his chairmanship for further negotiations. As usual, Pakistan agreed to all the proposals in principle, but India could not agree to any of them because they all ignored the root cause of the dispute. Since she would not modify her position on the legality of Kashmir's accession and Pakistan's aggression, she rejected Graham's suggestion for further negotiations under his auspices. By highlighting the irreconcilable views of the two opposing parties, the report called for a repetition of the crisis situation of the early years in the Council when India was regularly pilloried by pro-Pakistani elements for blocking the progress towards a settlement and nullifying all efforts of international mediation. Nonetheless, Graham's argument that direct talks between the parties at the highest level promised a solution to international difficulties was considered timely, as such a talk without any prior action in the Security Council would avoid a debate "embarrassing to both and damaging to the Commonwealth." Graham finally appealed to the parties to come together in the times "when thermonuclear power casts its shadows across the earth" and to the peoples of the world "to respond by transforming the forces of bitterness through the United Nations into creative cooperation in all fields."[15] Indeed, a utopian solution!

It was finally decided that the most hopeful course was direct discussions between the two parties without prior action by the Security Council. If this course could not be arranged or if the discussions broke down before September 1958, there should be a reference by the Security Council to the International Court of Justice or the General Assembly as the latter would be "less dangerous."[16]

Prime Minister Macmillan sent personal messages to Nehru and Noon on 18 May 1958 suggesting direct talks between them. It was suggested that the talks could go farther than the Kashmir question itself attempting to get to the root of the misunderstanding between them. Nehru in his reply said he could see no way to get out of the tangle as long as Pakistan possessed the territory she invaded and consistently spoke in terms of war. Referring to a "war psychosis" that had been created in Pakistan, he said early in June 1958 that six men of Indian border police were shot down in cold blood while negotiating under the white flag with their Pakistani counterparts along the border.[17] In his reply of 24 May to Macmillan, Noon gave a catalogue of Nehru's failures to fulfil his commitments. Since Nehru wanted the portion of Kashmir in the illegal possession of Pakistan to be delivered to India, Pakistan could not agree to any direct negotiations with him.

When the Kashmir debate was on at the Security Council, Pakistan suffered another political revolution though bloodless. The fifth Prime Minister of Pakistan, Suhrawardy, who succeeded Chaudhri Mohammad Ali in September 1956 and headed the Awami League-Republican Party coalition, had lost support in the National Assembly. He was forced to resign on 11 October 1957. President Iskandar Mirza appointed Ibrahim Ismail Chundrigar on 17 October as interim Prime Minister. He also headed a coalition Government that included many parties. Very soon the internal bickerings among the coalition partners became so acute as to force the seven-week old Government of Chundrigar to quit office on 11 December. Thereupon, Malik Feroz Khan Noon of the Republican Party who had won the election, was sworn in as the seventh Prime Minister of Pakistan on 16 December 1957. He held the reins of office until 7 October 1958 when Martial Law was enforced for the first time in Pakistan's history of eleven years by President Iskandar Mirza, who abrogated the Constitution of Pakistan, abolished political parties and appointed Mohammad Ayub Khan as the Chief Martial Law Administrator. It ought to be said to the credit of Noon, an Oxonian, who, at least on one occasion declared while challenging the Pakistani zealots: "If you think you can wage a war with India standing on your own feet, you can come and do it...I shall not lead the country to war because I know war will destroy both countries and solve no problems." After 1955, he was the first Prime Minister to hold talks with Nehru at New Delhi in a most cordial and friendly atmosphere. But this cordiality also was short-lived.

Some of the statements which President Iskandar Mirza made to the British Prime Minister a month after installing the new Cabinet of Noon in December 1957 were certainly a revelation. He told Macmillan that he had "no very high opinion of Jinnah," who, in his estimation was "a typical Bombay lawyer;" Liaquat "who posed as a country gentleman," really came from India and his major drawback was that he was "priest ridden;" his successors were all "second rate men;" and the Kashmir problem was "completely muddled by both Jinnah and Liaquat Ali."[18]

Abominable Lack of Knowledge

The events of 1957 showed no indication of any change in the less than honest attitude of Britain towards India. The messages of the well-informed

Malcolm MacDonald, UK High Commissioner in India, to Prime Minister Macmillan, conveying the extent to which the British attitude had antagonised India, hardly made any dent in the latter. Even Douglas-Home, Commonwealth Secretary, evinced no real concern about the near certainty of a permanent estrangement between India and Britain. The fact of the matter was that the top brass of the British administration including the Prime Minister had very little knowledge of the history of Kashmir. Nor were they conversant with the British policy on Kashmir which was laid down by the Labour Government in 1947-48. There was no change in the decade-old policy except that the anti-India attitude was "pressed with greater vigour and venom."

The basic policy of the British rule in India being *divide-et-impera*, the rulers upheld it faithfully by favouring the Muslims against the Hindus. After the partition, this differential treatment was openly exhibited on the Kashmir issue. India identified with the Hindu was meted out a step-motherly treatment where the Indo-Pakistan relations were concerned. All the Labour leaders including Hugh Gaitskell toed the pro-Pakistan line adopted by the British Government, the only exception being Aneurin Bevan. These men always tended to dismiss the Indian view points regardless of their merit when they related to Pakistan. Even when it became necessary for Macmillan to show an interest in the Kashmir crisis, he allowed himself to be guided by the Foreign Secretary Selwyn Lloyd and the Commonwealth Secretary Douglas-Home. It was a chain of ignorance coupled with indifference. These Secretaries were only slightly better informed than the Prime Minister and there were occasions when they also exhibited annoying ignorance of elementary facts. These ministers in turn relied heavily on the information supplied to them by the bureaucrats below them who too had no accurate knowledge of the issue. Added to these was the influence of the prevalent Tory sentiment. How then could they be expected to show sympathy towards India? In the words of the renowned Indian journalist, K.S. Shelvankar: "Whatever the complex motivations, there is a solid front against India on Kashmir – it stretches from RHS Crossman on the left to Tory diehards like Julian Amery on the right and includes London *Times* and *Manchester Guardian* as well as confirmed anti-Indian organs such as the *Daily Telegraph* and the *Daily Express*."[19]

Actually during the summer of 1958 Pakistan took no formal step to include the Kashmir question on the agenda of the Security Council. This was because trouble was once again brewing in her land. Following hard on the heels of the political upheaval of October 1957 came another *coup d'etat* on 7 October 1958. The ten-month old Noon's ministry was sacked by President

Iskandar Mirza who imposed Martial Law on Pakistan. In the absence of a rebellion, there was no justification to place the country under Martial Law. The *Dawn* wrote that only the fear of God would bring about a lasting cure in Pakistan. It was seen that Ayub was made the Chief Martial Law Administrator on 7 October. On 27 October, he unceremoniously dismissed President Iskandar Mirza and sent him to exile, thus tearing up "the remnants of legality." However, the world was made to believe that on 27 October 1958, President Iskandar Mirza decided to step aside and hand over all powers to Ayub. The latter announced that Pakistan would have a Presidential type of Government. He called himself the Supreme Arbiter of the State that Jinnah had founded in 1947, assuring the Muslims that "Pakistan would be more democratic than India." He issued an order to the effect that the post of Prime Minister had been abolished. All the eight ministers sworn in earlier were resworn to form the first Presidential Cabinet. The Pakistan Radio also announced that "Major General Iskandar Mirza, who relinquished the Office of President, left Karachi for Quetta on a holiday accompanied by his Begum." This seizure of power ended a semblance of responsible Government in Pakistan. Nehru remarked that "for the first time, dictatorial rule was established in a member country of the Commonwealth." The western democracies showed no alarm over the development in Pakistan because the new Government maintained in tact its treaties with the West. The Canadian Premier called it a passing phase. This led the *Dawn* to editorially comment that while the western nations approved the event, "a very blind and very deaf man in New Delhi" could not appreciate the value of the *coup* in Pakistan and further stated that far from being "frightened or dismayed, our people almost fell in love with Martial Law..." The continuous flow of Western military aid to Pakistan contributed to the creation of "a vested interest for the army and undermined any opposition political party which ventured to criticise the foreign policy of the Government."[20]

The Indo-Pakistan relations on Kashmir appeared very bleak at this point of time. Britain was becoming increasingly despondent about the inability of the Security Council to resolve the issue even after a decade. In her judgment, the Security Council's total failure to act on the Kashmir question had reduced its capacity to bring about an understanding between the feuding parties to a vanishing point. Britain's earnest hope was that Pakistan would not bring the Kashmir issue again to the Security Council since the best chance of a settlement lay only in a process of hard bargaining between President Ayub and Prime Minister Nehru.

Pakistan appeared to relegate the issue to the background bedevilled as she was by domestic problems of great dimensions.

As for India, she remained aggrieved and affronted. During the whole decade, the Security Council never even discussed, leave alone accept, India's contention that Kashmir was legally acceded to her and that Pakistan was an unvarnished aggressor.

References

1. *SWJN*, Vol. 28, pp. 246-63.
2. *The Hindu*, 20 May 1955.
3. *Ibid*, 19 Oct. 1955.
4. Khrushchev's Speech at Srinagar, 11 Dec. 1955, DO/35/6578.
5. Joint Statement of Indian and Soviet Leaders, 14 Dec. 1955, DO/35/6579.
6. Boundary line established in the Hindu Kush in 1893 running through the tribal lands between Afghanistan and British India. Named after Sir Mortimer Durand, who induced Abdur Rahman Khan, the Amir of Afghanistan, to agree to this boundary line which settled the Indo-Afghanistan Frontier for the rest of the British period. After partition, it marked the boundary between Afghanistan and Pakistan.
7. Text of protest, 27 April 1956, FO/371/123674.
8. *The Hindu*, 26 April 1956.
9. Suhrawardy's Speech, 17 May 1957, FO/371/129775.
10. *The Hindu*, 5 Feb. 1957.
11. *Ibid*, 20 Feb. 1957.
12. Macmillan's Conference with Eisenhower, 23 March 1957, PREM/11/1836.
13. Personal Minute of Prime Minister, 5 July 1957, FO/371/129763.
14. Kashmir : Background Note (Secret), DO/35/8876.
15. UKD to UN to FO, 29 March 1958, PREM/11/2364.
16. Brief prepared by CRO for Washington Discussions, 11 April 1958, DO/35/8876.
17. Nehru to Machillan, 7 June 1958, PREM/11/2364.
18. Record of Prime Minister's discussion with I. Mirza, 15 Jan, 1958, DO/35/8935.
19. K.S. Shelvankar, "Indo-British Relations," *The Hindu*, 21 Feb. 1957.
20. *Ibid*, 22 Nov. 1958.

12

The Four Unproductive Years

After the failure of Graham's last mission to the sub-continent in April 1958, no further move was made by Pakistan on the Kashmir question for several months. Only on 13 January 1959, Pakistan indicated to Britain and other members of the Security Council except Russia, her intention to take the Kashmir question again to the Security Council in the following April. She wanted to take the last report of Graham so as to effect the demilitarisation of Kashmir as a preliminary to a plebiscite. Canada viewed the resumption of the Kashmir question with alarm as the acrimonious debates in the Security Council would do no good to anyone. Britain felt that, apart from other dangers, Pakistan's reopening of the Kashmir crisis in the Security Council would imperil the chances of finding a solution to the river water issue which was on hand then. America said that if the past incidents were any indication, nothing could be gained by another debate on Kashmir in the Security Council leading to one more resolution. Holding a debate on Kashmir before the International Bank for Reconstruction and Development (IBRD) discussions would have a deplorable effect on the latter at a time when the problem seemed more susceptible of solution. Thus, no member of the Council was in favour of Pakistan's decision to raise the issue afresh. It was later revealed that Pakistan's approach to the Council members was intended as a *balon d'essai* and that her Government had in fact no firm ideas in mind about the move it was contemplating at that stage.[1]

Transient Change in Attitudes

Surprisingly, this time round, there seemed to be a noticeable change in the attitude of Britain towards India on the Kashmir question. At long last, she wisely decided that the keynote of her policy towards Indo-Pakistan relations on Kashmir should be marked by impartiality and equal treatment. It took more than a decade for her to realise that her influence and Commonwealth link with India would be in jeopardy if she continued to take sides in the Kashmir dispute and that her role in finding settlements to the Indo-Pakistan disputes must be that of a friend and mediator and not of a judge.[2] Keen on resolving the water dispute first, Britain like other powers was anxious that Pakistan should put off the Kashmir question till the last as it was an issue on which she could expect no change in India's decision. Britain perceived that it was incumbent on her to steer Pakistan away from Kashmir until the whole series of other problems with India were resolved to her benefit. Britain also felt that Pakistan should find herself "strong enough to reconcile her people pretty well to living with what they have got of Kashmir."[3] It must be remembered that this favourable attitude of Britain towards India was ephemeral.

There was a welcome change, for a very short while though, even in the Pakistani administration's attitude towards India. In August 1959, President Ayub wrote to K.M. Cariappa, former Chief of Staff of the Indian Army, expressing his desire to improve relations with India. He stated:

> "I would like to emphasise that it should not be inferred that simply because we have not agreed in signing a 'No War Declaration,' we are planning conquest or military adventure against India. Nothing is farther from our thoughts... Take the Kashmir dispute itself. We are after twelve years still waiting for a peaceful solution. If we had been thinking of a settlement through war, surely during this long period there would have been many an opportunity to resort to it."

On 1 September 1959, Ayub met Nehru at the Palam Airport in New Delhi during his journey between West and East Pakistan. The meeting that followed was friendly and cordial. It was the first meeting of the Pakistani Head of the State with the Indian Prime Minister since the October 1958 revolution. In the Joint *Communiqué* issued after an hour of informal talks at this meeting both agreed to conduct their relations with each other on a "rational and planned basis" and settle their outstanding problems "with justice and fair play, in the spirit of friendliness, cooperation and good neighbourliness."[4]

The canal waters and border talks were also proceeding well. The financial talks could not be termed bad. Only the Kashmir issue remained unsolved. But in this also, the British found in Ayub signs of flexibility. These indicated, according to Britain, a mood to accept a solution, even if it might not satisfy all aspirations "provided it can be 'dressed up' so as to suggest that Pakistan had not conceded as much as she might really be doing."[5]

Britain knew that whoever presided at the helm of affairs in Pakistan would find the Kashmir question insoluble. So, the wisest course would be to delay the matter as many times as Pakistan aired the need for action in the Security Council in order to avoid her case going by default. But Britain took the firm decision that its reaction to such proposals in future would be to persuade the Pakistanis to leave the matter where it was; if it became very difficult to avoid any action by the Security Council, there should be prior consultations with the US on the means of holding the Pakistanis to an "anodyne resolution." This was considered a reasonable approach as at that point of time it would be most unrealistic to expect India to make any substantial concession on Kashmir. The most that might be considered would be a settlement roughly on the CFL and this would mean that Pakistan would be forced to abandon her claims to Kashmir. This was the only course open and Britain would bring this home to the Pakistanis at the appropriate time in consultation with the US. In doing so, Britain would lay emphasis on the gains of Pakistan: progress over the Indus waters, visible Indo-Pakistan cooperation, prosperity and contentment in Pakistan on account of wise administration, an end to the irritating border incidents and India's undertaking to facilitate communications between East and West Pakistan. If the events developed along these lines, Pakistan would not have difficulty in bringing round its public to accept a *de facto* partition of Kashmir on the CFL.

There was a noticeable change for better in America's attitude also towards India though this too was short-lived. Eisenhower's visit to India in December 1959, proved eminently helpful. On the eve of his departure from the sub-continent, the Pakistani leaders presented him with a memorandum setting forth their stand on the Kashmir dispute and exhorted him to use his good offices to influence India to accept a settlement. But the President declined to interfere in the affair. He realised more than ever before the great need of western democracies to help India realise her aspirations. He was convinced of the genuineness of India's criticism of American aid to Pakistan as it arose from the fear that it might urge Pakistan to commit aggression against India again. Eisenhower told Nehru emphatically that his administration would not for a moment tolerate American arms being used by the Pakistanis to attack India. The Americans had effective sanctions against this because Pakistan "could not maintain a war for a week" without additional American help, he said and explained that Pakistan did not have sufficient ammunition for her American weapons to operate for longer than a week. After reaching Washington, the President urged that American aid to India should be enhanced.[6] *But Eisenhower did not say that America would put on hold further aid to Pakistan.*

Slowly Pakistan was growing restive. There were signs of agitation among the public at the lack of interest among the members of the Security Council to raise the Kashmir problem in the forum. Britain felt that any appeal to the UN to renew this sensitive issue would mean inviting trouble. Besides, experience over the years had shown that the Security Council could not find a solution for Kashmir. But everyone was certain that Pakistan would again press for the issue to be reopened at the UN.

In March 1961, President Kennedy's Roving Ambassador Averell Harriman visited both India and Pakistan. In Pakistan, he was subjected to a barrage of questions on Kashmir. He clarified that both parties being the friends of the US, the latter would not take sides and get involved in the dispute; that the military aid to Pakistan was to fight "the common enemy" and not India; and that both should sit together and sort out the problem of Kashmir just as they did in the case of the Indus water dispute. Of course he made it clear that it was his personal view.

The deep resentment at the statements of Harriman prompted Pakistan to indulge in an avalanche of accusations against America. Kennedy's administration came under fire from responsible men who charged that it had "assumed predilection for neutrals – notably India – and indifference towards pacts." Bitter criticisms voiced in sections of the Press primarily in the *Dawn* did not carry corrective statements from the official sources.[7]

When Ayub met Harriman later on 31 March, he said that the Ambassador and the US administration were "much too sympathetic to India." He was also critical of the proposed American aid to India. He further hinted to Harriman that just as India had looked to Russia for support on the Kashmir issue, so might Pakistan look to China![8]

The subsequent visit by Lyndon Johnson in May 1961 to the sub-continent did not appear to have improved matters in Pakistan's view. Angered over what it perceived to be America's new Democrat Government's efforts to foist Nehru's leadership on a "reluctant Asia," the Pakistani Press violently attacked Johnson. Its charges were based on the report in the *Times* of 1 June 1961 that Johnson on his return to Washington "urged Nehru at Kennedy's request to extend his leadership to other areas in South East Asia." This was wrongly interpreted to mean that America's new Government was indifferent to its ally Pakistan and wooing her enemy number one - India. Consumed by doubts and misgivings about the new Government's foreign policy, the Pakistani Press poured unlimited scorn on what they called the "Harvard intellectuals" who were in charge of the foreign policy. They were characterised as "pro-Indian," "pro-neutralist," "lukewarm towards America's existing alliances," "starry-eyed," "naive" and "largely out of touch with reality."[9]

On 10 July 1961, Ayub had a meeting with the British Prime Minister Harold Macmillan at the Admiralty House in London on his way to the US to meet President Kennedy. He had a litany of complaints against America. He told Macmillan that America's proposed amendment to the Mutual Security Act to allow supply of arms to neutrals was being made for the sake of India. He further reported that only 12½ per cent of the Indian army was massed against China to combat the Chinese frontier conflicts and that the rest was concentrated against Pakistan. On his return from America, Ayub was in a much better frame of mind. While passing through London, he sent a personal message to the British Prime Minister that President Kennedy had assured US support to Pakistan as and when the Kashmir question was brought up in the UN, categorically told him that America had "no intention of giving arms aid to India at present" and, more importantly, gave the assurance that if India needed military assistance to fight China, he would do nothing without first consulting Pakistan.[10] Subsequent events proved that Kennedy remained true to his promise to Pakistan to the last.

Pakistan had in fact no clear idea about a practicable and acceptable solution for Kashmir. Britain knew this though she treated Pakistan as if she were the aggrieved party. Britain also knew that the prospects of a mutually acceptable solution were unlikely in the foreseeable future. In fact, she wondered why at all the Pakistanis were constantly contemplating reopening the Kashmir issue at the UN when they were not sure of the gain they would derive by this course. Britain could never understand what Pakistan meant by a solution that would guarantee her "minimum economic and strategic interests." Moreover, the Pakistani leaders talked in different languages. Addressing a news conference in New York, Zafrullah said there was no intention of raising the Indo-Pakistan differences in the General Assembly of the UN. The Foreign Secretary Dehlavi on the other hand, when asked by journalists in Bombay to comment on Zafrullah's statement, told that the Kashmir issue had long been before the UN and would be raised sometime or other. This meant that Pakistan would keep alive the Kashmir question at least by a succession of public statements. Ayub was undoubtedly disillusioned that Pakistan's overtures and the progress made in other spheres with India, could not induce the latter to "move an iota on Kashmir." He was keen to revive the issue after Nehru's return from the US in November 1961.[11]

Ayub had also been writing to Macmillan suggesting that the Security Council should proceed to determine the state of implementation of the UNCIP's resolution of 13 August 1948. He stressed the need for a third party as no useful purpose would be served through bilateral discussions between the parties.

Revival of War Threats by Pakistan

It was clear from the activities of Pakistan that the absence of any serious debate or discussion or resolution on Kashmir in the Security Council after the failure of Graham's last mission undertaken in 1958 did not mean that she was quiescent. Feeling very uneasy that the prospect of a favourable settlement on Kashmir appeared gloomy, Pakistan was exploring all means to reopen the question at the Security Council. Zafrullah, an avowed foe of India, left no stone unturned to fabricate a case against her so as to keep alive his indictment of India. Nehru's reaffirmation of his one and only demand that Pakistan, the aggressor, should vacate aggression from the Indian territory was misinterpreted as India's threat of war on Pakistan. In blowing out of proportion every such statement of Nehru, Pakistan conveniently ignored her contemptuous disregard of India's gesture of goodwill to sign a "No War" pact with her. It was ridiculous that Pakistan raised the cry of an Indian invasion despite the continued presence of the UN observers on the CFL. The President of Azad Kashmir was equally vociferous in his unceasing threat to march his forces across the CFL to achieve his goal of liberating the whole of Kashmir.

These unhealthy activities and irresponsible utterances were not unexpected of Pakistan given her habit to resort to confrontational speeches against India to divert public attention from internal disorder. It was her time-honoured device to beat the Kashmir drum to offset the domestic turbulence. It was the time when the people of Pakistan were eagerly expecting the announcement of a new Constitution for the country. The military dictator was not prepared to address himself to this despite knowing that he would become unpopular over the issue. There were other problems too including the presidential election in Azad Kashmir. However, it was Pakistan's good fortune that an event that took place in India in December 1961, gave an impetus to her venomous propaganda against India. It was the liberation of the Indian territories of Goa, Daman and Diu from the Portuguese yoke. The border tensions and guerrilla warfare of fourteen years against Portugal were of no avail. The mass *satyagraha* launched in August 1955 to enter Goa also failed. Portugal sought to claim a sort of divine right to rule over the Indian territories of Goa, Daman and Diu.[12] India had to wait for six more years when on 18-19 December 1961, the Indian troops succeeded in entering Goa and liberating the Portuguese pockets in India. The attack met with little resistance and the Portuguese authorities surrendered to the Indian forces. The three liberated pockets were merged with India in 1962 after 451 years of Portuguese colonial rule. Many factors like the patriotic sentiment of the people of India, the strong influence exerted on India by the Africans who had been suffering horrors at the hands of the Portuguese in Angola (in South West Africa) and the personality of Krishna Menon contributed to the victory at Goa. After Goa's integration with India, the independence of India became complete.

The initial anti-India feeling generated in the West by the merger of Portuguese Indian pockets with India was exploited by Pakistan. She became very friendly with Portugal. She assiduously cultivated contacts with the Iberian Peninsula – Spain and Portugal. While the President of Pakistan visited Lisbon, his Interior Minister went to Madrid to carry on anti-India campaign in those places. Not one to let the opportunity presented by Goa slip, Pakistan expressed alarm at the Indian action and pressed for a discussion on Kashmir in the Security Council on the flimsy ground that India might have similar designs on Kashmir.

Incredibly, to Pakistan's sore disappointment, her cries had fallen flat in the Security Council. In January 1962, she requested the Council to convene a meeting to continue the Kashmir question from where the discussions had ended on 28 March 1958. C.S. Jha, India's Permanent Representative to the UN, wrote to the President of the Security Council to reject Pakistan's request for a meeting on Kashmir as it had already "fully heard" the arguments by both parties and was satisfied that there was no threat from India as alleged by Pakistan. India firmly held that the *raison d'etre* for Pakistan's request did not exist. The British delegation also did its best at carefully chosen occasions to discourage Pakistan from reviving the Kashmir issue at the UN on the ground that it would do her no good but only raise the temperature. The British knew that some form of arbitration or another mission would still be acceptable to Pakistan. But knowing that either of these would be unpalatable to India, the British delegation was against promoting such a proposal. America also did her best to dissuade Pakistan from taking the matter back to the Security Council as there was no likelihood of achieving anything constructive. Besides, having had a second thought over the liberation of Goa by India from Portuguese rule, the West did not react favourably to Pakistan's attitude towards India's role in it. Henry Kissinger, President Kennedy's Special Assistant on International Affairs, who was in India in June 1962 was reported to have remarked at a press conference in New Delhi that America would not spite India because of Goa. These were a severe blow to Pakistan's plan to raise the "imaginary Indian bogey in Kashmir." Another agreeable surprise to India was the statement of the British President of the Security Council Patrick Dean that there could be no meeting until the Indian elections were over.

Meanwhile, on 18 January 1962, Zulfikar Ali Bhutto, Pakistan's Minister for Fuel, Power and Natural Resources, called on the Duke of Devonshire, Parliamentary Under Secretary at the CRO, to urge the British Government to support Pakistan's proposal to reopen the Kashmir question once again at the Security Council. The Duke, while expressing his Government's sympathy for Pakistan, asked Bhutto if it would not be wiser to wait until the Indian elections were over. Bhutto's answer was that it would be for Pakistan's advantage to go ahead whilst the events in Goa remained fresh in public memory. Bhutto emphasised the same fact in vain when he met Lansdowne of the Foreign Office the same day.[13] It almost looked as if the ardour with which the resolutions on Kashmir were earlier sponsored by the Western bloc to support Pakistan's claims was no longer there. But the subsequent events proved that their concern for Pakistan had not in the least diminished.

At this juncture, President Kennedy in a private capacity suggested mediation by Eugene Black, President of the World Bank in the Kashmir dispute. Pakistan accepted the offer. India could not. While thanking Kennedy for his genuine desire to end the Kashmir imbroglio, Nehru said that direct negotiations between the parties in a moderate and restrained atmosphere would be preferred. He further wrote that the 1960 invitation to Ayub was still open but talks on "any other step" could not be held until the Indian elections were over.[14]

Western Bloc's Abortive Attempts

On 1 February 1962, yielding to Pakistan's persistent complaint that there was no substantive debate on the Kashmir question, Britain and America arranged for a meeting of the Security Council. In doing so, they ignored India's plea against a meeting. India refused to have talks as long as Pakistan continued to agitate for discussions. The British delegation told its Indian counterpart that it could not completely displease Pakistan! However, though the Council met, the discussion on Kashmir was put off much to the annoyance of Zafrullah. He suffered a double defeat at least for the moment: he failed to secure a full-scale discussion on Kashmir and he failed to get a sponsor even for a mild resolution on the issue. After hearing Zafrullah for 80 minutes and C.S. Jha for a short while, the Council adjourned on the initiative of its President Adlai Stevenson of the US who declared that the Kashmir question could be considered "sometime after 1 March when the Indian elections would be over" and that the next meeting should be called only after consultation with the members of the Council and the concerned parties.

Adlai Stevenson's declaration could not be taken to mean that he would always be inclined to consider India's demand judiciously. After adjourning the meeting on 1 February, Britain and America could not remain complacent on Kashmir. There were persistent pressures from Pakistan to renew discussions at the Council. They were however careful enough not to get embroiled in the issue directly. So, in April 1962, they approached U Thant, Secretary General of the UN, to take up the responsibility of handling the subject under a Security Council directive. But the Secretary General did not favour the suggestion. As a result, the traditional sponsors of the Kashmir resolutions, who were always favourable to Pakistan, had to seek the help of other smaller members to place the matter before the Security Council. The big powers found themselves in the greatest difficulty of pacifying Pakistan who went so far as to demand the annulment of Kashmir's accession to India! It was astounding that none of the big powers warned Pakistan against such a violent demand. On 27 April, Zafrullah came up with some suggestions which included calling Graham to bring his report up-to-date for the Security Council to consider it. Zafrullah threatened that if the Council did not oblige him, Pakistan would launch a war that would not be confined to Kashmir as it was in 1948.[15]

On 3 May 1962, Krishna Menon told the Security Council that Pakistan was "injecting an entirely new and dangerous element into Kashmir" by preparing to negotiate with Peking to demarcate the border between the Pakistan occupied Kashmir and Sinkiang. These negotiations were planned for the mere pleasure of tormenting India at a critical time. Countering Zafrullah's harangue to rake up the dead and buried question of Kashmir's accession to

India, Krishna Menon clarified that if the issue remained unsolved for so long a time, Pakistan was the sole cause for it. She refused to implement the UNCIP resolutions which were intended to set the stage for a plebiscite. Menon did not spare the Security Council either for its failure to face up squarely to India's complaint of Pakistani aggression and order her to vacate it forthwith. During this long period of a decade and a half, the situation in the area had changed unalterably. Jarring had already realised this and recorded it in his report. Menon assured the Council that India would not resort to force but definitely resist further aggression.

Praises were showered on Krishna Menon when he completed his speech. Since this was a rare gesture, the compliments paid by a British officer had better be said in his own words:

> "Krishna Menon...spoke well, amusingly and appealed to the public in the gallery. He made quite a number of cracks against the British (and the Americans and at least once the Russians) but in an apparently entirely good-hearted manner. He was certainly much easier to listen to than Zafrullah, and although they both went on too long, Krishna Menon kept his audience most of the time. I would certainly give the honours of the debate to Krishna in delivery, if not in content and my impression was that he was more convincing generally than Zafrullah. He was not looking particularly well (but then he never does) but there was nothing in his speech or delivery to suggest a diminution of his mental power."[16]

Strongly supporting India, Soviet Russia said that the plebiscite question had "lapsed itself," since conditions for it were not fulfilled by Pakistan. The Security Council adjourned *sine die* without adopting a resolution and without fixing a date for its next meeting.

The general impression even of the British who attended this session was that the Pakistanis hardly realised that they were overstepping their limits in the Security Council. The members in general felt that raising the Kashmir issue at that juncture by Pakistan was "a holding tactic" in view of the impending elections. Her rantings in the Council would make the Pakistani public believe that the Government was sincerely tackling the problem at the international forum.

Pakistan's failure to get the Security Council adopt a resolution on Kashmir did not at all deter her from pursuing her attempts. Her obstinacy to reactivate the issue in the Security Council at all costs was attributed by some to her anxiety to have the debate in the absence of India's Defence Minister

Krishna Menon who would be pre-occupied with affairs in Delhi. The big powers also did not think differently on this. It could be because they were frightened of his most competent advocacy of India's case on Kashmir. "Judging from the trend of events, it looks as though that even if the majority of the members of the Security Council would not support Pakistan's stand, not many would like Mr. Menon to go away with a victory," remarked an Indian correspondent.

The British officialdom took an unseemly delight in delineating the character of Krishna Menon. Their comments on and remarks about his performances in the Security Council and elsewhere, conveniently glossing over the truth or justice of his arguments, betrayed the widespread prejudice against Menon. Probing into the various causes that made Menon exercise such "an effective, and more often, destructive influence" over Nehru, Gore-Booth wrote

> "......the nearest reason that makes sense is that he has an uncanny faculty for rationalising Mr. Nehru's instincts and prejudices. I like to think of him fancifully as a sort of modern incarnation of the God of Siva (sic) who...is the God of both creation and destruction. In international affairs, he appears to take the latter function extremely seriously, though it must be added that in his capacity as Defence Minister, he also pays attention to the creative aspect."[17]

On 23 May, T.N. Kaul, Indian High Commissioner to UK, called on Foreign Secretary Douglas-Home to brief him on the agreement between Pakistan and China over parts of Kashmir which were acknowledged by Britain to lie within Indian sovereignty. He said that Zafrullah's indirect but serious threats in the Security Council, the various notes India had been receiving from China especially the one sent on 30 April demanding the withdrawal of the two newly-established Indian check posts in Ladakh and the Pakistani pressure for an early resumption of the Kashmir debate in the Security Council were not sheer coincidence, but deliberately planned to cause maximum embarrassment to India. Kaul told Douglas-Home that India was ever ready to negotiate directly with Pakistan on a bilateral basis but not under "this kind of pressure."[18]

When the Security Council met on 15 June after a lapse of about six weeks, Adlai Stevenson, the American delegate did a somersault wholly supporting Pakistan against India. But to the surprise of many, for the first time in the fourteen years since 1948, the British delegate Patrick Dean, categorically announced: "Our view is that the dispute can be settled by negotiations between the two parties because neither the Security Council nor any other outside body could come out with a solution."

But, Patrick Dean's announcement had no impact on Pakistan. Her mad rush to resume the Kashmir debate in the Security Council was going on indefinitely. On 22 June 1962, to appease Pakistan by offering her a forum for mere propaganda, the US got Ireland sponsor a resolution on Kashmir favourable to Pakistan. Initially, the resolution was arranged to be sponsored by five of the non-permanent members of the Security Council, namely, Ireland, Chile, Venezuela, Ghana and the UAR. But when all the five backed out of their agreement to sponsor the motion, it appeared very likely that the debate in the Council would peter out with no resolution being tabled — a situation that would have proved disastrous for Pakistan. President Kennedy thereupon personally pressed the Irish Government to advise its representative to table the resolution on his own.

The resolution loaded against India urged "the Governments of India and Pakistan to enter into negotiations on the question of Kashmir at the earliest convenient time with a view to its ultimate settlement in accordance with Article 33 and other relevant provisions of the Charter of the UN." All Western powers, two Latin American countries and Kuomintang China voted for it. The UAR and Ghana, non-aligned members of the Council, abstained. Russia's ally Rumania opposed it. But the Security Council failed to adopt the motion because it was vetoed by the Soviet Union. The following is a humourous description of this episode by Eswar Sagar, the columnist of *The Hindu* under the sub-title "Unhappy Gesture:"

> "The resolution which failed to-day had a mixed parentage. Inspired by Pakistan in the first place, conceived by the 'Little Five' (Ireland, Ghana, UAR, Chile and Venezuela) and nurtured by the US, it nearly became an orphan. When the 'Little Five' abandoned it, the US was left with the baby and during the last 48 hours, the latter was hard put to it to find someone other than itself, to sponsor it. It concentrated on Ireland and the latter finally succumbed."[19]

At one stage, the US delegate told Krishna Menon that in deference to India's wishes, they dropped any reference to third party mediation from the resolution. Menon told him that it was clear from the final draft that they did make an attempt to bring it by "back door" since the resolution recommended measures such as arbitration, mediation and other means which were provided under Article 33 of the UN Charter.[20] It was the hope of all right thinking persons that the whole sorry episode would have convinced Pakistan of the futility and purposelessness of raising the Kashmir issue again in the Security Council.

Commenting on the US tactics in the Security Council, which misfired, Patrick Dean wrote that they provided a fine opportunity to Krishna Menon and the Soviet Union "to attack the whole basis of discussion and to represent the handling of the issue as an American attempt to needle India." It was also his view that they afforded further scope to Russia "to leave with the Afro-Asians here an impression that the US had introduced cold war manoeuvring into the Kashmir dispute."[21]

During a Foreign Affairs debate in the Rajya Sabha on the 23 June, Nehru said that the way the Americans and the British delegates spoke and voted in the Security Council the previous day ignoring all facts on Kashmir had "hurt and injured" India very much. He also said that it was India's misfortune that "the work done for years, the work of creating that goodwill, which we value so much, is washed out by a stroke of the pen or a vote given or a speech made."

When the British Government was examining the various means of easing the tension between India and Pakistan over Kashmir, it made quite a few inferences. One such deduction was that in view of the continued Chinese pressure in the region, Pakistan would be induced to redeploy her forces against external threats instead of confronting India. But Pakistan's unneighbourly activities at a time, when India faced a grave danger from China, belied Britain's hope.

References

1. UK HC (P) to CRO, 20 Jan. 1959, FO/371/144466.
2. W.A.W. Clarke of CRO to Roger Stevens of FO, 24 Aug. 1959, FO/371/144467.
3. Minute of Commonwealth Secretary, 28 Oct. 1959, DO/35/8989.
4. *Ibid*, UK HC (P) to CRO, 16 Sep. 1959.
5. *Ibid*, L.B. Walsh Atkins to H.A. Twist, CRO, 19 Jan. 1960.
6. Malcolm MacDonald's talk with Ellsworth Bunker, 14 Jan. 1960, DO/35/8999.
7. Walsh Atkins, UK HC (P) to N. Pritchard, CRO, 30 March 1961, DO/196/132.
8. Walsh Atkins, UK HC (P) to N. Pritchard, CRO, 5 April 1961, DO/196/128.
9. UK HC (P) to Duncan Sandys, 2 June 1961; and to CRO, 15 June 1961, DO/196/132.

10. *Ibid,* Record of a conversation at Admiralty House, 10 July 1961 between Macmillan and Ayub Khan.
11. Walsh Atkins to Commonwealth Secretary, 6 Sep. 1961, DO/196/138.
12. Dadra and Nagar Haveli in Western India, which were also under the control of Portugal, launched an indigenous freedom movement in 1954 which forced the Portuguese to abandon them to India.
13. Bhutto's meetings with Duke of Devonshire and Lansdowne, 18 Jan. 1962, DO/196/139.
14. *Ibid,* G.L Simmons, UK HC (I) to Walker (CRO), 2 Feb. 1962.
15. *The Hindu,* 29 April 1962.
16. R. Walker (CRO) to R.C.C. Hunt, UK HC (P), 10 May 1962, DO/196/140.
17. P.H. Gore-Booth, UK HC (I) to Alexander Clutterbuck, 10 Nov. 1961, DO/181/6.
18. FO to UKD to UN, 23 May 1962, FO/371/164875.
19. *The Hindu,* 24 June 1962.
20. UK HC (I) to CRO, 28 June 1962, FO/371/164876.
21. *Ibid,* Patrick Dean to Home, 9 July 1962.

13

Rude Break With Age Old Relations

Despite enjoying a "colossal natural rampart" with vast seas on the two lower and highest mountains on the two upper sides to protect her, India remained assailable to external attacks from time immemorial. This vulnerability posed a perennial problem for the British Indian Government. Ever since she established her suzerainty over India, what afflicted Britain most in her foreign relations was Russophobia. Britain feared that in view of her proximity to India, Russia would come through the mountain passes and claim India for the Czars! To this was added the Sinophobia – the fear of invasion of India by a renascent China. Unlike Russophobia, invasion of China could not be dismissed as a mere phobia. Problem from China was very real and kept British Indian Government preoccupied with it almost till the end of its rule in India.

India and China, the two "Asian Giants," has a common frontier running over a distance of 3,200 kilometres along the Himalayan range. Kashmir adjoins the Chinese province of Sinkiang and is strategically situated between the two countries. Most of the Sino-Indian frontier lies between India and Tibet.

A brief account of the plateau of Ladakh in Kashmir, one of the most elevated regions in the world, merits special mention. It is a no man's land lying across a high mountain pass east of Srinagar and the Vale of Kashmir, at a height of 17,400 feet. An extension of the Tibetan plateau, Ladakh is culturally and geographically a bridge to Tibet as Tibet is to China. In the early decades of the nineteenth century, this desert land was closely related to Tibet by proximity and custom and so distantly related to then "exiguous Chinese

Empire." In 1841, Gulab Singh, ruler of the State of Jammu, invaded Ladakh. Though his forces succeeded in crushing the Tibetan defenders, half-way through the battle, with the onset of the deadly winter, the invaders were almost frozen to death. The next year Gulab Singh retrieved his position and concluded a peace treaty with the Tibetans by which each side had agreed to respect the other's territorial rights. Strangely, the agreement did not say what those rights were! This was because the Asians did not bother about precise boundary designations in those days as did the Europeans.

In 1846, Kashmir itself fell to the British and Gulab Singh was made its ruler. The transmountain plateau of Ladakh which he conquered became part of Kashmir and of the British Empire. But the line between the British Indian and the Chinese Tibetan territory was never settled. The Chinese Government was unwilling to risk agreeing to anything. The British were unsure which territory it would be wise for them to have. Only in the 1860s, for the first time, W.H. Johnson, an enterprising surveyor visited the territory and proposed a boundary far to the north and east of Kashmir. The next step in this direction was in 1897 when Major General John Ardagh, Director of Military Intelligence of the British General Staff, worked out a rough approximation of this line, overriding the objection of some. The resultant Johnson-Ardagh Line encompassed the Aksai Chin, a dreadful desolate land of stone and sand in Ladakh about 17,000 feet high, which was virtually an uninhabited area. "Sovereign India" inherited this unnotable and unsettled border but she was not sure where exactly it lay.[1]

The McMahon Line

The celebrated McMahon Line formed India's frontier with Tibet from the trijunction of Bhutan, Tibet and India eastwards towards the Burmese border. It was first delineated on a map that accompanied an exchange of letters in March 1914 between the British Plenipotentiary Henry McMahon and the Tibetan Plenipotentiary Lonchen Shatra who attended the Simla (now Shimla) Conference of 1913-14 at the invitation of British India. It was a Tripartite Conference between British India, Tibet and China to settle matters like concessions and extra-territorial rights in Tibet. The Conference was held under the presidency of the Foreign Secretary to the Government of India. On 3 July 1914, the Simla Convention between China, Tibet and British India was initialled by the representatives of the three countries. By this, Tibet was divided into two zones and the suzerainty of China over both was recognised. China agreed to recognise the complete autonomy of "outer Tibet," skirting the Indian frontier and including Lhasa, Shigatse and Chando and abstain from all interference in its administration and also to abstain from sending troops, stationing civil or military officers or establishing Chinese colonies there. The frontier between Tibet and Assam in British India and the map and the line on which this claim was based were named after McMahon, who was the chief negotiator. This line which brought all of North East Frontier Agency (NEFA) including the Tawang[2] tract into India, ran from the eastern border of Bhutan along the crest of the Himalayas until it reached the great bend in the Brahmaputra River where the latter issued forth from its Tibetan course into the Assam Valley. India's border with China in the NEFA region had been well established since very early times. What came to be called the McMahon Line, which separated India from Tibet, was a line of the high ridges that divided the watersheds. This had been "acknowledged as the border by history, tradition and treaties" long before it was named the McMahon Line.

Notwithstanding McMahon's competence, the McMahon Line was not without flaw. In the first place, it was never demarcated on the ground. Secondly, the delineation was on a map of comparatively small scale of 1:500,000. Naturally, its accuracy was open to question. The demarcation as it approached Bhutan failed to follow the peaks and became a simple straight line. There were therefore discrepancies between the line on the ground and the line on the original map. In furnishing the background information about the McMahon Line, the British Foreign Office warned that there could be strips of territory several miles wide which both India and China might claim as their own.[3]

At the end of the Simla Conference in July 1914, just weeks before the First World War, the Tibetans, in view of their *de facto* independence from China at that time, accepted the McMahon Line. The dealings of Britain with Tibet ended with the offer of the Dalai Lama, the country's temporal and spiritual ruler, to send assistance to Britain during the global war. The delegates of the Chinese Republican Government refused to sign the agreement on the status and boundaries of Tibet on the ground that Tibet which was under China's control *de jure* had no power to make treaties.

The traditional friendship between India and China which was more than two millennia old appeared to be growing even after 1947. Students of Indian history are only too familiar with the visits of the learned Chinese pilgrims like Fa Hein (fourth century), and Yuwan Chuwang (seventh century) to India – the cradle of Buddhism – to worship at the sacred Buddhist centres of pilgrimage and study the Buddhist literature *in situ*. Nehru who had an intimate knowledge of this phenomenal friendship was also closely following the revolutionary changes taking place in that country since the second quarter of the twentieth century: the birth of the Chinese National Party (Kuomintang) by Sun Yat-Sen, the establishment of the Chinese Nationalist Government at Nanking and the Civil War in which the Chinese Communists defeated the Nationalist Government, drove it to the Island of Formosa (now Taiwan) and proclaimed on 1 October 1949 the People's Republic of China. Since India believed that every country should have the right to choose its own "political and economic structure and to live its own life," the Indian Government recognised the new Government of China within three months of its establishment. Nehru had the warmest regard for China and fondly referred to her as "India's sister in ancient history." India relentlessly argued with other Commonwealth countries that the right course was to recognise Communist China. Britain also did the same though later her relations with China became complicated on account of America's reaction to her recognition of Communist China.

Since India firmly believed that China would not resort to armed attack on Tibet, she was rudely shocked when China invaded her in October 1950, defeating her poorly equipped troops and claiming to "liberate" three million Tibetans from the "imperialist yoke." The major impact of China's aggression was on Ladakh in Kashmir. Rubbing shoulders with the communist occupied Chinese Turkestan and Western Tibet, Ladakh had racial, spiritual and cultural ties with Tibet. For centuries, Lhasa had been Ladakh's Mecca and the Ladakhi Buddhists owed spiritual allegiance to the Dalai Lama as their spiritual *guru*. In fact, Ladakh was known as "Little Tibet." China's occupation of Tibet ended Ladakh's trade with Tibet and snapped her spiritual links with Lhasa. India's protest note against this unlawful occupation and caution that this act would only provide a handle to those, who opposed China's entry into the UN, were not heeded. In fact, China curtly replied that she would not tolerate foreign interference in a matter that was purely domestic! This accusation certainly offended Nehru who sincerely desired to start a new phase in world affairs in conjunction with his powerful neighbour.

China's immediate reaction to India's strong criticism of her invasion of Tibet was one of suspicion of India's motives for sympathising with Tibet. This was totally unwarranted as India was entirely opposed to extra-territorial rights in another country. Territorial expansion was the policy of the British regime in India which was carried out by force of arms in Tibet in the beginning of the twentieth century. This definitely brought much harm to the Tibetans.

The British policy in Tibet was based on their long-drawn-out rivalry with Russia in Central Asia. Right through the nineteenth century, Britain feared that Czarist Russia might come down through Kashmir or through Afghanistan into India. But during the period under review, it was an idle and meaningless menace. Even the Maharaja of Kashmir did not consider it necessary to protect the eastern borders of Kashmir and Ladakh.

China – An Insidious Enemy

The reactions in India to China's Tibetan invasion did not appear to have impaired the millennia old relations between the two countries. In April 1954, there was a Sino-Indian Agreement on trade with Tibet in which for the first time the principle of *Panch Sheel* ("the five tenets") was enunciated. The tenets were: (i) non-aggression, (ii) non-interference, (iii) recognition of each other's territory, (iv) mutual help and (v) peaceful co-existence. In June 1954, the warm welcome extended by India to Chou En-Lai, during his first visit to the country, proved historic. The principle of *Panch Sheel* was reiterated in the Joint *Communiqué* issued at the end of the Chinese leader's visit. When Nehru visited China in October of the same year, he received an extraordinary welcome there. These events signified to Nehru that China earnestly desired that the Sino-Indian relationship should flourish in the years to come. Nehru was said to be almost "lyrical" about the economic development of the Chinese People's Republic. The *Panch Sheel* was loudly trumpeted.

Nehru availed himself of the opportunity which his visit to China afforded to point out to Chou En-Lai in a good neighbourly way that certain Chinese maps still showed portions of Burma and India as Chinese territory. China published maps showing 1,32,090 square kilometres of Indian territory in the Himalayan region from Ladakh to the Assam border, as parts of China. Initially she offered many unbelievable excuses and explanations for the wrongful inclusion of Indian territory. Then she told they were old maps and the Government was yet to draw the new ones! In the next four years, there was no major problem between India and China save the border incidents in the Ladakh area.

It was unfortunate that India failed to perceive that the much talked of friendship between the two countries was an illusion. She committed a Himalayan blunder in not visiting the unsettled line between the British Indian and the Chinese–Tibetan territory until she heard of China's trespass on this area thus violating India's territorial integrity. Nehru made a statement touching this only in 1962. He recalled then that he told Chou En-Lai from his own evidence that some time in 1955 or 56 when he went to the airfield at Ladakh, no Chinese was found anywhere in the vicinity. But when he went there a second time, he found them atop a hill near the airfield which meant that they had come there since. Chou gave no answer to this. Nehru said that "apart from any claims based on history, the Chinese were not there (then) and they are there now. It was a peaceful frontier (then) and it is not a peaceful frontier now."[4] No sign of infiltration was noticed anywhere up to 1956. The patrol parties did not visit the northeastern part of the Aksai Chin area. They did not actually traverse the portion of the road within the Aksai Chin itself to notice any Chinese infiltration.

This total negligence of the Indian Government was exploited by the Chinese who in 1956-57 were vigorously building a military road across Aksai Chin connecting western Tibet with Sinkiang in the Indian territory. This Yehcheng-Garlok Road also called the Sinkiang-Tibet Highway was reported to be 1170 kilometres long. It was formally declared open on 6 October 1957. Since then, China's policy towards India was being governed by four factors: (a) the vital need for the Aksai Chin road; (b) the need to physically isolate Tibet from India; (c) the belief they could win over the Tibetan loyalty by reviving and establishing the Tibet's traditional territorial claims against India; and (d) the basic need to bring pressure on India herself and to humiliate her in order to maintain China's supremacy in the Asian region.

It was a pity that while the Chinese laid much stress on the construction of this road which they regarded as vital, its implications to India's security in the Ladakh region was not at any level properly understood. This highway was to serve the Chinese as a supply line for their campaign of repression in Tibet. India was blissfully ignorant of these happenings until the late 1950s when rumours of the road project reached New Delhi. The Chinese cartographic claims covered about 1,03,600 square kilometres of Indian territory some of which including Aksai Chin had already been occupied. Alarmed by this, India made arrangements for patrols to go to the frontier in all directions.[5]

Only in 1958, to confirm the "impressive trespass" of China, India chose to send patrolmen to the McMahon Line. One of these patrol men was reported to have "promptly disappeared into Chinese hands." This strained the Sino-Indian relations considerably. While Nehru insisted on the legal validity of the McMahon Line, China viewed all the agreements entered into by the colonial regime as symbols of past "imperial aggression." Britain also supported the view of the Government of India that the frontiers that India took over on attaining independence were those that Britain had long recognised as correct frontiers. The British Foreign Secretary affirmed that "this view is not changed by the fact that India is no longer British and that the Chinese have chosen to dispute those frontiers." Implicit in the Foreign Secretary's statement was the acceptance of the fact of India's case. Again while deploring the attacks of China against a fellow member of the Commonwealth in the General Assembly of the UN, the Foreign Secretary said emphatically, "The British Government have always recognised the McMahon Line as the frontier of India and, of course, continue to do so."[6] The US also endorsed this view though it cautiously refrained from airing it publicly. China herself was most inconsistent in assessing the position of the McMahon Line. Though she called it illegal, earlier she herself had in many ways acknowledged that Line as the border.[7]

China's refusal to allow Nehru to visit Lhasa cooled the relations between the two countries further. China was most unhappy at the obstinate resistance of the Dalai Lama and his theocratic leaders to her efforts to establish communist cadres in Tibet. She imputed this failure to India whose support the Tibetan leaders always sought and secured. She conceived a sinister design to stop the Tibetans from turning to India. It was a dual device to discourage the ruler of Tibet from approaching India for succour on the one hand and to make it very difficult for India to lend him any help on the other. China began her game by exerting extreme pressure continuously on Tibet. This drove the restive Tibetans, who were bent upon throwing overboard the Chinese yoke, stage a revolt in March 1959. This was the Khampa rebellion which China quelled with an iron hand. She overran Tibet and launched a veritable reign of terror resulting in the flight of the Dalai Lama to India with 30,000 "rebels." This aggravated China's hostility towards India who gave asylum to the Dalai Lama and his men. The Dalai Lama, who was only 24 then, entered India from Lhasa on his own volition. He first landed in Tezpur from where he made a statement that he had voluntarily left Tibet for India. But China alleged that he was made to make the statement by India.

A few days after the Lama's arrival, many more Tibetans crossed into the Kameng Frontier Division of the NEFA. India agreed to give them asylum. The Lama was accommodated in Mussorie where Nehru met him. China charged that Kalimpong was the centre of the rebellion, simply because the area had a large number of people of Tibetan stock who were Indian nationals but deeply devoted to the Dalai Lama. Rebutting China's charge as wholly unjustified, Nehru said, "to say that a small group of persons sitting in Kalimpong organised a major upheaval in Tibet seems to me to make a large draft on imagination and slur over obvious facts." He further said that the revolt started in an area in China proper adjoining Tibet in 1956 itself and slowly spread to Tibet to inject a powerful impression into the minds of the many Tibetans who kept away from the revolt.[8] As Nehru explained, trouble started in the Kham and Amdo areas inhabited by Buddhists owing allegiance to the Dalai Lama. Their revolt against the Chinese rule started as early as 1956. The Dalai Lama himself had no clear idea of the rebellion since the territories were no longer under his control.

The first serious clash between the Chinese and the Indian troops occurred in August 1959 when the Chinese seized Longju on the McMahon Line. China's cartographic claims for large areas of the Indian territory have already been referred to. In September 1959, she put forward claims to the 1,03,600 square kilometres of Indian territory on the periphery of the Indian frontier in the western, central and eastern sectors. The exchange of diplomatic notes that followed between Peking and New Delhi, which were initially friendly, became acerbic and finally angry. China's notes were violently worded challenging India to settle the Sino-Indian frontier by negotiations as it had never been delimited. This meant repudiation of the McMahon Line on the NEFA and consequently torpedoing India's legitimate claim to the NEFA area.

The second serious clash took place in October 1959 when the Chinese killed and captured many Indian policemen in Ladakh. China's high-handed activities triggered off the righteous indignation of India. There was a public outcry for revenge attacks against the aggressor. In April 1960, Prime Minister Chou En-Lai received a frigid welcome when he came to New Delhi to negotiate a settlement. Negotiations were afoot for five days. Since the Indian Parliament as well as the public were in no mood for any concessions to China, the talks ended in a stalemate.

China's Unabashed Aggression

All sagacious and right-minded persons viewed alarmingly the behaviour of such an ancient and great nation in Asia as China towards an equally ancient, great and above all friendly neighbour like India. China's main disputes with India were over two inhospitable terrains. One was the 41,440 square kilometres of the uninhabitable land in the northern portion of Ladakh known as Aksai Chin, also called the Soda Plain; the other was the deeply wooded 90,650 square kilometres of NEFA populated alternately thick and sparse. It was really puzzling why was China so adamant about acquiring just a toehold on such "bare and bitter" areas, where not even a blade of grass would grow, at the cost of antagonising India with whom she had had very peaceful, cultural and commercial ties for millennia? The one and only valid answer to China's utter disregard for such an age old friendship was her growing jealousy towards India. She looked upon India as her deadly rival. In the wake of her independence, despite the innumerable problems that she had to grapple with, India had, under Nehru's stewardship, earned for herself a pride of place in the comity of Afro-Asian nations. Nehru could perceive the link between the liberty of India and the liberty of other parts of Asia from the western colonial yoke. His fervent hope was to see that India's independence was followed by the resurgence of the whole continent of Asia. Nehru was both a politician when he fought the British and a statesman when he developed a smooth policy of international relationship by establishing good ties with Asian and neo-African States.

In the 1950s, only India enjoyed a strong and stable democracy and was hailed as "a beacon for democrats everywhere in Asia." India's many acts aimed at promoting peace like the convening of the Afro-Asian Conferences, playing the peace-maker unobtrusively in Indo-China, Korea and other places and the commendable role in solving the Suez Canal crisis, to mention but a few, were India's unique and timely contributions in the international arena. The years immediately following her independence were a glorious period with India commanding the respect and affection of the Afro-Asians. Even the west recognised Nehru's stature as a great statesman and held him in high esteem. The great British philosopher Bertrand Russell, haunted by the nuclear nightmare, declared that Nehru stood "for sanity and peace in a critical moment of human history. Perhaps it is he who would lead us out of the dark night of fear into a happy day." Even the British officialdom which was ever ready to carp at Nehru, especially on the Kashmir issue, did acknowledge his secure place in history as a leader who used his power, prestige and influence among the nations to enlarge the area of peace in the world. All these were too much for China to stomach.

Closer friendship, cooperation and mutual assistance between the two Asian nations would, apart from benefiting their own countries, help to guarantee the peace and progress in Asia and the world at large. Both could jointly contribute substantially to the welfare of humanity as a whole. But China refused to shake hands with India. She wanted to be the dominant power in Asia. Attainment of Great Power Status would entitle her to speak for the whole of Asia in regard to all the problems faced by that continent. Her aspiration might be legitimate but there was no justification for trying to achieve it through unfair means. China's twin objectives were: to secure the roads passing through Ladakh from Sinkiang to Tibet and to become the leading power in Asia. The spectacular success achieved initially in her first goal encouraged her to fulfil her second ambition of replacing India as the leading power in Asia. To achieve this, she planned to destroy India's prestige in the international arena, particularly in Nepal and Bhutan, hinder India's economic development, demonstrate to the Soviet Union the advantage of aggressive policies and encourage the communist parties in other Asian States to follow Peking rather than Moscow. Indisputably, China's ultimate aim seemed to be the construction of an empire of satellite Communist States throughout South East Asia owing ideological allegiance to her. To achieve this, she had to stifle India's growing power in Asia by engaging her in a debilitating war which would ruin her prospects for economic development completely.

Towards the end of 1961, Peking began her Press campaign of defamation of Nehru. What triggered this was the victory Nehru scored at the Conference of the Non-Aligned countries in Belgrade in September 1961 to discuss the frontier questions. The theses that China staunchly upheld were advanced by President Sukarno of Indonesia at this meet. But they were all beaten down by Nehru and Krishna Menon. As a result, Sukarno had to carry to Kennedy the India drafted peace appeal which he (Sukarno) scorned first.[9]

Pakistan which looked upon India as its inveterate enemy was out to fish in troubled waters. Her perfidy, though not unexpected, made the situation ominous for India. In May 1962, China and Pakistan simultaneously announced that they would negotiate a provisional border settlement and enter into a treaty of friendship by which their mutual frontiers would be aligned and delimited. The boundary was that of northwestern Kashmir as Pakistan had no common border with China. That part of Kashmir had been under the forcible occupation of Pakistan since 1948. It was substantiated that this provisional demarcation would be replaced in due course after reaching a settlement on the Indo-Pakistan dispute on Kashmir, by a formal boundary treaty between China and "the sovereign countries concerned." The Peking-Pindi announcement was made against a doubly disturbed background. It could not be taken in isolation from either the long-standing Kashmir dispute between India and Pakistan which was still unresolved or the newly inflamed frontier conflict between India and China.

On 7 May1962, referring to the announcement by Pakistan and China, Nehru told the Parliament that the two countries would make a provisional demarcation of the boundary west of the Karakoram Pass which amounted to interference in India's legal rights and sovereignty over Kashmir. He said India did not recognise any agreement between the two.

Pakistan's agreement with China was regarded a perfidy by her military allies. When President Kennedy told some American publishers that the US power was being used by her military allies in support of their national disputes, he referred in particular to Pakistan and the Kashmir dispute. The Pakistani Press criticised this remark. Privately America felt that the Kashmir dispute should be frozen on the existing cease-fire line. But it was a great pity that this was not expressed in public. America also, like Britain, was against incurring the displeasure of Pakistan.

On 9 September 1962, the Chinese troops crossed the Thag La Ridge, the highest watershed that constituted the McMahon Line and established themselves in a corner of territory where India, Tibet and Bhutan met. The Chinese had laid claims previously to this territory but it appeared they were occupied and administered by the Indians. Firing broke out on 20 September. China wanted to warn India that her claims extended to Ladakh and NEFA. To strengthen her claim, she sent a note on 3 October 1962 insisting that any talks between them should cover the whole of the Sino-Indian boundary. India replied that there could be no talks until the Chinese had withdrawn from the NEFA and taken measures to restore the *status quo* along the traditional boundary in the western sector.[10]

Full Dress Invasion

What began in 1957 as frontier skirmishes snowballed into a massive invasion of India by large Chinese forces. As it is not necessary to recount the war in detail only the principal events of the military campaign are narrated. Intrusions were taking place south of the McMahon Line and on 12 October 1962, Nehru declared that the Indian army had orders to stop the violations of the frontier by the Chinese army by pushing them back. On Saturday, 20 October 1962 at sunrise, about 30,000 Chinese troops unleashed an unprovoked and undeclared war against India in pursuance of China's expansionist policy. It may not be out of place to mention here, one of the "grim coincidental happenings" in the east and the west. Exactly in the third week of October 1962, on almost the same day, when the two huge Asian nations – India and China – went to war in the Himalayas, the two super powers – the US and the USSR – confronted each other over the island of Cuba and the world seemed perilously close to a nuclear war.

China was bent on settling a frontier favourable to her. Her army crossed the McMahon Line at several strategic points on a full dress invasion of India simultaneously launching an offensive in Ladakh. Nehru characterised this atrocious act as "unabashed aggression by an unscrupulous opponent." The Chinese overpowered Indian frontier posts in the NEFA which were on the Indian side of the McMahon Line. They also overwhelmed many frontier posts established by India in Ladakh. And they were poised to overrun Chushul in Ladakh. Once this was achieved there would be nothing to stop them till they reached Leh, the headquarters of Ladakh. Apart from being driven away from several posts in Ladakh, the Indian forces had also to abandon their major strong point at the Daulat Beg Oldi – the highest landing airstrip in the world at 17,000 feet altitude, near the Karakoram pass. Though the Indian soldiers fought gallantly, they were vastly outnumbered by the Chinese. There were others factors too for their inability to offer effective resistance. The attack was unexpected. India was totally unprepared to meet such a massive attack. The climate around the Chushul in Ladakh was ferocious at that period of the year. The soldiers had neither proper winter clothing nor the modern armour to fight in the NEFA mountains. Their weapons were obsolete and training inadequate. Untrained and ill-equipped to fight at such high altitudes of between 15,000 and 20,000 feet, they could not contain the far superior enemy forces.

Malcolm MacDonald, then Co-Chairman of the International Conference on Laos, had talks with Chou and Chen Yi on the Indo-China border question early in November 1962. The Chinese leaders said that Britain naturally supported India's stand on the question. To which MacDonald said that Britain was supporting India not only because they were both members of the Commonwealth but because she agreed with India's view as to where the frontier lay. Britain therefore shared India's view that it was the Chinese and not the Indians who were guilty of aggression. At the end of the meeting, Chou showed MacDonald the original map signed by McMahon and the Tibetan representative which showed the line right up to the Bhutan border. He said he presented Britain a copy of the map in London which should be there unless India had it in Delhi. He also said that China received her copy from the Tibetans in Lhasa. But it was at variance with the Indian claim as to the position of the line at the Bhutan end.[11]

On 8 November, the Lok Sabha passed a resolution proclaiming an emergency on account of the Chinese invasion. Speaking on the McMahon Line, Nehru said:

> "This line by whatever name it was called has been in existence now in our maps, in our practice, in our constitution, in our organisation for nearly 50 years... We have not gone one inch beyond the McMahon Line nor have we coveted another's territory...they (Chinese) have invaded an area not in their possession ever in the history of the last 10,000 years..."

On the same day – 8 November 1962 – President Kennedy sent a message to Ayub to the effect that he would find some way of letting Nehru know privately that Pakistan would not take advantage of any Indian withdrawal of the Indian forces on the Kashmir front to mount an attack on her.[12]

Kennedy had already, ten days earlier, sent a letter to Ayub focussing on the dangers that threatened the whole sub-continent if China succeeded in establishing herself in strength on the southern slopes of the Himalayas. Since the help coming forth to India from America or other western countries would be insignificant, she would be forced to withdraw one or two divisions from her existing positions in Kashmir. In such a situation, Kennedy wanted Ayub to "display a high degree of sportsmanship by sending some signal to Nehru" assuring that Pakistan would not exploit the situation to move against Kashmir.[13] Such entreaties even from the President of America had no impact on the President of Pakistan.

India did not expect that Pakistan, who was inflamed by anger over not getting the whole of Kashmir, would rush to India's help at her hour of great peril. But what hurt her was that Pakistan did not conceal her malicious pleasure at the hazard her neighbour was facing over the clash with China. It was a clear manifestation of the deplorable behaviour of a neighbour who, until 1947, was a part of India. Britain was not very helpful either. Her perfidy during the Chinese war was exposed when she asserted herself against large scale arms deliveries to India and succeeded in clamping a low ceiling at Nassau on American aid to India.[14] Even this act of Britain did not satisfy Pakistan who feared that the decision regarding the proposed ceiling was fraught with serious consequences to the security of Pakistan.[15]

On 14 November, the Lok Sabha passed another resolution dealing with the Chinese aggression and invasion. This was passed unanimously. A more significant factor was its passage in an unusual manner by all the members of the Parliament standing and pledging themselves to what the motion contained.

Having seized Ladakh and occupied the portion of the territory they claimed in October, the Chinese forces marched towards Tezpur in Assam, seized it and mounted another massive attack on the Indian position at the Sela Pass and at Walong in the second week of November. On 18 November, the Indian forces withdrew from these places and a little later from Bomdila, following its fall to the Chinese on 19 November. There was the chilling prospect of losing the Digboi oil field and the whole of Assam on either side of the River Brahmaputra. The Chinese violence appeared to be unending.

Nehru was in a state of profound shock. There never was a time when he felt so desolate. The events of October-November 1962 were such as to overwhelm even a man of such boundless energy, calibre and tact as Nehru. He was facing a national calamity. India's fate appeared dismal. To Nehru no cost was too great to save his motherland from an unscrupulous neighbour like China who was manoeuvring for her fall. In such a critical moment, when he was in a state of great panic, the only course the anguished Prime Minister could think of to weather the storm was to turn to the American President. He sent two letters in quick succession to President Kennedy on 19 November. The first letter was delivered in the morning and the second in the afternoon to the President by the Indian Ambassador B.K. Nehru. The following is the full text of Nehru's second letter to Kennedy:

"Dear Mr. President,

Within a few hours of despatching my earlier message of today, the situation in the N.E.F.A. Command has deteriorated still further. Bomdila has fallen and the retreating forces from Sela have been trapped between the Sela Ridge and Bomdila. A serious threat has developed to our Digboi oil fields in Assam. With the advance of the Chinese in massive strength, the entire Brahmaputra Valley is seriously threatened and unless something is done immediately to stem the tide, the whole of Assam, Tripura, Manipur and Nagaland would also pass into Chinese hands.

2. The Chinese have poised massive forces in the Chumbi Valley between Sikkim and Bhutan and another invasion from that direction appears imminent. Our areas further north west on the border with Tibet in the States of U.P., Punjab and Himachal Pradesh are also threatened. In Ladakh, as I have said in my earlier communication, Chushul is under heavy attack and shelling of the airfield at Chushul has already commenced. We have also noticed increasing air activity by the Chinese Air Force in Tibet.

3 Hitherto we have restricted our requests for assistance to essential equipment and we are most grateful for the assistance which has been so readily given to us. We did not ask for most comprehensive assistance particularly air assistance because of the wider implications of such assistance in the global context and we did not want to embarrass our friends.

4 The situation that has developed is, however, really desperate. We have to have more comprehensive assistance if the Chinese are to be prevented from taking over the whole of Eastern India. Any delay in the assistance reaching us will result in nothing short of a catastrophe for our country.

5. We have repeatedly felt the need of using air arm in support of our land forces, but have been unable to do so as in the present state of our air and radar equipment we have no defence against retaliatory action by the Chinese.

6. I, therefore, request that immediate support be given to strengthen our air arm sufficiently to stem the tide of Chinese advance.

7. I am advised that for providing adequate air defence a minimum of 12 squadrons of supersonic all-weather fighters are essential. We have no modern radar cover in the country. For this also we seek your assistance. Our needs are most immediate. The United States Air Force personnel will have to man these fighters and radar installations while our personnel are being trained. United States fighters and transport planes manned by United States personnel will be used for the present to protect our cities and installations from Chinese air attacks and to maintain our communications. We should, if this is possible, also like United States planes manned by United States personnel to assist the Indian Air Force in air battles with the Chinese Air Force over Indian areas where air action by the I.A.F. against Chinese communication lines, supplies and troop concentration may lead to counter air action by the Chinese.

8. Any air action to be taken against the Chinese beyond the limits of our country, e.g. in Tibet, will be taken by I.A.F. planes manned by Indian personnel.

9. Determined as we are to liberate all parts of our territory which may pass into the hands of the Chinese aggressors it is clear that sooner or later we would have to neutralise their bases and

airfields by striking from the air. For this purpose I request you to consider assisting us with two squadrons of bombers of B-47 type. To man this indispensable arm we would like to send immediately our pilots and technicians for training in the United States.

10. The Chinese threat as it has developed involves not merely the survival of India, but the survival of free and independent Governments in the whole of this sub-continent or in Asia. The domestic quarrels regarding small areas or territorial borders between the countries in this sub-continent or in Asia have no relevance whatever in the context of the developing Chinese invasion. I would emphasise particularly that all the assistance or equipment given to us to meet our dire need will be used entirely for resistance against the Chinese. I have made this clear in a letter I sent to President Ayub Khan of Pakistan. I am asking our Ambassador to give you a copy of this letter.
11. We are confident that your great country will in this hour of our trial help us in our fight for survival and for the survival of freedom and independence in this sub-continent as well as the rest of Asia. We on our part are determined to spare no effort until the threat posed by Chinese expansionist and aggressive militarism to freedom and independence is completely eliminated.[16]

With kind regards
Yours Sincerely,
Jawaharlal Nehru.

Conveying the contents of these letters to Ormsby Gore, British Ambassador to the US over phone, Kennedy said that Nehru's requests to the US were "far-reaching in the extreme." He had a feeling that Nehru's "appreciation" of the situation was "not entirely sound." And what was more important, Kennedy confided in Gore that "it was of vital importance that our knowledge of the text (of the letter) not becoming known to Indians." Thus, the US administration treated the letters as top-secret.

Avoidable Furore

Few in India had any knowledge of the existence of the letters of Nehru. Even if it were a public secret, no sane person would fail to appreciate the most perilous situation in which the Prime Minister found himself when he penned the letters. But, as ill-luck would have it, there was a storm of protest when the incident was made public. The disclosure of Nehru's request to Kennedy in November 1962 for American air protection against the Chinese was made for the first time by Sudhir Ghosh in the Indian Parliament on 15 March 1965. He said India was completely overwhelmed by Communist China that the Prime Minister "the father of non-alignment" was driven to ask for American air protection and that Kennedy responded by ordering "one of the American aircraft carriers to proceed to the Bay of Bengal."

A loud protest followed this remark and all hell broke loose. Sudhir Ghosh, an admirer of Nehru, was not critical of the non-alignment policy. He made the statement in the sense that while he believed in India's non-alignment between the US and the USSR, he did not understand how she could remain non-aligned between China and the US. Strengthening his statement, he also said that in an hour of great menace from China, the Prime Minister shrewdly realised that there could be "no non-alignment where Communist China was concerned." But this part of his speech was drowned in the tumult in the Parliament. What Ghosh said was a compliment to Nehru and not in any sense derogatory. Ghosh was shocked at the outcome of his statement. There was political storm in the lobbies of the Parliament and in the Press lasting for a fortnight. There were editorial articles in some of the leading newspapers.[17]

The pressure against Sudhir Ghosh's statement was so vehement as to force Prime Minister Lal Bahadur Shastri to deny that Nehru ever requested Kennedy for an American aircraft carrier and that there was a US carrier anywhere near Calcutta. In denying the fact Shastri disregarded Ghosh's advice to check the fact with Chester Bowles, American Ambassador to India. The latter confirmed on 10 June 1966 at a meeting of the Indian Army, Navy and Air Force Officers that "The US Government did have the document (Panditji's appeal to President Kennedy for air protection). The document was in Washington and it could be produced if the Government of India so desired."[18] According to Nehru's biographer, the celebrated historian S. Gopal, the Prime Minister wrote the two letters without consulting his Cabinet colleagues or officials save the Foreign Secretary. But, Gopal too had only summarised the contents of the letters without reproducing their full text "leaving it open to question whether the summary was accurate and faithful."[19]

Kennedy promptly responded to Nehru's letter by alerting the US Sixth Fleet in the Mediterranean and its Seventh Fleet in the Pacific. Possibly, a carrier was set on the move. During a subsequent cross-examination of Dean

Rusk by Senator Mundt, it was made unambiguously clear that India did ask America for air protection and that the latter did respond to it.[20]

On 21 November, within 48 hours after despatch of Nehru's letters to Kennedy, China announced a unilateral cease-fire and also her withdrawal to a considerable distance. Thus the Sino-Indian war came "wholly and abruptly" to an end. It was very possible that China had scented America's military help to India. G.K. Galbraith recorded on 22 November, "Yesterday, like a thief in the night, peace arrived."[21] For India, who had no army and who had suffered extensive loss of material, a breathing space was no doubt much needed. But in view of the discrepancies and contradictions in China's peace proposal, Nehru wrote to Chou En-Lai on 1 December seeking clarifications and also proposing for the latter's acceptance the restoration of the *status quo* prior to 8 September 1962, which was the least needed to create "the necessary atmosphere for reverting to peaceful process." Meanwhile, anxious to promote world peace, six non-aligned countries – Ceylon, Burma, Cambodia, Indonesia, Ghana and the United Arab Republic – convened a conference at Colombo from 10 to 12 December 1962. Proposals were put forward by the Prime Minister of Ceylon, the leader of the six nations, to stabilise the cease-fire and resume direct negotiations. After clarification of the proposals by representatives of three countries of the Colombo Conference, India accepted them but China did not. And in open violation of the proposals, she established seven civil posts in the western sector, placed stone cairns along the so-called "Line of Control," and increased her military strength along the Indian border. In fine, in December 1962, China was in possession of 36,260 square kilometres of Indian territory in Ladakh and 5180 sqaure kilometres in the NEFA. What was worse, she was supplying arms to Pakistan and training Pakistani military personnel.

There was opposition in the Parliament against the 8 September position agreed by Nehru. The opposition parties repeatedly reminded the Government of the Parliament's commitment only to the resolution of 14 November which was adopted unanimously and which expressed the nation's determination not to rest until the invader was driven out of the Indian soil altogether. The opposition was inclined to treat the 8 September position as irrelevant as accepting it would create the erroneous impression that the Parliament was supporting it as a permanent boundary between India and China. In the prevailing climate when Nehru revealed his commitment to the Ceylon Premier about the acceptance of the Colombo proposals, many Congress members themselves were not in its favour. They felt that further negotiations with

China would be construed that India had become complacent and slackened the defence efforts. They also felt that such a course would confuse the friendly countries who were keen to help India. But they could not summon courage to flout the Prime Minister publicly.

It is highly relevant here to speak of the folly of some officials who failed to muster courage to pass on their forebodings to the higher authorities concerned. It is difficult to fathom the rationale behind the disinclination or failure of even people in high and responsible positions to alert the concerned men/departments about vital matters they are in the know of about the security of the country. The behaviour of the Chief of the General Staff of the Indian Armed Forces, General Brij Kaul, is a classic instance. When Chester Bowles, a former US Ambassador to India, made a brief visit to the country in March 1962, Brij Kaul, at his own request, met him. He apprised Bowles of an expected attack of India by Communist China between July and October of that year. He wanted to know from Bowles what the US could be expected to do to help India. When Bowles appeared sceptical about such an attack, Kaul insisted that the Chinese troop movements into Tibet and the "carefully calculated build up of tensions" bore ample evidence to their "move from the negotiating table to the battlefield." When asked whether the Prime Minister knew that he was discussing these possibilities with Bowles, Kaul answered in the negative. He also did not follow Bowles's specific suggestion to discuss the matter with Ambassador Galbraith who would put the question to Washington. When, after the war, Nehru was told of this his regret was, "I wish he (Brij Kaul) had told me too."[22]

Krishna Menon's Exit

The reaction of the people of India to their country's defeat and the collapse of the Indian outposts was too sharp and startling. There was a strong condemnation of China throughout the country. The public was in no mood to allow any concession to China. The significant increase in the representation of the Jan Sangh in the Parliament, especially in the Hindi-belt, was a well-defined message that the public would not tolerate any concession to China. There were public utterances on the necessity of China's "vacating her aggression" as a condition for further negotiations. In fact, apart from possible American intervention, the unexpected anger of the Indian public also contributed to the Chinese offer of cease-fire and withdrawal.

The violence of the public feeling turned against Krishna Menon, the Defence Minister, who was held responsible for India's tarnished performance in the war. He became the butt of all attacks against bad administration of defence, deficiency in equipment and many other drawbacks in the Indian defences responsible for the unpreparedness of the army to meet the enemy. He was particularly condemned by the disgruntled army officers as being directly responsible for the calamity and hence unfit to hold the defence portfolio. He was also deplored for his "Pakistan is the real enemy" policy. Nehru was unhappy over this loud outcry at home and even resented the accusations levelled against Menon. Since the volume of criticism against him impeded his work, Menon himself resigned in November 1962 after serving as India's Defence Minister for five years and a half. The strength and persistence of the pressure on him from his own party as well as the higher civil service forced Nehru to accept Menon's resignation. Though Nehru was also blamed for misreading the perilous situation on the northern borders of India, the nation soon forgave its beloved Prime Minister. To a person of such transparent sincerity as Nehru, who was tirelessly championing China's cause in all world fora, China's treachery gave the severest shock from which he practically never recovered. Y.B. Chavan, Chief Minister of Maharashtra, was drafted to replace Krishna Menon.

There was however a lot of criticism both in India and abroad about Nehru's earlier acts in according recognition to the People's Republic of China without making it conditional on the latter guaranteeing the autonomy of Tibet and accepting the validity of the McMahon Line frontier. But Nehru's reasonable contention for the recognition of new China was that India could not ignore a major event in the history of a country with whom she had 3219 kilometres of common frontier.

After the "naked aggression" by a neighbour who India had trusted, the Indian public had become more united than ever before. The entire country empathised with the distress of the Indian leadership. Members of Parliament who represented the people were in an uncompromising mood. There was a fierce determination not to suffer any more humiliation from any quarter – be it Communist China or Pakistan. They were firm in their resolve to build the best system of defence for India of which they were capable. Immediately following Nehru's emotional broadcast warning the nation to prepare itself for a long struggle with China, there was a spontaneous surge of emotion throughout India. All parties pledged support to the Government; Trade Unions did likewise; temples made huge monetary contributions; Citizens Committees were set up in all cities; all ranks of society contributed to the National Defence

Fund that was quickly established; and knitting for the "jawans" became a major female industry. Austerity was observed in all governmental functions. In Delhi, "the atmosphere quickly approached that of the capital of a country at war." It is noteworthy that China did not at all expect so intense a surge of national feeling which she witnessed in India in the wake of her unprovoked and undeclared war on India.

India knew that Krishna Menon's exit alone would not change the position of India's defence. India's urgent needs were a thorough reorganisation of the entire defence system and provision of all equipments needed for the forces to successfully complete the task of throwing back the invader. The one most edifying lesson the Government of India learned from this war was the great and urgent need to improve the military might of India in commensurate with her vast size and exposed geographical position with two hostile neighbours. Galbraith, who was in India throughout the catastrophe recorded in December 1962 that the Indian army had recovered its balance and that its "morale is improving, the soldiers are rough, hard and well-trained and discipline is good. Nevertheless, it is well that the Chinese stopped (but) they could do a great deal of damage if they decide to come again...My instinct is the danger of a new and major adventure is receding though I assume the Chinese have not given up their evil intentions."[23]

References

1. Malcolm MacDonald's talk with Ellsworth Bunker, 14 Jan. 1960, DO/35/8999.
2. Known for the large Buddhist monastery, the Tawang tract was under the administration of Tibet. In contrast with the tribal regions, it was a settled and culturally relatively advanced area.
3. FO to HM's Representatives, 30 Oct. 1962, FO/1061/135(A).
4. Statement in Rajya Sabha, 22 Aug. 1962.
5. B.N. Mullick, *My Years with Nehru: The Chinese Betrayal,* p. 201.
6. Statement made on 27 Sep. 1962, DO/196/165.
7. W.J.E. Norton, FO to J.M. Dutton, CRO, 21 Aug. 1962, FO/196/164.
8. *Speeches of Jawaharlal Nehru 1957-63,* Vol. Four, p. 190.
9. *The Economist,* 12 May 1962.
10. Paul Gore-Booth, UK HC (I) to Commonwealth Secy., 28 Dec. 1962, DO/196/171.
11. Report on MacDonald's talks with Chou, 5 & 10 Nov. 1962, DO/196/167 & DO/ 196/168.

12. Kennedy to Ayub Khan, 8 Nov. 1962, DO/196/187.
13. D. Ormsby Gore to FO, 29 Oct. 1962, DO/196/166.
14. K.C. Khanna, "Indo-British Relations," *Times of India*, 2 April 1966.
15. Ayub to Macmillan, 24 Dec. 1962, DO/196/147.
16. Jawaharlal Nehru to Kennedy, 19 Nov. 1962, FO/371/164880.
17. Sudhir Ghosh, *Gandhi's Emissary*, pp. 291 & 92.
18. *Ibid*, p. 298.
19. Atlaf Gauhar, *Ayub Khan*, p. 357.
20. *Gandhi's Emissary, op. cit.*, pp. 291 & 98.
21. J.K. Galbraith, *Ambassador's Journal A Personal Account of Kennedy Years*, p. 490.
22. Chester Bowles, *Mission To India A Search For Alternatives In Asia*, p. 85.
23. *Ambassador's Journal, op. cit.*, pp. 510 & 11.

14

West's Conditional Military Aid to India

In May 1962, when China's attack on India seemed imminent, Pakistan and China announced their intention to hold border negotiations in regard to the boundary between China's Sinkiang and the contiguous Kashmiri areas which was under the actual control of Pakistan. Pakistan wanted to seek political mileage out of the turbulent situation India was facing. What both contemplated was an interference with India's sovereignty over Kashmir. Obviously, both China and Pakistan were as keen on scoring points off India as to settle matters between themselves. China, it must be borne in mind, did not back Pakistan's full claims to Kashmir. Anti-communist and western-allied Pakistan's wooing of China was "a boost" to Pakistan and "a blow" to India. As *The Economist* observed, it was "a boost and a blow which reveal, very interestingly, that membership of 'militarist- Western blocks' is no bar to – and non-alignment on the purest *Panch-Shila* principles no guarantee of – the favour of a communist power interested in making trouble among its neighbours."[1]

Kashmir Made "Core Issue"

Both Communist China and militarist Pakistan rejoiced at the deep sense of gloom prevailing in India. Both were delighted to find India struggle between the devil and the deep sea. While stepping up its pressure on the Chinese forces which had intruded in the east, the Indian army had also to look to the west where the newly elected President of Azad Kashmir and his cohorts had revived more vehemently than ever before their talk of the "war of liberation" in Kashmir.

On 22 October 1962 – two days after China launched her attack on India, Nehru wrote to Ayub informing him of China's aggression which was endangering the peace and stability of the region in which Pakistan was "vitally concerned." Nehru sent communications about the Chinese aggression to all Heads of States except Portugal and 63 countries responded conveying their sympathy and support to India. In his very friendly reply to Nehru, Ayub wrote that Pakistan was wedded to peace with all her neighbours especially India and hoped that the conflict with China could be peacefully resolved. Nehru wrote to Ayub again on 12 November that the Chinese aggression was no mere frontier incident but an invasion of India on a massive scale. He further said that the help given by friendly countries by way of defence equipment and stores would be utilised solely to resist the Chinese aggression. There was no response to this letter. Shockingly, contrary to his own statements in his earlier friendly letter to Nehru, Ayub organised on 16 November, a day of protest against Western aid to India. The anger was triggered by the help Britain rushed to India to fight the Chinese without regard to Pakistan's reactions. There were allegations that the aid was being used by India to attack Pakistan. Ill-feeling in both wings of Pakistan were inflamed by vicious articles in the Press particularly the vernacular ones and by the rash utterances of leaders of every political hue. There were also demonstrations against both Britain and America.[2] The allegations were mostly based on false information supplied by Musa, Commander-in-Chief of Pakistan. He spread the rumour that mere border skirmishes with China were wantonly magnified by India to obtain arms from the West to be used against Pakistan. Whereas Britain had delivered a meagre quantity of small arms and ammunitions to India, Musa made the hyperbolic statement that India had received arms on a "fantastic scale" and that Britain had delivered to her more arms in eight days than what she supplied to Pakistan in eight years. On being informed of this false propaganda, the CRO told the British High Commissioner in Karachi to reveal to Musa that just 2000 automatic rifles and 3 million rounds of ammunition amounting in all to £1,50,000 were delivered to India.[3]

What puzzled India was the leakage of military secrets. Perhaps what India considered as military secrets were not so in other countries. As a renowned Indian correspondent wrote: "In the United States and to some extent in Britain everything relating to India is an open secret."[4] From the statements Ayub often made regarding western arms aid to India, it was very clear that Britain and America did keep him informed of what had been supplied and what were proposed to be supplied by them to India.

It was interesting and perhaps significant that even while explaining to Ayub the great need to help India when she was in a highly critical situation, Macmillan made his statements very guardedly. In his letter to Ayub, he wrote that in extending military aid to India, he was "particularly mindful of the interests and understandable anxieties of Pakistan...I well understand the emotions which have been roused among your people...I hope that together you and we (the British) will be able to...prevent popular feelings from endangering the deep friendship which exits between Pakistan and Britain..."[5]

At the BBC Television interview on 22 October 1962 when Nehru was asked what sort of aid, military or otherwise, he would take from America or Britain, his clear answer was: "We don't intend to ask for any free aid. We may of course buy things from them on suitable terms, but we have always avoided taking any free military aid from any country."[6] But Pakistan refused to consider all this.

The unsettlement of the Kashmir imbroglio coupled with the insensate propaganda of Pakistan against India certainly placed Britain and America in a great dilemma. No doubt both were shocked at Chinese aggression and both expressed sympathy with India. But when it came to helping India with military aid to repel the Chinese attack both were very cautious to ensure that Pakistan did not take umbrage because the Kashmir question was hanging fire for fourteen years. Pakistan had already set afloat the rumour that there was no major attack on India by China and that India herself was in favour of negotiated settlement with China. India felt that the two issues not being interrelated, it was not correct or even justifiable to link them while considering India's request for military aid. Both the powers – Britain and America, argued that they had to consider public feelings and apprehensions. Britain knew that the very likely attack by China on the Chumbi Valley would have a serious impact on India and that they had to provide arms to India to meet such a contingency. Yet, not to offend Pakistan, she informed India that all her military supplies including the future ones were subject to the same conditions as those laid down by the Americans under the US Mutual Security Act of 1954. India agreed.

The American authorities were no less concerned about keeping Pakistan in good humour. In fact, Dean Rusk was critical of Nehru's second midnight letter to Kennedy written in great desperation. He sent his

Ambassador in India a long telegram which was largely devoted to raising questions. He asked: "Will the Indians take a sensible view of Pakistan? Will they be more concerned about the problems of communism in Asia? (Why) no one hereabouts has thought of South Asia for weeks? What about mobilising the resources of the Commonwealth? What about the UN?" It was very clear that Rusk grievously underrated the ruinous situation India was in. Otherwise, he would not have ended the telegram with the prediction that the Chinese would not, as India feared, press forward on all fronts.[7]

The two Western powers could not reach a consensus about the simple matter of extending help to a large democracy in distress. They were much concerned about how Pakistan would react to it. Galbraith told them in all frankness that if India was to feel secure enough to face China, it was necessary to ensure that her mind was taken off the Kashmir issue. Macmillan viewed this suggestion with an amount of scepticism and told Kennedy that "in my view, it would have a reverse effect; the more secure the Indians felt, the more intransigent they would be with the Pakistanis, who would then turn to the Chinese."[8]

The Anglo-American ominous policy of playing the two disputants against each other on Kashmir emboldened Pakistan not to budge an inch on her stand on the issue. The whole world knew and Britain and America also knew that India would never launch an aggression against anyone. Yet Ayub did not shrink from stating in an interview with an American television that India's latest arms build-up was primarily directed against Pakistan "in keeping with her record of intimidating her smaller neighbours." Both Britain and America knew that Pakistan's statement was ill-conceived because Pakistan's proclivity for promoting militancy across the border was universally known. Yet, they failed to check her intrigues. Britain and America were also perturbed that despite being an active member of the SEATO, which was forged to contain communist China's expansionism, Pakistan's support to China in her aggression against India had gone to the extent of signing border and trade pacts with her (China). Pakistan had an unshakeable belief that Western aid to India in the existing emergency endangered her own security. With this erroneous impression having become implanted in her mind, even efforts by India to defend herself against China were misread by Pakistan as preparations to attack her. Knowing this stark reality, the Western powers, instead of dispelling the Pakistani illusions about India, took her line of reasoning and wanted the Kashmir question to be cleared out of the way so as to smoothen the flow of military aid to India.

Overconcern for Pakistan

Two political-cum-military missions from America and Britain visited India soon after China announced her plan of unilateral cease-fire on 21 November 1962. They were headed by Averell Harriman of the US and Duncan Sandys, British Commonwealth Secretary. Aided by their top military advisers, they were to make an assessment of India's immediate military requirements and also to study Indian reactions at various levels to the Chinese cease-fire proposal so as to ascertain to what extent India could carry on the struggle against China.

The military missions agreed to reequip the battered divisions of the Indian Army which had suffered by the Chinese onslaught. But Ayub stated in a later broadcast that the Western powers had agreed to equip "six new Indian divisions," which was not correct. Immediately after the Chinese attack, American planes loaded only with small arms were sent and Britain also did the same. As Harriman stated the loss of equipment suffered by the Indian Army in NEFA was much more than what had been supplied by both Britain and America.[9]

While discussing the supply of arms from abroad, India made it clear that she had no wish to ask for arms from abroad which could be produced in India and that she was already taking action to step up the output of her ordnance factories and to expand in other ways her manufacturing capacity. Instead of examining this, the Western powers most inappropriately evinced an interest in another subject which pertained to India's relation with Pakistan on Kashmir. It was entirely out of context at that moment and hence should not have been mixed up with granting military aid to India. Linking the two subjects which were not inter-related was totally incorrect and unjustified. In fact, there was a strong feeling among the public in India that the Western powers under the pressure of Pakistan were making too much of the need for a settlement on Kashmir before taking a decision on the supply of fighters and bombers. When Duncan Sandys met Nehru in Delhi on 24 November, he linked up the subject of arms aid with Kashmir. He stressed the urgent need to settle the Kashmir dispute first as that would enable both India and Pakistan to present a united front against the common external threat to the sub-continent and release the military forces which were being wasted in guarding themselves against one another. Nehru readily recognised the desirability of a settlement on Kashmir but said the time was not opportune for it. The people of India, who were already humiliated by the defeat of their forces by the Chinese, were in no mood to make concessions over Kashmir as that would mean surrender to the Pakistani blackmail. He also said that India could never forgive Pakistan for flirting with China while the Chinese troops were attacking her.

In their discussions with the Indian Prime Minister, both Duncan Sandys and Averell Harriman attributed the difficulty in giving long-term military aid to India to the unwillingness of certain sections of the peoples of Britain and America. They would be unhappy to find an appreciable part of the Indian army deployed not for defence against China but for defence against Pakistan. By this, they drove home the point that in the face of the Chinese threat to the whole sub-continent, a new attempt had necessarily to be made to settle the differences between India and Pakistan, meaning the Kashmir issue.

Britain, more a friend of Pakistan than of India, was hesitant to extend support for a long term programme of military assistance to India as that would enrage Pakistan. Duncan Sandys requested that India should create conditions for Britain to help her without "irretrievably embittering our relations with Pakistan." Nehru plainly told Duncan Sandys of the impossibility of handing over the Vale to Pakistan. Though Kashmir had a special status as a State, it was an integral part of the complex Indian Union. Removing it away would mean taking a plank out of the Indian Union which would deal out a severe blow to the building up process of the country including that of Kashmir which had been accomplished in over fifteen years. Ruling out plebiscite which Pakistan was pressing, Nehru said that the Vale being predominantly Muslim, would feel it their duty to vote for Pakistan on religious grounds. An electoral campaign conducted on religious lines would have serious repercussions in India. There might be a fierce communal strife throughout India of which Kashmir was an essential part. This would "undermine the secular character of the Indian State and weaken the whole fabric of Indian unity built up over the years," Nehru said. However, he agreed to meet Ayub or have a meeting at ministerial level for an unrestricted discussion of the whole problem. Nehru particularly spoke of the possible cooperation between the two countries in defence.[10] As for Pakistan, she was not at all in favour of the Anglo-American proposal for bilateral talks to resolve the Kashmir issue because the intention was for India and Pakistan to present a united front against China with whom she was negotiating to demarcate the common boundary between China and northern Kashmir.

Duncan Sandys met Ayub also, spoke to him convincingly and succeeded in getting both Nehru and Ayub issue the following Joint Statement:

> "On 29 November 1962, the President of Pakistan and the Prime Minister of India have agreed that a renewed effort should be made

to resolve the outstanding differences between their two countries on Kashmir and other related matters so as to enable India and Pakistan to live side by side in peace and friendship. In consequence, they have decided to start discussions at an early date with the object of reaching an honourable and equitable settlement. These will be conducted initially at the ministerial level. At the appropriate stage direct talks will be held between Prime Minister Nehru and President Ayub Khan."

There was a strong undercurrent of unhappiness among the public in Pakistan about the Joint Statement. The primary purpose of the discussions which were to begin from December 1962 was to secure the disengagement of the Indian and Pakistani forces facing each other on the Kashmir front so as to enable India to deploy her troops to meet the Chinese menace. This being unpalatable to Pakistan, she vented her anger on India. Even the innocuous statements of the Indian Prime Minister were misinterpreted in Pakistan particularly by the Members of the Pakistan Parliament. Nehru's statement in the Lok Sabha that "India would not bypass or ignore her basic principles" and that any change in the *status quo* in Kashmir would be harmful was seized upon as a complete vindication of all Pakistan's suspicions of "Indian duplicity and insincerity." It was said that Nehru would reject any solution on Kashmir which would involve a change in the *status quo*. It was a tendentious interpretation of Nehru's statement to raise the emotional temperature of the Pakistani public. The Pakistan Government had allowed itself to be misled and a motion of censure on it was being tabled in the Parliament at Rawalpindi.

Duncan Sandys knew that Nehru's statement was not intended to convey the meaning attributed to it. But the Pakistan Government refused to hold talks unless Duncan Sandys returned to Delhi and obtained a clarification from Nehru. The Pakistani Press persisted in believing that so long as Nehru was the Prime Minister, hopes of a settlement on Kashmir acceptable to both were extremely bleak. Despite knowing that India's acceptance to enter the discussions without preconditions was a definite advance on her previous position, the Pakistani Press continued to be suspicious and sceptical. The fear that the scepticism of the Pakistan Parliament might sabotage the contemplated peace process drove Duncan Sandys to fly back to Delhi forthwith and request Nehru to dispel any misunderstanding. He briefed Nehru about the wrong interpretation that had been put upon his words in the Lok Sabha. Sandys was much relieved when Nehru obliged by issuing what Duncan termed "a most helpful statement." It made clear that Nehru had no intention of placing any restrictions on the scope of the proposed talks or refusing to consider any solution that Pakistan might wish to propose. This welcome statement reached Rawalpindi just in time to be announced in the Parliament. This did help to clear the earlier suspicions. More importantly, it helped the Pakistan Government to keep the situation in the country under control.

On reaching England, Duncan Sandys told the British Parliament: "During my stay in Delhi, I concluded an agreement with the Indian Government, one of the purposes of which was to reassure Pakistan that arms supplied to India to meet Chinese aggression would be used for no other purpose..."[11]

Harriman stated in his report that Ayub had "permitted and encouraged the stirring up of emotion in the Pakistani Press." This prompted him to draw the conclusion that a settlement of Kashmir on acceptable terms would be the only thing that would change the attitude of Ayub.[12]

Ayub told Sandys and Harriman that it was of paramount importance to make Nehru realise that since the emergency was over, India should not expect any further aid from Britain until she settled the vexed Kashmir question. Repeating this in a letter to Prime Minister Macmillan, he asked the UK Government to bring continued pressure on Nehru before the commencement of negotiations. He threatened that the alarm in Pakistan over the arms aid to India would aggravate if the volume of aid was increased without settling the Kashmir issue and cautioned that the alarm and criticism in the Pakistani public opinion could not be discounted. He also wanted Macmillan to persuade India to reach a peaceful settlement with China and dissuade it from launching a military adventure to evict the Chinese. Ayub concluded his letter thus: "The British know as well as we do that the Hindu will only listen if circumstances compel him to do so and I am convinced that to-day the compulsion of events will make him listen to reason."[13]

The minatory talks and letters of Ayub drove Macmillan to write to Nehru from Nassau in December 1962 how very difficult it was for Britain and America to help India "without gravely damaging our relations with Pakistan." He also expressed concern about public in Britain and America as their opinion would be "dampened if many resources are immobilised on the Pakistan border, which would otherwise be available for defence against China.[14] In his letter to Ayub on the same date, Macmillan assured him that the military aid of Britain and America to India would be "tailored to the precise requirements" to meet the Chinese threat, as assessed by the military experts. There was also the further assurance that the equipment they provided would be used exclusively to meet the danger of Chinese aggression.[15]

Six Rounds of Talks

There were altogether six rounds of ministerial talks between Zulfiquar Ali Bhutto, Pakistan's Minister for Industries, Natural Resources and Works and Sardar Swaran Singh, India's Minister for Railways. The first round of the talks was held in Rawalpindi from 26 to 28 December 1962. Of course, there were no high hopes of a settlement. Both parties admitted that the Kashmir problem overshadowed all other differences between them. At the very outset, elaborating on the need to resolve the outstanding differences and live in peace as friendly neighbours, Swaran Singh said that the campaign of the Pakistani Press and the public against India, which was becoming more and more virulent, hurt India's feelings. Bhutto in his speech reiterated that the Kashmir issue was the source of all "ill-will and bitterness" and then made the blunt statement that if India's approach to the problem lay in asserting that the State was an integral part of India, then there would be no basis for negotiation.[16] It was agreed by both parties that plebiscite in any form being impracticable, a political solution had to be found to settle the problem.

When the Rawalpindi talks were in progress, Gundevia, India's Commonwealth Secretary, in his talk with the UK High Commissioner to Pakistan said that if the Pakistanis did not insist on a plebiscite, the Indians would offer a "territorial redistribution." He meant by this a settlement along the CFL with possibly some special economic and other concessions for Pakistan in the Indian two-thirds of the territory. India had already told both Harriman and Sandys unambiguously that she could never part with the Vale and therefore, there was absolutely no chance of any solution based on that idea. So the only real solution was for each side to keep what it already held. In fact, about a fortnight earlier, Belcher, UK Deputy High Commissioner in New Delhi, had a talk on Kashmir with Gundevia when the latter was in the company of G. Parthasarathy, India's High Commissioner to Pakistan. Belcher said that Nehru was interested in Galbraith's idea of taking the sting out of the sovereignty issue by the development of some kind of enjoyment of the attributes of sovereignty in the interests of the people of Kashmir themselves. They thought of some kind of condominium though they were unsure of its "practicable possibility." Nevertheless both Gundevia and Parthasarathy were plainly interested in it and were ready to discuss the idea with Pakistan. But the snag was that both felt, no doubt reasonably, that even a sane suggestion, coming from the Indians, would be suspect in the eyes of the Pakistanis. It was therefore decided that the idea should be sold to the Pakistanis so that they would themselves bring it forward at the appropriate moment. Gundevia said

"There would be no question about our willingness to discuss it. Indeed Galbraith has half sold it to Nehru already." Nothing however was heard subsequently of the condominium proposal.[17]

While India was anxious to explore the possibilities of a settlement on Kashmir, Pakistan was moving in the direction of reaching a settlement with China even by sacrificing an area of about 9583 square kilometres in the Hunza region. It was under this shadow that the first round of ministerial talks began. On the night of 26 December 1962, the day the ministerial talks opened in Rawalpindi – there was a surprise announcement that China and Pakistan had reached a complete agreement in principle on the alignment of their "common border" (which was in fact the Azad Kashmir border). The Pakistani Ambassador in Peking was empowered to go ahead with the negotiations if a reasonably satisfactory basis had been achieved. A simultaneous announcement was made in Peking on the same night. The Indian delegation, which was sore and suspicious about the announcement, was told by the UK High Commissioner in Pakistan that it was China's plan to wreck the Indo-Pakistan talks.[18]

Nehru regretted much the announcement which he felt did not augur well for the future rounds of talks. Public opinion in India regarded the announcement and its timing as a definite attempt to "pressurise India to seek accommodation under threat of force."[19]

The second round of ministerial talks was held in New Delhi in January 1963. The plebiscite idea was covered again at this round. Whether the plebiscite should be for the whole State of Jammu and Kashmir or region-wise or limited to the Valley was reviewed at considerable length, very unnecessarily and as usual, it appeared an insurmountable problem to solve. India would not agree to a settlement that would upset the Valley's existing status. Pakistan, already in forcible occupation of Gilgit, Gilgit Agency, Baltistan and a third of Jammu, asserted that what she possessed in Kashmir was hers by her own right and that she should have more.

However, there was no breakdown of the talks. Both parties agreed that a political solution acceptable to them had to be found. This decision facilitated the continuance of another round of talks. There was a Joint Statement issued at the end of the discussion to the effect that: "The two Ministers held ten meetings on the 16, 17, 18 and 19 January at which various aspects of the Kashmir problem were discussed...The discussions were frank and cordial and the attitude of the two sides was constructive throughout." It was decided to have the third round of talks in Karachi in February 1963.

Pakistan's claim that what she held in Kashmir was hers by right and that she was legitimately entitled to more was dangerous. It was most unfortunate that India did nothing to counter this claim. Commenting on this failure on the part of India, *The Hindu* wrote "To imagine that truth will ultimately prevail, is good philosophy. But it does not seem to produce results in a world where nations are preoccupied with their own immediate problems."[20]

Before the Karachi talks, Philip Talbot, the US Assistant Secretary of State, visited India. He said nothing new but simply repeated that America was not making the Kashmir settlement a condition for American military aid. But he also said in the same breath that the Congressional thinking in the US on military aid to India would depend on her reaching an agreement with Pakistan on the Kashmir question. Both Britain and America often used this contradictory statement to assuage the grief of India. While talking to T.T. Krishnamachari about military aid, the US President assured him that that problem was not linked to the Kashmir issue but that he hoped that India would definitely pursue her efforts to reach a settlement with Pakistan. Similarly, the British Prime Minister also told him that Britain did not link Kashmir to military aid "but the two questions were certainly connected."[21] In other words, India's coming to terms with Pakistan on Kashmir was mandatory for military aid. The US which was embarrassed by Pakistan's flirtations with China felt that the only way by which Pakistan could be drawn away from China's influence was by forcing India to reach an accommodation with Pakistan on Kashmir. Pakistan exulted at the Western pressure on India. She was sure that India, who was in dire need of Western military aid, had no option but to agree to the conditions laid down by the West. If Pakistan had thought that she would soon have the whole of Kashmir, she was sadly mistaken.

The third round of talks in Karachi was held from 8 to 11 February 1963. The extravagant demand made by the Pakistan Government at these meetings stunned the Pakistanis themselves. The demand embraced practically the whole of the undivided Jammu and Kashmir State with the exception of the Katua district and half of the Udhampur district in the southeastern tip of Jammu. In short, out of total area of 2,22,236 square kilometres for the whole of the State of Kashmir, the area offered to India was less than 5180 square kilometres! This ridiculous offer made by Pakistan constituted her idea of a political settlement with India. There was an unbridgeable gulf between what Pakistan demanded and what India would offer. The day before the meeting commenced, Bhutto told the UK High Commissioner that he would accept no solution calling for a division of the Vale of Kashmir and that the Pakistanis were no chattels to be disposed of without regard for their desires. He told the US Ambassador McConnaughy also that he would rather break off the talks than accept the partition of the Vale. He warned him that if the UK and the US advocated such a proposal, its "effect on Western position here would be disastrous." In a private talk with the UK High Commissioner, Gundevia denounced Bhutto's proposal regarding the Vale as "a shabby bargaining manoeuvre worthy only of the bazaar."[22]

Bhutto was furious over India's refusal to accept the Vale as a disputed territory. As he always did when his proposals failed to carry weight, he said, in a more intimidatory tone that since the problem was not solved either in the UN or bilaterally, the only way open to him was to adopt what he described as "Pakistan Solution," meaning a possible direct action.

The Joint *Communique* issued at the end of the meeting on 11 February merely said that the Ministers held several meetings and agreed that a further exchange of views was necessary. Pakistan was reluctant to have another round of talks if India did not offer more liberal proposals. India would not agree to any conditions imposed on her by Pakistan. Finally, however, both managed to agree on a fourth round of talks without pre-conditions on 12 March in Calcutta.

Even the bosom friends of Pakistan – Britain and America – had not the least doubt that to the Pakistani politicians the possession of Kashmir by means fair or foul and hatred of India and the Hindus through false propaganda were the only useful weapons to keep Pakistan in tact and themselves in power. India had never been in favour of talks, discussions and negotiations on the Kashmir crisis since she knew they would achieve nothing worthwhile with both parties sticking to their guns. If, with all the misgivings gnawing her mind, India agreed to enter the fourth round of dismal talks, it was because she was anxious to convince the world that she was genuine about reaching a settlement on reasonable terms with Pakistan.

The wide gulf between Pakistan's arbitrary claims and India's reasonable offers was not narrowed at the fourth round of talks in Calcutta. In fact, a good deal of time during this meeting was occupied by the Sino-Pakistan Border Agreement leaving very little time to discuss Kashmir. Though this would have served as a convincing excuse for India to break off the talks, she did not do so. Nothing was accomplished on the Kashmir question. There could be no settlement as long as Pakistan was bent on appropriating the whole of Kashmir. It was during this time at Calcutta, Bhutto told Galbraith and Gore-Booth that Pakistan claimed the whole of Kashmir except two districts in

Jammu. Commenting on this, Gore-Booth wrote "This was an absurd claim and the Pakistanis pretty well admitted as much...Our efforts to him to make a sensible suggestion failed."[23] Impressed by whatever had been achieved, the conferees set another date in late April for one more round – the fifth one – again in Karachi and adjourned. Prime Minister Macmillan expressed to Nehru his disappointment at the absence of progress in the talks at Calcutta. Dwelling on the benefits that would accrue to both the countries through progress towards a settlement, he urged Nehru to make every attempt at the next round of talks in Karachi so as to break the existing deadlock.[24]

On the eve of the fifth round of talks in Karachi, Bhutto issued a warning to the West. It contained some most unrealistic demands: (i) Pakistan would reconsider her alliances with the West if she did not receive all she wanted in Kashmir; (ii) any further Western military aid to India must be made conditional on a settlement of the Kashmir dispute; and (iii) the Western allies should deny long-term arms assistance to India unless his demand for practically the entire Valley of Kashmir was conceded in full. He refused to consider the Chinese attack on India because, in his opinion, there was no threat at all from China to India who was suffering from "war hysteria."[25] India, for her part, held firmly to her stand that she would cooperate with Pakistan to work out a solution only if it did not upset Kashmir's status as one of the fifteen States of the Indian Federation.

Unlike the previous four rounds of talks, at the fifth round in Karachi, India could sense distinct stiffening in Pakistan's attitude towards her. There was no cordiality in the tone of the Pakistani authorities either. Pakistan had completely abandoned the idea of a political settlement and pressed her earlier demands for the Valley along with the Buddhist majority area of Ladakh and the catchment areas of the Jhelum and the Chenab. Pakistan chose to ask for Ladakh in the shocking context of the Indo-China war knowing well that only India who had control over the Valley could defend Ladakh against China. Pakistan was not unaware that her Western friends would not countenance her demands when even what she had been occupying was "not legitimately hers but the fruits of aggression." The Karachi meeting achieved nothing since Pakistan's "unreasonable and overweening" demands could not be met. Bhutto peremptorily demanded the whole of the Vale for Pakistan. Anything short of this was "a 1000 per cent out of question." The failure of the five rounds of talks indicated beyond doubt the unwisdom of any more attempt to reach an agreement on the Kashmir question. Still there was no breakdown of talks. It was agreed to continue the discussions in New Delhi on 15 May 1963.

Galbraith said that the achievement of the five rounds of talks was "a hardening in the hard-core bargaining position of each country. Bhutto had now started insisting on Pakistan's claim to Ladakh. It became clear that even a remote possibility of flexibility on the part of India in regard to the Vale had been lost." The Ambassador came to the inevitable conclusion that the time "to plan for failure" had come. He recommended a year's standstill in the talks so that they might not peter out with no hope of renewal.[26]

Before the sixth round of talks, there took place an unusual visit of three top-level leaders from Britain – Mountbatten, Duncan Sandys and George Selkirk, High Commissioner for South East Asia – to India in May 1963. Though all the three leaders had discussions with Nehru, Mountbatten met him several times and had talks on many subjects. But his main object was to find some way to get the talks on Kashmir out of the "dead end" into which they were sure to run in the sixth round of talks in New Delhi. It was expected that Mountbatten would use his close personal relationship with Nehru to explore the ground. The proposal they contemplated centred round the appointment of a mediator. Initially, Nehru was unresponsive but after two talks, it emerged that he might consider the appointment of a mediator. But Nehru let Mountbatten know that he had a "ticklish time" with his colleagues about resorting to mediation. Subsequently, the visitors made an approach to Ayub regarding the proposal but he wanted time to reach a final decision on it.

On 15 May, both the delegations met in New Delhi for the sixth round of talks. Actually, the discussions had hardly begun when Bhutto suddenly announced his decision to cut short his stay in Delhi which led to the breakdown of the negotiations. It was evident that Bhutto was aware of the mediatory efforts being made in the West. The discussions on 16 May, moved on to a suggestion put forth by India to the following effect: "Both sides should accept that agreement could not be reached over Kashmir but that a big step towards resolving outstanding disagreements and suspicions could be taken by reaching an agreement on disengagement of forces coupled with a no war declaration." Pakistan replied that since she had no aggressive designs against India, a "No War" declaration was uncalled for. She harped on the reactions to such a declaration from her public which would further embitter her relations with India. Thereupon, the following *Communiqué* was issued: "At the end of the last meeting which concluded to-day, the two Ministers recorded their regret that no agreement could be reached on the settlement of the Kashmir dispute."

The ministerial talks on Kashmir finally broke down. Both the Ministers met the Press separately and both indicated the mediation proposals made to their Governments. Bhutto's conference was marred towards the end when he completely abandoned politeness and suavity and switched over to abusing India for her "arrogance, obstinacy and sophistry." He even suggested that the "Indian Kashmiris would be unwilling to share in national resistance to China."[27]

The abrupt termination of the talks synchronised with the simultaneous announcements from Washington and London on the attempts being made for mediation in Kashmir. For the Pakistan Government, these timely announcements were a blessing in disguise as they prevented any adverse reactions in Pakistan to the breakdown of the talks.

Unparalleled Tension

India was getting agitated over the delay on receiving long-term military aid from the Western bloc. Lot of thinking was done by America and Britain also about giving long-term aid to India though the recognition of the need to help her arose from different reasons. America, a vehement opponent of communism, would not let China persist in her massive and unjustifiable military aggression against India. Her assistance to India related to her policy of containing international communism. In a private talk with Nehru, Rusk said in no uncertain language that there could be no compromise where America was concerned over communist China's threat to the entire sub-continent. It was only in the context of the Chinese threat that America was desirous to promote friendly relations between India and Pakistan, he emphasised. Britain's policy towards military aid to India, on the other hand, had no bearing on the Chinese menace. This fact did not figure in Duncan Sandy's talk with Nehru. Britain had recognised Communist China and had diplomatic relations with her. She was even contemplating on trade with China, the future of Hong Kong and the formation of Malaysia. Then she had to consider the important question of finding resources to assist India, who was a member of the Commonwealth. The only common concern of both powers in extending long term military aid to India was that they should do it without incurring the wrath of Pakistan. It was the apprehension about the adverse impact of their good gesture on Pakistan that forced the powers to drag their feet on a vital issue. But neither Britain nor America boldly and clearly spelt out the fact that Pakistan's stern warning against any long term arms aid to India contributed to their inability to come to a decision.

It was a fact that the authorities of the two Western countries found themselves in a very difficult situation in regard to military aid to India. At the meeting at Nassau, the Canadian Prime Minister, John Diefenbaker, suggested a modest amount of $ 120 million as the extent of assistance to be given to India who had already received miscellaneous supplies to the value about $ 20 million. This had to be shared equally between the US on the one side and the UK, Canada and Australia on the other. But the snag was that all being democratic countries, had to get legislative sanction.[28] Besides, there was a group among the Congressmen in the US which was pro-Pakistan. Influenced by Pakistan, they were bitterly hostile even to continued US economic aid to India. Many of them, who were critical of India's policy of non-alignment, hinted that India who was not in any military alliance must be content with economic aid. Also factors like the Chinese cease-fire proposal, the six power meeting at Colombo and India's desire for a peaceful settlement confused even India's friends among the Congressmen about the need for the military aid. In December 1962, Senator Russell of Georgia said that India should not get arms aid because she would promptly lose the weapons to the Chinese. In February 1963, in a private interview with President Kennedy in Washington, the Pakistani Ambassador told him that the only hope for a settlement in Kashmir was for the US "to jump in with both feet and tell the Indians that they must surrender the Valley or have a plebiscite." The President declined.[29] Pakistan refused to realise that India had to have the Valley as a base for operations in Ladakh and that otherwise there was every possibility of the Chinese grabbing it.

The British Government which had fixed a ceiling on military aid could not grant anything in excess of it. It was significant that Pakistan's Foreign Secretary was already on a mission to Britain and other European countries to press Pakistan's viewpoint on extending military aid to India.[30] Though India also had highly capable men like Secretary General R.K. Nehru, Ambassador B.K. Nehru in Washington and High Commissioner M.C. Chagla in Britain, the Pakistani lobby was much more active.

Throughout 1963 and 1964, the Pakistan Government was building up with its public a spectre of hostile bellicose India brimming with Western arms to attack Pakistan. This was a thesis that contained not a particle of truth. Britain herself knew and had even stated but not publicly that the Indian arms were less modern and lethal than the latest arms Pakistan had received from America. Besides, the Indians allowed the US/UK inspection of their location and use to ensure they were used exclusively for defence against China.

The Western bloc's delay in conveying its decision on military aid caused immense mental agony to India at a time of turmoil. The Indian Government therefore decided at the end of February 1963 to send T.T. Krishnamachari, India's Minister for Economic and Defence Coordination, to Britain and the US for a high level exchange of views regarding long term military requirements. When due to unknown reasons, the date for Krishnamachari's visit was postponed several times, there were serious doubts in India if the trip would take place at all. True, there were two reasons which justified the delay in finalising the date. One was the reports of the military missions that came to India in November 1962 to study the situation were not ready; and the Governments concerned, after their receipt, would need time to study them and formulate their policies. The other was that both the US and UK were really marking time to see if any progress was registered in the series of talks held in India and Pakistan on Kashmir. The British and American diplomats in India and Pakistan were evincing an "embarrassingly open interest" in the negotiations. It was a known fact that unlike their counterparts in India, the UK High Commissioner to Pakistan Morrice James and the US Ambassador to Pakistan, McConnaughy were less objective and more partisan in their attitude towards India. All of a sudden, they came out with a vague proposal that the Kashmir Valley should be internationalised. These two diplomats were conspicuously absent from the fifth round of talks going on in Karachi. Without any hesitation they presented the proposal with a copy of it sent to the Indian High Commissioner in Pakistan. On the last day of the talks, Pakistan attempted to raise a discussion on the proposal because it was designed to benefit Pakistan at India's expense. This triggered off much indignation and Nehru wrote to both Kennedy and Macmillan expressing India's deep resentment against the partisan attitude shown by the diplomats of Britain and America in Pakistan. He told them firmly that if they felt embarrassing to help India at a critical time without a settlement on Kashmir, he would not definitely persist in his request for long term arms aid. Fortunately, the timely arrival of Mountbatten in India ended an embarrassing situation. As referred to earlier, there were discussions in the first week of May 1963 between Nehru on one side and Duncan Sandys and the US Secretary of State Dean Rusk on the other in Delhi at which Mountbatten succeeded in smoothening the atmosphere. They assured Nehru that the Kashmir question would not be linked with military aid. Rusk informed Nehru that the US Government would welcome Krishnamachari's trip to Washington. Macmillan informed Nehru through Duncan Sandys that Krishnamachari's visit to London would be useful.

The Delhi discussions resulted in the finalisation of Krishnamachari's visit to the West. But they did not really delink the two issues completely. Only there was a change in the language which was milder. The West now urged that "a settlement in Kashmir would facilitate" the grant of long term military aid. It was most unfortunate that the big powers unduly delayed sending friendly India succour which should have been done in December 1962 itself when the Chinese aggression in India dominated world thinking.

At the time when the bilateral talks were going on in different places in India and Pakistan, Bhutto, then Minister for External Affairs, was in Peking from 26 February to 5 March as China's guest. This definitely meant that China was once again at her game of driving a wedge between India and Pakistan. It was said that in pursuance of the announcements of 1962, the negotiations held later in Peking in October and the subsequent "agreement in principle" reached in December, both the Governments signed an agreement in Peking. This agreement delineated the boundary between Sinkiang and the territory Pakistan grabbed from India in 1948. Deploring this "unedifying performance" of Pakistan, certain circles in Britain expressed the worry that Pakistan was becoming "dangerously amenable to China's blandishments." Dwelling on the situation that was potentially explosive in the Indian sub-continent, Garvey of the Foreign Office wrote to the Commonwealth Secretary from Peking that the agreement signed by Bhutto "cooked the goose of the Kashmir negotiations."[31]

In July 1963, in his speech at the National Assembly, Bhutto warned the Western powers that any attack of Pakistan by India with Western military aid "would no longer involve the security and territorial integrity of Pakistan alone but would equally involve the largest State of Asia," an obvious reference to China. This categorical statement, the first of its kind from Bhutto, was a clear indication that Rawalpindi and Peking had already reached some sort of an understanding on mutual defence.[32]

When Bhutto was asked to clarify his statement, he denied the existence of any defence or security arrangement between Pakistan and China but said that his statement was based on a remark the "Chinese official" made to him that China would be "highly disturbed" if India attacked Pakistan. Bhutto's declaration in the National Assembly was unambiguous. He also told the American Ambassador in Pakistan that the US should establish a ceiling on arms aid to India and also arrange "some selected increment" in the military aid programme to Pakistan.[33] It must be remembered that Pakistan had already received on a grant basis $850 million worth of American military equipment.

Bhutto also objected to the word "massive" attached to arms aid to India. Any military aid programme that included tanks, heavy artillery, bombers and fighters was normally described as massive and American military aid to Pakistan also was called so. Still, out of regard for Pakistan's feelings, America and Britain dropped these items from the supply list to India.[34]

The Pakistani demands instilled fear into Prime Minister Macmillan that she might leave the Western alliance to make common cause with China. And if the Chinese moved into East Pakistan, they could paralyse India. When he discussed the matter with his Foreign and Commonwealth Secretaries, the former said that Iskander Mirza maintained that "President Ayub had made a mistake when China invaded India. He ought to have offered Pakistan's military support to India." This statement should be taken with a pinch of salt given the relations between the two Pakistani leaders.

Kennedy's Avowed Aim Frustrated

Kennedy was frustrated by the total lack of progress registered on the Kashmir question by the six rounds of negotiations held in different places in India and Pakistan. Keeping in view the critical situation faced by India and her felt need for security, he decided to give her substantial military aid despite the sure impact of it on the US-Pakistan relations. When his Secretary of Defence Robert McNamara proposed at a White House meeting on 25 April, a total of $300 million as aid to India for the next three years as against the $1.6 billion for which India was lobbying, Kennedy quickly retorted saying: "Let's not be penny-wise about India. Let's not let them get into a position where they feel that they can't cope with the Chicoms (Chinese Communists) and Paks (Pakistanis) on top of their problems." On 9 May, at the National Security Council meeting, Kennedy approved a plan to provide radar facilities to strengthen India's air defences. He also decided to consider a guarantee of India's territorial integrity. To make public the intent to hold off further Chinese attack, Kennedy proposed the conduct of intermittent air defence exercises in India in tandem with Britain.[35]

The decision of the Kennedy administration to increase considerably the military assistance to India despite the breakdown of the Indo-Pakistan talks on Kashmir, infuriated Pakistan whose relations with Washington became seriously strained. Pakistan openly flirted with China and announced the proposal to establish an air link with her. Anxious to clear the air, Kennedy sent his Under Secretary of State George Ball to Pakistan for discussions with Ayub. During the talks held from 3 to 5 September 1963, Ayub bluntly said that anything more than the meagre assistance contemplated earlier to India, would jeopardise Pakistan's security. He reiterated that if Pakistan agreed to the American proposal for mediation made in May 1963, it would definitely improve the US-Pak relations but its impact on Pakistani public would be disastrous. It would lead to "disturbances and disruptions" in his country. There would be strong public outbursts of feeling about the failure to "penalise" India for her obstruction which would be very hard to contain.[36] He referred to Nehru's statement in the Rajya Sabha on 3 September that "any change in Kashmir would have disastrous consequences" and asserted that Nehru could not be expected to change his position especially after the assurance of the American military aid. Ball frankly emphasised the need to contain Communist China's aggression but also assured that Pakistan could always rely on America's help if she were attacked by India or any other country. But he warned Ayub that any further step by Pakistan to strengthen her relations with Communist China would "require an adjustment of policies on both sides" and "a very close re-examination" of the existing US-Pak relations.[37]

Ayub minced no words in telling Ball that India had no intention of fighting the Chinese and that the West's policy of arming India would rebound disastrously not only on Pakistan but also on the West. On 5 September, in a prepared statement Ayub made it clear that Pakistan did not wish "the matter (meaning Kashmir) to be pursued."[38]

At a Press Conference in Washington on 12 September 1963, President Kennedy's attention was drawn to Pakistan's alliance with Communist China which was believed to be the result of America's arming India further. The President's answer was that if China attacked India and the country was

> "fragmented and defeated, that would be a most destructive blow to the balance of power. On the other hand, everything we give to India adversely affects the balance of power with Pakistan which is a much smaller country. So we are dealing with a very very complicated problem because the hostility between them is so deep... We had hoped that the settlement of the Kashmir dispute would bring about an improvement in the relations between the two countries, but Kashmir is farther from being settled to-day than it was six months ago..."

In mid-November 1963, when Chester Bowles had been six months the Ambassador to India, he had talks with Nehru about the US military assistance to India and reported it to Kennedy. The President was mightily pleased to support India regardless of Pakistan's relations with her. It was decided to place this before the National Security Council meeting to be held on 26 November 1963. It was a great tragedy that four days before the meeting was to be convened – on 22 November 1963, Kennedy was assassinated at Dallas in Texas. Chester Bowles discussed the matter regarding the aid with Dean Rusk and McNamara and despite pressures from Pakistan against any military aid to India, they succeeded in convincing Lyndon Johnson of the great need to help India. By mid-March 1964, it appeared almost certain that a favourable decision would be taken to extend aid to India to the tune of $100 million annually for five tears. But Pentagon was not prepared to risk American base at Peshawar. In the meantime, Nehru passed away on 27 May 1964. India was at her wit's end having waited in vain for eighteen months. When it became known that opposition to extend military aid was gathering force in America, India wisely turned to the Soviet Union which readily supplied MIG-21 planes. In mid-August, "the same Indian Military Negotiating Team with whom the US had very nearly reached an agreement in Washington departed for Moscow and two weeks later returned with all it asked for and more."[39]

Meanwhile, in December 1963, it was announced that Chou En-Lai would be visiting Pakistan in February 1964. This provoked the wrath of Duncan Sandys because during his meeting with Bhutto for a frank talk on international affairs in London in October, the latter did not mention this to him. He had strong misgivings about the outcome of Chou's visit as it would only serve to exacerbate the feelings between India and Pakistan. There was the real risk of all their efforts to forge an understanding between the feuding parties getting out of hand.[40]America was also unhappy at Chinese leaders "friendly visit" to Pakistan who was allied with the West against Communist aggressive aims.[41]

As if the long succession of adversities with which India was already heavily overcast was not enough, there occurred an extra-ordinary event in Kashmir in December 1963 which was considered sacrilegious. The Prophet's Hair kept under the custody of the Hazratbal Mosque in Srinagar was stolen. As expected, it roused communal passions. There was a violent demand for its recovery. Nehru lost no time in sending Mullick, Chief of Intelligence Bureau, to take steps for the recovery of the relic. Karan Singh also made a trip to Srinagar in January 1964, visited the Mosque and also organised prayers in temples. Fortunately, Mullick traced down the lifters of the Relic and quietly arranged for it to be restored to the Mosque. The event was thus settled as the Sacred Relic was lost and was found.

Pakistan was determined not to let slip an uneasy situation in Srinagar, which, though a thing of the past, could still be exploited by her to her advantage. It was to Pakistan's advantage that immediately following the Holy Relic episode, a grave problem presented itself in East Pakistan where, on 24 January 1964, in a major communal flare-up over 1000 persons of the Hindu community including women and children were slaughtered. The suggestion of the President of India that a joint appeal by the leaders of India and Pakistan would restore communal peace was rejected by Ayub on the plea that he had already appealed to his people. He was not really interested in lessening the domestic tension. Instead, he magnified out of proportion the Holy Relic incident and presented to the UN a different picture linking up the two totally unrelated incidents. In his letter to the UN, Ayub alleged that the Hazratbal Mosque episode was not merely religious but an outburst of the pent-up feelings of entire Kashmir against New Delhi. Bhutto, Pakistan's representative in the UN, quickly began his all too familiar job of activating the Kashmir question in the Security Council on the ground that it was an urgent necessity. The missing of the Prophet's Relic in Srinagar had absolutely no relation to the disturbances in East Pakistan which were the direct result of the massacre of the Hindus. Nothing could be more absurd or illogical than correlating the two totally unrelated incidents.

References

1. *The Economist,* 12 May 1962.
2. UK HC (P) to CRO, 16 Nov. 1962, DO/196/187.
3. *Ibid,* CRO to UK HC (P), 16 Nov. 1962.
4. K. Rangaswami, "Western Military Aid to India," *The Hindu,* 14 Jan. 1963.
5. Macmillan to Ayub, 18 Nov. 1962, DO/196/187.
6. BBC Television Feature in Panorama concerning India's Dispute with Communist China, 22 Oct. 1962, DO/196/165.
7. J.K. Galbraith, *Ambassador's Journal*, p. 489.
8. Harold Macmillan, *At The End Of The Day 1961-1963*, p. 234.
9. *The Hindu,* 14 Jan. 1963.
10. From UK HC (I) to CRO, 27 Nov. 1962, DO/196/146.
11. *Ibid,* Duncan Sandy's Statement, 3 Dec. 1962.
12. *Ibid,* R.T.D. Ledward (British Embassy in Washington) to C.S. Pickard (CRO) 12 Dec. 1962.
13. *Ibid,* Ayub to Macmillan, 17 Dec. 1962.

14. *Ibid,* Macmillan to Nehru, 23 Dec. 1962.
15 *Ibid,* Macmillan to Ayub, 23 Dec. 1962.
16. UK HC (P) to CRO, 28 Dec. 1962, FO/371/164877.
17. *Y.D. Gundevia Papers.*
18. FO to certain of Her Majesty's Representatives, 31 Dec. 1962. FO/371/170637
19. Nehru to Macmillan, 31 Dec. 1962, DO/196/147.
20. *The Hindu,* 29 April 1963.
21. Record of Meeting at the Admiralty House between Prime Minister and TTK, 30 May 1963, PREM/11/4867.
22. UK HC (P) to CRO, 7 & 10 Feb. 1963, DO/196//149.
23. Paul Gore-Booth's Note, Sep. 1965, DO/96/224.
24. Macmillan to Nehru, 6 April 1963, DO/196/150.
25. *The Hindu,* 20 April 1963.
26. UK HC (I) to CRO, 26 April 1963, DO/196/151.
27. UK HC (I) to CRO, 18 May 1963, DO/196/152.
28. *The Hindu,* 14 Jan. 1963.
29. *Ambassador's Journal, op. cit.,* pp. 535 & 42.
30. *The Hindu,* 14 Jan. 1963.
31. Garvey to Home, March 1963, DO/196/131
32. *Times,* London, 18 July 1963
33. UK HC (P) to CRO, 19 July 1963, DO/196/129.
34. *Ibid,* 20 July 1963.
35. *Foreign Relations of the US (FRUS) 1961-1963,* Vol. XIX, pp. 283 & 93.
36. UK HC (P) to CRO, 6 Sep. 1963, DO/196/129.
37. FRUS, *op. cit.,* p. 332.
38. Ball's discussions with the President, Foreign Minister and Pakistani officials between 3 and 5 Sep. 1963 in Karachi, DO/196/129.
39. Chester Bowles, *Mission to India,* pp. 95, 96 & 98.
40. CRO to UK HC (P), 7 Dec. 1963, DO/196/107.
41. *Ibid,* Statement by Spokesman of the US Department of State, 11 Dec. 1963.

15

Pakistan's Continued Belligerence

The UN failed to find a solution to the Kashmir problem even after a lapse of fifteen years. It could never succeed because in the case of Kashmir it was functioning under a heavy handicap. It was subservient to the Western bloc especially Britain. Its approach to the problem could therefore be never fair or unbiased and its policy could not but be one-sided and partial to Pakistan. It was therefore little wonder that the Security Council stubbornly refused to address itself to the fundamental issue involved and persisted in treating the offender and the defender alike. It brought forth proposals the implementation of which would benefit the aggressor. India's rejection of the proposals which were detrimental to Kashmir's cause made Pakistan too angrily hostile towards India.

Feeling very uneasy about her having allowed the Kashmir question to lie dormant for nearly two years, Pakistan resorted to her usual method of pressurising the Security Council. Adhering to the normal procedure, Bhutto readied himself to alert the Security Council on the "grave situation" that had arisen in the State of Jammu and Kashmir. He spoke of a widespread resentment amongst a large section of the people of Kashmir against the "Indian-dominated Government." His letter of 16 January 1964 to the President, Security Council, portrayed Kashmir as a seething cauldron of chaos and anarchy. Of his long catalogue of what he perceived to be unlawful acts of the Government of India in Kashmir, at least two merit mention. One was the Indian Government's directive to change the designations of the *Sadr-i-Riyasat* and the Prime

Minister into Governor and Chief Minister respectively to conform to the pattern obtained in the rest of India. This was construed to be a deliberate defiance by India of the Security Council's resolutions of 30 March 1951 and 24 January 1957 with a view to integrating the "India-occupied" Kashmir with the Indian Union. The other imputation was the "vicious climate" India had created in Kashmir where such thuggish acts as the theft of the Sacred Hair of the Prophet flourished. He complained that this sacrilege had resulted in massive demonstrations and uninterrupted rebellion. The long and short of Bhutto's complaint was that India was conspiring to reduce the Muslim majority in Kashmir. He further stated that "unlawful acts" in Kashmir leading to serious communal disturbances were causing tension in Azad Kashmir.[1] Ayub also described the theft of the Holy Relic as a conspiracy planned by the Indian Government to continue the repression and persecution of the Muslims of "occupied Kashmir."

In truth, evidence of communal conflicts during the Hazratbal incident was totally absent. Both the communities joined in the agitation over the loss of the Sacred Hair and neither community indulged in the usual destruction of each other's property.[2] This was an unusual feature of the agitation.

Britain was not in favour of a meeting of the Security Council at that point of time and much less a resolution there on Kashmir as demanded by Pakistan. Still, she arranged a meeting so as not to "embitter Pakistan unnecessarily." At the Security Council meeting on 5 February 1964, M.C. Chagla, who was the only speaker, said that there was no justification at all to bring in Kashmir to the Council. It was one more move of Pakistan's relentless "hate-India" campaign, aimed at weakening and dividing India in order to possess illegally an area which was as much a part of India as Bombay. Nothing would induce any Government in India to sign the death warrant of India's unity, he said. However, as a gesture of goodwill, Chagla said that India would cooperate with Pakistan and meet her more than half way provided she renounced her "India-bashing" attitude.

Patrick Dean's Offensive Speech

Bhutto would not budge from his stand. He would not stop condemning India. He would not rest unless a resolution on Kashmir was tabled in the Security Council. Failure to do so would be a far severer blow to the West as Pakistan would then regard China as her saviour, he threatened. Bhutto even sent a draft resolution which he wanted Britain and her allies to sponsor. It was common knowledge that India would not accept it. India had already conveyed to Britain her strong objection to any resolution on Kashmir in the Security Council. Since America and France were strongly opposed to reactivating the Kashmir issue, Britain was in a quandary. She felt that if a resolution could not be introduced in the Council, it should at least work for a consensus statement to avoid extreme reactions from Pakistan. With this view, she decided that the statement she was contemplating should refer to the previous resolutions on Kashmir and appeal to both parties to resume bilateral talks to resolve the immediate problems and consider the desirability of mediation.[3] Based on these lines, Patrick Dean of the British Delegation in New York drafted his speech to be delivered at the Council. His speech included the holding of a plebiscite in Kashmir. In the corrected form of his speech by the Foreign Office, there was no direct reference to plebiscite but consulting the wish of the people of Kashmir was not ruled out.

When the Security Council met on 10 February 1964, Patrick Dean reopened the buried solution of a plebiscite in Kashmir just to please Pakistan. It was intended to help Pakistan not to budge on her demand to extract her pound of flesh from India at gunpoint. Otherwise, it was incomprehensible as to why Patrick, who, along with Adlai Stevenson, subscribed to the theory of bilateral negotiations between the two parties, should in the same breath proclaim that plebiscite was the best solution. In his speech of 10 February, referring to the Security Council resolution of 24 January 1957, he argued: "My Government stands firmly by the principles enunciated in that resolution to-day. We consider it unrealistic to consider the status of Kashmir purely in terms of the legal effect of the Maharaja's Instrument of Accession...It is impossible to leave out of consideration fifteen years of discussion in this Council and the decision taken by it." Countering the contention that a dispute no longer existed in Kashmir where there was nothing to be negotiated, he asserted: "A dispute does exist which should be made subject to negotiation with due regard to previous Security Council resolutions and to the wishes of the people most directly concerned, namely, the people of Kashmir."

By his readvocacy of a plebiscite in the whole of Kashmir, Patrick Dean encouraged Pakistan not to accept any alternate solution. He also chose to ignore the commendable progress made by Kashmir politically and economically as a full and equal member of the Indian Union since her accession in 1947. These achievements had to be considered by the Security Council if it was really interested in making a constructive contribution to a peaceful settlement. That this was not done was a glaring omission on the part of the Council. Added to this was the double speak so frequently indulged in by the

Anglo-American group in the Council. While subscribing to the theory that the two parties should reach a mutually agreed solution to Kashmir, the group also harped on holding a plebiscite which Pakistan had been relentlessly demanding.

As expected, Pakistan regarded Patrick Dean's speech as "robust and refreshing." Agha Hilaly, Pakistan High Commissioner in London, praised Patrick for expressing "the essentials in clear, forthright terms." Through him Bhutto, who was impressed by the speech, conveyed his thanks to the Commonwealth Secretary. It created a great impression in Bhutto as the British delegate had given the straightforward support to Pakistan's case on Kashmir. This was yet another case where transparency was at a discount. Saville Garner gave prior indication to Hilaly the lines on which Patrick would speak.[4]

Incredibly, on 20 February – exactly ten days after his speech in the Security Council – Patrick Dean condemned Bhutto's cynical approach to communal riots. He said that the most distasteful aspect of Bhutto's policy towards both Britain and India was his "willingness to use any stick to beat the Indians with such as communal riotings, Hazratbal and evictions, whether or not the issue could be shown to have connection with the Pakistani case over Kashmir."[5]

Patrick's speech in the Security Council on 10 February which was most unfair to India did arouse resentment. Particularly his references to Kashmir's accession and past resolutions of the Council did evoke a hostile response from India. The past resolutions some of which were sixteen years old had become obsolete. They were not welcome to India. Plebiscite could not be held because of Pakistan's refusal to implement the provisions of the UNCIP resolutions and stop aggression against India. Patrick Dean conveniently omitted any reference to this in his speech.

India was furious against the two points in Patrick's speech: (a) calling into question the legality of Kashmir's accession to India and (b) equating India and Pakistan in regard to communal carnage. Reactions in the official circles and in the Indian Press presaged a sharp and sudden deterioration in the Indo-British relations which were already far from friendly. Mountbatten who complained to the Foreign Office about Patrick's speech wanted to know if the British Government had changed its policy[6]. The Foreign Office affirmed that there was no change in the British Government's policy and also clarified that all that Patrick meant was that there was a dispute before the Security Council which still remained unsolved.[7] The British official circles which were against resurrecting the idea of a resolution in the Council felt that the right middle course would be a "consensus."[8]

The controversy created by Patrick Dean in the Security Council figured in the Indian Parliament also. The speech of Krishna Menon, easily one of his best, gave unmistakable proof of the feeling of offence caused by Britain's handling of the Kashmir question. He dismissed the consensus theory as a trick to avoid veto. He attacked the British temerity in challenging Kashmir's accession to India. He condemned Britain's persistence in equating Pakistan with India. He ridiculed Britain's advocacy of self-determination in the light of her own actions in Southern Rhodesia[9] and Cyprus. He asserted that Britain's attitude in the Security Council was part of a process of getting back her lost Empire "by back door."[10]

Patrick did not bother about India's reactions. He was happy that Pakistan was impressed by his speech and that was enough. It was not his job to please both Pakistan and India. The Indian Delegation in New York felt that the speech especially the portion relating to Kashmir's status caused the "greatest offence" to India. Since Patrick's speech was pro-Pakistan and anti-India and was at variance with the British Prime Minister's assurance of non-involvement, Chagla, members of the Indian delegation to the UN and most of the Indian Press correspondents boycotted the reception hosted by Patrick on 12 February.

Questioning the veracity of Patrick's statement about Kashmir's status Chagla said at a Press Conference on 17 February, "I thought England believed in the rule of law. After all we were relying on an Act of Parliament – of the British Parliament. England should have stood by a law that her Parliament passed."[11]

The Security Council's "exercise in futility" exposed Pakistan's trick to use the UN as a body for propaganda and also for deepening the Kashmir crisis. She raised the cry that India had rashly triggered an "extremely tense and explosive situation" in Kashmir against which the Council had to take immediate steps. No other country on earth than Pakistan would have had the guts to bring in such a complaint against India in the world forum when, in truth, hardly six weeks before, an Indian patrol was ambushed and massacred by Pakistan on the Kashmir border. Since Pakistan had got into the habit of crying wolf over the Kashmir issue to whip up the communal sentiment, the members of the Council barring the two new comers from Africa – Morocco and Ivory Coast – were evidently disgusted with her hullabaloo. The attitude of the majority in the Council was made clear by the leisurely discussions of the Kashmir question for over a fortnight at the end of which it was adjourned *sine die*, reaching as usual, no decision.

Pakistan's Debacle

Though, the prevailing climate in the Security Council was most unfavourable for a resolution on Kashmir, Pakistan was firm on a resolution and discussion on the issue there. The delay in arranging for discussions irritated Pakistan. Her hostility towards India grew as the issue dragged on. Since the chances to convince the US President or the British Commonwealth Secretary to bring in a resolution appeared extremely remote, Bhutto himself drafted a resolution. Pakistan was keen to place clearly on record that the Kashmir issue was not closed as India argued. Bhutto's resolution reaffirmed the various resolutions of the Security Council and of the UNCIP. Apart from this, his resolution also contained elements of self-determination for Kashmir and UN mediation through the Secretary General. Copies of the draft were sent to all members of the Council. When Patrick sought instructions from London on how to vote on the Pakistani resolution, he was not authorised to vote for it without further consultation.[12] It was clear that the British officialdom was not in favour of Bhutto's resolution.

On 16 February, the President of the Security Council, after consulting other non-communist members of the Council, put a formula which referred to "the principles enshrined in the Charter of the UN and its past proceedings in the matter." This was a consensus statement which was secured in preference to a resolution. The two African members (Morocco and Ivory Coast) were emphatic about the inclusion of the plebiscite in the statement. It was shown to Chagla and Bhutto. Chagla, who was exasperated at this, refused to consider any reference, no matter how indirectly phrased, to past UN actions or proceedings as they had become obsolete with the passage of time. Feeling there was no point in discussing the summing up further, Bhutto decided to table his draft resolution on 17 February. The British delegation was confident that the resolution would secure the 7 votes required.

In the US view, it would be difficult if its Government favoured a resolution strongly in favour of Pakistan who was acting in collusion with Communist China. As Dean Rusk said candidly, the US was no longer in favour of Pakistan's efforts to bring pressure to bear on Delhi through other countries. America was not happy about Pakistan's exploitation of India's weak position in the wake of the Chinese invasion and of Nehru's illness.[13]

In its message to the UK Delegation, the Foreign Office stated that if a vote on Bhutto's resolution was "regrettably inevitable," the British should vote for it provided the US also did so. Having known that the US Ambassador was urging his Government not vote for it, the message ended thus: "It is essential that we and the Americans should keep in step."[14]

Knowing perhaps the fate of his resolution, on the morning of 17 March instead of tabling his resolution at the Security Council, Bhutto asked for an adjournment for a few days. Chagla stoutly opposed adjournment. He was dragged from India on the ground that there was "a grave emergency" in Kashmir. Since Pakistan herself had wished for a postponement, he asked what had become of the "grave emergency." The meeting was adjourned under Rule 33 (3) of the Rules of Procedure until 5 May 1964.

The unpleasantness created in India by the whole episode was conveyed to London by Gore-Booth, UK High Commissioner in India. He wrote that there was "a serious setback to our (British) position here (in India) with the Government, Parliament and the general public. Bhutto's unexpected return to Karachi and adjournment of the debate have saved us from the even more widespread and deeply felt bitterness that would have followed a vote for a Pakistani resolution."[15]

Gore-Booth also warned that resorting to a plebiscite to decide Kashmir's status would bring about a "wholesale bloodshed" and the catastrophe would not just be confined to Kashmir. If the plebiscite went in favour of Pakistan, the violence unleashed by the extremist Hindus against the 50 million Indian Muslims in reprisal would be such as to defy the best efforts of the authorities to control. Gore-Booth justified Nehru's fear that plebiscite would be a wrong step. [16] It was plain from India's reactions to the activities in the Security Council that Britain had temporarily lost even the appearance of impartiality where the Kashmir question was concerned. Terence O'Brien of the UK High Commission in India made an open statement that "Britain's influence in India has seldom been so savagely reduced as it has been following our intervention in the Security Council on 10 February."[17]

R.A. Butler, British Foreign Secretary, sounded a dismal note that there would be no early solution to the Kashmir question and that the tension over it had been heightened by western aid to India. As if in answer to this, Philip Talbot of the US clarified that the extent of the US military aid to India was relatively small and was just marginal to the Indian defence effort. He also pointed out that the US military assistance to Pakistan was the "backbone of the Pakistani military structure" and that the US economic aid to Pakistan on a per capita basis was twice what it was to India.[18]

At the meeting on 5 May, Bhutto stated that the Security Council might find it useful to give a hearing to Sheikh Abdullah who had been released in April when the charges against him were withdrawn. He requested the President to take steps to invite him to appear before the Council. Abdullah, who described the suggestion of Bhutto as fantastic, said that it was totally unacceptable to India. In his speech, Chagla who was the only speaker said that India's grievance was the indulgent attitude of Pakistan's allies which constituted the greatest obstacle to a solution of the Kashmir dispute. He said the real issue before the Council was not Kashmir's status but its turning a blind eye to Pakistan's aggression. Referring to Abdullah's release he said it was a tribute to democracy and freedom in India. He disproved the thesis that Kashmir was in revolt. He concluded by appealing to the Council to understand that the differences between India and Pakistan could be solved only by them. The chances of a settlement were more without the intervention by third parties.[19] At the Council's next meeting on 14 May, most of the members expressed the view that a solution to the Kashmir problem could be found only through bilateral talks between India and Pakistan.

When the Council met on 20 May 1964, there was a "summing up" by its President Roger Seydoux of France to the effect that the Secretary General would give useful assistance to the parties to facilitate the resumption of negotiations on Kashmir. Chagla opposed it. Telling the Council that India was not bound by the summing up, he called for bilateral talks. In a rare agreement before the Council, both India and Pakistan made it clear that what the President said was only a summing up and not a consensus or a resolution and did not bind the parties. After this, the Council adjourned its debate on Kashmir *sine die* without arriving at any conclusion.

A Stimulated Hatred

Interestingly, the Chinese who had hitherto taken the line that the Kashmir problem should be settled bilaterally between India and Pakistan suddenly gave it up in favour of the theory of a plebiscite. By the boundary agreement already negotiated with Pakistan, the latter had conceded to China 5180 square kilometres of the Kashmir territory which she had illegally seized from India. Since Bhutto's visit to Peking in March 1963, both the countries had been vigorously pursuing their efforts to develop fresh links with each other. The Sino-Pakistan air agreement signed in August 1963 marked a further step in this process. During their visit to Rawalpindi, where they stayed from 18 to 26 February, both the Prime Minister and the Foreign Minister of China went far towards committing Chinese support to Pakistan over Kashmir. In support of Pakistan's demand for a plebisc in Kashmir, both issued a Joint *Communiqué* which was signed on 7 March 1)64. China allowed Pakistan to state therein that the Kashmir question shoul be solved in accordance with the wishes of the people of Kashmir as "pledged to them by India and Pakistan." It was most odd that Pakistan who had grabbed a large portion of the Indian territory of Kashmir by force and China who broke all her promises of autonomy to Tibet and mercilessly drove all her leaders out of their country, should prattle on consulting the wishes of the people of Kashmir about the accession of their State.

For Pakistan the most important part of the *Communiqué* concerned the Sino-Indian border dispute and above all Kashmir. But the motive behind China's call for a plebiscite in Kashmir was to grab the Buddhist Ladakh whose people would definitely not eager to be a part of either an independent Valley or of Pakistan. If in the plebiscite, the Muslim majority Valley voted to accede to Pakistan, India would withdraw her troops from Ladakh and surrender the region to Communist China. Nehru who was condemned for having allowed the "rape of Tibet" by Communist China would become the butt of a more severe indictment for sacrificing Ladakh. This would doubtless smirch India's reputation in international circles and affect the nation's morale for years. China was clearly thinking along these lines. Thus, the Chinese leaders' visit to Pakistan though "unsensational," had done further harm to the already bleak prospect of the Indo-Pakistan reconciliation.

The position of Pakistan would be no better either. If China occupied Ladakh, "the Chinese dragon would be right round Pakistan's neck." In their "anti-Indian frenzy," the Pakistani leaders failed to think of the "fatal folly" they would be committing, if they believed that China's endorsement of their view on this issue was conceived in a spirit of helping Pakistan's interests.[20] China's change of idea had a deeper significance than what Pakistan thought. If ultimately, there was a serious change in the status of Kashmir, could she not exploit it to her own advantage?

Pakistan had a taste of China's flawed proposal when Chen Yi, the Chinese Foreign Minister advised her to keep the Kashmir issue out of the Algiers Conference to be held. He explained that any such act might cause damage to the Afro-Asian solidarity and further said that China also could not raise there the border issue with India. The crux of this advice was that Pakistan would do well to stick to bilateral negotiations. Pakistan was most unhappy as she was banking on doing much at the Algiers Conference.[21]

Censure on Government for Poor Publicity

When the Indian Parliament met on 14 February 1964 to discuss Pakistan's atrocities in the Kashmir border, the members of all political parties being sick of Pakistan's hate-India campaign demanded that the Pakistani intruders should be chased into the Pakistani territory and punished. They had not forgotten that a sizeable portion of Kashmir was still in the unlawful occupation of Pakistan. The members also blamed India for not doing enough to put her genuine case abroad especially in Africa. Their complaint was well-founded. A plethora of instances can be cited to prove that India showed no inclination to counter the false reportings of the Pakistan Government and the Press about her in Pakistan and abroad. This casual attitude created a wrong impression in the outside world that India was the tormentor of Pakistan whereas the converse was the fact. Once Indira Gandhi bitterly complained to her father that the Azad Kashmir Radio was blaring out falsehoods about India unceasingly with India doing nothing to counteract them.

India's propaganda outside the country was no match at all to that of Pakistan. Purely by misinformation, Pakistan easily gained the sympathy of other nations. The Heads of many nations, who were not in the know of the real situation in Kashmir, sympathised with Pakistan. They were keen to resolve the question in the UN in her favour believing that she was being victimised by India.

Nehru himself regretfully referred to this defect in December 1947 itself when the tribal incursions into Kashmir continued uninterruptedly. Stating that Pakistan's publicity which was "entirely false" was done very ably, he lamented that: "Our publicity is feeble in the extreme. There is very little about Kashmir in our newspapers or on the Radio and whatever news there is make dull reading."

Some Heads of States seemed to have asked Mountbatten: "Why is it the apostle of liberty and self-determination (Nehru) insists on keeping four million Muslims in bondage against their will?"[22] India's lackadaisical attitude in this regard was most unfortunate. Many Indian statesmen and also western friends of India had expressed their concern about this nonchalant attitude of India's representatives abroad. During the war of 1965, India failed to give the right kind of publicity abroad keeping thereby the other countries in the dark about the actual happenings in India. The outcome of the war was very badly reported. The eminent statesman and administrator C.P. Ramaswami Aiyar, who was then touring Japan and England, was shocked to find in both countries a distorted account of the war. In England, the *Daily Telegraph* and the *Daily Mirror* reported that in the Indo-Pakistan war, India was the vanquished! He bluntly expressed his unhappiness at the failure of India's diplomats abroad to create an authentic picture of their country.

There is no denying that India had always been remiss in not projecting her case effectively to the world. Expressing concern over China's alignment with Pakistan in the game of undercutting India's position abroad, the Parliament at its meeting on 14 February called for redoubling India's efforts by her diplomatic missions.

Clash Over Rann of Kutch

The Government of Pakistan, which failed to introduce a resolution on the Kashmir dispute in the Security Council in February 1964, was out to find a pretext to reanimate its hostility to India. Since nothing came in handy, she created the opportunity by claiming sovereignty over the Rann of Kutch.

The Rann of Kutch is a barren strip of uninhabitable land of mudflats and wasteland at the seaward end of the boundary between West Pakistan and India. The name Rann is derived from the Sanskrit *Irina* meaning "salt waste." For one part of the year, it is a desert and for the other, a marshy swap covered by several feet of brackish water whipped in from the Arabian Sea by the southwest monsoon beginning in the month of May. Its area of about 9065 square kilometres was brought under dispute when opposing armies moved towards each other along the India/West Pakistan frontier. It is not known how such an area became the bone of contention between the neighbouring countries. The report that there might be rich oil deposits beneath the sand and marshes of the Rann could have been the cause. Public interest in Kutch as a potential oil field was stimulated by Morarji Desai's mail from Gujarat in April 1965. There was also Press speculation in India that oil might be present in the Rann or offshore from near it. In normal times, there would have been nothing astonishing about this given that many parts of India were geologically so formed that an oil prospecting survey in the Rann of Kutch could prove worthwhile.[23] But the deposits if there were any had never been exploited. Without the oil deposits, it is a useless area both economically and strategically.[24] For several months from April, it is impracticable to gain access to the firm ground on the northern edge of the Rann from the south and east where the former Princely State of Kutch (now part of Gujarat) lay; but it is wholly unimpeded from the north where lies Sind (now part of Pakistan).

The story of the Rann of Kutch may be traced to 1908 when there were claims and counter claims between the British Indian Province of Sind and the Ruler of Kutch regarding the boundary in the small western portion. A settlement was reached which was formalised in a resolution of the Government of Bombay and approved by the Government of India. The letters of the two Governments exchanged between September and November 1913 and the final resolution of 24 February 1914 amply indicated the authentic boundary. Pursuant of this resolution, demarcation on the ground by the emplacement of pillars was done with the full knowledge of the Commissioner of Sind, the Princely State of Kutch and the British Government as the Paramount Power. It extended to the tri-junction of Karachi and Hyderabad districts and the northern limits of the Rann which was a part of Kutch. By the resolution of 1914, a roughly triangular portion of territory was awarded to the Province of Sind which had become part of Pakistan after the partition of India in 1947. This very fact bore ample testimony to the validity of the resolution. All the subsequent documents issued by the Political Department of the Government of India clearly depicted the Rann of Kutch as falling within the Western India States' Agency and never as part of the Province of Sind.

The records of the British Indian Government up to 1947 were the only authentic and relevant original source of information for the purpose of determining the boundary in the sector. According to these records, the Rann of Kutch belonged to the Kutch State and since the latter came under the sovereignty of the Indian Union after 1947, the Rann of Kutch also belonged to India. It was the general belief that the boundary fixed by the British was "incontrovertible and inviolable." This boundary was depicted correctly in all official maps and documents including the official *Gazetteer of the Province of Sind* and the *Bombay Gazetteer*. In fine, the boundary between India and Pakistan in the Kutch-Sind sector was very clearly demarcated and delineated long before Pakistan was created.

Pakistan made unreasonable demands on the Rann of Kutch. Her fulminations over the sovereignty of the Rann may be said to have begun in 1948. Notes were exchanged at regular intervals between the Governments of India and Pakistan from July 1948 to January 1960. Each argued its case in voluminous detail showing a history of conflicting claims going back to at least a hundred years. In January 1960, the correspondence ended and talks were held between General Sheikh of Pakistan and Sardar Swaran Singh of India. Settlement was reached on the whole of the India-West Pakistan frontier except the Rann of Kutch where the demarcation had not been made. India wanted the demarcation to be done by professional surveyors of the boundary line as shown on the pre-partition maps which was already agreed. But Pakistan maintained that this boundary line was not agreed since the dispute involved several thousand square miles of territory down to the region of the 24th parallel which could be settled only by high level political talks.[25] Throughout the talks and negotiations, the Pakistani regular army freely attacked the Indian positions including the Sardar Post near Kanjarkot, a ruined fortress, and drove back the defenders. These initial successes encouraged Pakistan to continue her aggression. The Pakistanis felt very strongly about the history of posts in the area. They maintained that from 1947 to 1956 they had a post at Chad Bet – one of the larger bets in the Rann. Bhutto went so far as to say that he visited it with his father as a child when it was a Sind Police Post![26] India adopted only defensive measurers with great restraint at the points where Pakistan resorted to firings, clashes and intrusions on the Indo-Pakistan border both in the East and West. Still, talks against India and for Pakistan were rampant. At the meeting of the CENTO Council of Deputies on the Rann of Kutch, accusations were levelled against India by Turkey, Iran and other Muslim countries who did not know the full story. They were plainly partisan. Even Britain supposed that these declamations were arranged by Pakistan.[27]

Smokescreen

The following brief account of the Rann of Kutch episode would show that all manoeuvres of Pakistan in this territory were nothing more than a camouflage for her elaborately planned incursions into Kashmir. Pakistan's objective was war with India on the question of Kashmir. But India was against a large scale war with Pakistan. She would not definitely submit to aggression and military action by Pakistan in an area which, without doubt, the British Indian Government had always recognized as a part of Kutch and not of Sind.

The skirmishes over such a territory as the Rann of Kutch were so minor an affair that was hardly worth so many debates and discussions. It could have been settled without firing a single shot. But Pakistan's devilish design was to precipitate a war with India by linking it with the Kashmir entanglement. All her attacks on the Rann of Kutch were thus a preliminary trial of strength with the Indian army for restarting her relentless and deadly war on Kashmir. The dispute over the Rann of Kutch thus culminated in the second major Indo-Pakistan war on Kashmir. To achieve her great goal to grab the whole of Kashmir by keeping up the tension all along the Indo-Pakistan borders, Pakistan became friendly with all those who were India's opponents and worked hand-in-glove with China and Indonesia.

After 1960, no further talks were held on the Rann issue until mid-1965. Pakistan refused to submit her claim to scrutiny by experts on the strength of authoritative data and maps. Her Survey Department refused to attend a meeting organized by the Survey of India. She brazenly attempted to falsify the international border in this area and enforced her territorial pretensions by military means. The Government of India noted in its pamphlet Pakistan's Aggression in Kutch:

> "The boundary between Sind and Kutch having been clearly and repeatedly defined by the British Power and admitting of no controversy, arbitrary and baseless claims by Pakistan and its present efforts to enforce the claim through military aggression cannot constitute a dispute where none existed. It can only indicate territorial ambition on the part of Pakistan."[28]

Between 1948 and 1965, there occurred several minor and two major clashes. The first major clash was in 1956 when the Indian Border Police drove the Pakistani Border Police out of a post it had established at Chhad Bet. The second and the more serious engagement was in April 1965 when disagreement arose over the exact location of that sector of the Indo-Pakistan frontier which passed through the desolate swamp - the Rann of Kutch. The accounts of the clashes were so bewildering as to make it impossible to determine who the real culprit was. On 12 May 1964, three Pakistani nationals were found on the Indian territory in Kutch near Kanjarkot. Assuming that they might have unintentionally strayed into the area, the Government of India released them under the Indo-Pakistan Border Agreement of 1960. On 25 January and 10 February 1965, incursions were again noticed by India on her territory of Kanjarkot. On the first occasion, a Gujarat police patrol noticed a freshly laid 32 kilometres heavy vehicle track one mile and a half inside the Indian territory. The Pakistanis must have definitely taken some days to lay it. India's protest was lodged at the local level first and then at the Governmental level on 12 February 1965. But there was no response to these. On both occasions, Pakistan refused to come to the conference table. On 9 April, there was aggression on a large scale in the region of the 24th parallel despite the fact that this was never the boundary. This was incontestably proved by the fact that the line of stone pillars erected while implementing the decision taken by the Government of Bombay and the Government of India in 1913-14 ran up about 37 kilometres north of the 24th parallel.

After the 9 April incident, it was agreed by both parties that there should be a cease-fire in the Kutch-Sind border followed by talks. India agreed to the proposal of a cease-fire on condition that immediately after its announcement all troop movements would be stopped and disengagement ensured. In the prevailing situation it was essential that there should be the restoration of *status quo ante* on the Kutch border as a prelude to the later stages of a final settlement. The return to the 1 January 1965 position of the troops should commence immediately and be completed at the earliest.[29] Pakistan demanded restoration of *status quo* not as on 1 January 1965 but pre 1956. This was because she was in occupation of the Chhad Bet until 1956. Pakistan also refused to accept the Indian demand to withdraw from Kanjarkot. As a result, the talks remained deadlocked. And Pakistan's non-response to India's demand for the restoration of the *status quo ante* was intended to make further military advances!

The British Prime Minister Harold Wilson was deeply perturbed over the developments in the Rann of Kutch. He stated that the cease-fire arrangement was only "preparatory to a negotiated determination of the frontier." While Lal Bahadur Shastri accepted this statement, Ayub did not. Shastri even told the Lok Sabha on 28 April that he saw no reason why the simple fact of determining what was the actual boundary could not be settled across the table. Which made Wilson write to Ayub that since his statement "has been accepted by Shastri, I find it difficult, in the light of this, to accept your argument that the plan I propose would prejudice Pakistan's claim to territory in the Rann of Kutch..."[30]

War Afoot

By then, rumours were afloat that Pakistan had ordered a general mobilization which indicated the certainty of the dispute escalating into a major conflict. The Pakistanis were in an advantageous position as they had quicker and more secure communication facilities from their terrain. But the Indians could not simply hold on to their position in the northern area of the Rann where the inundation would start from the month of April. The military disadvantages which the geography of the territory imposed on India were exploited by Pakistan who had many advantages on the Kutch border. Her encroachments on Kutch therefore continued. Her armed personnel intruded into the Indian territory of the Kutch-Sind border in the Kanjarkot area. These intrusions spread over an area of 13,000 acres of Indian territory. It was clear that the main purpose of Pakistan was to establish the existence of a territorial dispute.

In March 1965, at a time when the dispute on the Rann of Kutch was at its height, Ayub accompanied by Bhutto visited Communist China. They stayed in Peking for eight days. The only information given about the purpose of their visit was that China would offer substantial credits to her. Ayub's emphasis in all his speeches on the "friendship" and "peaceful" aspirations of Communist China and repetition of these in the international propaganda excelled the glowing phases of the Sino-Indian friendship in the 1950s. During this visit of Ayub and Bhutto, the Chinese leaders for a second time subscribed to a *Communiqué* supporting a plebiscite in Kashmir. For the first time, the Chinese Foreign Minister made a statement on China's military support to Pakistan. But it was an equivocal statement without a pledge. The motive was obviously to intimidate India.

Britain was not happy about Pakistan's honey-moon with China. She felt that Pakistan was committing a profound mistake in getting closer and closer to China which could secure her at the most only short-term benefits. Her long-term interest, Britain knew, lay definitely in stable and friendly relations with India. But Wilson's anxieties about a grave threat to Pakistan from China were expressed only in private. Publicly, he showered his blessings copiously on Pakistan. On the eve of Ayub's visit to Peking, the Prime Minister wished him all success.[31] Encouraged by this sop, Pakistan as audacious as ever, charged India with the commission of aggression in the Rann of Kutch!

On 24 April 1965, at 7.00 am, Pakistan inducted a full military brigade with tank and heavy artillery into a four-pronged offensive against Indian positions at Bian Pet 48 kilometres east of Kanjarkot and 16 kilometres south of the Kutch-Sind border. It was an illegal occupation of the Indian territory in the Rann of Kutch. It was a violation of the Indo-Pakistan Border Agreement of 1960. It was a breach of the International Law and of the UN Charter. It was an act of "naked aggression against India."

The most tragic part of the whole conflict on the Rann of Kutch was Pakistan's blatant employment against India of the aid equipment donated by the US and the UK only to fight communism! Pakistan used not only American tanks but also 106mm recoilless guns in the fighting in Kutch.[32] Since 1947, Pakistan had been seeking and receiving decisive military support from the Western bloc and from 1960 from the opposite communist bloc also. When the clash between the patrols drawn from the two border police escalated into fighting between the two regular armies, the Pakistani army brought up its American tanks and from the edge of the dry ground to the north shelled the Indian positions in the Rann. On 18 April, these lightly held Indian positions were withdrawn since there was nothing but 40 miles of marshy ground behind them. Pakistan exulted in this "minor tactical retreat" by the Indians treating it a great victory for her.[33]

J.N. Chaudhury, Chief of the Indian Army Staff, summoned the American Chief of Military Supply Mission on 24 April and explained to him the very difficult situation that India was in. Since India had no armour in the area, her ability to contain this thrust by Pakistan was extremely limited. Chaudhury wanted to know how America would stop the misuse of her military aid equipments by Pakistan. At a subsequent meeting between the American Minister Green and the Indian Foreign Secretary C.S. Jha, the latter confirmed Chaudhury's apprehensions. Jha also said India looked to America to accept responsibility for arming Pakistan with weapons which were being used against India. He further indicated America's good offices to bring about a cease-fire would be welcome.[34]

The US informed Pakistan that her military operations could not be considered as "self-defence" even if the northern part of the Rann were a disputed territory. This impelled Pakistan to stop using the US military equipment under the cover of self-defence.

On 26 April, Pakistan's Foreign Secretary Aziz Ahmed clarified Pakistan's position over the Rann of Kutch and related matters when he declared that the Indo-Pakistan negotiations over the Rann of Kutch had reached "a dead-end."[35] Formerly of the ICS, Aziz Ahmed opted for Pakistan at the time of partition and brought with him "a full measure of bitterness against India and the Indians...(and) on anything to do with India, he was aggressively hostile."[36]

The British officialdom, as usual, blamed only India for the turmoil in the Rann of Kutch. She was accused of adopting a stubborn and uncompromising attitude. Granting that India was stubborn and uncompromising, could any other peace-loving nation placed in a similar situation have acted differently? It must however be said that, very unusually, Britain also said that Pakistan was determined to give maximum trouble to India to ensure that world opinion did not stop pressurising the Indian Government to reach a settlement on Kashmir.[37]

Speaking of Pakistan's anti-India propaganda which was always replete with half-truths and untruths, Shastri remarked "India can never compete with Pakistan in this respect." He also cautioned that if the Pakistani menace did not abate "we will have to fight it with the utmost strength at our command."[38]

On 28 April, Shastri stated that if Pakistan was not amenable to reason "the Indian Army would decide its own strategy and employ its own man power and equipment in the manner it deems best." Ayub replied that this meant a total war between the two countries. The Pakistani troops were moved right up to the Indo-Pakistan border and "soon more and more of them were thus employed eye-ball to eye-ball than at any time since independence."[39] When Wilson had a meeting with Shastri in London on 15 June 1965, he asked if he desired to meet Ayub or any other Pakistani official in London. Shastri replied that he doubted the value of any such meeting and preferred to deal through the UK authorities. He also said that Ayub had caused great harm to him (Shastri) and that his connection with China was particularly damaging.

Adhering to the advice of their Prime Minister, the British High Commissioners in India and Pakistan played a very crucial role in bringing the parties to the negotiating table. Morrice James had talks in Delhi and Rawalpindi. He told Ayub that a solution should be reached without a war. Ayub also realised that the people of Pakistan were not prepared for a war and that if it did break out, there would be a harsh revulsion against his regime. So, the only option open to Pakistan to come out of the predicament, which was her own making, was to accept the British-sponsored negotiations. They ensured, among other things, withdrawal of the Indian forces along the borders of the Punjab and East Pakistan. The question of timing of the disengagement of the two armies posed a problem. Since the fighting was a naked and unprovoked aggression by Pakistan, India insisted on expiation on the part of the former. She was firm that there could be no settlement until Pakistan first vacated her aggression. The position was that while Pakistan wanted disengagement in the Punjab as a *quid pro quo* for restoring the *status quo* in the Rann, India peremptorily ruled out any discussion on disengagement elsewhere until Pakistan had atoned for her aggression in the Rann.

There were many other minor points which Aziz Ahmed deliberately pressed on. Communications posed another great difficulty on account of the peculiar situation of the offices in Pakistan. A distance of 12 miles separated the two men who handled the negotiations – Ayub in Rawalpindi and Aziz Ahmed in Islamabad. Foreign Office in Karachi was 900 miles away but fortunately, Bhutto played no role in the negotiations. Ayub had a broader view of the problem than Aziz Ahmed who simply would not accept any proposal that would give anything at all to the Indian side. Inevitably, the negotiations ended in a deadlock. It was only towards the end of June, when Shastri and Ayub were brought together for personal contact with the British ministers and with each other in London that an agreement was reached finally. Even here, Aziz Ahmed did his best to create some problem or other. It was not until full sixty minutes before the signing ceremony did the Pakistanis accept the time for the proposed cease-fire.[40]

Agreement on Rann

On 30 June 1965, the agreement on the Rann of Kutch was signed by Shastri and Ayub in London where the two leaders had gone to attend the

Commonwealth Prime Ministers' Conference. Wilson played a leading role in bringing the two parties together to sign the agreement. Its preamble stated that the two countries had agreed to a cease-fire and to restore the *status quo* "in the confidence that this will also contribute to a reduction of the present tension along the entire Indo-Pakistan border." That Pakistan did not sign the agreement with the genuine intention of reducing the wider tension, the subsequent events testified.

On the same day - 30 June 1965 - Wilson informed the House of commons that the Governments of India and Pakistan had announced the signature of an agreement for a cease-fire and the restoration of the *status quo* in the Rann of Kutch as on 1 January 1965 and on the arrangements for the determination and demarcation of the border in that area.

The Agreement of June 1965 did not please all the political parties in India. The Jan Sangh demonstrated against the signing of the Agreement. India was blamed for having failed to secure the vacation of Pakistan's aggression and abdicated her sovereign rights over her own territory. There were misgivings about the cease-fire agreement because India had withdrawn from her own territory and Pakistan had acquired the right to patrol a strip of Indian territory. By this, the Government of India had accepted the view that a territorial dispute existed.[41] Shastri had a tough task in defending India's acceptance of the truce in the Parliament.

The cease-fire came into effect as provided for in Article (1) of the Agreement. As provided for in sub-paragraph (iii) of Article 3 of the Agreement, a three-member tribunal was constituted with Gunnar La Gergun of Sweden, the UN Secretary General's nominee as the Chairman. The other two members were Ales Bebler of Yugoslavia and Nasrullah Entezam of Iran nominated respectively by the Governments of India and Pakistan. The provision for recourse to a tribunal to decide the conflicting claims of territorial jurisdiction was unpopular in India. However, Shastri was wise enough to realise that an area of salt waste was not worth a war. So, he succeeded in making his view prevail upon the Cabinet and the Parliament. Without his strong decision, the constitution of a tribunal would not have been accepted by India. The Tribunal conducted meetings from 15 February 1966 to14 July 1967 and the Award was announced in February 1968. It unanimously rejected the Pakistani claim that the border lay along the 24th Parallel. One member upheld India's claim while the two others upheld it with some modifications in some sections of the boundary. By a majority, the tribunal held that about 8288 square kilometres lay on India's side of the boundary while about 777 square kilometres of the territory claimed by Pakistan lay on the Pakistani side of the boundary.[42] In other words, the Tribunal's arbitration award gave about 10 per cent of the territory to Pakistan and 90 percent to India. Both Governments accepted the Tribunal's findings though India was much disappointed that sovereignty had not been confirmed over the whole territory which was legitimately hers.

References

1. Bhutto to President, Security Council, 16 Jan. 1964, DO/196/339.
2. UK HC (I) to CRO, 11 Jan. 1964, DO/196/338.
3. FO to UKD to UN, 7 Feb. 1964, DO/196/339.
4. *Ibid,* Saville Garner to N. Pritchard, 13 Feb. 1964.
5. *Ibid*, Patrick Dean to FO, 20 Feb. 1964.
6. Mountbatten, Chief of Defence Staff to Harold Cassia of FO, 13 Feb. 1964, DO/196/425.
7. *Ibid*, J.J.S. Garner to Mountbatten, 20 Feb. 1964.
8. FO to UKD to UN, 13 Feb. 1964, DO/196/339.
9. Southern Rhodesia (now Zimbabwe) in Central Africa was only a British Colony then.
10. UK HC (I) to CRO, 15 Feb. 1964, DO/196/339.
11. *Ibid*, Chagla's Press Conference, 19 Feb. 1964.
12. *Ibid,* FO to UKD to UN, 15 Feb. 1964.
13. *Ibid*, Extract from the record of a meeting between R.A. Butler and Dean Rusk, 12 Feb. 1964.
14. *Ibid*, FO to UKD to UN, 17 Feb. 1964.
15. *Ibid*, UK HC (I) to CRO, 20 Feb. 1964.
16. *Ibid*, UK HC (I) Despatch No. 6, 26 Feb. 1964.
17. T.J. O'Brien, UK HC (1) to E.J. Emery (CRO), 16 April 1964, DO/196/345.
18. Record of Talbot's meeting with CRO officials, 28 Feb. 1964, DO/196/340.
19. *Ibid*, Chagla's Speech at Security Council, 5 May 1964.
20. K. Rangaswami, "Ladakh: Key to Kashmir Problem," *The Hindu*, 4 March 1964.
21. *Ibid*, 10 March 1964.
22. Record of conversation between Nehru and Mountbatten, 30 April & 2 May 1963, DO/196/153.
23. UK HC (I) to CRO, 14 April 1965, DO/196/361.
24. Extract from Russell Brines, *The Indo-Pakistan Conflict.*
25. "History of Rann of Kutch," 3 Aug 1965, PREM/13/393.

26. CRO to UK HC (I), 10 May 1965, DO/196/363.
27. *Ibid*, British Embassy in Ankara to CRO, 17 May 1965.
28. Note of Government of India, 11 May 1965, DO/196/364.
29. Lal Bahadur Shastri to Wilson, 28 April 1965, PREM/13/391.
30. *Ibid*, Wilson to Ayub Khan, 29 April 1965.
31. Wilson to Ayub Khan, 27 Feb. 1965, PREM/13/463.
32. *The Indo-Pakistan Conflict, op. cit.*
33. Morrice James, *Pakistan Chronicle*, p. 123.
34. UK HC (I) to CRO, 24 April, 1965, PREM/13/390.
35. UK HC (P) to CRO, 26 April 1965, PREM/13/391.
36. *Pakistan Chronicle, op. cit.*, p. 125.
37. *Ibid.*
38. UK HC (I) to CRO, 29 April 1965, PREM/13/391.
39. *Ibid.*
40. "History of the Rann of Kutch," op. cit.
41. Scott to CRO, 7 July 1965, DO/196/368.
42. Prime Minister Indira Gandhi's Statement in the Lok Sabha, 20 Feb. 1968.

16

The Second Pakistani Invasion of India 1965

When Pakistan signed the Rann of Kutch Agreement on 30 June 1965, she had in fact no intention to reduce tension along the Indo-Pakistan border as envisaged in the Agreement. As on all previous occasions, it was her extreme avarice to possess Kashmir – an inalienable part of India - that proved a *casus belli* to wage a war against India this time also. Even while Ayub was putting his signature to the Rann Agreement in London, Pakistan was vigorously organising massive armed infiltrations across the CFL in Jammu and Kashmir. In fact, Pakistan's elaborate preparations to attack Kashmir were going on simultaneously with the clash on the Rann of Kutch. The information received from various reliable sources including the statements obtained directly from the interrogation of the captured infiltrators established beyond an atom of doubt that the plan to invade Kashmir had been finalised even before the end of May 1965 and that several thousand infiltrators camouflaged as civilians had surreptitiously got into the Indian territory. On learning of the developments later, Shastri wrote that he was "horrified to learn that even when the Kutch negotiations were in progress, and there was so much talk of reducing tension, plans for the present invasion were being perfected."[1]

The documents the Indians seized from Commander Akhtar Hussain Malik of the Pakistani forces during the war also revealed that the preparations for the infiltration of a great magnitude had begun as early as May 1965, long before the Kutch agreement was signed. This caused "a somewhat disquieting reflection on President Ayub's good faith towards the (British) Prime Minister's role as mediator in the Kutch dispute," noted John Freeman, British High Commissioner in India.[2]

Ayub committed the greatest folly in allowing Pakistan's infiltration into Kashmir in August 1965. It was a misadventure leading inevitably to an unwinnable war with India over Kashmir. Guided by misguides, he did a serious mistake in believing that the Indian army would retreat as it did in the Rann and that, if the situation turned grave, India would be forced to accept international arbitration on Kashmir. This prediction proved totally inaccurate. Pakistan failed to realize that Kashmir was no uninhabited salt marsh like the Rann to be left to the invader. If Pakistan really thought that the Indian army had lost its cutting edge, she was woefully mistaken. Pakistan was equally wrong in concluding that India would refrain from fiercely resisting any international award on Kashmir favourable to Pakistan.

Miscarriage of a Marathon Move

A group of Pakistani officials, no doubt with the knowledge and approval of Ayub Khan, secretly planned what they called the "Operation Gibraltar." It was so named in commemoration of a Muslim capture of Gibraltar[3] in 711 A.D. It was an elaborate plan which involved guerrilla training for two weeks to hundreds of men drawn mostly from the POK component of the Pakistani army but supplemented by civilians who were called *Mujahidin* ("crusaders"). They were all organised in May 1965 in Murree in West Punjab under Malik. They were instructed by the Government of Pakistan to destroy bridges and vital roads and attack police stations and VIPs in Jammu and Kashmir. Apart form these, compulsory military training was given to the POK youths aged between 16 and 25.

By June 1965, Pakistan had created two forces: one consisting of lightly trained civilians - the *Mujahids*, which with a strength of 1,50,000, formed part of the Pakistani army and the other, a semi-military volunteer force of light armed Razakars with a strength of 8500 under the control of the Pakistani army along with other military units. These vicious preparations betrayed the degree to which Pakistan was frustrated over her repeated failures to grab Kashmir.

Pakistan launched this unprovoked attack against India on the basis of two hypothetical situations: (i) There would be some sort of an uprising or revolution in Kashmir and (ii) there would be some communal disturbances in India. Pakistan was firm in her belief that there could be no settlement of the

Kashmir question except through violence. And she chose the most opportune moment to strike. India was still recovering from the massive Chinese attack of October–November 1962. Prime Minister Shastri was in the grip of many problems including the greatest challenges to India's security and freedom by a truculent neighbour like Pakistan who had received generous arms aid from the West and gained the friendship of other enemies of peace like China.

On 12 May, Bhutto succeeded in convincing Ayub that if India was not provoked into an armed confrontation immediately, it would never be possible for Pakistan to do so later when India's military strength would become too formidable for Pakistan to tackle. Ayub who was too great an admirer of the young and "inventive minded" Bhutto faithfully listened to his suggestion. He was equally enamoured of the "virtues" of Aziz Ahmed also. He would readily accept the recommendations of these two men without weighing them against the saner advice readily available to him if only he cared to seek it. Ayub's immense trust in and ready receptivity to the unwholesome advice of Bhutto "an unscrupulous opportunist" and Aziz Ahmed, "a dangerous fanatic" where India was concerned, proved his undoing.[4]

Bhutto's Plan to resuscitate the Kashmir dispute by stirring up a rebellion that would create maximum turmoil in Kashmir appealed to Ayub. It being a more critical time for India, the upheaval generated by the planned rebellion in Kashmir would force the Western powers to intervene and pressurise India to accept mediation. This would, as it happened in the Rann of Kutch, "open up the Kashmir dispute to a self-executing solution."[5]

Bhutto and his cohorts presented to Ayub a very vibrant picture of the extreme situation their "Operation Gibraltar" would create in Kashmir. The entry of the main guerrilla force into Srinagar had been timed for 8 August when they would mingle with the huge crowd gathered to celebrate the festival of a saint. On 9 August, there would be a rally to commemorate the twelfth anniversary of Sheikh Abdullah's first arrest and dismissal as Prime Minister of Kashmir in 1953. There would definitely be an insurgence then between the supporters of Abdullah and those of Prime Minister G.M. Sadiq. Sadiq succeeded Shamsuddin, the immediate successor of Bakshi Ghulam Mohammad who, under the Kamaraj Plan, resigned voluntarily to devote himself to the reorganisation of the Congress at the grass-roots level. This was the supreme moment for the armed raiders to create a menacing situation. They would participate in the melee and gain control over it so as to incite the crowd to overthrow the Sadiq Government. They would tell the world that they had gone there to do a great good of supporting their co-religionists who were waging a war of liberation against the despotic rule of Sadiq. It is relevant to state here that harsher words were used against Abdullah from 1947 to 1953 and before that against Maharaja Hari Singh.

In the meantime, so went the account of the proposed invasion, the other forces would engage themselves in destructive activities apart from capturing the airfield and nearby radio station. The next step in Srinagar was to establish a pro-Pakistan revolutionary council to take over the political control of the State of Kashmir. The new regime would call upon Pakistan for help. With the start of counter action by India, which was a certainty, the regular Pakistani forces would join the infiltrators in their war of "liberation." This, in short, was Pakistan's plan which Shastri called "thinly disguised armed attack on Kashmir" to create turmoil, start a riot against the Sadiq Government, establish a pro-Pakistan regime and then invite Pakistan to help them to "liberate" Kashmir.

Bhutto thus marvellously succeeded in persuading Ayub to embark on the infiltration scheme which had set off the second Kashmir war. The simmering discontent over the non-possession of Kashmir, which had been building up in Pakistan ever since her birth, burst into flames for a second time on 5 August 1965. On that day began the massive infiltrations of the armed personnel from Pakistan who were well-organised and well-trained in sabotage and subversive warfare. This was a clear violation of the UN Charter, the Cease-Fire Agreement and all canons of international law and code of good neighbourliness.

Travelling on foot and at night across precipices and through dense jungles, the Pakistani invaders slipped into Kashmir as planned on 5 August at widely separated points. They then crossed unobtrusively four main areas along the entire stretch of the 470 mile CFL. According to reliable accounts, they were engaged in eight primary areas along the CFL while isolated bands were located at six points. They carried lethal equipments hidden beneath baggy clothes so as to enter Srinagar undetected. The elements penetrated four suburbs and maintained radio contact with their head quarters in the illegally occupied Azad Kashmir.

On 8 August, the Indian Foreign Secretary C.S. Jha summoned the U.S. Ambassador and the British High Commissioner to apprise them of the infiltration of about 1,200 Pakistani troops in civilian dress across the CFL in Kashmir on the night of 5-6 August. Since they were well armed and carried leaflets and posters exhorting the local population to insurrection, Jha wanted the Ambassador and the High Commissioner to try their utmost endeavour to call off the operation, as otherwise India would have to take preventive action. Very soon, the number of the infiltrators rose to 5000.

Pakistan's grand design – "Operation Gibraltar" – to seize Kashmir was however a dismal failure. Her tricky plans to invite an avalanche of agitators and demonstrators ended in a fiasco. Her efforts to foment lawlessness and exploit the extreme elements in Kashmir proved infructuous. Her attempts to rouse the fiercest passions of the Muslims in Srinagar were most unsuccessful as there was no inkling of unrest anywhere in Kashmir. In truth, the Kashmiris of the Vale were taken by surprise when the infiltrators burst in. "The whole world knows there was no revolt in Kashmir," said Shastri. This statement was confirmed by the reports of impartial eye-witnesses who were residents or on holiday in Kashmir. The reports said that the people of Srinagar and the valley did not rise in revolt on 9 August as Pakistan had hoped and expected and that these places were "relatively calm without a sign of armed combat and life was proceeding normally." Maulana Masoodi told Richard Critchfield of the *Washington Star* that Pakistan's attempt to ignite a revolt continued for three days but the Indian security forces proved too strong. Donald Chesworth, Correspondent, *Manchester Guardian,* wrote: "I was in the Kashmir Valley during much of the present trouble...But at no time did I come across any evidence that there was a Kashmiri revolt, spontaneous or otherwise." The *Baltimore Sun* reported that "there was no evidence of a popular rising against India or of repressive measures against the people."[6] The *Sydney Daily Telegraph* said that Pakistan's claim that "the present armed conflict (in Kashmir) is a purely internal rebellion against India stretches credulity a trifle too far."[7]

The other guerrilla units carried on their acts of sabotage like cutting Indian communications and severing Indian military roads in order to clear the way for larger number of infiltrators and to isolate Srinagar. There were casualties and prisoners were taken but there was no response from the Kashmiris at large. All these were confirmed by the Australian General R.H. Nimmo, Chief of the UNMOGIP in Kashmir. He further stated that the guerrillas were supplied by air-lifts.

India's Belated Response

It was generally held, and rightly too, that India failed to avail of the rarest of rare opportunities that presented itself then. She missed a prime opportunity to establish a convincing case for herself when there was clear proof of Pakistan's disguised aggression. There was sufficient indisputable evidence that she was the victim of attack. She could have easily enlisted world support by inviting foreign newsmen and diplomatic officials to inspect the evidence in Kashmir. There were also pressures to do so but India effectively resisted them all. The result was she had to "move into offensive defensive action."[8] Even as late as 13 August, India was content with condemning Pakistan for the infiltrations and suggesting Sino–Pakistan collusion when a powerful bellicose element in Pakistan, led by Bhutto and Aziz Ahmed, had precipitated the situation in Kashmir "in the belief that this would lead to British mediation."[9]

India's patience reached its limit only on 15 August when an unusual array of Pakistan artillery crossed from the Pakistani side of the CFL into Jammu and heavily shelled the Indian positions on the Srinagar–Leh Road. They killed 50 civilians including women and children and injured many more in addition to bombing a mosque. The *Times* of London, which was not friendly to India, published a photo of the desecrated mosque. The Indian armed forces went into action against the Pakistani army, knocked out several tanks and army vehicles. This was the first crossing of the CFL by the Indian army since the start of the guerrilla attack and the twelfth confirmed incident listed in the initial report of Nimmo. The Indian forces occupied three lofty mountain positions which they previously held in Kargil on the northern sector. They found these positions empty. The purpose of this thrust was to warn Pakistan that the Indian troops would strike back promptly against further provocation.

On 23 August, the Pakistani artillery moved close to the CFL and started shelling villages and the Indian troop's concentrations near Tithwal, Uri and Poonch. India retaliated with two more limited attacks into the POK. The other noteworthy exploits of the Indian troops were the capture of the strategic Pakistani positions including the important peak Pir Saheba on 24 August; the 8600 feet Haji Pir pass on 25 August; and the cutting off of a bulge of about 150 square miles on 10 September. The last one was left protruding into the Indian territory of Kashmir when the CFL was accepted. This bulge provided the main springboard for infiltrators bound for Srinagar.

On 24 August, the New Delhi Press announced in banner headlines the crossing of the CFL by the Indian forces which dislodged the Pakistani forces from two posts in Tithwal overlooking the road from Muzaffarabad after a brief encounter at a height of 9000 feet, two miles across the CFL. The announcement of this news by the Defence Minister Y.B. Chavan in the Lok Sabha was greeted with thunderous cheers by all including the opposition which showered praises on Government regardless of the censure debate that was in progress in the House. Pakistan developed cold feet at this. Her General was heard to say that if the Indians attacked the Tithwal-Uri-Poonch sector, the POK forces would not be strong enough to hold them. He was deeply concerned about holding Muzaffarabad at all costs for if that was captured the whole of the Kashmir movement in Pakistan would collapse. [10]

It was Pakistan's strong tank attack in the Bhimbar-Chhamb sector of Jammu by her regular forces supported by armour on 1 September that forced India to launch its diversionary attack in the Punjab in the direction of Lahore "the fabled city of religion and history," lying 15 miles from India. In the absence of heavy Indian tanks, the Indian Air Force brought in the Gnat jet fighter to stop the Pakistani advance. India strongly protested to America against Pakistan's use of American Patton tanks. In fact, Morrice James, British High Commissioner to Pakistan, frankly said that the events of 1965 might not have happened if Pakistan had not been built up militarily by the Americans to a point at which they could challenge the Indians.[11] Galbraith echoed the same view when he told the Senate Foreign Relations Committee in April 1966, that the cause for the 1965 war over Kashmir was American military aid. "The full consequences of the policy of indiscriminate arms aid have revealed themselves with a kind of heroic clarity in South Asia...The arms we supplied under this policy caused the war last autumn between India and Pakistan," he said.[12] There was also a Pakistani threat to the Indian capital. It was at this juncture that the Secretary General of the UN appealed to India to honour the CFL. To which India replied that she could not consider the appeal until Pakistan stopped armed infiltrations into Kashmir and guaranteed that there would be no recurrence of the existing situation. But Pakistan gave no assurance that the cease-fire and the CFL would be respected. This was evidence of Pakistan's intransigence.

On 4 September, the Chinese Foreign Minister Chen Yi made a transit stop in Karachi and held two sessions of talk totalling in all six hours with Bhutto and senior officials of the Foreign Ministry. But he gave only an "oblique support" but no "concrete reassurance" to Pakistan in his statement backing Pakistan's "just action" to repel the "Indian armed provocation".[13]

On 6 September, India launched a major attack across the international border towards Lahore. This was to retaliate against Pakistan's attack by a single Pakistani F 86-F Sabre jet on the anti-aircraft installations near Amritsar, the Sikh stronghold, on 5 September. The Indian attack, though limited, was regarded as the opening of a new front in the Punjab. Privately, the Government of India said that the attack was a military necessity to relieve the pressure on Akhnur and protect the India-Kashmir road which Pakistan intended to cut off.

When Chavan broke the news in the Parliament and told the members that the whole nation was one with the Government in this matter, the mood of India was extremely cheerful. This news caused more excitement in Delhi than any other news since 1947. Events after this date had had a more profound effect on life in the capital than the Chinese attack of October-November 1962.

In 1962, the mood in India was one of bewilderment at Chinese military victories. In 1965, there was no sense of bewilderment in fighting Pakistan. Although the fighting was reported fierce and indecisive from 6 September, there was a sense of confidence in India engendered by the knowledge that she was a much bigger country than Pakistan with a much bigger army. There were stringent black out orders. Bands of civil defence vigilantes roamed the streets at nights. Bad elements capable of fomenting troubles for their ends were rounded up in hundreds. The Anglo-Indian community which formed the stronghold of the army provided a considerable proportion of the war heroes. The nation was proud of its *Jawans* fighting against odds in the State of Jammu and Kashmir in an extremely difficult terrain as Kargil and Haji Pir areas.

On 7 September, India launched her second major offensive against Sialkot, an important railway and road centre when her troops crossed the international boundary from Sialkot to Kasure. Thus began the "All-out-war." Indian action was intended to reduce the Pakistani pressure on Akhnur, as Sialkot was militarily the most vital target. Akhnur was still definitely vulnerable but Agha Mohammed Yahya Khan, who replaced Malik, acted differently. Disregarding the specific orders to take Akhnur, he delayed action. India's diversionary strategy worked and Pakistan withdrew the bulk of her armoured strength from the Akhnur Sector to meet the new challenge. This strategy also prevented Pakistan's drive to New Delhi. The main reason for Pakistan's failure of the thrust against Akhnur, which was named "Operation Grand Slam," was the change of command. However, the Pakistani forces continued to occupy a sizeable portion of the Indian territory.

Defying UN Resolutions to Halt War

On 31 August 1965, U Thant, Secretary General of the UN, addressed an informal and confidential memorandum on the Pakistani infiltrations into the Indian State of Kashmir to all the members of the Security Council and supplied copies of it to India and Pakistan. The very next day – 1 September – Pakistan launched a brigade strength attack in the Chhamb Sector of Jammu and Kashmir. On 2 September, U Thant sent a message to both India and Pakistan to which India responded on 4 September while Pakistan did so on 6 September. On the same day - 2 September - there were reports from UNMOGIP indicating the continuance of violations of the cease-fire and CFL on both sides.

On 3 September, U Thant presented a report to the Security Council. Its portrayal of the war-torn Kashmir "jolted" its members. U Thant told them that Nimmo "has indicated to me that the series of violations that began on 5 August were to a considerable extent in subsequent days in the form of armed men, generally not in uniform, crossing the CFL from the Pakistan side for the purpose of armed action on the Indian side." According to U Thant's report, Nimmo had, on the basis of the investigations by the UN observers and "in the light of the extensive character of the raiding activities and their proximity to the CFL" reached the conclusion that "large scale infiltrations of heavily armed irregulars from Pakistan across the CFL took place on 5 August and subsequent days." A careful examination of the list of incidents attached to the Secretary General's report showed clearly and unambiguously that it was only after the first eleven Pakistani attacks that occurred between 5 and 14 August "each with increasing intensity and severity," did the Indian troops for the first time cross the CFL and reoccupy the position northeast of Kargil from which in May, in deference to the appeal of the Secretary General, they withdrew. This belated disclosure annoyed India. It vexed her to find that the Secretary General did not make the contents of Nimmo's reports covering the events from 5 August public until 3 September. U Thant had known from Nimmo of the mass crossings of the CFL by Pakistan from 5 August and the resultant casualties to 3 September when he tabled his report in the Security Council. The Secretary General had thus maintained silence over the untoward events. One account went that on 5 August, a shepherd boy apprised the police, of the entry of strangers into Tanmarg. The strangers, he said, were offering bribes to locals for giving information. The boy led the police to Salahuddin's base.[14]

The *Times of India* quoted a cancelled statement of U Thant which referred to numerous and widespread violations of the CFL "to an unprecedented degree" by highly armed, well trained and well led infiltrators supported by Pakistan. Some other papers editorially commented that UN's reactions to Pakistan's actions were "singularly anaemic and unproductive."

U Thant justified his silence on the ground of pursuing his peace-making efforts by quiet diplomacy without blaming any party for starting and continuing the fighting. What prompted him to shield a party that was erring egregiously? This will always remain unanswered. With the steady escalation of the war, he abandoned his policy of suppression of facts. It was most unfortunate that wisdom dawned on him so very belatedly.

U Thant also stated in his report that on 9 August after receiving Nimmo's wire that the situation was getting from bad to worse along the CFL, he told the representative of Pakistan to convey to his Government how seriously he was concerned about Pakistan's attacks. He also told the Indian representative to convey to his Government his appeal to exercise restraint in any retaliatory action from India's side. Whereas India conveyed her assurance orally through her representative, Pakistan gave no assurance.

On 4 September 1965, the Security Council passed a resolution calling upon both the parties to stop fighting, as that would be consistent with their obligations to themselves, the UN Charter and the world. In adopting the motion, the members sincerely hoped that it would get a response from the parties within three days but hardly half that period had ended when the Council got the dreadful news that the war was accelerating in its "insane speed" showing no sign of halting or abating.

On 6 September, the Security Council met again and adopted another resolution which the Secretary General himself carried to the sub-continent to explore the possibilities of bringing peace. He considered it the most momentous mission ever undertaken by a Secretary General of the UN. He intended to get back to New York by 14 September, complete his report and ask for a meeting of the Security Council on 17 September.[15] When Shastri learnt of this, he eagerly looked forward to U Thant's visit. The Secretary General stayed in New Delhi for three days from 12 September. There was no lack of cooperation from India. In fact, the diplomatic skill that Shastri displayed at the negotiations with U Thant in New Delhi were reported to be remarkable. But his visit proved no turning point in his efforts to secure a cease-fire. He returned to New York with his objective unfulfilled.

When the second resolution was adopted on 6 September, Dean Rusk telegraphed to both Swaran Singh and Bhutto urging them to accept the UN resolution. America was so displeased with Pakistan that she stopped despatching military equipment to her. An ammunition ship, which was on its way to Pakistan through the Suez Canal, was also diverted. Rusk was so disgusted as to say very confidently that Ayub might be "gambling" on a major internal disintegration in India; but, in the long run, India's numerical superiority would tell. He also said that Ayub was getting bad advice and that if there were Chinese-Pakistani collusion, he would be taking big risks.[16]

At this point of time, Ayub, absolutely confident of US support, requested Rusk to invoke the 1959 American assurance regarding aid to Pakistan. But Rusk replied that he did not accept Pakistani denials of infiltration across the CFL in Kashmir as he had abundant evidence from both the UNMOGIP and American intelligence sources that infiltration had taken place. The clear implication in his remark was that there was no basis for Ayub to invoke the 1959 assurance. But President Lyndon Johnson failed to take up a strong position in public.[17]

Wilson's Provocative Message to Shastri

On 6 September, a crucial meeting took place between the UK Minister of State and the Indian High Commissioner in Britain, Jivraj Mehta. The former carried a message from his Prime Minister to the Indian Prime Minister. After deploring the escalation in the fighting, the Minister handed to Mehta Prime Minister Wilson's message. Mehta flew into a rage when he found in it a statement expressing "horror" at India's action! "I am horrified" stated Wilson "at the rapid escalation of fighting between India and Pakistan culminating in the news that the Indian forces had on September 6 attacked Pakistani territory across the common international frontier between India and Pakistan in the Punjab. This attack was a most regrettable response to the resolution adopted by the Security Council on 4 September calling for a cease-fire."

Wilson's message was thoughtless and meaningless. It was done for the mere pleasure to smear India. Perhaps, like Pakistan, Wilson too thought that India was a soft nation and would always adhere strictly to Gandhiji's message of non-violence and peace. It was a great pity that neither Pakistan nor Britain was aware that Gandhiji had also said that a country had to defend itself against aggression. India acted throughout only in self-defence. Mehta said that Wilson who chose to pillory India for crossing the international boundary had not said a word in his message about the real culprit Pakistan who started the infiltration into Kashmir and committed many other atrocities. The Minister who delivered the message explained that the Prime Minister referred only to the new situation that developed on 6 September. Mehta countered him with the legalistic argument that Pakistan, who was the first to cross the international boundary in her drive towards Jammu and Akhnur and who should therefore have drawn a strong condemnation from Britain, had not even been mentioned by Wilson in his statement. This wrong statement about India would be read throughout the world and provoke the ire of the Indian Parliament. But the Minister maintained that the Indian attack of Lahore was a much more serious act than all the previous onslaughts of Pakistan on India!

When the Minister referred to U Thant's appeal, Mehta insisted that the least Britain could do to repair the damage done to India was to issue a condemnation of the illegal acts of Pakistan against India and Kashmir before the Government of India could agree to a cease-fire. Mehta bluntly told the Minister that the British Government had never dispassionately viewed India's genuine complaints about Pakistani violations of cease-fire agreements, which were always "ignored and fobbed off."[18] India protested against Wilson's adverse public comment which blamed India for extending the fighting with Pakistan. India described the statement as "one sided and unhelpful" because, amongst other things, Wilson failed to take into account the persistent Pakistani provocation in Kashmir since May 1965.[19] The message was badly received by Shastri as it was not based on a recognition of the circumstances, which had led up to India's retaliation. It aroused the resentment of a section of the cabinet whose spokesman was T.T. Krishnamachari.

Britain was unaware of how India was going out of the way to clarify some of Pakistan's unfounded suspicions. Pakistan complained that the Indian Government's extension of the operation of the Articles 356 and 357 of the Constitution of India (providing for President's Rule) to Kashmir would hamper the bilateral talks between the two Governments. This was because Britain interpreted the Indian Government's announcement to mean "to integrate Kashmir more fully into the Indian Union."[20] This was done at a time when Ayub was willing to give sufficient time to Shastri to settle down as Prime Minister and strengthen his internal position to make meaningful negotiations possible. There was nothing wrong in what India had done in her State but Pakistan was determined to exert more pressure on India. Shastri clarified that it was an internal matter to improve the Government of Kashmir and not related to his dialogue with Ayub. When the matter was raised again by Ayub during the Kutch negotiations, Shastri sent him a secret personal message to the effect that he was still ready to negotiate on Kashmir after he had faced the elections and incidentally "after the retirement of Aziz Ahmed" which would make the atmosphere easier and that the Constitutional provisions would not be allowed to stand in the way of anything to which they had agreed.[21] Disregarding all gestures of goodwill by India, Pakistan began committing aggression after aggression against her in total violation of the cease-fire. What hurt India much more than even the Pakistani invasion was that instead of directing Pakistan to withdraw her intruders from the Indian territory and help India to preserve peace, Wilson severely censured India for having resorted to defensive measures! Justice demanded a double condemnation of Pakistan from the British Prime Minister: first for criminal acts and second, for her failure to consult Britain, her ally in the CENTO, before embarking on her illegal infiltration followed by military attack across the CFL which alone provoked India to attack across the international frontier.

Wilson's statement upset many English officers of consequence. It was pointed out that London had not, until then, said a word about her disapproval of Pakistan's infiltrations into India. Britain, it was stressed, had to keep her record straight on this point, "especially as the armed infiltration had been the immediate basis for the Indian counteraction on a big scale."[22]

The Indian leaders including President Radhakrishnan expressed great anxiety over the Indo-British relations which were deteriorating rapidly. High Commissioner John Freeman wrote that it was of "crucial importance to prevent what I hope is a temporary phase from becoming a permanent liability to our policy and interest in India."

A soothing gesture did come from the British Prime Minister. On 17 September, ten days after sending his unsavoury message to the Indian Prime Minister, Wilson wrote a personal letter to Shastri which was clearly intended to thaw the frost that had come over Britain's relations with India. He praised Shastri for the distance he had gone towards agreeing to an unconditional cease-fire. "You have mercifully avoided communal troubles," he wrote. Wilson thus indirectly atoned for the folly committed.[23]

India Isolated

During the period of the war, it looked as if India, the victim of aggression, was isolated. Wilson did not act favourably even to India's action to seal off the infiltrators' entry routes. Turkey and Iran who were Pakistan's closest allies always spoke of India in harshest terms. They openly said that "India's actions" against Pakistan could never be condoned and pledged their support to Pakistan, their brother and ally. Commenting on the degenerating Pakistani-US relations, the Shah of Iran said that since the US held the key to the sub-continent, the Indian attack was an American inspired plot to unite the sub-continent under a Government subservient to the US.[24] Apart form their membership in the CENTO, their deep friendship and close association bound the three – Pakistan, Turkey and Iran – together.

As for Communist China, the harrowing situation that India was in on account of the Pakistani onslaught presented her the finest opportunity to restart her game of torturing India by her threatening gestures. On 8 September, she sent a note to the Government of India protesting against the alleged Indian incursions across the Sikkim border. On 16 September, she delivered an ultimatum to India that she should dismantle all her border installations on the China-Sikkim border within three days or face "grave consequences." On 19 September, the Chinese extended the ultimatum for a further period of three days. And this was to expire on the evening of 22 September. On the same date – 19 September, Ayub accompanied by Bhutto, made a secret visit to Peking (now Beijing). They had two long meetings with Chou En-Lai and Chen Yi. The Chinese leaders assured the Pakistani leaders of China's unconditional support to Pakistan in her war against India but on the understanding that Pakistan should be prepared to wage a long war in which there was the possibility of her losing some cities like Lahore. Since both Ayub and Bhutto were not prepared for this, they returned to Pakistan as secretly as they went.[25]

The Chinese troops were reported to be moving up in limited numbers to the border at points in Ladakh and in the Chumbi Valley near Sikkim. The Chinese ultimatum and troop movements put a grave responsibility on Ayub. If he encouraged the Chinese intervention or provided an opportunity for such an intervention by refusing to agree to the UN cease-fire, he would alienate Pakistan from the world. If Pakistan did not accept the cease-fire and India did, Pakistan would be in a highly critical position if China attacked India subsequently. The non-communist world would infer collusion between Pakistan and China against India and the whole World would hold Pakistan responsible for whatever disasters followed. As if to put an end to these worries, on 21 September, China called off the ultimatum to India which was to expire on 22 September on the pretext that the Indians had carried out her demands! In fact, even when China delivered her very first ultimatum to India on 16 September, the British Government dismissed it as a bluff. America asserted that Ayub who feared a massive US intervention on behalf of India and possibly even a world war pleaded with China to lay off. There were certain other tenable arguments supporting China's backing down on her aggressive stance. In the first place, China knew that a cease-fire between India and Pakistan was in prospect. Secondly, the precise nature of India's alleged military installations was never established. Thirdly her inability to exert "psychological pressure" on India by pinning down the Indian troops in the eastern sector so as to prevent their transfer to the Punjab where they might be deployed against Pakistan.

Though the Chinese seemed to have withdrawn their threat to Sikkim, they were digging in in Ladakh. They captured three Indian Policemen. There was thus the danger of the Chinese who were already on the Indian territory in Ladakh intervening in the war on the side of Pakistan. China had already declared her moral support to Pakistan whose cause she proclaimed was "just." She was loudly trumpeting that India was the aggressor from whose clutch none of her neighbours was safe. She also repeatedly upheld Kashmir's right to self-determination. China and Indonesia chose to interpret India's defensive action as "naked and criminal aggression against Pakistan...crude violation of international relations, grave threat to peace in Asia and another exposure of chauvinist and expansionist features of India's ruling circles."[26]

There was thus a wholesale support for the aggressor at the expense of the aggressed. As for Britain, she chose to dismiss the Pakistani incursions of roughly the first two weeks as minor skirmishes. Towards the end of August, no doubt she treated the events more seriously but her habit of juxtaposing what she called "Indian allegations" with the Pakistani denials became more pronounced.

Even India's friends including the USSR, whose solid support India enjoyed all along, failed to openly condemn the bare-faced aggression for which Pakistan denied responsibility. Russia remained strictly non-committal about the event despite knowing that Pakistan was guilty of unprovoked aggression against India. It was very possible that on account of the Sino-Soviet hostility, there was a major change in the Soviet policy from one of unequivocal support for India to one of even-handedness between India and Pakistan. When India could not halt Pakistan's 1 September attack in the Chhamb sector, which constituted a major threat to Indian life-line, India was left with no other military alternative but to go into counter action. The Indians were thus forced at every stage to escalate the struggle in self-defence. If India was expected to co-operate in stopping the war, she would certainly expect the western powers to start from the point at which Pakistan decided to solve a long term problem by force. This was the most just demand of India. India had never intended to conquer Pakistan. She was only working towards a military situation where she would be in a strong position for eventual negotiations and removal of infiltrators.

To halt the fighting, Britain took the ungenerous measure of banning supplies of arms to India immediately after India took the defensive position.

The British Foreign Secretary wrote to the British High Commissioner in Teheran in September that the UK Government had decided to suspend all military supplies to India and Pakistan "and in fact this applies more to India in our case".

About Western aid, India made it clear that while she had no objection to the US suspending any new commitments for economic aid, she would strongly deplore American decision under any circumstance to suspend delivery of PL 480 wheat. If a new PL 480 contract was not signed immediately, India's food situation would become serious by November 1965. If PL 480 was not resumed on time or if India, the defender, was singled out for hasher sanctions than Pakistan, the invader, the resultant bitterness would be very severe and deep. Jivraj Mehta also pointed out to Prime Minister Wilson that it was wrong to put an embargo on shipment of military equipments to India as his country was in dire need of them whereas Pakistan was receiving arms from both Iran and Turkey. Wilson replied that he did not want complications to arise on this account if the Security Council called for an arms embargo and there were ships with arms on the seas. Stating that the situation in Turkey and Iran also would change, Wilson said that Britain had made it clear to the CENTO allies that their organisation could not be invoked against another Commonwealth country.[27]

Escalation of war

America's disenchantment with Pakistan's unprovoked infiltration into the Indian territory angered her. The Pakistani public became more aggressive as it was made to believe by the military regime that India was the assailant. The Pakistani Press, uninhibited by any fear, freely indulged in India-baiting. The *Dawn* wrote "Hypocrites" in Western Capitalist countries, who professed to be fighting for freedom in Vietnam, were defending the "oppressors and tyrants and butchers of freedom in Kashmir." All these signalled that the Pakistan's war would not abate.

It looked as if the entire sub-continent would soon be engulfed in an appalling catastrophe. Agitated over the possibility of Pakistan's drive to New Delhi, India took to counter-action. On 8 September, she advanced westward in the desert along the border between Sind and Rajasthan. It was explained variedly as a diversionary thrust and an attempt to pin down the Pakistani forces in Karachi, west of the area of the desert advance. On the night of the same day, the Indian intelligence reported that the main Pakistani tank force was in the Sialkot sector and that under the cover of darkness her force equipped with heavy American Patton tanks, light American Shermans and medium French Chaffers opened an offensive. The Pattons were equipped with infra red "eyes" for night fighting. But India's heavy Centurion tanks, which were her best, were blind after sun-set. According to some accounts, there were more than 225 Pakistani tanks involved in this, which far outnumbered the Indian Centurions. A more important factor than this about which India had no complete knowledge was the secret installation of a tunnel by Pakistan beneath the waterway which facilitated the sending of a large force across the Bambansala-Ravi-Bedian (BRB) canal.

But India repulsed this most thrilling onslaught and thwarted Ayub's dream of "strolling up" to New Delhi. D.R. Mankekar says in his book on the 1965 war that if Pakistan "had succeeded, east of that point, up to Delhi, the Grand Trunk Road lay open, practically undefended with all our forces on the other side of the Beas - thus bringing within an ace of realisation of Ayub's dream of 'strolling up' to Delhi."[28]

After this, Pakistan diverted the tank attacks into the fields of sugar cane some of 9 feet high behind which a force of Indian Centurions crouched in ambush. While the newly created marshlands cut down Pakistan's speed and mobility, the high sugar cane fields reduced the visibility of the attacks. As a result, the superior gunnery range of the Pattons was curtailed. Another factor that happened by chance to the advantage of the Indian side was that while their tanks were hidden, the waving sugar cane exposed the position of the Pakistani pattons to the Indian forces. This facilitated the dug-in Indian tanks to open fire. They used the Canadian designed 76 mm high velocity tank guns. Pakistan's offensive was halted. The Pakistani forces fell back to Khem-Karan where they dug in.[29]

In the meantime the battle for Sialkot, 50 miles northeast of Lahore was developing into a biggest tank engagement since the Second World War. This extensive and ferocious 15-day battle fought across flat land was the biggest engagement during this war. It was a very important war in which both claimed victory.

U Thant's Report

It was seen that U Thant's mission to the sub-continent to call for a halt to hostilities in accordance with the Security Council's resolutions of 4 and 6 September was a failure. Halting hostilities was the sole concern of the Council and it was determined not to sidetrack from this main objective. But U Thant could not secure the withdrawal of troops of either side from the occupied territory. The preliminary report of his visit to the sub-continent completed on 16 September was placed before the council on 18 September. The terms of his second letter to the Prime Minister of India and the President of Pakistan attached to the report was a disagreeable surprise to many members as they contained the following words: "I note, however, that both Governments have added to their replies to my request for an unconditional cease-fire, conditions and qualifications upon which I have no right under the Security Council resolutions, to give firm undertakings."[30] This was a distortion of fact. It gave no indication of the essential differences between the ready willingness of one party namely India to accept the cease-fire and reluctant response of the other namely Pakistan to it. India's readiness and willingness to accept the Security Council's proposal for an immediate cease-fire contrasted with the consistently unhelpful attitude of Pakistan. It was also seen that to the Secretary General's appeal of 9 August, Pakistan gave no assurance that the case-fire and the CFL would be respected. India on the other hand gave the assurance that she would exercise restraint in her retaliatory acts and respect the cease-fire agreement and the CFL if Pakistan did likewise.

On 16 September in view of the steadily deteriorating situation, the Secretary General gave the Council a prepared statement detailing all the cease-fire violations which was designed for public release. The draft was given to the representatives of both India and Pakistan for the information of their Governments. Both reacted promptly. India expressed no objection to its release but suggested some modifications in it part of which U Thant found unacceptable. But the Government of Pakistan adopted a strongly negative attitude about the statement on the ground that it was favourable to India. It pointed out that the draft "dealt only with the current cease-fire situation without presenting the political background of the broad issue and thus was lacking in balance since a cease-fire alone supports the *status quo* to India's benefit."[31] Ayub openly stated that he would welcome only a "purposeful cease-fire" which would provide for "a self-executing arrangement for the final settlement of the Kashmir dispute which is the root cause of the India-Pakistan conflict." Criticising the proposal of "cease-fire without condition," Ayub said that soon after the cease-fire, the Security Council would proceed to implement the resolution of 6 September by which there would be an immediate withdrawal of all armed Pakistan personnel to the Pakistan side of the CFL by strengthening the UNMOGIP. This, he emphasised, "would result in restoring India's military grip over Kashmir. We would thus merely revert to the same explosive position which triggered the present conflict." Ayub ended his reply by veering round to the conclusion that for a cease-fire to be meaningful it was imperative to evolve "an effective machinery and procedures which would finally resolve the Kashmir dispute."[32]

When the Security Council met on 18 September, the Pakistani Minister gave a litany of the enormous miseries and human tragedies his country had suffered during the fighting. He claimed that these were but "the symptoms of an ancient malignancy." He wanted the Security Council to go to the root cause of the trouble which lay in India's refusal to have a plebiscite to which she agreed in 1948. A member quipped that this was Pakistan's "time-honoured refrain."

When his turn came, the member of the Malaysian delegation, Ramani said :

> "I have not the slightest doubt that the Minister of India does have his own story to tell of unspeakable tragedies. In human terms, it should tug at our hearts and stir our souls with revulsion for war; and pity and compassion for those that are unwilling legatees of the misery, starvation, homelessness and suffering innumerable let loose by war, a situation in which swift death would be a great mercy. I trust that this mental picture alone will give this debate a sense of urgency as nothing else can."

Cease-Fire

At its meeting on 20 September, the Security Council passed a strongly worded resolution. For the first time in UN's history, the resolution demanded that cease-fire should take effect on Wednesday 22 September at 07.00 hours GMT and called upon both Governments to issue orders for a cease-fire at that moment and a subsequent withdrawal of all armed personnel back to the positions held by them before 5 August 1965. It was passed by 10-0, Jordan alone abstaining. The American Ambassador in Pakistan pressed Ayub very hard to accept the cease-fire resolution.[33] Bhutto told the Commonwealth Secretary that Ayub had not yet decided on accepting the resolution and that he wanted to secure an amendment to it. The amendment was to delete reference to 5 August 1965 which implied that Pakistan had started the "present hostilities." He wanted it to be changed into "in August" or "position before the outbreak of hostilities."[34] A clear case of the culprit being the chooser! Bhutto for his part, pointed to Goldberg, President of the Security Council, two deficiencies in the Resolution: (i) Reference to 5 August was an indictment of Pakistan; and (ii) Absence of any reference to the past resolutions of the UN. Goldberg indicated to Bhutto that his interpretation of the reference to 5

August was incorrect as the resolution merely indicated that the parties were required to withdraw behind the CFL and the international boundary. He further said that the Council made no adjudication of aggression by either party. Regarding the second "deficiency" mentioned by Bhutto he said that not all members of the Council supported its earlier resolutions; the Council had neither endorsed nor abandoned them but they remained on record. He added that all the members of the Council had taken the resolution in good faith.

The Security Council had an emergency meeting at 02.35 hours at Bhutto's request to announce Pakistan's answer to the resolution. He announced that Pakistan had issued cease-fire orders to take effect that night at 12.05 hours West Pakistan time, provided India did the same. Bhutto was very angry with Morrice James who played a vital role in persuading Ayub to agree to the cease-fire. He felt that Morrice had ruined all his plans.[35] Both before and after his announcement at the Security Council, Bhutto, well-known for his arrogant rhetoric especially in his speeches in the Security Council, indulged in a mud-slinging campaign against both India and the Security Council. He began with a rash, injudicious and almost hysterical tirade against India; thundered that Pakistan would fight to the end for its "just cause"; called the Security Council's resolution unsatisfactory; accused the Council of playing with the Kashmir issue for eighteen years; and threatened that Pakistan would give the Council one last chance but if it failed to put its full force behind a solution, his country would leave the UN and set a time limit for this process. He ended with the warning that he would "wage a war for a thousand years, a war of defence."[36]

After the President welcomed the decision of both the Governments to the cease-fire, India asked for reasonable notice of the new cease-fire time and the Council fixed it at not later than 22.00 GMT on 22 September and adjourned. The Secretary General recruited about 90 observers to police the CFL south of Kashmir and doubled the number of observers within Kashmir itself.

There were different verdicts of the result of the war. According to some, Indians won a significant victory. Foreign opinion was that it ended in a draw. In the judgment of "impartial experts," India displayed "greater skill and better strategy in the use of amour" than Pakistan. Whoever was the victor, the loss was considerable on both sides.

On the whole, the result of the war was badly reported abroad. There were distorted versions of even the details of the war. Foreign correspondents, especially the British "played up Pakistani Reports and blacked out (India's) success". *The Hindu* wrote:

"There can be no gainsaying the fact that at the cease-fire, we stand deep in Pakistani territory while Pakistan's plans to seize Kashmir, capture Amritsar and drive to Delhi have fizzled out. We have destroyed so large a part of the Pakistani war machine that it will be a long time before Rawalpindi can think of another assault on India...Perhaps the most remarkable feature of this war has been the determination and discipline of our armed forces that have confined themselves to severely limited objectives without trying to gain territory or seize inhabited cities. This also has been misrepresented abroad as a failure on our part but we may rest content with the attainment of our purpose which was to break the strength of the enemy and teach him that aggression does not pay."[37]

The hostilities between the armies of 600 million people in the sub-continent constituted a huge problem which could not be allowed to go on endlessly. Fortunately, there was a rare global unanimity on the decision to impose a quick peace on the parties. India who never started the war was throughout more amenable than Pakistan to an early cease-fire. However, she stuck to her stand that Kashmir was non negotiable and that the only possible give and take in this case was withdrawal from the territory won during the war. Pakistan eventually agreed to halt the war but with a "public face-saving promise that the UN would seek a future political settlement." India stated that the call for case-fire had to be on Pakistan and not on India who had not once but twice accepted the Secretary General's proposals to cease hostilities at a particular date and a particular time.

Dwelling on the testing time of seven weeks during which India made huge scarifies in blood and armour and paying tributes to the imperishable heroism of the civilian population in Kashmir, the Punjab and other places and glorious role of the defence forces, *The Hindu* wrote: "If there is one lesson Pakistan has to learn from its adventure of the past two months, it is that no military solution of the Kashmir problem will be possible." Pakistan refused to learn this.

Though the war came to an end, the subsequent events revealed that Pakistan attached very little importance to the cease-fire. That she was still in a belligerent mood was evident from the threat of Ayub and Bhutto of a wider conflagration in the future. The view of opinion leaders was that while the conflict between the two armed forces had come to an end what was much more important than this was to bring to an end "the deeper conflict between a theocratic state and a secular state, between a free democracy and a guided democracy" and that the answer to this lay in "peaceful co-existence."

Renewal of Attacks

From 21 September - one day before the cease-fire agreement, the whole of Karachi was in a state ferment with students marching in procession chanting pro-Pakistan, pro-China and pro-Indonesia and anti-India, anti-Britain and anti-America slogans. In Jakarta, 500 youths whose passions were roused to fever heat ransacked the Indian Embassy and shouted the slogan "Crush India." The authorities did not stop them.

On 23 September, in his broadcast to the nation, Shastri said that the hostilities between India and Pakistan that began on 5 August with Pakistan's infiltration had come to an end "but let us not mistake it for the dawn of peace." He said that the cease-fire had been put off by 15 hours because of Pakistan's delay in agreeing to it. He also referred to Pakistan's bombing of the civilian population in Amritsar in broad daylight causing much loss of life and property, after having informed the Security Council of her acceptance of the cease-fire.

To quote Shastri:

> "We have no quarrel with the people of Pakistan (We) wish them well...even in the fighting that just ended all our attacks were directed against the Pakistani war machine. We have not bombed civilians, not shelled Lahore, and did not retaliate against air raids from East Pakistan...Not attacked Karachi even though most of the aircrafts that were used to attack our territory, had their base there. In contrast, the Pakistanis had chased and shot down an unarmed civilian plane carrying the Chief Minister of Gujarat and his wife. They had thrown bombs on the civilian population of Rajasthan, Gujarat and Punjab...After unleashing a planned massive attack of India, thus compelling us to take measures, Pakistan is deliberately carrying on a false propaganda that India is out to destroy Pakistan."[38]

Having learnt that the cease-fire was not holding, the Security Council passed another resolution on 27 September which demanded the parties to "urgently honour commitments to the Council to observe the cease-fire" and "withdraw all armed personnel as necessary steps in the full implementation" of the resolution of 20 September 1965.

The Pakistani army maintained that its Government had not yet agreed to the withdrawal of troops and that the agreement thus far was only on the cease-fire. Pakistan would withdraw her troops to their side of the CFL only when an agreement on the general withdrawal of troops was reached between the Governments of India and Pakistan.[39] It was clear that Pakistan had no idea of withdrawing her troops until she found meaningful progress towards a settlement on Kashmir. India also declined to withdraw no doubt because they first wanted guarantee about infiltrators. This meant continuance of fighting which threatened to get out of hand.

It all came to this. While both Governments accepted cease-fire, neither had accepted any obligation to withdraw its forces. The crux of the matter was that Pakistan's unabashed aggression against India had not even halted. To achieve this, it was not enough if the cease-fire was rigorously observed and the withdrawal of the Pakistani troops effected but all infiltrators must be withdrawn too. If Pakistan did this, India in her magnanimity, would certainly listen to the views of other countries. A similar view was expressed by Vijayalakshmi Pandit in Paris when Shastri sent her there for explanatory talks with the French Government.[40]

Apart from the communal killings, the domestic situation in both countries was far from satisfactory. The economies of both countries were in bad shape. India's food crisis, which could not be solved without western aid, worried Britain who felt that the Soviet Union would come to her rescue. India could get adequate aid only from the US. But Lyndon Johnson's Government took a tough stand to withhold both military and economic aid at least until there was a compliance with the U.N. resolution. Even after compliance, the question of resumption of American aid would depend on a number of conditions including progress towards a settlement on Kashmir. Britain however was not in favour of applying a complete withholding of aid as the US Government was doing. Because of her Commonwealth connection, Britain did not have the same freedom of action as the US.

When the violations of cease-fire did not stop and there were no symptoms of withdrawal of troops, the Security Council met again and adopted another resolution on 5 November 1965. By this, the Security Council called upon the two Governments to instruct their armed personnel "to cooperate with the United Nations and cease all military activity." The resolution also envisaged the appointment of a representative of the Secretary General to meet the representatives of India and Pakistan "to formulate an agreed plan and schedule of withdrawals." With the consent of the two Governments, the Secretary General appointed Brigadier General Tulio Marambio, Director of the Chilean War Academy as his representative.

The war brought a welcome change in the attitude of two nations towards India. Iran and Australia were hitherto strong opponents of India. The Shah of Iran, a close friend of Pakistan who always castigated India, changed his attitude and made appeals to Pakistan to stop the senseless fighting against India on Kashmir.[41] There was a much greater change in the attitude of Robert Menzies, Prime Minister of Australia, who had all along been with Pakistan and strongly felt that Nehru put India in the wrong by refusing to agree to a plebiscite. This war thoroughly modified his view in this regard. He realised that because of Pakistan's flirtations with China, solution of the Kashmir problem in Pakistan's favour would involve extension of China's sphere of influence in the sub-continent. Chatterjee, the energetic Indian High Commissioner to Australia, was responsible for this change in Menzies's attitude. He assiduously propagated that the outcome of the war should not be such as to allow Chinese influence to spread to Kashmir and that, in particular, Indians should continue to control the road to Ladakh.[42]

References

1. Shastri to Wilson, 10 Sep. 1965, PREM/13/394.
2. UK HC (I) to Commonwealth Secretary, 2 Oct. 1965, PREM/13/395.
3. Known in ancient times as Calpe, Gibraltar (occupying a narrow peninsula of Spain's Southern Mediterranean coast), took its present name from the Arabic *Gobel el Tariq* (Mount of Tarik) from the Tarik leader of the expedition that landed there on 30 April 711 AD which marked the starting of the Moorish conquest of the Iberian Peninsula.
4. UK HC (P) to Commonwealth Secretary, 3 Feb. 1966, DO/196/219.
5. Morrice James, *Pakistan Chronicle*, p. 129.
6. *The Baltimore Sun*, 12 Aug. 1965.
7. *Sydney Daily Telegraph*, 13 Aug. 1965.
8. Russell Brines, *The Indo-Pakistani conflict.* The author was an ace foreign correspondent with 30 years experience in covering Asia. This book which was the result of his observation of the Indo-Pakistan War of 1965 from close quarters in India was banned by Pakistan. Extracts from the book are in the possession of the Adyar Library, Chennai.
9. Rumbold's account of the Indo-Pakistan War, FCO/37/916.
10. UK HC (P) to CRO, 1 Sep. 1965, PREM/13/393.
11. Morrice James to Freeman, 1 Feb. 1966, DO/196/484.
12. *Tribune*, 29 April 1966.
13. UK HC (P) to CRO, 6 Sep. 1965, PREM/13/394.
14. Victoria Schofield, *Kashmir in Conflict – India, Pakistan and the unending war*, p. 110.
15. FO to UKD to UN, 8 Sep. 1965, DO/ 196/384.

16. Dean Rusk to FO, 6 Sep. 1965, PREM/13/393.
17. *Ibid*, UK Embassy, Washington to FO, 6 Sep. 1965.
18. *Ibid*, Record of meeting between Minister of State and Dr. Mehta, 6 Sep. 1965.
19. *Times of India*, 8 Sep. 1965; UK HC (1) to CRO, 8 Sep. 1965, DO/196/384.
20. Draft Paper (Confdl), South East Asia Department, FCO/37/174.
21. UK HC (1) to CRO, 7 Sep. 1965, PREM/13/393.
22. Gore-Booth to Pickard, 8 Sep. 1965, DO/196/385.
23. CRO to UK HC (I), 17 Sep. 1965, PREM/13/394.
24. UK HC (P) to CRO, 8 September 1965, DO/196/384.
25. Altaf Gauhar, *Ayub Khan: Pakistan's First Military Ruler*, p. 236.
26. UK Ambassador (Teheran) to FO, 9 Sept. 1965, PREM/13/394.
27. *Ibid*, Record of Conversation between Prime Minister and Indian HC to UK, 15 Sept. 1965.
28. Cited in *Indo Pakistan conflict, op. cit.*
29. *Ibid.*
30. Documents/S 6683, 16 Sept. 1965, Para 10.
31. *Ibid*, S 6651/Paras. 9 & 10.
32. *Ibid*, S/6683/Paras. 9 to 14.
33. UKD to UN to FO, 20 Sep. 1965, PREM/13/395.
34. *Ibid*, CRO to UK HC (P), 21 Sep. 1965.
35. Minute dated 13 Oct. 1967, FCO/37/185.
36. UKD to UN to FO, 22 Sep. 1965, PREM/13/395.
37. *A Hundred Years of The Hindu*, p. 761.
38. Lal Bahadur Shastri's Broadcast on the AIR on 23 Sep. 1965. PREM/13/395.
39. *Ibid*, UKD to UN to FO, 26 Sep. 1965.
40. *Ibid*, P. Reilly, UK Ambassador (Paris) to FO, 4 Oct. 1965.
41. UK Ambassador (Teheran) to CRO, 14 Sep. 1965, DO/196/385.
42. C. Johnston, UK HC (Australia) to CRO, 16 Sep. 1965, PREM/13/394.

17

Tashkent and After

Bhutto's violent utterances at the Security Council on 20 September 1965 were adequate proof of Pakistan's intention not to implement the UN's call for cease-fire. By this order both sides had to make the cease-fire effective forthwith and withdraw all their armed personnel. Pakistan accepted it only grudgingly. The acceptance was but a tactical manoeuvre to gain time to set in order the shattered Pakistani forces and to keep them ready to strike Kashmir again when the time was propitious. Pakistan ensured that tension was kept up all along the CFL. There were infringements of the cease-fire all the way from Tithwal to Rajasthan. Massive preparations were afoot to train the Pakistani irregulars to resume the attack on Kashmir. Pakistan was also shopping for war material in Turkey, Iran, Indonesia, Portugal, France, West Germany and Japan.

This was not the first occasion when the Security Council had a taste of Pakistan's violations of cease-fire agreements. It was strange that even after its experience of Pakistan's incessant intransigence, the Council should have trusted her word to agree to a cease-fire. The UN was not to blame for this. It was after all, a tool of Western imperialism especially of Britain, who was ever anxious to placate Pakistan at whatever cost to India.

Bhutto's frequent assertions and Pakistan's persistent violations of the cease-fire left India in no doubt of Pakistan's sincerity. The Security Council's past record as to its capacity to enforce its decisions in this regard was not encouraging. In such a circumstance, India's ready response to withdrawal of her forces would expose her to the risk of fresh Pakistani attacks.

There were occasions where Pakistan refused to withdraw from the Indian positions even at the request of the UN's Chief Military Observer.

The Pakistani forces refused to remain frozen at the positions they occupied at the moment of the announcement of the cease-fire. In fact, they continuously endeavoured to improve their positions by both open and clandestine occupation of new positions east of the line held by them on 22 September in order to " present a *fait accompli*" to the UN observers. The Government of India refused to permit such patent violations. It also refused to recognise positions occupied by the Pakistani forces after the announcement of cease-fire on 22 September. The only area in Rajasthan occupied by Pakistan at the time when the cease-fire came into operation was the border outpost of Munabao. In pointing out this, G. Parthasarathy, Ambassador Extraordinary and Plenipotentiary Permanent Representative of India to the UN told the Secretary General that the idea of "telescoping cease-fire and withdrawals into a single operation" was contrary to the resolutions of the Security Council and was therefore unacceptable to India.[1]

Bhutto's Degrading Melodrama

At the meeting of the Security Council on 25 October, Bhutto's behaviour was worse than what it was on 20 September. He continued his offensive and abusive remarks about India that hardly had any parallel in the annals of the UN for their vulgarity. When his invectives became so outrageous as to force the Indian delegation to walk out, he jeered at them saying: "The Indian dogs have run away from the Security Council Chamber but not from Kashmir." This must have undoubtedly shocked all the Members of the Council. Yet none dared to ask him to stop. Nor did the President, known for his indecisiveness, choose to call him to order and demand for the withdrawal of his obnoxious remarks.

The wrangle created by Bhutto in the Council on 25 October by his misuse of the forum, his uninterrupted vituperation against India for two hours, his threats to leave the UN and India's walk-out and refusal to attend the next meeting of the Council on 27 October might have given Bhutto a fleeting tactical victory. But the ugly events of the day did not certainly redound to the prestige of the Security Council.

Since India stayed away from the debate of the Security Council on 27 October, there was a brief debate in the Council on 29 October. On the same day, there were also diplomatic exchanges outside it. In the Council, Britain strongly and unequivocally endorsed India's stand that the Council should devote itself to military disengagement and not to political issues or the internal affairs of Kashmir. Russia also bluntly said that without the participation of one of the affected parties, no positive results could be reached. This was a double blow to Pakistan: her joy over India's absence was short-lived and her hope to ingratiate herself with the Soviet Union was shattered.

Commenting on the revolting incidents in the world forum, India's President Radhakrishnan said that "if the UN failed to act in a just and honourable way, the fate of the League of Nations is there to warn us." The conflict between Ethiopia and Italy marked the beginning of the end of the League which could not act justly and honourably. He expressed the hope that the UN would not submit to anything false or unjust but insist on the implementation of the cease-fire and withdrawal of all Pakistani armed personnel from the Indian territory.[2]

The situation in the sub–continent remained highly unstable. The relations between India and Pakistan had reached the very nadir since Pakistan launched the armed attack against India on 5 August 1965. The fear of Pakistan achieving her aims by "bluster and blackmail," was very much there. Countries interested in peace in the sub-continent agreed that this situation should not be allowed to continue.

Tashkent Agreement

When the sub-continent faced a grave situation, the Russians came forward to offer their good offices. It was given to the Soviet Premier Aleksey Kosygin to bring about in January 1966 reconciliation between Shastri and Ayub at Tashkent, capital of the Uzbek Soviet Socialist Republic. The Russian offer to mediate was made as early as 21 September 1965. L.K. Jha, Shastri's close confidant informed the UK High Commissioner John Freeman that Shastri and the Cabinet were seriously thinking of accepting Kosygin's offer. In December, during his meeting with Ayub in London, Prime Minister Wilson discussed the prospects of a meeting at Tashkent. About the same time, Morrice James, UK High Commissioner to Pakistan, discussed the Soviet offer with Bhutto. The latter replied that the Government of Pakistan was determined not to get sidetracked into spending its time exclusively on "minor issues." He also said that the meeting should last 4 to 10 days![3] The Government of Pakistan agreed to go to Tashkent because it understood that Britain and America had lost their initiative in the Security Council and that, if it rejected the Soviet offer at this difficult hour, there was no other course open to Pakistan.

Kosygin's friendly move was welcome to both the UK and the US. In fact, Freeman wrote to his Government in September that Britain should do nothing to frustrate the good services offered by the Soviet Union. When Dean Rusk was asked if he had any objection to such a meeting, he said he had none. On the contrary, he was happy to involve the Russians in the problem that had been round their necks for 18 years.[4] In fact America genuinely felt that what the two warring countries really needed to do was to concentrate on efficient food production and economic development rather than on senseless arms race.

Kosygin's offer to settle the Kashmir dispute marked the first ever attempt at "enjoining patience and encouraging bilateral relations." The Russians proceeded very cautiously and displayed considerable diplomatic skill in keeping the Indian side in good humour. They did succeed in maintaining in tact their long friendship and goodwill with India despite the change from the previous Soviet stand of wholehearted support for the Indian cause on Kashmir to a more neutral position.

In January 1966, Shastri and Ayub met at Tashkent and held discussions. On 10 January, in the presence of Kosygin and Bulganin, the Tashkent Declaration was signed in the Conference Hall of the Uzbek Government by Prime Minister Shastri on behalf of India and President Ayub on behalf of Pakistan. Bhutto "sat through the half-hour function glum-faced. His hostility to the Declaration was writ large on his face," reported the *Hindustan Standard*.[5] The nine point Joint Declaration provided among other things for good neighbourly relations between India and Pakistan in accordance with the UN Charter, withdrawal of all armed personnel of the two countries not later than 25 February 1966 to the positions they held prior to 5 August 1965, observance by both of cease-fire terms on the CFL, non-interference in the internal affairs of each other, discouragement of propaganda directed against each other and settlement of disputes peacefully and not through war. The Declaration was admittedly a significant contribution to peace in the sub-continent though the mention of no-war pact and renunciation of guerrilla aggression in Kashmir was conspicuous by its absence. It certainly marked the starting of a new era in the relations between the two hostile neighbours. "If Ayub means to honour what the Joint Declaration he had signed implies," wrote *The Hindu*, "we have reason to hope there will be no more of this infiltration business. Unless this is ended once and for all, there can be no peace in the region."[6]

The Declaration gave the impression that both the countries would bury the hatchet and settle their differences by peaceful means. The spirit of *Panch Sheel* was enshrined in the Declaration.

After signing the Declaration, Shastri appeared to have had supper with Ayub before retiring to bed when he remarked: "We fought the war gallantly and I want to fight for peace gallantly."[7]

Prime Minister Shastri was not destined to return to India as a hero. He suddenly died of heart attack at 3 am on 11 January 1966, at Tashkent. His countrymen could only see the body of their great national leader on 12 January in New Delhi.

A costly war which was Pakistan's own making did not help her to add an inch of territory to what she had already grabbed during the war of 1947-48 and continued to retain illegally. Pakistan understood that though the Kashmiris might not have been happy with India, they would never "surrender their unique culture and identity to Pakistan." In other words, "*Kashmiriyat* survived the war of 1965."[8]

Normal relations appeared to return to the sub-continent after the Tashkent Declaration. The army leaders of both India and Pakistan deserved tributes for their remarkable implementation of the Agreement on the withdrawal of troops in letter and spirit. Both General Chaudhuri of India and General Musa of Pakistan demonstrated amazing speed and cordiality in the disengagement of the two armies, withdrawal of armed personnel to the positions they occupied before 5 August 1965 and a general lessening of tension along the long meandering borders between the two countries. Well-meaning people on both sides hoped that the two armies would further consolidate the gains of Tashkent by deciding to stop the stationing of troops in close proximity to the border. This expectation, as *The Statesman* observed:

> "arose from an interesting, if somewhat strange, fact peculiar to India and Pakistan: sudden spurts of goodwill and good neighbourliness between the two countries seem as genuine and as strong as the frequent bouts of bitterness, hostility and conflict. At Tashkent, even at a time when the talks between them were teetering on the brink of failure, neither Mr. Shastri nor President Ayub had any doubt about the other's sincerity about wanting to establish... honourable peace between the two countries..."[9]

By the Security Council's resolution of 5 November 1965, U Thant's nominee Tulio Marambio of the Chilean War Academy, who was to formulate the schedule for the withdrawal of the forces, met the representatives of India and Pakistan in February 1966. He was pleased to find that the withdrawals had taken place within the agreed time limit.

Normal Relations - A Mirage

The smooth withdrawal of troops did not mean that the parties concerned were satisfied with the outcome of the entire Tashkent Declaration. Both had their own grievances against it. In India, though the dissatisfaction with the Declaration was common among the general public, many parties were particularly unhappy with the withdrawal of the Indian troops from Haji Pir Pass, Tithwal and Kargil. The return of the territories to Pakistan caused much misgiving among Shastri's Cabinet colleagues. In fact the decision regarding this was taken by Shastri even before he left for Tashkent. He took the decision personally on the advice of L.K. Jha, his Secretary, Y.B. Chavan, Defence Minister and General Chaudhuri (COAS). The reaction of the Socialist parties was too hostile. The Congress, the Swatantra party and the right wing of the Communist Party of India endorsed the Declaration. Even in the Congress, the general opinion was that there was some objection which, if Shastri had not died, would have been much stronger than what it was. Anyway, the declaration was honoured and the tone of the Republic Day Parade on 26 January 1966 in Delhi was such as to fit in with the spirit of Tashkent.

As for Pakistan, it is needless to stress the strong opposition of her public to the Declaration. The resistance from the areas in the Punjab was very powerful as they had borne the brunt of the fighting. Within three weeks of the completion of the withdrawal of their forces on 25 February 1966, Pakistan had forsaken the Tashkent spirit. Ayub's position was becoming shaky. Fortunately, he was saved from facing the wrath of the Punjab as the venue for the March session of National Assembly was East Pakistan. Ayub was sore that the promise offered by the Tashkent Declaration had not been fully realised. At the time of the first anniversary of the Tashkent Declaration, Ayub told Kosygin that he had failed to convince India that Kashmir was a disputed territory and as such it was central to any negotiations with her. India had always maintained that Kashmir was not a disputed territory and therefore could not be discussed as such. India had made it plain that she was ready to discuss any subject under dispute with Pakistan but that Kashmir was not negotiable.

India had never minced words when she affirmed and reaffirmed the two vital factors in relation to Kashmir: (i) With the passage of time the UN resolutions had ceased to have any relevance to the progress that Kashmir had made over the years; and (ii) the general elections held in the State had to be considered as equivalent to the popular consultation envisaged when the Maharaja's accession of Kashmir to India was accepted. But Pakistan adamantly refuted India's contentions. There was another decisive factor that was completely lost sight of. Before the war, the Government of India as well as informed public opinion had a real fear that the Pakistani army with its superior war equipment supplied by America would defeat the Indian army in a military confrontation and drive into New Delhi. But that fear was banished after the war and India emerged from the war much stronger than Pakistan. Having added considerably to her military strength after the war, India was confident she could hold and defeat the Pakistani forces in another military encounter.

Against this background of the results of the 1965 war, India saw no need to compromise on her traditional stand on Kashmir. If, notwithstanding the changed atmosphere, Pakistan chose to raise the Kashmir issue again at the Security Council, the British Delegation would have to concentrate exclusively on the resolutions of 20 September and 5 November 1965 and the Tashkent Declaration of 10 January 1966 as the framework within which India and Pakistan should themselves find a solution. This was the uniform opinion of all major powers with the exception of China. Pakistan was certainly aware of this. Yet she would not budge from her stand that until the Kashmir problem was solved the relationship with India would be one of stresses and strains.

Ayub was angry with Kosygin and accused him of ignoring his responsibilities and obligations by continuing the arms supplies to India. The motive behind this charge was to give the Russians a prod to further action in settling the Kashmir question. Britain also knew only too well that this drama was "no more than a predictable statement of Pakistan's attitude intended as much for domestic and international consumption as for the Russian Government."[10] The Anniversary of the Tashkent Declaration afforded the Pakistani Press also a chance to persist in its insinuations of "India's dishonesty" and wild accusation that India "killed" the Tashkent sprit by her refusal to negotiate on Kashmir.

America was displeased with Pakistan's persistence in her hostility towards India. Since the economies of both the countries were in bad shape, she wanted Pakistan to put the Kashmir imbroglio "on ice" and concentrate on the economic development of her country. Since many worthwhile joint economic projects required the co-operation of both nations, the US urged Pakistan to address herself to constructive activities which would also help reduce her escalating defence expenditure appreciably. Anyway, the Pakistan Government, which linked every Indo-Pakistan problem with Kashmir, could not be brought to think on American lines. It refused to concede that India was in a perilous situation consequent upon the Chinese aggression and that any concession to Pakistan at that stage would gravely weaken India's defences against China. It also refused to accept that, until the Sino-Indian border dispute was resolved, the Indian Government could not be expected to adopt a soft line towards Pakistan who it tended to regard as an accomplice of China. Again, it did not strike the Pakistan Government that in the secular context of the Indian Government, Kashmir had to remain only in the Indian Union in the interest of the communal harmony of the 50 million Muslims scattered throughout India.

Britain feared that Pakistan might go straight to the Security Council once the military withdrawals were complete. At a secret meeting held in Karachi on 1 and 2 February 1966, between the British High Commissioners to India and Pakistan, it was decided that Britain should do everything possible to avoid the Kashmir issue coming before the Security Council. If the British failed in their effort, they should take no prominent part in the proceedings of the Council but should get that body invite the Russians to continue their good offices. It was also agreed that they should impress on Pakistan the limited power they had and their inability to play a significant role in settling the issue. Freeman was keen to let Pakistan understand Britain's need to rebuild her influence in Delhi. He also warned that Britain would carry a very grave responsibility if she encouraged Pakistan to believe that eventually she was bound to get the Vale.

With little progress registered in the interaction between India and Pakistan even after the Tashkent Declaration, normalisation of relations between them proved, as on previous occasions, deceptive. The only two minor matters settled were the resumption of telecommunications and the acceptance by both sides of the three member Tribunal Award on the Rann of Kutch. Otherwise, the Indo-Pakistan relations remained as bitter as ever.

Change of Guard in Pakistan

The span of the first eleven years (1947-1958) in Pakistan's history is generally characterized as a period of "drift and muddle." In 1958, Ayub made himself President. He was no doubt a dictator and the Constitution which he himself drafted and imposed on the country in 1962, placed overwhelming powers in his hands. Still, the first seven years of his reign from 1958 to 1965 proved a "purposeful and productive period." On 2 January 1965, he was re-elected President of Pakistan for another term of five years (1965 to 1970) when he polled 63 per cent of all valid votes defeating Jinnah's sister Fatima

Jinnah. But the fact that Fatima, though beaten in both wings of Pakistan, had won larger number of votes than he expected, convinced Ayub of the opposition to his regime. He was not unaware of his dictatorial governance. He was well aware that there would be large-scale protest against it and that things would not all be so smooth in future.

The ill-fated unprovoked war Ayub waged against India thanks to the bad advice and wrong counselling of Bhutto and Aziz Ahmed led to his downfall. He realised that this was "a substantial policy blunder." Bhutto, the incurable optimist, was more than confident that India would be totally ruined in the war and that Pakistan's possession of the Vale was only a matter of time. But the war had shaken Ayub's regime to its roots. The consequences of the war were very severe. In September 1965, when Pakistan's invasion of India was in full swing, the US suddenly suspended the supply of economic and military aid to both India and Pakistan. This suspension hurt Pakistan more than India. In 1966, America lifted the ban on non-lethal weapons but there was inordinate delay in their release. In April 1967, the US announced its new decision by which military aid would be brought to an end but spares would be considered on a case by case basis. It was clear to Pakistan that she could no longer rely upon America for aid. In retaliation, the irate Ayub Government announced that the US would have to give up its vital communications base near Peshawar. The Government also informed the US of the cancellation of the lease on the base at Badaber in Peshawar with effect from mid-1969.[11]

Though the US had stopped military supplies, Communist China was supplying arms to Pakistan which enabled her to replace those lost in fighting the war. China was also providing Pakistan essential political and psychological support. But china was doing all this in her own interests in the future of Kashmir. She could gain politically only by keeping the dispute between India and Pakistan alive. The dispute afforded her the opportunity to further her influence in the sub-continent and weaken both the quarrelling parties economically. Shrewd Ayub gauged all this. There were two other factors which strengthened his doubt about the continuance of Chinese help. One was that China could not spare time to Pakistan, pre-occupied as she was, with her own "Cultural Revolution."[12] The other was Bhutto, who was primarily responsible for cementing the alliance between Pakistan and China, had been sacked by Ayub in July 1966. After this, the relations between the two countries could not be called cordial. Ayub became sufficiently alert to the dangers of getting very close to Communist China.

Having managed to make good the losses sustained in men and arms during the war and also added considerably to her striking power by new recruits to the army, Pakistan started again her war-like utterances against India. There was concentration of Pakistani troops along India's border. The April 1967 decision of the US to resume the supply of military spares coupled with the aid she was receiving from other countries encouraged Pakistan's bellicosity. In April 1967, Pakistan spurned an Indian offer of bilateral negotiations to scale down the arms build up in the sub-continent. Prime Minister Indira Gandhi's statement in a broadcast that the "seeds of disputes were sown after Pakistan and Israel came into being and Western countries also militarily equipped Israel as they equipped Pakistan,"[13] intensified Pakistan's animosity against India. This statement was nothing more than an emphasis on well-known historical facts. But it infuriated Pakistan so much that she called it "a malicious and ill intentioned analogy" which was bound to strengthen the feeling that India was still unreconciled to the partition of India. It was further averred that India's professed desire to promote good relations with Pakistan was a mere eye-wash. The British High Commissioner in India John Freeman resolutely repudiated this contention of Pakistan. He bluntly said that it was the Pakistan Government that was carrying on a sustained campaign during the West Asian crisis to distract public attention in foreign countries from India's firm stand on the calamity.[14] To add to the volatile situation was the *Autobiography* of Ayub published about this time which reflected no prospect of rapprochement between the two nations.

On 16 August 1968, Indira Gandhi renewed her non-aggression pact with Pakistan. It was a renewal of what her father and her predecessor Shastri had offered several times earlier. Pakistan's response to this offer was also the same as before. In his broadcast on 1 September 1968, Ayub declared that a "No War" pact without settling the vexed Kashmir question was "unrealistic and meaningless and amount to misleading and hoodwinking the world."[15]

In the domestic sphere, Ayub's popularity had declined considerably by this time. In November 1967, Bhutto, who was sacked by Ayub, launched his People's Party. At its first convention on 30 November and 1 December 1967, he thundered: "Give me the authority and I shall take Jammu and Kashmir." His utterances against India reeked of communalism. Students' unrest, which was not political initially, began to assume political overtones. There was widespread discontent with Auyb's authoritarian administration which was associated with corruption. The political instability was exploited by Ayub's political opponents especially Bhutto who was still in jail. Thus Pakistan was getting plunged in one crisis after another. For a while Ayub managed to contain the student unrest. He also ensured that the general situation quietened down a little in December 1968 with the help of the army, police and civil service. But all this was short lived. In view of the disorder in both wings of Pakistan, Ayub decided against attending the Commonwealth Prime Ministers' Conference in London.

Ayub's own Constitution of 1962 conferred on the President enormous powers. Police harassment of opposition leaders, press controls, nepotism, bribery and many other obnoxious acts were rampant. People were totally apathetic towards their own political system; the economy had virtually ground to a halt; religious and ethnic feuds posed a menace to public order and safety; the Khan of Kalat was leading his own Baluchi Army in open rebellion against the Government; banditry was widespread and politicians were as self-defeatingly querulous as ever. However, no act of Ayub's Government was so unpopular as its failure to involve East Pakistan in the decision making. Unquestionably, a step-motherly treatment was meted out to the East wing of the nation by the Government. There was a "perceptible string of political disintegration in Pakistan followed by economic and social dislocation."[16] It was clear to all that the fall of Ayub's Government was only a question of time.

With mounting tensions over several issues and his credibility having reached an irreversible low, Ayub announced his resignation as the President of Pakistan on 25 March 1969. He called upon General Yahya Khan, Commander-in-Chief of the Army, to fulfil his constitutional responsibilities. Ayub said: "It hurts me deeply to say that the situation now is no longer under the control of the Government. All Government institutions have become victims of coercion, fear and intimidation..."

Declaration of a state of Martial Law was left to Yahya who, on the same day - 25 March 1969, issued a Proclamation implementing Martial Law, abrogating the Constitution (including the dismissal of the National and Provincial Ministries and dissolution of the National and Provincial Assemblies) and providing for the continuance of the existing laws and administrative machinery including civil service. Political parties were not abolished now as they were in 1958 under Iskander Mirza's presidency. This was the second round of Martial Law in Pakistan in slightly over a decade.

An air of uncertainty about the future of the country was lingering in Pakistan. There was a strong doubt whether any alternative regime could tackle the problems that bedevilled the country better than the previous Governments.

End of Estranged Relationship

It was an open secret that the relations between India and Britain had never been very friendly and that the British Government made no efforts to be fair to India in dealing with Kashmir. India had not forgotten the hypocrisy of the British who, despite their expressions of benevolence and enlightenment, endlessly harped on safeguarding the minority rights for no other reason than "to sabotage the idea of an independent India by encouraging the Muslim truculence." After India's independence, the unfriendliness became more visible on the question of the status of Kashmir. Any British regime whether Labour or Tory, looked at Indo-British relations mainly in terms of Indo-Pakistan equations. India had the first taste of it about a couple of months after partition. Britain's reaction to Pakistan's naked trespass into the Indian territory in October 1947 was not as it should have been. Even later, despite the chain of aggressions committed by Pakistan, Britain refused to understand that a potential for a horrendous repeat of the 1947 incursion existed. The British had no inclination to waste their precious time to listen calmly to the sane arguments from the Indian side and take a dispassionate view of the Kashmir dispute. Instead, they had a strong tendency to beat down the arguments of the Indian representatives on Kashmir regardless of their merit. V.K. Krishna Menon, for instance, was such an anathema to the British that once Malcolm MacDonald described him as more than an "infernal nuisance." He was even considered a menace to good relations between India and Britain.[17] The whole business of the British Government was to discredit India's legitimate claim to Kashmir and prejudice public opinion in Britain.

War or no war, in Britain's view, Pakistan must hold the key to all disputes with India. Britain would have no discussion or meeting with India unless Pakistan was also present. To cite an instance, in December 1964, Shastri was to visit London form 2 to 6 December 1964. When the holding of the meeting was confirmed, the first thing that Britain did was to wire to Pakistan immediately and extend an invitation to Ayub also to visit London on those dates.[18] There were occasions when India was simply taken for granted by Britain. For instance, in the case of the Rann of Kutch, there were backroom talks with Wilson. This deepened the British conviction that India would meekly accept any interpretation of Whitehall's "impartiality" in the Indo-Pakistan disputes.

Of the many episodes that had deleterious effects on the Indo-British relations, the one that generated immeasurable ill-feeling in India was the message of Prime Minister Wilson to Shastri. Reference has been made in

Chapter 16 to this indecorous message of 6 September 1965 and the violent reactions to it in India. Some in Britain tended to regard the incident lightly. But the public and governmental reactions were definitely substantial.[19] The soft letter Wilson sent to Shastri ten days after his outrageous message was but a short-term palliative.

British officers in India were well aware of the constant reproaches from Indians, particularly those from the political circles, about the "hostile" and "pro-Pakistani' attitude of Britain during the war of 1965. They were very angry with the British Press as well as the BBC for their unfair comments and untrue reports about the military operations during the 1965 war. Whitehall was surprised at India's reaction and pooh-poohed it as "something that was regrettable but would pass off."[20]

The battered state of relations between the two countries drove some high ranking British officers both in India and Britain to repair the damage. John Freeman, British High Commissioner in India, played a key role in this. To assuage Indian feelings over Wilson's blunder, he explained to the Indian Government that Wilson's statement of 6 September was made out of ignorance of Pakistan's attack in the Chhamb sector the previous day (5 September) owing to a temporary failure of communication. But this adroit theory of Freeman was torpedoed by Wilson himself by another clumsy act which added fuel to the fire of 6 September which was just beginning to die down. On 21 December 1965, he sent a letter to Francis Noel-Baker, Member of Parliament, setting forth the reasons for sending such a message to Shastri on 6 September. He asserted therein that he had learnt from the message which originated from UN sources that "the whole of the Indian Army, less than four divisions, was attacking in the Punjab."[21]

Wilson's letter carried the charge that there was undoubtedly a tendency on the part of some Indians to exaggerate the implications of his message and to "read more into it than was ever intended." He justified his act on the ground that public reaction in Britain to the news of Indian attack demanded it because it came immediately after the UN appeal to a cease-fire. Wilson grieved that the Indians had overlooked some of his kind gestures especially his support to them during the Chinese aggression and his speech to this effect at Guild hall on 15 November 1965.[22]

Britain's relations with India touched the rock-bottom of bitterness on 5 January 1966 when Francis Noel-Baker published the Prime Minister's letter to him and stirred up a real hornet's nest. Publication of the letter did no good to anyone but further damaged the Prime Minister's prestige in India. In the wake of the publication of his letter by Francis Noel-Baker, British influence in India sank to a very low point. Britain felt that the view of all Indians except those of the ministerial circles was that the British Government was committed to Pakistan in the Kashmir affair and that this commitment coloured the whole spectrum of their relations with India.[23] The adverse impact on India of Wilson's message and the publication of his letter by Francis Noel-Baker continued and India long remained embittered and unappeased.

Strangely enough, in his *Memoirs,* Wilson had admitted in a short passage that his statement of 6 September 1965 about the outbreak of full-scale hostilities in the Punjab between India and Pakistan had been too tough. He further stated he had been "over persuaded" by a group of pro-Pakistan officials in the Commonwealth Relations Office and added that "they did not stay there long." In a subsequent appearance on Independent Television, he repeated the charge that he had been ill-advised.[24]

On 2 April 1966, Wilson met Indira Gandhi at the London Airport in a warm atmosphere. The meeting enabled both to leave the "sterile arguments" behind and let bygones be bygones so that a new chapter of cordial relations could be opened. Wilson told Indira Gandhi that he must take full responsibility for the 6 September message and the Wilson-Noel-Baker correspondence. The assessment of Freeman who had a personal talk with Indira Gandhi later in April was that there was really no reunion of minds after Wilson's face to face meeting with Indira Gandhi. He said Wilson went so far as to tender a personal apology "at least for the words in which the British policy was announced...I was forced to conclude that whatever the value of the personal meeting may have been, there was absolutely no meeting of minds between the two Prime Ministers." [25]

Though the chain of unpleasant events had practically undone the careful work of Freeman and others both in India and Britain, the well-wishers of India did not abandon their efforts to restore good relationship between the two nations. Freeman's correspondence with Britain both before and after the 6 September incident were replete with references to the prevailing anti-British feeling in India. India was particularly offended when Britain strongly backed Pakistan in her war against India in 1965 knowing well that she was not only the aggressor but also an "instrument of Chinese policy" and a "territorially frustrated power anxious to upset the *status quo*." Freeman's correspondence reiterated his anxiety to end the rift at all costs. He even recommended once that he should be authorised to sign the £14 million loan to India the negotiations for which was on the point of conclusion when hostilities broke out in August 1965.[26]

As one of the ablest to mend fences, Freeman dinned into the ears of the concerned persons the futility of dragging on the Kashmir question in a vain attempt to find a settlement that would give the Vale to Pakistan. Underscoring the truth that the problem would never be settled unless Britain took account of the latest events, Freeman wrote that Pakistan

> "attempted to secure a military solution (to Kashmir) and has decisively failed...Personally, I do not see the slightest chance of India's ever accepting that the Vale should either go to Pakistan or become independent. On the contrary, it is certain that she will refuse such a solution and oppose those who promote it by every available means. The loss of Kashmir would thus have to be imposed on India by a threat of force so formidable as to be irresistible. Is it in our interests – short or long term – to support such a policy? On the contrary, the security of the West as a whole might be seriously threatened if China were allowed to secure an accessible land frontier with Pakistān from which she could pose a major and permanent threat to the Punjab."[27]

The genuine efforts of Freeman and other British officers who had first hand knowledge of the Kashmir affairs to establish Indo-British relations on a firmer and sounder basis did bear fruit. A consensus of opinion was building up in Britain that thereafter she must avoid getting directly involved in Indo-Pakistan friction. It was realised that any "ineffectual intervention" or "conspicuous involvement" was sure to damage Britain's interests in India. It was agreed to adopt a policy of non-involvement in the Indo-Pakistan disputes as Britain's guiding principle in the prevailing situation.[28] There were letters from Morrice James, successor of Freeman also to HMG harping on the fact that the relations between the two countries, though improved, were still not satisfactory. He referred to the sound principles of India's foreign policy as evolved by Nehru and wrote appreciatively of its main principles of non-alignment, anti-colonialism and the Gandhian concept of peace. He also wrote convincingly in defence of the two main factors uppermost in India's mind at that point of time, namely, "the protection of her frontier against China and the containment and outwitting of Pakistan."

The determination of the British friends of India to bring about a change in the British policy culminated in the visit to India of Michael Stewart in his capacity as the Secretary of State for Foreign and Commonwealth Affairs. He sojourned in India from 2 to 8 December 1968. The timing of his visit was opportune. His meetings with the Indian dignitaries proved propitious. Stewart emphasized the great need to establish a "mature relationship" between India and Britain — a phrase that hit the headlines of the Indian newspapers the next day. This theme dominated his whole visit. On the Indian side, the Home Minister Chavan, Minister of State for External Affairs B.R. Bhagat and Foreign Secretary T.N. Kaul, played a significant role at the meetings. Stewart called on many Indian leaders including C. Rajagopalachari, the first Indian Governor General of independent India, President Zakir Hussain and Morarji Desai, Deputy Prime Minister. Loan agreement worth £20 million in completion of Britain's pledge of £35 million worth of aid to India for that financial year was signed.[29]

The most significant feature of the visit of Michael Stewart was the announcement he made of the change in the British foreign policy especially in relation to Kashmir. It was his categorical statement that Britain had "neither the right, nor the duty, nor indeed the power to intervene in India-Pakistan disputes."

References

1. G. Parthasarathy to the Secretary General, 8 Oct. 1965, DO/196/388.
2. *The Hindu*, 31 Oct. 1965.
3. Morrice James to CRO, 30 Dec. 1965, PREM/13/398.
4. From UK Embassy, Washington to FO, 11 Oct. 1965, PREM/13/462.
5. Quoted in M.J. Akbar, *Kashmir Behind the Vale*, p. 175.
6. *The Hindu*, 11 Jan. 1965.
7. Ayub's meeting with Prime Minister Wilson, 24 Nov. 1966, PREM/13/1045.
8. *Kashmir Behind the Vale*, *op. cit.*, P. 172.
9. *The Statesman*, New Delhi, 28 Jan. 1966.
10. UK HC (P) to CRO, 18 Jan. 1967, FCO/37/239.
11. Background Note by CRO, FCO/37/189.
12. It was launched on 13 August 1966 by Mao Tse-tung (1893-1976), Chairman of the Communist Party of China to release the revolutionary fervour of the Chinese youth who formed themselves into Red Guards and set about extirpating all revisionism and westernism. It ended only with its founder's death in 1976.
13. Broadcast, 10 June 1967 from Ambikapur in Madhya Pradesh.
14. UK HC (I) to HC (P) (Date not given), FCO/37/24.
15. UK HC (P) to CRO, 2 Sep. 1968, FCO/37/189.
16. Report of the Canadian HC in Islamabad to the Under Secretary of State for External Affairs, Ottawa, Canada, 22 April 1969, FCO/37/472.

17. Malcolm MacDonald to Douglas-Home, 18 Sep. 1957, DO/35/9014.
18. UK HC (I) to HC (P), 9 Nov. 1964, PREM/13/390.
19. Freeman to Herbert Bowden, 3 March 1967, FCO/37/70.
20. K.C. Khanna "Indo-British Relations," *Times of India*, 2 April 1966.
21. Wilson to Francis Noel-Baker, 21 Dec. 1965, DO/196/559.
22. *Ibid.*
23. A.A. Duff (CRO) to Commonwealth Secretary, 26, Jan. 1967, FCO/37/239.
24. Algernon Rumbold to Stanley Tomlinson (FCO), 12 Nov. 1971, FCO/37/916.
25. Freeman's meeting with Indira Gandhi, 14, April, 1966, DO/196/ 217.
26. UKD to UN to FO, 22 Sep. 1965, PREM /13/395.
27. *Ibid*, UK HC (I) to CRO, 23 Sep. 1965.
28. Freeman to George Thompson, Foreign and Commonwealth Secretary, 26 June 1968, FCO/37/383.
29. *Ibid*, UK HC (1) to Foreign & CW Secretary, 20, Dec. 1968.

18

Pakistan Dismembered

Yahya Khan, who assumed the Presidency of Pakistan in March 1969, inherited a highly unstable Government and an extremely fragile economy not to speak of the host of other problems threatening the country. Instead of addressing himself to these challenges, the military dictator gave top priority to foreign relations. The new Government was particularly anxious to avail itself of the earliest opportunity to strengthen its ties with Communist China which had become rather weak in the last years of Ayub's regime. The overtures made to Pakistan by the US and the Soviet Union to join any anti-China regional organization went unheeded. Kosygin's brief stop-over in Pakistan in May 1969 to convince Yahya of the undesirability of getting close to China proved ineffective. Pakistan regarded Russia's drive for a closer economic and military regional cooperation in Asia as a manoeuvre to destroy the ties between Pakistan and China. Pakistan was ready "to risk a cooling off of ties with the Soviet Union and new tensions with New Delhi to protect its alliance with China."

Air Marshal Nur Khan was sent by Pakistan on a week-long visit to Peking in August 1969 which was construed by the outside world as an attempt to thwart Russia's plan to bring about an Asian collective security system aimed at containing Communist China.[1] In fact, Nur Khan's visit was more in connection with Pakistan's rejection of India's strongly worded note against the new road Pakistan was constructing with Chinese help in the POK. The road would run from the Sinkiang-Gilgit "Silk Route" to the Chinese trunk route connecting Kashgar in Sinkiang and Lhasa in Tibet. India called it "a sinister military move against India." Pakistan hardly took note of India's protest.[2] Nur Khan's visit to Peking was also intended to dispel any possible misunderstandings by China of Pakistan's foreign policy. When the new Republican American President Richard Nixon visited Lahore on 1 August 1969, Pakistan took extra care to ensure that China did not view it with hostility. Starting from 1953, Nixon had made six trips to Pakistan. Emphasis was laid on Nixon's status as "an old friend of Pakistan." His latest visit left the strong impression that it was the beginning of the end of strained relations between the two countries under the two previous Democrat Presidents and that the question of lifting the arms embargo was under consideration.

As for Pakistan's relations with India, the "unsettlement" of the Kashmir issue was continually agitating her mind. Since she could not bring in a resolution on the subject at the Security Council then as on previous occasions, she resorted to a world-wide false propaganda campaign. Through her representative at the UN Headquarters, Yahya's administration made the unconscionable allegations that India was systematically annihilating a large number of Muslims in India and that the Congress Party was encouraging the communal and bloodthirsty Hindu organisations. The representative circulated amongst selected members of the Security Council letters which carried allegations about India's "monstrous human wrongs" like the persecution of Muslims who were a "beleaguered minority" there. Pakistan also made the highly incredible charge that India was driving out her Muslim population while actually the Census of India for 1951 and 1961 showed an increase of 25.6 per cent in the population of Muslims as against an overall increase of 21.5 per cent in the population of India. This trend continued throughout the 1960s.[3]

This was not the first time Pakistan was indulging in such nasty allegations. The only difference this time was the inclusion of the Sikhs, Nagas and Mizos also besides Muslims in its list of minority communities. The allegation of the annihilation of Muslims in India coincided with the mass exodus of Hindus to India of whom 1,19,771 were from East Pakistan. They crossed into the Indian States of West Bengal, Assam and Tripura that surrounded East Pakistan seeking refuge from January to mid-June 1970.[4] In keeping with her sectarian policy based on the pernicious two-nation theory, Pakistan indulged in creating disunity among the different communities in India in order to realise her territorial and other ambitions in India. She believed that if she set up the entire Muslim community in India against the Hindus, India would be gravely weakened.

On the Home Front

Under the new Martial Law regime of Yahya, political parties were not abolished in Pakistan. Even the subsequent regulations did no more than impose restrictions on public meetings. Yahya gave the impression that while he was very anxious to bring back civil rule, what stood in the way of the surrender of power by the army was the failure of the 15 parties in Pakistan to agree on the shape of the new constitution. Among the many parties in Pakistan, the Awami League of East Pakistan which had a chequered life deserves special mention. It was founded on 23 June 1949 as the East Pakistan Awami (People's) Muslim League (EPAL for short) at Dacca in opposition to the Muslim League which until then was the main ruling party in Pakistan. The elected President of the EPAL was Maulana Abdul Humid Khan, leftist peasant leader of the old Assam Muslim League. Its Vice President and Joint Secretary were Ataur Rehman and Sheikh Mujibur Rahman.

Right from the day of the birth of Pakistan, its East wing was an aggrieved lot. Actually, the aetiology of Bangladesh should be traced to the beginning of the twentieth century when Curzon partitioned Bengal. The motive behind the 1905 partition was to segregate the Hindus and Muslims of Bengal. But after 1947, though the people of both wings of Pakistan were Muslims, the Punjab-dominated West Pakistan treated East Pakistan, which was actually larger in size, as a colony. West Pakistan, which was a clique of a few opulent families supporting the military caste, assumed imperial airs and posed itself as the master of entire Pakistan. It flourished at the expense of the east wing. The three capitals of Pakistan – Karachi first, Rawalpindi then and Islamabad later – have all been in the west. A bulk of the federal expenditure was incurred in the west. Relegated to the status of second class citizens, the East Pakistanis often looked back nostalgically to the pre-partition days when the Hindus, Muslims and Christians of Bengal spoke the same Bengali language and had broadly the same tastes in food or clothing.

In 1952, the EPAL demanded in vain that Bengali and not Urdu should be the official language of East Pakistan. It was instantly reminded of what Jinnah declared four years earlier. On 21 March 1948, Jinnah announced at a public meeting in Dacca, "Urdu is going to be the *lingua franca* of this country...Anyone who says anything else is an enemy of Pakistan."[5] Three days later, on 24 March, while addressing the Dacca University Convocation,

Jinnah reiterated that "in Pakistan, there shall be one State Language and that shall be Urdu." This was considered very "undemocratic" as the majority of the Pakistanis spoke Bengali "one of the richest languages of the Indo-Pak sub-continent." In 1954, the EPAL scored a sweeping victory in the polls over the Muslim League reducing it to nought in East Pakistan. After 1955, the party was thrown open to non-Muslims also. In the meantime, many parties sprang up in Pakistan with the name "Awami" attached to them – the All-Pakistan Awami League, All-Pakistan Jinnah-Awami Muslim League, National Awami League, National Awami Party (NAP) etc. In 1958, the EPAL claimed a membership of 1.8 million in East Pakistan.

During the first five years of its birth, when Bengalis were in control of political power in Pakistan, the Punjabi dominant civil and military bureaucracy was scheming to nullify their influence. In Pakistan, the army was so powerful as to make and unmake governments. The first Bengali Prime Minister Khwaja Nazimuddin who enjoyed the confidence of the Parliament was dismissed after holding office for a year and a half by the Punjabi Governor General Ghulam Mohammad. The Second Bengali Prime Minister Mohammad Ali Bogra practically remained a prisoner of the Punjabi ruling elite from the date of his installation. After suffering one ignominy after another, he was dismissed after two years in office by Ghulam Mohammad's successor Iskander Mirza. The last Bengali Prime Minister Suhrawardy was dismissed after a year and half in office again by President Iskander Mirza without giving him an opportunity to test his strength in the Parliament.

A constitution providing for a federal Parliamentary form adopted at last in 1956 was denied a chance to come to fruition owing to Iskander Mirza's conspiratorial policy and interference of the Punjabi controlled army and government services. When preparations for the general elections under the new Constitution were being made, the first army *coup* came about in October 1958 and Ayub became the supreme arbiter of the State. Thereafter, there was military dictatorship in Pakistan for 12 years when in December 1970, the first general elections were held. The results of the elections and their aftermath are discussed elsewhere in this chapter. Despite its numerical superiority, East Pakistan patiently pocketed the many injustices perpetrated on it by the west for 23 years. Finally, the worm turned.

In 1958, when Martial Law was declared, President Iskander Mirza banned all political parties. Consequently, the EPAL was out of action until its political life was revived in 1962 when the new National Assembly met on 8 June of that year and announced the end of Martial Law. In the early years of this decade of increasing political demoralisation, Mujib had a tough time preserving an uneasy balance between the extremist Bhashani on the one hand and the moderate Ataur Rehman on the other.

The office bearers of the revived EPAL were elected from both the Provinces. Nawabzada Nasrullah Khan, a West Pakistani, became its President but the party became weak in West Pakistan. Mujib, who was the General Secretary, was in fact the leader of the party in East Pakistan. In July 1964, the EPAL joined a group of opposition parties including the NAP. This grouping, called the "Combined Opposition Parties" (COP), was to contest the 1965 Basic Democratic elections for the National and Provincial Assemblies. In the Presidential election, Ayub won defeating Fatima Jinnah, who contested on the COP's ticket. In the National Assembly elections also, the COP was defeated. It did not contest the provincial elections in West Pakistan. In East Pakistan also, the opposition did not fare well.

Mujib's Six-Point Programme

After the 1965 war, Ayub's popularity waned considerably in East Pakistan which was very unhappy over its isolation and lack of defence as a result of the war. Since Kashmir was not a popular issue in East Pakistan, the Tashkent Declaration was welcomed there. In February 1966, there was a conference of the opposition parties at Lahore which was attended by the EPAL. Mujib introduced there a six-point programme which was to become the guiding document of his party ever since. It provided for a federation of Pakistan with Parliamentary Government and a supreme legislature directly elected on the basis of universal suffrage. The Federal Government would deal only with defence and foreign affairs. The Provinces would have separate currencies and powers of taxation and revenue collection. There was to be a separate militia or para-military force for East Pakistan. These six points of Mujib were but a crystallisation of East Pakistan's demands for regional autonomy first put forward in the original Awami League manifesto of 1954. Its election demands then included autonomy, freedom to export jute and abolition of Indo-Pakistan passport and visa. It had long been demanding these because West Pakistan was treating East Pakistan as its colony.

To the Bengali agitators, the six-point programme formed the basis for any relationship between the two wings of Pakistan. But the Lahore Conference of February 1966 rejected this programme and Mujib replied by refusing to support any of the resolutions of the Conference. This led to a split in the opposition which exposed the gulf between the two wings of Pakistan. These developments infuriated Ayub who arrested Mujib in April 1966 under the Defence of Pakistan Rules. This did not deter the EPAL. It sponsored a Province-wise *hartal* which revealed the genuine mass support for the six-point programme. The political struggle continued throughout the year and more and more Awami League leaders were arrested. Political parties critical of Mujib's six-points formed themselves into the Pakistan Democratic Movement (PDM). In August 1967, this movement brought about a split in the EPAL between the extremists and moderates led respectively by Mujib and Nasrullah Khan. The former was called the Anti - PDM "Six-Point" Awami League and the latter the Pro-PDM Awami League. Nasrullah's Party, which was of no importance, merged within two years in the Pakistan Democratic Party.

In January 1969, once again all the opposition parties including the "Six Point" Awami League combined together to form the Democratic Action Committee in Dacca. It issued a Manifesto which denounced the "autocratic and one-man dictatorship" of Ayub and called for a boycott of elections. It avoided controversial questions, but decided to wage "a relentless, non-violent, organised and disciplined mass revolt" against military dictatorship. On 1 February 1969, when mass strike and violence ensued, Ayub agreed to meet the leaders of the opposition at a Round Table Conference and also released political prisoners including Mujib detained under the Defence of Pakistan Rules. However, realising that democratisation of the country in the existing situation was impracticable, Ayub resigned on 25 March 1969.

On 28 November 1969, Yahya announced that in October 1970 Pakistan would have the first general elections in its life of 23 years to elect a National Assembly which would frame a Constitution within the time limit of 120 days. On 30 March, he published the Legal Framework Order which outlined the basic form the new Constitution was to take. The new National Assembly would have 313 members. The provinces were to be represented on the basis of the 1961 census. East Pakistan would therefore have 169 and the whole of West Pakistan 144 Seats. Pakistan would be a Federal Islamic Republic. By this time, the EPAL had grown so influential as to cause alarm in West Pakistan which was stoutly opposed to the Six-Point Programme. An acrimonious quarrel between the two wings was anticipated when the Constituent Assembly emerged. The radical extremists within the EPAL favoured outright secession.

On 15 August 1970, the Government announced a postponement of elections from October to December owing to floods in East Pakistan. In December, despite the cyclone disaster, the elections were not allowed to be postponed for a second time. There was a bitter feeling among the public by the Centre's handling of the disaster. In the election for the National Assembly, the EPAL won a landslide victory bagging 167 of the 169 seats in East Pakistan. Bhutto's PPP won 81 of the 144 seats in West Pakistan. In the Provincial Assembly elections held on 17 December, the EPAL secured 268 of the 279 seats in East Pakistan and Bhutto's PPP was dominant in the Punjab and Sind Provincial Assemblies. The popular verdict was loud and clear. The general elections thus confirmed the emergence of the two dominant political figures – Mujib and Bhutto – with clear mandates to speak respectively for the 75 million East Pakistanis and the 60 million West Pakistanis.[6] Mujib's EPAL having secured an absolute majority in the National Assembly, was in a position to form a stable government and frame its Constitution. Deeply committed to his six-point programme, Mujib would take any attempt to compromise on them as a betrayal. He demanded fair deal for the Bengalis. But that became impossible since both the major parties differed on several points. Mujib's scheme of federal government was unacceptable to Bhutto. Bhutto's demand on first settling the Kashmir question with India was unacceptable to Mujib who believed him (Bhutto) to be pro-Chinese. Mujib was opposed to aggressive militant approach to the Kashmir dispute. It was clear that they would not reach an agreement about a Constitution.

A Despicable Act

Between 27 and 30 January 1971, talks were held in Dacca between the two leaders but nothing came of it. Mujib's opposition to Bhutto's demand for settling the Kashmir question before forming a stable government in Pakistan made the cantankerous military regime very furious. Its anger turned against India. It was determined to do something or other to throw India into turmoil until Kashmir was handed to Pakistan. Once such a thought was planted in its mind, it was none too difficult for that unneighbourly neighbour to hatch plans.

On 30 January 1971, an Indian Airlines Fokker Friendship Aircraft flying form Srinagar to Jammu with 23 passengers and four crew members was hijacked by two young Kashmiris of the POK – Mohammed Hashim Quershi and Mohammed Ashraf – and diverted at gunpoint to Lahore. The Indian passengers and crew were got off the aircraft safely but were held up in Lahore. The responsibility for organising the hijacking was claimed in Pakistan by the Jammu and Kashmir National Liberation Front (JKNLF) which issued a statement from Karachi to this effect. It was stated to be a retaliatory measure against the arrest of Sheikh Abdullah who was packed off to Ooty in South

India in 1965 and mounting Indian pressure in the Vale of Kashmir. Since the two hijackers had the strong support of Bhutto and certain other politicians, it was feared that they might destroy the aircraft.[7] At the instigation of the higher-ups there were violent demonstrations of the Azad Kashmiri students in Lahore and Peshawar demanding that the aircraft should be handed over to POK and the passengers held as hostages. On 2 February, the aircraft was blown up by the two hijackers.[8] Pakistan refused to return the hijackers to India on the ground that they were not Indian nationals. The stranded passengers and the crew were repatriated to India after more than 48 hours by road.

Bhutto was reported to have instructed the representatives of the PPP in Lahore well in advance to establish contacts with the JKNLF to assist the hijackers in every possible way. Bhutto said though the two hijackers were not Pakistani nationals, they were Kashmiris who enjoyed full freedom in Pakistan. And so, the question of granting them political asylum did not arise. He justified the hijacking on the ground it was part of the Kashmiri struggle for self-determination and reiterated that the PPP would always give full support to them.[9]

India retaliated to the hijacking by the cancellation of overflight rights across India to Pakistani military aircrafts. If Pakistan did not pay compensation or hand over the hijackers to her, India said she would not be in a position to hold talks with the Pakistanis about the restoration of overflight rights until after the elections. When Yahya approached the British Prime Minister Edward Heath in this connection, he said that it was a matter in which Britain would not involve herself. He also condemned the hijacking.[10] Because Heath did not support the hijacking, the British High commissioner Cyril Pickard was summoned by the Marital Law authorities, given a dressing down and threatened that Britain's investment of £50 million in West Pakistan would be confiscated if she did not change her line. According to the Indian Press, this led the British Press, the Government and the BBC to come in support of Islamabad against Mujib![11]

Pakistan described the two hijackers as "Kashmiri Crusaders." One of them was stated to be a member of the para military border security force. The BBC Urdu Service carried articles stating among other things that Sheikh Abdullah's son Tariq Abdullah had links with the hijackers.[12]

On 15 April 1971, the Commission of Enquiry under Justice Nurul Anfin appointed by the Government of Pakistan on Lahore hijack gave the shallow verdict that the Government of Pakistan was not responsible for the hijack.

What was worse, it gave the ruling that the hijack was actually arranged by the Indian Intelligence Agencies "to provide a reason to ban overflights on the Indian territory by Pakistan aircrafts."[13]

Monstrous Tyranny

On 13 February, Yahya announced that the National Assembly would meet in Dacca on 3 March. The EPAL promptly formulated a Constitution on the basis of the six points to be presented at the meeting. Bhutto declared that he would boycott the National Assembly Session on 3 March unless Mujib modified his six points. He even threatened that his PPP would launch a movement "from the Khyber to Karachi." Mujib would not modify his six points because in January 1971, he had taken an oath in public on the *Quran* that he would not deviate from his declared intention to base the Constitution on the six points. There would therefore be no climb down on his part in the face of West Pakistan's pressure. Pakistan held India responsible for this. There were many Bengali politicians at the Centre who accused India of "shameless intervention" in East Pakistan affairs and condemned Mujib as a conspirator bent upon partitioning Pakistan and "aligning East Pakistan with the Hindu cult."[14]

The EPAL did its best to reach a peaceful solution of the Pakistani crisis by the transfer of power to elected representatives and withdrawal of Martial Law which were Mujib's pre-requisites for any settlement. Since the EPAL consisted of Bengalis led by Mujib, vested interests of West Pakistan decided to nullify the election results.

On 1 March 1971, Yahya announced the postponement of the National Assembly session under the pretext of giving the leaders some more time to bring about an agreement. This postponement convinced Mujib that the West Pakistan leaders were conspiring to maintain domination over East Pakistan. Protesting against the postponement, he called for a *hartal* in East Pakistan on 3 March. On 4 March, he called for an indefinite mass civil disobedience movement – non-payment of taxes to and non-cooperation with the Government. He rejected Yahya's invitation to attend a meeting of the political leaders on 10 March. On 6 March in his broadest to the nation, Yahya announced another postponement of the National Assembly session to 25 March and also his determination to prevent the break-up of Pakistan at all costs. But disturbances in East Pakistan intensified. Despite the alarming situation, Mujib did not proclaim the independence of East Pakistan. He refused to attend the National Assembly session unless Martial Law was withdrawn and power transferred to the elected representatives of the people. At this point, secession seemed imminent.

On 15 March, Yahya arrived in Dacca for further consultations with the East Pakistani leaders to reach some compromise between his pledge to preserve the integrity of Pakistan and the Bengali demand for autonomy. On 21 March, Bhutto also flew to Dacca. But the talks between the leaders of the two wings ended in a deadlock. The National Assembly was never called into session. For, on 22 March, for the third time, its session was postponed, this time *sine die*. Simultaneously, he announced the removal of the intelligent, capable and popular Vice Admiral Ahsan as the Governor of East Pakistan. There was a huge public outcry against his removal.

Initially, Yahya's approach to the problem was certainly positive. He permitted the holding of the elections and promised transfer of power to the elected representatives after the elections. But when the mandate of the people was overwhelmingly for the EPAL, his authoritarian mindset got the better of him and he tended to endlessly postpone the convening of the National Assembly instead of welcoming the people's verdict with good grace. Even after a lapse of three months after the elections, the National Assembly was not convened. Yahya secretly left East Pakistan on the night of 25 March leaving instructions with the army under the new military Governor Tikka Khan, to crush the EPAL.[15] On his way back, Yahya visited Bhutto at Larkana.

At mid-night on 25 March, Tikka Khan faithfully following the orders of Yahya unleashed military action against a sleeping nation with tanks, artillery, machine guns and flame throwers. The army took control of Dacca and fighting flared up in other cities. Much of the Awami leadership was either arrested or shot at. All political activity throughout the province was forbidden. The EPAL was banned as a party and its leader spirited away to West Pakistan.

Actually Bangla Desh was born on 25 March 1971 amidst the genocidal attacks let loose by Tikka Khan to thwart the inalienable and fundamental rights of the Bengalis. The Bengalis of East Pakistan realised that living together with the West Pakistanis was impossible thereafter. The elected representatives declared East Pakistan independent and renamed it "Bangla Desh." The British High Commissioner in Pakistan said: "The people of Bangla Desh through their elected representatives and with their blood have given the verdict in favour of independent Bangladesh."[16] Highlighting this event against the background of the carnage unleashed by the West Pakistan war mongers, K.R. Srinivasa Iyengar, a great litterateur of his generation, wrote satirically that by the last week of March 1971 "it must have been clear to all except the purblind war lords of Pakistan and their colour blind accomplices at Washington that the Old Pakistan was as dead as Humpty Dumpty in the Poem:

Humpty Dumpty
Sat on a wall
Humpty Dumpty
Had a great fall
And all Yahya's arms
And Bhutto's alarums
Cannot put Humpty Dumpty
Together again. [17]

The birth of the separate State of Bangladesh marked the end of Jinnah's Pakistan which consisted of the two territories of East and West Pakistan separated by a 1000 miles of India. The formal ceremony of the Declaration of Independence of Bangla Desh took place on 17 April 1971 at Mujibnagar. The Proclamation of Independence dated 10 April 1971 provided for a Constituent Assembly and declared Sheikh Mujibur Rahman, President of the People's Republic of Bangla Desh and Syed Nasrul Islam, Vice president. Since Mujib was in prison, Syed assumed the Acting Presidency of the Government.

Severely hurt by the tyranny let loose in East Pakistan by the West Pakistan Military junta, which had the backing of the great democracy of America under President Nixon, Keating, US Ambassador to India, sent a telegram to his Secretary of State, carrying the following:

> "Am deeply shocked at massacre by Pakistani military in East Pakistan. Appalled at possibility these atrocities are being committed with American equipment. Greatly concerned (about) allegations of US association with reign of military terror...USG (A) should promptly, publicly and prominently deplore this brutality. (B) Should privately let it on line with GOP...and (C) Should announce unilateral abrogation of one-time exception military supply agreement and suspension of all military deliveries under 1967 Restrictive Policy spare parts...Most important these actions be taken now...prior to...emergence of horrible truths...and communist initiatives to exploit situation. This is time when principles make best politics." [18]

Mujib called the Pakistani assault on East Pakistan the "greatest massacre of a people in history."[19]

There was news of the imposition of blackout by Yahya's Government during the massacres. The reason for this order was to hide the systematic butchery of thousands of civilians in the East Pakistan by the West Pakistan army since March. Eight West Pakistani journalists were allowed to see the conduct of the militarists operation and report to the people of West Pakistan the "great job the army was doing." A top journalist of the *Morning News*, Anthony Mascarenhas, a Goan Christian, one of the eight journalists, was so aghast at what he witnessed that he chose to exile himself from his country in order to tell the world the fate of East Pakistan.[20]

Mass Exodus to India

In the regular butchery of unarmed people on 25 March under the lead of Tikka Khan, the Pakistani army of 70,000 effortlessly subdued the poorly equipped, disorganized and "sullen and hostile" Bengal populace. The move to crush the dissidents resulted in the casualties of thousands of civilians including students associated with the local nationalist movement. The army's main targets were Hindus and leaders of Bengali thought. The Hindus were killed simply because they were Hindus. Major cities and principal lines of communication came under the control of the Pakistan Government which could not however eliminate the Bengali opposition or contain the guerrilla activities.

One million lives were taken and nine million fled East Pakistan to the neighbouring India, risking cholera and famine. Approximately, 50,000 refugees per day were leaving East Pakistan for India.[21] The inflow of refugees imposed colossal burden on India. It posed a major threat to international peace and security. India was facing this huge problem for a second time since 1947. Yet, the Government of India was determined as it did on the previous occasion to treat the refugees civilly. Notwithstanding the enormous strain the exodus placed on the Indian economy, public sympathy for the plight of the fellow Bengalis, induced the Government to grant them entry into India. India knew that there was very little prospect of their returning home until a political settlement was reached which alone would ensure their safety.

Britain felt certain that Bengali nationalism would assert itself again. She would not therefore alienate Bengali opinion. In fact, Britain knew that it was Pakistan's policy to invade India under some pretext or other to grab Kashmir. The fact that Britain always stood by Pakistan did not mean that she was unaware of the truth that the attack always came from Pakistan upon India. Only she did not express it publicity even once. Also to placate Pakistan, she did not mind hurting India. This was the policy she adhered to strictly from 1947 to the end of the Second Indo-Pakistan War. With the conspicuous change in her foreign policy after the 1965 war, she stated candidly who was to be faulted. From 1947 to 1960, Zafrullah played a key role in the Kashmir affairs. During the 1947 incursions of the thuggish tribals into Kashmir, he abetted their evil deeds first and later allowed the Pakistani army to enter the fray. From the 1960s the policy to invade India to take Kashmir was designed by Bhutto. The 1965 war imposed an unsustainable load on the economy of the country. This in turn contributed to political instability. Bhutto again played a crucial role in the events that led to the downfall of Ayub's regime early in 1969. Yahya had power thrust upon him. Under his military regime, the political malaise continued to grow until the whole political system broke down on 25 March 1971 for which also Bhutto must be accorded a major share of the blame.[22]

Care of the refugees cost the Indian government $1,300,000 per day. Less than one half of this was provided by the international community.[23] The Indian Government hoped that pressure from the UN and other concerned countries on Pakistan would end the army occupation of East Pakistan leading to the establishment there of the civilian government by the EPAL. When the Government realised its hope was not achievable, its only option was to gear up for a more direct course of lending active support to the guerrilla campaign of the Bangla Desh Liberation Army. Pakistan promptly accused India of being primarily responsible for continuing the agitation in East Pakistan to realise her objective of destroying Pakistan.

Yahya's brutalities in East Pakistan had evoked such widespread notice as to earn him a bad reputation and unfavourable publicity. Anxious to improve his image before the commencement of the 26th session of the UN, he effected some changes. He replaced the military Government of Tikka Khan in East Pakistan with a civilian administration under the popular Bengali civilian A.M. Malik; announced a general amnesty for most of those who committed offences during the agitation; accepted representatives of the UN to supervise the return of the refugees and co-ordinate relief operations in East Pakistan.[24] These concessions may have brought some fleeting relief. There was certainly no indication in the territory that the fundamental cause for tension had been wiped out or the real menace of war had passed out. Food problem was expected to be very acute by the end of 1971.

It was a great pity that many countries refused to see the events in the right perspective and condemn Pakistan for her brutalities. The Government of India knew that it could not rely on Nixon's America either to moderate Pakistani actions or lend support to India in any form if Pakistan started a war. Conscious of external Muslim sympathy for Pakistan, India looked for a powerful and trustworthy friend. In such a circumstance, her choice was to activate the dormant treaty with the USSR. Since the Soviet Union was also willing, a

Treaty of Peace, Friendship and Cooperation was signed between India and the USSR on 9 August 1971. Its object was to reduce the likelihood of war.

Pakistan did not stop her infiltration into India. She had no scruples about constantly violating the cease-fire agreement in Jammu and Kashmir. On 6 November, two Pakistani personnel mounted on camels broke into the Rann of Kutch but took to their heels when Indian patrols from the Sardar Post opened fire.[25] The Urdu papers carried violently worded editorials urging war against India. There were attacks and counter attacks. In his address to the nation on the Radio, Yahya, the pseudo prophet, said very confidently that if war broke out Pakistan would emerge triumphant. He said: "Victory did not depend on superiority of numbers and weapons but on religious faith. Pakistan has the sympathy and support abroad...Allah being on Pakistan's side, final victory is certain." Britain described this as "a predictable chest-thumping exhortation."[26] Pakistan alleged that there was a general Indian ground attack in the west but the British High Commissioner there confirmed there was no evidence to support the allegation.[27]

The Fifteen-Day War

Greatly perturbed by the blood bath that Pakistan had perpetrated on her east wing, the Indian Parliament passed a resolution on 31 March 1971 expressing its "profound sympathy for and solidarity with" the people of Bangla Desh in their "struggle for democratic way of life." The resolution pressed for an immediate cessation of the genocide of the defenceless people whose leader was languishing in prison in West Pakistan.

Meanwhile the Mukti Bahini Liberation Forces, the military organisation of Bangla Desh, was showing its unique fighting prowess. Its brave leaders, throughout their long guerrilla warfare, succeeded in confining the West Pakistani enemy to strongly defended cantonments and military bases. They were largely teenagers wearing cotton shirts – in most cases torn – hiding in haystacks, the only cover for them in the cold nights and eating dry rice, cucumber and molasses. Unable to remain silent spectators of the cruelties inflicted on the Bangla Deshis, the Indian Border Security Force and Indian troops supported the Mukti Bahini to step up its counter attacks against the Pakistani military. Immediately, Pakistan cried hoarse that India was launching an all-out offensive against East Pakistan. India's support to the Mukti Bahini in a series of concerted attacks was to demonstrate to the Pakistani Army that in the eastern province it lacked sufficient strength to hold the border against sustained attack.

Stung by the swift actions of the Mukti Bahini in Bangla Desh and the heavy blows dealt with by the Indian army to retaliate against Pakistan's shelling of the border towns in India, Pakistan declared *jihad* on India on 3 December 1971. Prime Minister Indira Gandhi told the nation over the All India Radio shortly after mid-night on 3 December that at the moment of great peril for the country, Pakistan had launched a full-scale war against India. The Pakistani Air Force had suddenly and without any provocation, struck at India's airfields at Amritsar, Pathankot, Srinagar, Avantipur, Uttarlai, Jodhpur, Ambala and Agra while her ground forces were shelling India's defence position in Sulaimanki, Khem Karan, Poonch and other sectors. The Prime Minister said:

> "Since March last, we have borne the heaviest of burdens and withstood the greatest of pressures in a tremendous effort to urge the world to help to bring about a peaceful solution and prevent the annihilation of an entire people, whose only crime was to vote democratically. But the world ignored the basic causes and concerned itself only with certain repercussions...A courageous band of freedom fighters have staked their all in defence of the value for which we also have struggled and which are basic to our way of life.
>
> "The war on Bangle Desh has become a war on India and this imposes upon me, my Government and the people of India awful responsibility. We have no other option but to put our country on a war footing. We are prepared for any eventuality...Aggression must be met and the people of India will meet it with fortitude and determination, with discipline and the utmost unity. Jai Hind."

Later that night, President V.V. Giri proclaimed a national emergency. It was the second emergency. The first one was declared on 26 October 1962 in the wake of the Chinese aggression and continued till the second Pakistani invasion of India in 1965. This third Indo-Pakistan war started by Pakistan on the evening of Friday the 3 December ended on Friday the 17 December 1971.

The fiercest fighting throughout the battle was centred on the Chhamb sector. Yahya's vicious plan according to the documents captured by the Indian army was to rush to Akhnur in a bid to cut off Jammu from the rest of India. But his great expectations were blasted by the Indian Air Force which played an admirable role in the battle of Chhamb. The fighting was over by 11 December with disastrous results to Pakistan. On the Kashmir front, the Indian forces took 17 posts in the Kargil sector, took possession of two important heights between Hajeera and Kotli in the Poonch sector and repulsed the

Pakistani shelling in Tithwal and Kumali in the Uri sector. However, the West Pakistani forces in East Pakistan refused to surrender disregarding the appeals and warnings of General Manekshaw, Chief of the Army Staff. On 11 December, he appealed to them to surrender without delay. By another message on 13 December, he said that failure to surrender would mean "the death of many poor soldiers." The IAF dropped leaflets in Dacca carrying Manekshaw's final warning to the beleaguered Pakistani troops to surrender. On 14 December, the Pakistani Governor Malik and other civilian authorities abdicated in favour of the Bangla Desh regime. On 16 December, the Pakistani forces in Bangla Desh capitulated and Dacca fell.

Lt. Gen. Niazi, the Pakistan Commander, signed the surrender documents in Dacca. On 17 December, over 32,000 Pakistani armed forces personnel surrendered to the Indian forces in East Pakistan. In Dacca alone 23,000 troops and 1000 officers surrendered.

Yahya whose pastime it was to call India an "unscrupulous hostile neighbour" and her veteran leaders "Warlords of Bharat" and who delighted in subjecting Pakistan's brethren in the East wing to "terror and tribulation," accepted India's unilateral proposal of a cease-fire. Though initially he called the peace offer a trick, he accepted it on 16 December after Islamabad's military rule in Bangla Desh came to a humiliating end. Still he remained arrogant and in his broadcast to the nation said that though he was accepting the cease–fire in the interest of peace, his "Holy *Jihad*" against India would continue. On 17 December, Yahya ordered his troops on the West Pakistan border to cease-fire with effect from that day. The *New York Times* wrote that "Yahya must realise that Bangla Desh exists; Bangla Desh cannot be negotiated away...His American allies have a duty to tell him that he should face reality rather than declare a *jihad*...the time for lecturing Delhi is long past."[28]

In Pakistan, there were psychological tensions created by the loss of East Pakistan which was a severe below to Jinnah's concept of Pakistan as the largest Islamic nation and a sure refuge for the Muslims of the Indian sub-continent. By itself, Pakistan minus East Pakistan was only the third largest group of Muslims in the Indian sub-continent. The Pakistani authorities also feared the severe shock and anger with which their nation would receive the damaging consequences of the war. There were worrying reports of the popular mood which had become so hostile to the Yahya administration. For until then, the people were misled by the Pakistani Press and the Radio that a military victory was certain. Many Pakistani officials themselves felt such official propaganda a curse as they raised popular expectations to fever pitch.

The reaction to the result of the war was expected to be one of disbelief, anger and violence. Even aggressive demonstrations against foreign missions were not ruled out.

The cease-fire took effect from 8 pm on 17 December. In sheer desperation at the outcome of the war, President Nixon with the assistance of Kissinger played the dirtiest game against India. He cancelled the remaining outstanding ammunition licences for India and also suspended $87.6 million worth of aid that was on the pipeline because of India's "continuing incursions into East Pakistan." Determined to keep Yahya in the saddle, Nixon did not even stop military aid to a country that was indulging in genocidal crimes. Britain and France, on the other hand, refused to sell arms to Pakistan which they knew would be used against India. They did not also suspend supplies of some vital spares to India. France withdrew her technicians who were training the Pakistani ground crews in the maintenance of the *Mirage* aircraft after Yahya launched his pre-emptive air strike. West Germany also did not go along with the US either in ignoring the ghastly incidents in Bangla Desh or accusing India of aggression when she was compelled to take military action against Pakistan.[29]

Lamentable Letdown

When the Indo-Pakistan war was being waged, Nixon decided to take the matter to the UN. But many members including Britain and France were against the move. Russia was determined to stonewall and oppose any resolution forcing a cease-fire. But the US President was keen on getting resolutions passed in the Security Council to satisfy Pakistan. Yahya's motive behind widening the conflict was to create a situation where the international community could be mobilised through the UN to get India halt the war giving thereby the West Pakistani troops in Bangla Desh the much needed respite. There were signs of Yahya planning an attack on a larger scale on Kashmir. As per a clandestine report, a convoy of Chinese small arms was *en route* to Gilgit. There was an earlier report of the Chinese undertaking to arm two Pakistani divisions. [30]

The Security Council met on 5 December to discuss with the representatives of India and Pakistan the deteriorating situation in the sub-continent. In his statement in the House of Commons on 7 December, the Foreign and Commonwealth Secretary said that the Security Council met for eight hours in an attempt to bring a resolution calling for a cease-fire and an end to hostilities. Britain abstained as she knew the resolution before the

Council would not pass.[31] The Soviet Union exercised its veto twice within 48 hours on 5 December to kill the US-backed resolution that called for a cease-fire and withdrawal by both India and Pakistan of their forces. This was 107th time that the Soviet exercised its veto in the Security Council. The 8-power resolution got the backing of China but Britain and France abstained because they knew it was devoid of reality. In their view, a resolution that did not command unanimity in the Council was meaningless.

Britain was already committed to a policy not only of neutrality, but also of non-intervention in Indo-Pakistan disputes. She now openly declared that she would not cancel military aid to India even during the war. The BBC's reportings of the war also were favourable to India. The *Times of India* observed: "It is perhaps for the fist time since the partition that in a conflict between India and Pakistan, British public opinion as reflected in the mass media has been on the whole in favour of this country."[32] The Soviet Union said that the US resolution was one-sided and equated India with Pakistan. India had stated unequivocally that any resolution that did not bring about West Pakistani military withdrawals from Bangla Desh would be unacceptable to her. She welcomed the Soviet statement asking the great powers to keep their hands off the Hindustan Peninsula and expressed "shock and surprise" at the American attitude in the Security Council.

Commenting on the happenings in the UN, *The Hindu* observed that the Security Council would have undoubtedly disgraced itself had it "adopted the US inspired resolutions which, taken in conjunction with the supporting statement made by the US representative Mr. George Bush and by a State Department spokesman in Washington, would have made an aggressor of the victim and an exemplary UN member of a murderous military junta..."[33] America's new born anxiety to end the carnage would have been meaningful had it come nine months earlier when Yahya's military junta was committing unparalleled human annihilation in East Pakistan.

On the whole, seven cease-fire resolutions were brought before the UN in an attempt to achieve an international consensus on what was to be done about the war. The resolution of the General Assembly on 7 December and that of the Security Council on 21 December after the termination of the war, had no significance. Inspired by the US Administration, they were all intensely pro-Pakistan and rabidly anti-India. They were pushed through but none was acted upon.[34] They were oblivious to the realities of the situation. They were "slanderous and scandalous" but happily the people of America did not toe the President's line.

India's anger against the US was aggravated when the nuclear powered aircraft carrier "Enterprise" and a task force of destroyers and amphibious ships from the Seventh Fleet sailed into the Bay of Bengal. This was clearly intended to intimidate India to accept the cease-fire and halt its march to Dacca. This incited anti-American feelings in India. There were demonstrations and the Prime Minister had a tough time in pacifying the incensed demonstrators. She also managed to disallow a debate in the Parliament on the anti-American moves. In her letter to Nixon, Indira Gandhi discreetly refrained from scoring any points against him beyond what was needed to establish India's view of American culpability. The letter was more in the nature of intimation to the American President of India's readiness to cooperate with the US to mend fences with it if the latter would reciprocate.[35] While India's foreign policy would remain the same with its main planks of non-alignment and anti-colonialism, she would focus on developing closer bilateral relations wherever possible to put the country's interest on a firmer foundation.

Britain made a fairly reasonable assessment of the changed situation while giving an outline of her policy on the Indian sub-continent. In the new context of its division into three – India, West Pakistan and Bangla Desh – a report in the Foreign and Commonwealth Office stated that one could be certain of the political future of only India at that stage. It also said that India would be "the most stable of the three entities in the sub-continent, the most powerful and, to western interests, the most important." Britain did not believe as did America that India would destroy West Pakistan. She was absolutely right. India would not succumb to the temptation to use force herself in an attempt to eject the Pakistanis from the POK areas. In fact India felt she was secure in her position of the territory which really mattered to her. Britain accepted India's statement that she would not seek territorial gains as a result of her victory. Britain however felt that there was a possibility of her (India) trying to secure a minor adjustment to the 1965 CFL in Kashmir which would enable her to retain or demilitarise the Kargil Heights. In the case of West Pakistan, Britain felt that there was a possibility of this weakened, embittered and frustrated country to leave the Commonwealth.

As for President Nixon, his war policy had come under sharp criticism in the US itself. Since his image as the statesman of the "era of negotiation" had been tarnished by his intervention in the Indo-Pakistan war, the British report stated that it would not be "in the general Western interests that the US should identify its prestige with the rump of Pakistan or promote friendship with China at the cost of a quarrel with the Soviet Union and India..."[36]

Triumph of Justice

On 20 December, Bhutto assumed the office of President and Chief Martial Law Administrator in succession to Yahya who had resigned. He assumed these titles because in the absence of a Constitution in Pakistan it was only in this way Bhutto could take legitimate powers for the time being.

It was significant that just about a month before this event, Bhutto made a categorical demand for immediate transfer of power into his hands. On 23 November 1971, he said at the Lahore airport that if the Indo-Pakistan situation was to be taken to the Security Council, he alone had the right to represent Pakistan at the UN. He emphatically declared that he was the "leader of the people" and that he was "conversant with the working of the General Assembly." He further said that "the hour is (sic) struck" and hence power had to be handed over to his party. Otherwise, he threatened as usual, his party would not be responsible for any developments.[37] Russia instantly signified to the UK Delegation in New York her strong opposition to any meeting of the Security Council on the basis of equating India and Pakistan.[38]

Mujib, who was in Lyallpur jail, was taken away from there by Bhutto and put under house arrest. On 3 January 1972, Bhutto announced his decision to release him unconditionally in response to world opinion. It marked the end of Mujib's eighth and last prison term which lasted more than nine months. He defied death during this period under the blood thirsty Yahya's regime. On 8 January 1972, Mujib was flown to London. On Monday, 10 January, he was in New Delhi. India had already recognised Bangla Desh on 6 December 1971. After a brief halt in New Delhi, Mujib reached Dacca the same day. Monday the tenth January became a golden Monday in the history of Bangla Desh. There was a red carpet welcome in Dacca to *Bangabandhu/Bangapita* as Mujib was variously called. Mujib was treated to an enormous popular acclaim.

References

1. UK HC (P) to Michael Stewart, 12 Aug. 1969, FCO/37/489; *Guardian* 26 May 1969.
2. Werner Adam, "An Unholy Alliance," *Far Eastern Economic Review*, 7 August 1969.
3. *Aide Memoire*, Govt. of India 13 Aug. 1970, FCO/37/697.
4. *Ibid.*
5. *The Hindu*, 17 Dec. 1971.
6. "India-Pakistan Crisis," 21 Sep. 1971, FCO/37/924.

7. Note of H.C. Byatt, 1 Feb. 1971, FCO/37/914.
8. *Ibid*, UK HC (P) to FO, 2 Feb. 1971.
9. *Ibid*, UK HC (P) to FO, 4 Feb. 1971.
10. *Ibid*, UK HC (1) FO, 9 Feb. 1971.
11. *The Motherland* and *Patriot*, 2 April 1971; UK HC (1) to FCO, April 1971, FCO/37/928.
12. UK HC (1) to FCO, 5 Feb. 1971, FCO/37/914.
13. UK HC (P) to FCO, 23 April 1971, FCO/37/915.
14. UK HC (P) to FCO, 16 Feb. 1971, FCO/ 37/870.
15. "Indo-Pakistan Crisis," *op. cit.*
16. "The case for Bangladesh," by UK HC (P), 12 Oct. 1971, FCO/37/87.
17. K.R. Srinivasa Iyengar "Bangla Desh: Saga of Blood and Tears," *The Hindu*, 12 Dec. 1971.
18. Keating to SoS, 29 March 1971, Dept. of State, Pol. 23–9 PAK.
19. J.S.B. Arora, *War with Pakistan 1971*, p. 18.
20. *The Hindu*, 15 June 1971.
21. "Indo-Pakistan Crisis," *op. cit.*
22. UK HC (P) to FCO, 13 April 1971, FCO/37/870.
23. "India Pakistan Crisis," *op. cit.*
24. *Ibid.*
25. *Hindustan Times*, 6 Nov. '71.
26. UK HC (P) to FCO, 1 Dec. 1971, FCO/37/943.
27. *Ibid*, UK HC (P) to FCO, 5 Dec. 1971.
28. *New York Times*, 16 Dec. 1971, cited in J.B.S. Arora, *War with Pakistan* 1971, p. 149.
29. India, Pakistan and Burma Association, Confidential Report, FCO/37/1091.
30. UK HC (P) to FCO, 5 Dec. 1971, FCO/37/924.
31. Statement of the Secretary of State in the House of Commons, 7 DEC. 1971, FCO/37/943.
32. *Times of India*, 6 Dec. 1971.
33. *The Hindu*, 7 Dec. 1971.
34. India, Pakistan and Burma Association, Confidential Report, *op, cit.*
35. *Ibid.*
36. "British Policy on the Sub-Continent," Paper prepared by FCO, 18 Dec. 1971, FCO 37/1756.
37. UK HC (P) to FCO, 24 Nov. 1971, FCO/37/924.
38. *Ibid*, UKD to UN to FCO, 26 Nov. 1971.

19

Epilogue

In October 1971, about a month before the outbreak of the Third Indo-Pakistan War, Indira Gandhi made a five-day visit to Britain. Her trip was undertaken not to secure from Britain more help for the refugees who were flooding into India at the rate of 40,000 to 50,000 a day. Nor did she visit Britain expecting a sea change in the latter's attitude towards India after her categorical declaration of non-intervention in Indo-Pakistan affairs. Though there was certainly a change in the British policy where Kashmir was concerned, the Government of India never expected Britain to give her full commitment to a just cause. As for the Prime Minister of India, she never trusted the British completely. It was seen in Chapter 17 that behind the facade of exchange of pleasantries at the London airport in 1966, there was really no meeting of the minds between the Prime Ministers of India and Britain. Indira Gandhi was certainly aware that behind the British diplomacy, there was the hidden truth that Britain would not like India to emerge as a pre-eminent power in the sub-continent. Besides, at that point of time, Britain's energies were more devoted to going into the Common Market[1] for "economic resurgence and to find a new *raison d'etre* as the leader of a European super State."[2] She had therefore neither the time nor the inclination to involve herself in the affairs of the Indian sub-continent.

The purpose behind Indira Gandhi's visit to Britain was to convey to that Government the depth of the Indian feeling on the Bangla Desh issue and to clarify the main features of the crisis created by Pakistan's internal problems and their impact on India. On these two points, she succeeded to an appreciable degree. She told Prime Minister Edward Heath clearly and concisely that

Pakistan alone was the master for the prevalent perilous situation in the sub-continent and that it was Pakistan's diversionary tactic to project India-Pakistan hostility rather than her own shortfalls in East Pakistan that constituted the main cause of the new tension. Indira Gandhi's accurate presentation of the facts would have certainly denied the Pakistani leaders any scope to twist the facts. Her five-day journey enabled Britain to have a clear-cut idea of the developments in East Pakistan and their repercussions on India. This was a "great gain" and for this alone Indira Gandhi's visit "was well worth while. It has established that New Delhi expects more than sympathy, appropriate pressure and action to persuade Islamabad that there is no alternative to accepting political realities in East Bengal."[3]

Simla Agreement

After the surrender of the West Pakistani Army to the Indian forces on 17 December 1971, Bhutto, as President of a truncated Pakistan, keenly felt the need to have talks with India. Since Pakistan was at a grave disadvantage after her humiliating defeat at India's hands, Bhutto was anxious to preserve what remained of his country's honour. His primary concern was the repatriation of nearly 95,000 Pakistani prisoners of war in India including those charged with war crimes. But any talk on the issue of those on charges of war crimes had to include Bangla Desh also. The Prime Ministers of India and Bangla Desh had in a joint declaration stated that the trials of the war criminals would "bring the guilty persons to justice and would bring home to the world at large the enormity of the suffering of the people of Bangla Desh." For Bangla Desh to participate in the talks, Pakistan's recognition of the new nation was indispensable. Seventy five nations had already established their embassies in Dacca. The greatest obstacle to recognition was that dictators made in the mould of Bhutto could not be expected to climb down so easily and shake hands with a "secessionist."

When Bhutto declared his desire to have friendly relations with India, Indira Gandhi sent a letter to the UN Secretary General on 14 February 1972 conveying her acceptance to hold direct talks with Bhutto "at any time, at any level and without pre-conditions." It was then decided that both Indira Gandhi and Bhutto should meet and sort out the problems. Perturbed over the "multiple inconsistencies" in Bhutto's public utterances, Indira Gandhi concluded that, as a precaution, the proposed summit meeting must be preceded by preliminary talks at official level. She suggested to Bhutto that special emissaries of both Governments should meet initially to settle the modalities for the summit to ensure its success.[4] Bhutto agreed and accordingly pre-summit talks were held between the Indian delegation led by D.P. Dhar, Chairman, Policy Planning Committee, Ministry of External Affairs and the Pakistani delegation led by Aziz Ahmed at Murree in Pakistan from 26 to 29 April 1972. This is how the British High Commissioner P.T. Garvey rated the heads of the two delegations: Dhar as "a wily Kashmiri, not yet quite a Minister" and Aziz as a "hard-nosed Indophobe."[5] Utter confusion reigned on both sides during the talks. The path to the summit was felt to be "frustratingly serpentine." The talks came within an ace of deadlock when a last minute talk of Dhar with Bhutto saved the situation and the delegations parted with an agreement on the agenda for the summit which was scheduled to begin at Simla on 28 June1972.

There ensued five days of cliff-hanging negotiations from 28 June 1972 in the historic hill resort of Simla. On the eve of the summit, both Indira Gandhi and Bhutto expressed that they did not expect much to come out of the meeting. The negotiations almost foundered over the differences in approach to the crucial Kashmir issue. India preferred to defer a definite settlement on Kashmir provided the eventual negotiations would be purely bilateral and would not disturb the *status quo.* By contrast, Bhutto was intent on liquidating piecemeal the consequences of the 1971 war and to move step by step on practical measures to normalise relations without renouncing his position on Kashmir and making commitments on future behaviour. Negotiations were going very tough. There were exchanges of drafts achieving no acknowledged progress. Time was running out and predictions of an imminent demise of the negotiations began to multiply.

By a curious twist of fate, an understanding was reached and the summit was salvaged after two meetings between the two leaders who until then remained off the stage with only the officials doing most of the talks. At half past midnight on 2-3 July, P.N. Haksar, Indira Gandhi's Principal Secretary, who had taken the place of D.P. Dhar, announced that agreement had been reached. This was followed by the signing of the famous Simla Agreement by Prime Minister Indira Gandhi and President Bhutto. Both the Governments agreed to end the conflict and confrontation that had hitherto marred their relations; promote a friendly and harmonious relationship; establish durable peace in order to address themselves to the welfare of the people and like matters; and to maintain the *status quo* in Jammu and Kashmir as on 17 December 1971. In Jammu and Kashmir, both sides should respect the Line of Control (LOC) resulting from the cease-fire of 17 December 1971 without prejudice to the recognised position of either side. Neither side should seek to alter it unilaterally irrespective of mutual differences and legal interpretations. Thus both settled for a bilateral approach to sort out their pending problems. By any standard, the Simla Agreement could be called a modest triumph for both the parties. India felt that Bhutto's attitude was genuine and sincere. Mrs. Gandhi was convinced of his peaceful intentions. He appeared to abandon all hope of war with India and India derived some comfort from this.

The Simla Agreement was ratified by Pakistan and India on 15 and 28 July respectively. Withdrawal of troops was to begin in August with India vacating 13,310 square kilometres of Pakistani territory and Pakistan vacating 179 square kilometres of Indian territory.

> Britain remarked: "The Simla Agreement though not legally watertight, represents an exchange of commitments...Neither side got entirely what they wanted on Kashmir, but overall both sides made concessions and secured demonstrable gains...It is easy to be pessimistic about India and Pakistan. There are still formidable problems ahead. Both sides apparently wanted to make a new start. The Simla Agreement is a hopeful development which we can heartily welcome."[6]

On 24 August 1972, dwelling on the need to develop the Pakistani side of the LOC, Bhutto said in Gilgit that the real competition lay in winning the hearts and minds of the people through service and not in winning territory through war. He did not fail to express with confidence that the reunion of Kashmir would definitely come about, "if not in his life time, after him." His threats on Kashmir, though mild, did not abate. On 5 Mach 1973, he made a statement in Islamabad which was contrary to the Simla Agreement on Kashmir. What he said indicated that Pakistani stand on Kashmir remained clear-cut. He said that without a "free and impartial plebiscite" in Kashmir, Pakistan would not "sanction" any regime there "whatever the degree of autonomy from Delhi that such a regime might enjoy." He also said that Pakistan was not "tied to Sheikh Abdullah or the Plebiscite Front" and that she rested her case "squarely on the UN Resolutions of 1948 and 1949." However, there were grounds to believe that regardless of the statements of Bhutto, the official Pakistani attitude in the wake of the 1971 war was less militaristic than before.[7] In fact some of the articles appearing in the Pakistani press after the Simla Accord ruled out the possibility of another war or round of hostilities at least for some time.

Bhutto started creating a problem over the repatriation of the Pakistani prisoners in India with criminal charges. By the joint Indo-Bangla Desh

Agreement of 17 April 1973, they were to be tried in Dacca. But he obstinately refused their trial on the plea that the Dacca authorities were not competent for the task. He was yet to recognise Bangla Desh. Though he had signed the Simla Agreement, his animosity towards India had by no means lessened. The following is a verbatim transcript of an interview with Bhutto on BBC TV on 24 July 1973 at 11 p.m.

A Hart: You have made from time to time, as all politicians do, extreme statements. You have talked about a thousand year war with India. Now was that to the gallery or that ...?

President Bhutto: No, Not at all. We have had a thousand years of hostility, you know. There has been no confrontation which is as old as the confrontation between India and Pakistan, neither between the Carthage and Rome, nor between Britain and France, nor between the Russians and Americans, nor between the Arabs and the Israelis. Ours is the oldest confrontation. So we have had a thousand years of hostility in the past and in the future we hope that this does not happen but we are an old civilization.[8]

Bhutto's statements were very convincing evidence of the impact on him of the works of British authors like the famous archaeologist Mortimer Wheeler. Wheeler titled his book published in 1950 – three years after the birth of Pakistan – as *Five Thousand Years of Pakistan*!

Bhutto recognised Bangladesh only on 21 February 1974 at the Islamic Summit in Lahore which enabled Mujib to take his place at the Summit. The question of repatriation of the war criminals was settled two months later at a tripartite meeting of India, Pakistan and Bangla Desh. This removed a major stumbling block to the normalisation of relations in the sub-continent.

Ill-Conceived Kargil War

Until 1999, that is to say, for nearly three decades after the Simla Agreement, there was no major conflict between India and Pakistan. This did not mean that the people of Kashmir were allowed to live in comfort and peace. There was no change in Pakistan's conviction that the possession of Kashmir in its entirety was a supreme necessity for her. To reach her goal, she cared very little for justice or humanity or truth. Breaches of the accord on the LOC, killing of the Hindus including women and children and abduction of the girls of the Pandit families were a routine feature. In all these dreadful activities, the complicity of the Pakistani authorities was very clear.

What was enacted by Pakistan in the beginning of 1999 in Kargil was a most treacherous drama at a most crucial time for both India and Pakistan.

Prime Minister Atal Behari Vajpayee was undertaking a "Bus *Yatra*" from the Wagah border to Lahore on 19 February 1999. While travelling, Vajpayee beckoned to the reputed journalist, author, diplomat and parliamentarian Kuldip Nayar, who was accompanying him and told him that about the same time 26 Hindus were done to death by militants near Rajouri and Udhampur. The Prime Minister was so anguished by the killings that he doubted if there was any purpose in furthering the bilateral talks. Kuldip Nayar reassured him that the militants were resorting to such heinous acts to stall the talks between the two leaders.[9]

Even as Vajpayee was taking a good will message to Lahore, to share a vision of peace and stability between the two neighbours and to reaffirm India's faith in the Simla Agreement, Pakistan was sending her troops in the guise of *Mujahideens* and occupied strategic areas like Mashkoh, Dras, Kaksar and Batalik.[10] By this treacherous method, initially the infiltrators succeeded in creating the impression that it was the Indian troops which were fighting an internal war against separatists.

The awful lack of concern on the part of Indian Intelligence about a hostile mountainous area traditionally regarded "an area for infiltration," greatly encouraged the invaders. After a belated realisation, the Indian armed forces were entrusted with the task of literally fighting a well-entrenched enemy in a hostile terrain and they carried out the command marvellously well. Later, the Indian Air Force also entered the fray which Pakistan did not expect. Its bombardment of mountain-top targets with pin-point accuracy was a rare performance. The whole world watched India's first televised war as the territory was being recaptured peak by peak.

In early July 1999, the beleaguered Pakistani Prime Minister Nawaz Sharif telephoned President Clinton of the US for an urgent meeting to discuss the dangerous stand-off between India and Pakistan. He told the President that the trouble began when the Pakistani forces under the Command of General Pervez Musharraf crossed the LOC which had been recognised and generally observed as the boundary between the two countries in Kashmir since the Simla Agreement of 1972. Sharif requested Clinton's good offices not only to resolve the unexpected crisis but help mediate with India on the question of Kashmir itself. But Clinton told him that since India was strongly against any third party involvement, he was not in a position to help Sharif. He told him candidly that while Sharif was always welcome to Washington, he had to come there bearing in mind two things: (1) he had to agree to withdraw his troops back across the LOC and (2) he (Clinton) would not agree to intervene in the Kashmir dispute, especially under circumstances that appeared to reward Pakistan's wrongful incursion. Sharif did go to Washington on 4 July and a joint statement was issued stating that steps would be taken to restore the LOC and that America would support and encourage the resumption and intensification of bilateral talks once violence had stopped.[11]

Rumination

Pakistan has waged as many as four wars on India since 1947 and it would be naive to assume that she would make no more war on India. All along, the whole world knew who the culprit was. Yet, none demanded Pakistan to halt and vacate its aggression. The point to ponder is whether India could have acted differently in 1947. Could she have taken action, even if drastic, to end the conflict once and for ever? Considering the timing of the first invasion just two months after India became free and the horrific communal mayhem that rocked both India and Pakistan at that time, Nehru could not be faulted. The British documents refer, not without grounds, to the dissatisfaction of some of the Indian leaders and high ranking officers with the policy Nehru pursued on Kashmir. Some Congressmen even felt that among the ham-handed actions of the Congress since 1937 which paved the way to a considerable degree to the partition of India, the costliest blunder was taking away Kashmir from the charge of Vallabhbhai Patel who held the crucial portfolios of Home and States apart from the post of Deputy Prime Minister. On 23 December 1947, Nehru sent a letter to Patel informing him of his decision to take away Kashmir from him and place it under the charge of N. Gopalaswamy Ayyangar.

Patel was a brilliant tactician and a talented administrator who accomplished with consummate skill the herculean task of integrating the 562 Princely Indian States into the political structure of India. This was acclaimed as his master achievement. Nehru's decision to take away the key issue of Kashmir from Patel at a most critical time astounded many. Patel, who was naturally outraged at this, immediately penned his resignation as a member of the Government. Fortunately, Gandhiji's intervention stopped the letter from being delivered. According to Patel's biographer, B. Krishna, Patel once told H.V. Kamath that if Nehru and Gopalaswamy Ayyangar had not made Kashmir their close preserve by separating it from his portfolio, "I would have tackled the problem as purposefully as I had already done in Hyderabad."[12] Given his track record, Patel only spoke the truth. Many veterans openly stated that Patel would have tackled the problem in the best manner possible. Even some Englishmen believed that Patel was the only man capable of forcing Nehru reach a settlement on Kashmir. After Patel's death in December 1950, many in the British official circles felt there was practically none who was able to stand up to Nehru on the Kashmir question.[13] This was absolutely true.

After Patel, Nehru was the only man who stood firm on Kashmir. Many agreed that his was the authentic voice that spoke for Kashmir. He did make a number of concessions to Pakistan much to the annoyance of many political parties in India. Not waging a war on Pakistan to retrieve from her the portions of Kashmir under her forcible occupation was itself an act of excessive tolerance on the part of India. But on the maintenance of *status quo* in Kashmir as it was after the raid of 1947, he was firm and unyielding. The western bloc in the Security Council knew it. They understood there was no point in Pakistan taking the issue again and again to the Security Council when it was clear that Nehru would not budge from his stand. But they failed to dissuade Pakistan from needlessly reactivating the issue at the Council several times.

Nehru remained steadfast in his stand despite the multiple problems he faced and the denunciations heaped on him from many including Sheikh Abdullah who failed to stay loyal to him. Nehru's Prime Ministership was not a bed of roses but of thorns. True to the axiom "Uneasy lies the head that wears a crown," he had to face innumerable unprecedented problems. Starting with the senseless killings in the wake of the birth of Pakistan for no other reason than that one was not a Muslim or a Hindu to the end of his life in 1964, he had to face a sea of troubles. Yet, nothing could deflect him from giving up the cause of Kashmir whose accession was legal and binding. He left no one in doubt that the presence of the Indian troops there could not be questioned. In entering the Indian State to support the raiders, the Pakistani army had committed an aggression and until that was set right Pakistan would have no *locus standi* in the dispute, he asserted. Nehru was very conscious that any false move on Kashmir would spark off a communal explosion in India against Muslims which he would be unable to control. Nehru's concern for the Muslims in India was genuine.

There were criticisms from some quarters in India that in 1947 itself the matter could have been settled easily since the Indian forces were definitely in a position to drive out the Pakistani forces. Nehru was blamed for his failure to avail himself of the opportune moment. Nehru did not do so because the Pakistani forces could not be driven beyond the border without bombing the Pakistani bases. This would mean an attack on Pakistan which would result in a full-scale war between the two countries. Nehru was right in scotching such thoughts. But his going to the UN on Mountbatten's insistence was definitely a great mistake and Nehru admitted it.

Another criticism levelled against Nehru in this context was his choice of V.K. Krishna Menon to high posts and the excessive faith he reposed in him. In truth, Menon's activities as free India's first High Commissioner to Britain and as leader of the Indian Delegation to the UN bore ample testimony to his total dedication to the cause of India's freedom first and to the cause of her progress later. It could never be denied that members of the Indian Delegation to the UN Security Council were men of sterling qualities known for their depth of knowledge and erudition. For instance, the speeches of the great Jurist B.N. Rau during discussions on Kashmir would be brief but aggressive always making an impression in the august body. But it was only Krishna Menon who introduced heat and strength into the Indian arguments on Kashmir. Though all the speeches of Menon on Kashmir were outstanding, those delivered in 1957 in the Security Council were memorable. In January-February of that year when discussions on the subject were at fever pitch, Menon spoke for hours on end. Once, despite being racked by fatigue, he refused to give up and thundered:

> "Why is it that we have never heard voices in connection with the freedom of people under the suppression and tyranny of Pakistani authorities on the other side of the cease-fire line? Why is it that we have not heard here that in ten years these people have not seen a ballot paper? With what voice can either the Security Council or anyone coming before it demand a plebiscite for a people on our side who exercise franchise, who have freedom of speech, who function under a hundred local bodies?"

In another speech delivered during that year which was considered brilliant by friends and foes alike, Menon stoutly opposed the move to induct UN troops into Kashmir. After Menon's marathon performance, the Soviet Union vetoed the mischievous Anglo-American resolution. In another moving speech at the Security Council on 3 May 1962 highlighting the fact that Kashmir's accession to India was full, irrevocable and perpetual, Menon said: "On no condition shall we trade our sovereignty. On no condition shall we sell our heritage. On no condition shall we open our door for the disruption or disintegration of India."

Earlier in 1954, at the Geneva Conference "Nehru's invisible presence was felt through Krishna Menon's agency." Menon's performance at Geneva to negotiate for peace in both Korea and Indo-China was widely acclaimed. In later years, Nehru relied largely on Krishna Menon in the conduct of foreign policy, especially in the UN. A reputed biographer of Nehru says that "Krishna

Menon was the only modern mind in the Cabinet, besides Krishnamachari." Nehru found Menon's ingenuity very useful. This was not liked by many including some in the Congress. Though Menon had a share in India's defeat in the Chinese War, it must be admitted that he brought new vigour to the office as Defence Minister and also helped to develop India's arms industry. But because of the reverses suffered by India in the war, he was held solely responsible for the debacle. When the opposition to him snowballed, Nehru had to drop Menon whose loyalty to the country was unquestionable.

After Nehru, Pakistan invaded India thrice – in 1965, 1971 and 1999 and was defeated in all the battles. Of late, some people have been offering what they think are possible solutions to the Kashmir problem. It would be of interest to know that recently Pakistan also evinced an interest in putting forward a solution. In 2006, for the first time, the Pakistan Government abandoned the plebiscite proposal and threw the UN resolutions on Kashmir to the "dustbin of history." After this, the Pakistan President Pervez Musharraf suggested the separation of Kashmir from Jammu on the basis of religion. India could not but reject the proposal on the ground that "the ethos of pluralism, India's proud possession since the time of the struggle for independence, will be destroyed if such a division takes place."[14] There can be no panacea for the problem as long as Pakistan persists in her demand for the Vale of Kashmir.

Sri Aurobindo's Prophecy

It would be most appropriate in the present situation to remember the utterance made by a great *yogi* on 15 August 1947 when India gained independence from the yoke of British imperialism. It was indeed a great day in the life of the nation. The transfer of power was smooth and India was jubilant. Still, joyful India was weighed down by the unpleasant fact that she was free not as one whole nation but as a great nation cut into two parts. In India's view Independence was indivisible. When with mixed feelings the nation was celebrating this auspicious day which coincided with the 75th birth day of Sri Aurobindo, the sage made a historic pronouncement in Pondicherry (now Puducherry). He told the public at large his firm conviction that the partition was not permanent. Countering the general belief that the division of India was a "settled fact," Sri Aurobindo said:

> "It is to be hoped this settled fact will not be accepted as settled for ever or anything more than a temporary expedient...The partition must go. Let us hope that they may come about naturally, by an

> increasing recognition of the necessity not only of peace and concord but by the practice of common action and the creation of means for that purpose. In this way, unity may finally come about under whatever form – the exact form may have a pragmatic but not a fundamental importance. But by whatever means, in whatever way, the division must go; unity must and will be achieved, for it is necessary for the greatness of India's future."

Sri Aurobindo, the intellectual revolutionary turned *yogi,* was an authentic and inspired prophet. From 1910 when he landed on the shores of Pondicherry abjuring violence to 1950 when he attained *samadi,* very seldom he intervened in political matters. On such occasions, his forecasts of the future shape of things to come, which were born out of an extraordinary calibre of mind, proved true. It was India's misfortune that his prophecies and recommendations were not given the weightage they merited. Two instances deserve mention in this context. One was when the Second World War broke out and England forced on India the war with which she was not concerned either directly or indirectly. Since India was declared belligerent without the consent of her people and without consulting the legislative bodies, the Indian National Congress refused to offer cooperation to the Government. Sri Aurobindo did not agree with the view of the Congress that Britain was waging the war for imperialist end. To the utter surprise of many close to him, and indignation of his own countrymen, Sri Aurobindo along with the Mother, contributed to the Viceroy's War Purposes Fund. It was done "as a token of complete adhesion to the Allied cause." In doing so, for the first time he made clear to the nation that the war was being fought "in defence of civilization and its highest attained social, cultural and spiritual values and the whole future of humanity…"[15] This singular gesture might have earned Sri Aurobindo protests and calumnies. But did not the events after the war prove him right?

The second instance when Sri Aurobindo intervened in a political matter was during the visit to India in March 1942 of Sir Stafford Cripps, Lord of the Privy Seal and Leader of the House of Commons. At that time, there was no indication of Britain deciding to leave India. Prime Minister Winston Churchill sent Cripps to explain to the Indian leaders the solution agreed upon by the War Cabinet to end the Indian crisis: It was the offer of Dominion Status providing for the creation of a new Indian Union which should take its place as a Dominion of the Commonwealth owing allegiance to the Crown as an equal partner with the UK and other Dominions at the end of the War. The Cripps offer was rejected by Gandhiji and Nehru. Instantly, Sri Aurobindo intervened. Discerning the advantages the offer had for India at that time, he advised the Congress against rejecting it. He could see that though Britain and her allies were passing through the dark days of war, they were certainly going to win the war and that, after the war, Britain would voluntarily leave India without India having to work for it. Sri Aurobindo sent the following message forthwith to the Congress leaders in Delhi through his trusted disciple Doraiswamy, a lawyer from Madras:

> "If the Congress can get Dominion Status without any fighting or struggle...I do not see why it should not accept it...It can build our defence after that and when that is ready, it can easily cut off the British connection...When you can secede at your will from the British connection, it is practically independence."

The Mother also voiced the same opinion. But the Congress leaders, perhaps still angry with Sri Aurobindo for his total withdrawal from politics, did not accept his suggestion. A biographer of the Mother wrote: "So the golden moment passed and with it the last real chance of establishing a united Independent India. *The rejection of the offer was a prelude to the partition.*"[16]

The events of the past 62 years have demonstrated how difficult it is to find a solution to the Kashmir problem. However, one cannot rule out a short term solution which will serve the interests of both the parties besides enabling the Kashmiris to live in peace. The solution lies in sincerely adhering to the present LOC which was agreed as the border between India and Pakistan in Kashmir. Nehru clearly perceived as early as 1948 that there could be no military solution to the Kashmir dispute and that any solution for Kashmir worth its name must have a broad consensus of the people of both countries and, more importantly, of the people of Kashmir. Nehru expressed this clearly to Liaquat when he met him in London and Paris in 1948. He repeated this offer to Pakistan in later years also. But the Pakistani leaders believed in achieving their end militarily and failed thoroughly in all their attempts to grab Kashmir.

Curiously enough, the former British Prime Minister Attlee himself made a bold statement about this after his visit to India towards the end of 1956. He visited Kashmir also then. After his talks with Nehru and Prime Minister Bakshi Ghulam Mohammad of Kashmir, he wrote an article about the impressions of his visit which appeared in the *Evening Star*. He had stated therein:

> "I gather that the tension of a few years ago has relaxed and that everyone in Kashmir and Jammu, apart from the territories occupied

by Pakistan, is convinced that the present division of the country has come to stay...Altogether my impression is that judging by results, the present regime is successful. It is also thoroughly democratic with local self-government all the way from the village. I think that Kashmir has definitely opted for union with India."[17]

There is of course a long term solution. Emulating Abraham Lincoln who would never have a "half free and half slave America," our leaders should have exercised "indomitable patience" and waited till they had one united independent India instead of a fractured independent India. But this was not done. The prediction of an authentic prophet like Sri Aurobindo which was made after the partition cannot be brushed aside. India and Pakistan should greet the unseen with cheer and wait for the day when certainly the two peoples will realise the folly of the past and reunite. It may take a century or more for this to happen but a century is not a long period in the life of a nation as ancient as India. Reunion is the only lasting and permanent solution to all the problems now being faced by both India and Pakistan.

References

1. European Common Market established by the Treaty of Rome in 1957. The UK joined it in 1973.
2. Nihal Singh, "UK's Attitude Unchanged," *The Statesman*, 4 Nov. 1971.
3. *Ibid.*
4. Indira Gandhi to Bhutto, 30 March 1972, PREM/15/1810.
5. P.T. Garvey, UK HC(I) to Secy. of State, FCO, 14 July 1972, FCO/37/1149.
6. *Ibid.*
7. C.R. Budd, British Embassy (Islamabad), to D.H. Doble, SAD, FCO, 14 March 1973, FCO/37/1351.
8. FCO/37/1339.
9. Kuldip Nayar, *Scoop Inside Stories from the Partition to the Present*, p. 211.
10. Jagmohan, *My Frozen Turbulence in Kashmir*, pp. 743 & 44.
11. Bill Clinton, *My Life*, pp. 864 & 65.
12. La. Su. Rengarajan, "Patel's Role in Freedom Struggle" (Review Article of B. Krishna's *India's Bismarck – Sardar Vallabhbhai Patel*), *The Hindu*, 20 May, 2008.
13. UK HC (I) to CRO, 23 Jan 1951, FL/ 1015/ 53.
14. *Deccan Chronicle*, 1 Jan. 2007.
15. Georges Van Vrekhem, *The Mother The Story Of Her Life*, pp. 291 & 92.

16. Wilfred, *The Mother*, p. 62 cited in *The Mother The Story Of Her Life*, p. 293; Sudhir Ghosh, *Gandhi's Emissary*, p. 278. Emphasis Author's.
17. *Evening Star*, 20 Nov. 1956, quoted in *The Hindu*, 26 Nov. 1956.

Bibliography

Primary Sources

United Kingdom

1. **National Archives**
   Records of the Cabinet, Prime Minister's Office, Foreign Office, Colonial Office, Commonwealth Office and Foreign and Commonwealth Relations Office – 1947-72.
2. **British Library (OIOC)**
   Corfield Collections
3. **National Army Museum**
   Roy Bucher Papers
4. **Churchill Library**
   Philip Noel-Baker Correspondence

India

1. **Nehru Memorial Museum and Library, New Delhi**
   Vijayalakshmi Pandit Papers
   Y.D. Gundevia Papers
2. **Parliament Library. New Delhi**
   The Hindu
   Hindustan Times
   The Statesman
   Times, London
3. **Adyar Library and Research Centre, Chennai**
   New India

Secondary Sources

Books

A Hundred Years of The Hindu: The Epic Story of Indian Nationalism, Kasturi & Sons Ltd., Madras, 1978.

Adyar Library Bulletin, Vol. XXXI – XXXII – 1967-68, *Dr. V. Raghavan Felicitation Volume.*

Akbar Khan DSO, *Raiders in Kashmir*, Pak Publishers Ltd., Karachi, 1970.

Akbar, M.J. *Kashmir Behind the Vale*, Roli Books Pvt. Ltd., New Delhi, 2003.

Anand, A.S. *The Constitution of Jammu and Kashmir: Its Developments and Comments*, Universal Book Traders, 1991.

Annual Report, Archaeological Survey of India, 1915-1916, Calcutta, 1918.

Arora, J.S.B. *War with Pakistan 1971*, Army Publishers, Delhi.

Azad, Maulana Abul Kalam. *India Wins Freedom: The Complete Version*, Orient Longmans, 1988.

Bamzai, P. N. K. *Culture and Political History of Kashmir*, Vol. Three, M D Publications Pvt. Ltd., New Delhi, 1994.

Basham, A.L. *The Wonder that was India*, Rupa & Co., 1987.

Birdwood, Lord. *A continent Decides*, Robert Hale Ltd., London, 1953.

Bowles, Chester. *Mission to India: A Search for Alternatives in Asia*, B.I. Publications, New Delhi, 1974.

Brecher, Michael. *Nehru - A Political Biography*, OUP, *1969.*

Brecher, Michael. *The Struggle for Kashmir*, Ryerson Press, 1953.

Brines, Russell. *The Indo-Pakistan Conflict*, London, Pall Mall, 1968.

Chagla, M.C. *Kashmir 1947-1965*, Publications Division, Government of India, New Delhi, 1965.

Chopra, P.N. *The Sardar of India*, Allied Publishers Ltd., New Delhi.

Clinton, Bill. *My Life*, Hutchinson, The Random House Group Ltd., London, 2004.

Coupland, R. *The Constitutional Problem in India*, Part II, OUP, 1944.

Das Gupta, C. *War and Diplomacy in Kashmir, 1947-48*, Sage Publications, New Delhi, 2002.

Devarajan, *Vainavamum Aazhvarkalum* (Tamil), Part 2, Sri Shenbaka Padippagam, Madras.

Dhar, K.N. *Glimpses of Kashmiri Culture*, Series I, Sri Paramananda Research Institute, Kashmir, 1975.

Dictionary of World History, Butler & Tanner Ltd., 1973.

Dixit, J.N. *India-Pakistan in War & Peace*, Defence Spectrum Books, Dehra Dun, 2002.

Documents on Kashmir Problem, Edited by M.S. Deora and R. Grover, Vols. I to X1V, Discovery Publishing House, New Delhi.

Foreign Relations of the United States (FRUS), 1947, Vol. III, 1972.

Foreign Relations of the United States (FRUS), 1948, Vol. V, Part I, pp. 291-294.

Foreign Relations of the US (FRUS) 1961-1963, Vol. XIX,

Frank, Katherine. *Life of Indira Nehru Gandhi*, HarperCollins *Publishers*, 2001.

Galbraith, J.K. *Ambassador's Journal: A Personal Account of the Kennedy Years,* Hamish Hamilton, London, 1969.

Garrett, John. *A Classical Dictionary of India*, Rupa & C0., 1994.

Gauhar, Altaf. *Ayub Khan: Pakistan's First Military Ruler,* University Press Ltd, 1996.

Ghosh, Sudhir. *Gandhi's Emissary*, Routledge, New Delhi, 2008.

Gwasha Lal, P. *A Short History of Kashmir from the earliest times to the Present day,* Srinagar, Kashmir, 1932.

Hansard (House of Lords), 30 Nov. 1955.

History of Kashmir, Christian Literature Society for India, 1920.

Hudson, H.V. *The Great Divide: Britain-India-Pakistan,* Hutchinson of London, 1968.

India 2009 A Reference Annual, Publication Division, Government of India, New Delhi.

Jagmohan. *My Frozen Turbulence in Kashmir*, Allied Publishers (Pvt) Ltd., New Delhi, 2007.

Jha, Prem Shankar. *The origin of a Dispute, Kashmir 1947*, OUP, New Delhi, 2003.

Kak, B.L. *The Fall of Gilgit The Untold Story of Indo-Pak Affairs from Jinnah to Bhutto (1947-1977)*, Light and Life Publishers, 1977.

Kapur M.L. *Kashmir Sold and Snatched,* Published by the author, 1968.

Keith, A.B. *A History of Sanskrit Literature*, OUP, 1941.

Korbel, Josef. *Danger In Kashmir*, Princeton University Press, 1966.

Krishna, B. *Sardar Vallabhbhai Patel India's Iron Man,* Indus, 1995.

Larry Collin and Dominique Lapierre. *Mountbatten and the Partition of India, 22 March-15 August 1947*, Vikas Publishing House Pvt., Ltd., New Delhi.

Larry Collins and Dominique Lapierre. *Freedom At Midnight,* Vikas Publishing House Pvt., Ltd., New Delhi.

Literary Cultures in History, Reconstructed from South Asia, Edited by Sheldon Pollock University of California Press, 2003.

Macmillan, Harold. *At The End Of The Day 1961-1963*, Macmillan, 1973.

Mahajan, M.C. *Looking back*, Har-Anand Publications India, 1994.

Margaret-Bourke-White. *Interview with India*, Phoenix House Ltd., London, 1950.

Mellor, Andrew. *India Since Partition*, Turnstile Press, 1951.

Mitra, Debala. *Pandrethan, Avantipur and Martand*, Published by D.G., ASI, New Delhi.

Moon, Penderel. *Divide and Quit :An Eyewitness Account of the Partition of India*, OUP, 1998.

Moon, Penderel. *Wavell: The Viceroy's Journal*, OUP, London, 1973.

Moraes, Frank. *Jawaharlal Nehru A Biography*, The Macmillan Company, New York, 1956.

Morrice, James. *Pakistan Chronicle*, Hurst & Co, London, 1993.

Mullick, B.N. *My Years With Nehru: The Chinese Betrayal*, Allied Publishers, 1971.

Nagarajan, K.S. *Contribution of Kashmir to Sanskrit Literature*, Printed by V.B. Soobiah & Sons, 1970.

Nayar, Kuldip. *Scoop! Inside Stories From the Partition to the Present*, HarperCollins *Publishers* India, New Delhi, 2007.

Nehru, Jawaharlal. *Glimpses of World History*, Jawaharlal Nehru Memorial Fund, New Delhi, OUP, 1982.

Nehru, Jawaharlal. *The Discovery of India*, Jawaharlal Nehru Memorial Fund, New Delhi, OUP, 1981.

Noorani, A.G. *The Kashmir Question*, Manaktalas, Bombay, 1964.

Oxford Dictionary of National Biography, Vol, 29.

Pandit, Ranjit Sitaram. *Rajatarangini The Saga of the Kings of Kashmir*, Sahitya Academy, New Delhi, 1977.

Praveen Swami. *India, Pakistan and The Secret Jihad: The Covert War in Kashmir*, 1947-2004, Routledge, Abingdon, Oxon, 2007.

Sardar Patel's Correspondence 1945–50, New Light on Kashmir, Edited by Durga Das, Navajivan Publishing House, Ahmedabad, 1971.

Schofield, Victoria. *Kashmir in Conflict – India, Pakistan and the Unending War*, Tauris & Co Ltd, London, 2003.

Selected Works of Jawaharlal Nehru, (*SWJN*) Second Series, Vols. 1 to 39.

Sender, Henry. *The Kashmiri Pandits – A Study of Cultural Choice in North India*, OUP, 1988.

Shiva Rau, B. *Framing of India's Constitution – A Study*, IIPA, New Delhi.

Singh, Karan. *Heir Apparent An Autobiography,* OUP, Delhi, 1983.

Singh, Karan. *Jammu And Kashmir 1949-64- Select Correspondence Between Jawaharlal Nehru And Karan Singh*, Penguin Books India, 2006.

Singh, Raghubir. *Kashmir, Garden of Himalayas,* Thames & Hudson, 1983.

Smith, Vincent. *The Oxford History of India*, The Clarendon Press, Oxford, 1928.

Speeches of Jawaharlal Nehru 1957-63, Vol. Four, Publications Division, Government of India, New Delhi.

Stein, M.A., *Kalhana's Rajatarangini A Chronicle of Kings of Kashmir,* Motilal Banarsidass Publishers Pvt. Ltd., Delhi.

Tavleen Singh. *Kashmir: A Tragedy of Errors*, Penguin Books India Pvt. Ltd., 1995.

Tendulkar, D.G. *Mahatma: Life of Mohandas Karamchand Gandhi*, Vol. IV, The Publications Division, Government of India, 1988.

The Variegated Plumage Encounters with Indian Philosophy, A Commemoration Volume in honour of Pandit Jankinath Kaul "Kamal," Edited by N.B. Patil, Sat Samagam Research Institute, J.K. & Motilal Banarsidass Publishers Pvt Ltd, Delhi, 2003.

The Cambridge History of India, Vol. IV, S. Chand & Co. Pvt. Ltd., 1987.

The Earth Has No Corners, Felicitation Volume on the 70th Birthday of Dr. Karan Singh, Edited by K.L. Nandan, Shipra Publications, Delhi, 2001.

The Gazetteer of India, History and Culture, Edited by P.N. Chopra, Vol. Two, Publication Division, Government of India, New Delhi, 1997.

The Hindu Speaks, Interpress, Bombay, 1978.

The Indian Annual Register, July-December 1937.

The Transfer of Power, 1942-7, Ed. Nicholas Mansergh, Vol. XI, HMSO, London.

Trench, Charles Chenevix. *Viceroy's Agent,* Jonathan Cape London, 1987.

Tyson, Geoffrey. *Nehru: The Years of Power*, Jaico Publishing House, Bombay, 1970.

Vijay Kumar. *Anglo-American Plot against Kashmir*, People's Publishing House Ltd., Bombay, 1954.

Wheeler, REM. *Five Thousand Years of Pakistan*, Christopher Johnson (publishers) Ltd., 1950.

Wilson Harold. *Memoirs: The Making of a Prime Minister 1916-64*, Weidenfeld & Nicolson & Michael Joseph, 1986.

Wolpert, Stanley. *Nehru A Tryst with Destiny*, OUP, 1996.

Younghusband, Sir Francis. *The History of Kashmir*, A&C Black Ltd., 1017.

Zakaria, Rafiq. *The man who divided India: An insight into Jinnah's leadership and its aftermath*, Popular Prakashan, Mumbai, 2001.
Ziegler, Philip. *Mountbatten The Official Biography*, Collins, London, 1985.

Periodicals & Newspapers

Daily Telegraph
Dawn.
Frontline
Hindustan Times
Indian Review
Manchester Guardian
Modern Review
New York Times
Sydney Daily Telegraph
The Baltimore Sun
The Economist
The Hindu
The Mail
The Statesman
The Sunday Standard
Times, London
Washington Post

Index

C

D

E

F

G

N

V

W

Y

Z